HARVESTING LABOUR

Rethinking Canada in the World

SERIES EDITORS: IAN MCKAY AND SEAN MILLS

Supported by the Wilson Institute for Canadian History at McMaster University, this series is committed to books that rethink Canadian history from transnational and global perspectives. It enlarges approaches to the study of Canada in the world by exploring how Canadian history has long been a dynamic product of global currents and forces. The series will also reinvigorate understanding of Canada's role as an international actor and how Canadians have contributed to intellectual, political, cultural, social, and material exchanges around the world.

Volumes included in the series explore the ideas, movements, people, and institutions that have transcended political boundaries and territories to shape Canadian society and the state. These include both state and non-state actors, and phenomena such as international migration, diaspora politics, religious movements, evolving conceptions of human rights and civil society, popular culture, technology, epidemics, wars, and global finance and trade.

The series charts a new direction by exploring networks of transmission and exchange from a standpoint that is not solely national or international, expanding the history of Canada's engagement with the world.

http://wilson.humanities.mcmaster.ca

HARVESTING LABOUR

*Tobacco and the Global Making
of Canada's Agricultural Workforce*

EDWARD DUNSWORTH

McGill-Queen's University Press
Montreal & Kingston | London | Chicago

ISBN 978-0-2280-1123-1 (cloth)
ISBN 978-0-2280-1124-8 (paper)
ISBN 978-0-2280-1269-6 (ePDF)
ISBN 978-0-2280-1270-2 (ePUB)

Legal deposit third quarter 2022
Bibliothèque nationale du Québec

Printed in Canada on acid-free paper that is 100% ancient forest free
(100% post-consumer recycled), processed chlorine free

This book has been published with the help of a grant from the Canadian
Federation for the Humanities and Social Sciences, through the Awards to
Scholarly Publications Program, using funds provided by the Social Sciences
and Humanities Research Council of Canada.

We acknowledge the support of the Canada Council for the Arts.
Nous remercions le Conseil des arts du Canada de son soutien.

Library and Archives Canada Cataloguing in Publication

Title: Harvesting labour : tobacco and the global making of Canada's agricul-
    tural workforce / Edward Dunsworth.
Names: Dunsworth, Edward, author.
Series: Rethinking Canada in the world ; 12.
Description: Series statement: Rethinking Canada in the world ; 12 | Includes
    bibliographical references and index.
Identifiers: Canadiana (print) 20220219192 | Canadiana (ebook) 20220219389 |
    ISBN 9780228011248 (paper) | ISBN 9780228011231 (cloth) | ISBN 9780228012696
    (ePDF) | ISBN 9780228012702 (ePUB)
Subjects: LCSH: Tobacco workers—Ontario—History—20th century. | LCSH:
    Agricultural laborers, Foreign—Ontario—History—20th century. | LCSH:
    Tobacco farms—Ontario—History—20th century. | LCSH: Agricultural
    laborers—Canada—History—20th century. | LCSH: Labor supply—Canada
    —History—20th century.
Classification: LCC HD8039.T62 C3 2022 | DDC 338.1/737109713—dc23

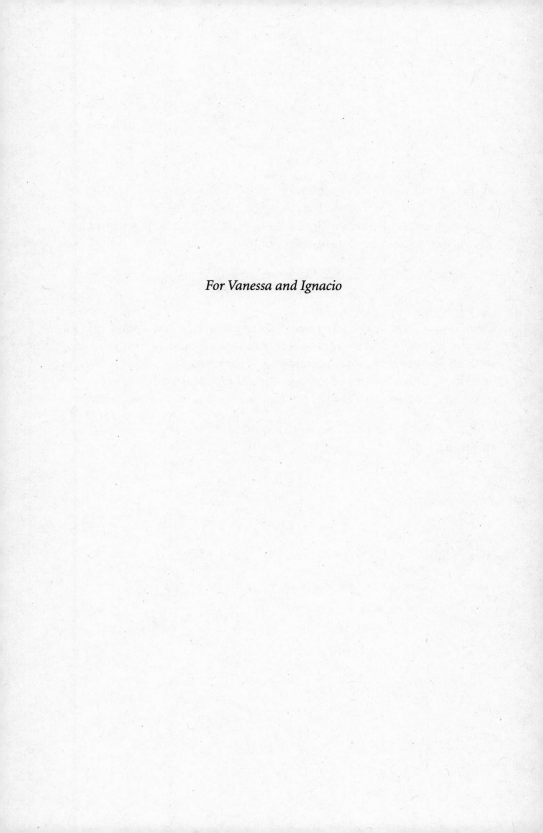

For Vanessa and Ignacio

At some point you gotta expand on a story. You can't just give it focus, you gotta give it scope. Shit doesn't just happen in a void, there're ripples and consequences and even with all that there's still a whole fucking world going on, whether you're doing something or not.

– Alex Pierce, character in Marlon James's *Brief History of Seven Killings*

There is no future working in tobacco. I have worked in it 25 years. If I had worked instead in a factory I would be getting a pension, but for tobacco work all you can show for it is poor health, the result of working long hours in all kinds of bad weather. How true these sayings the poor will get poorer and the rich richer. This is what is happening in this part of the country.

– Anonymous woman tobacco worker quoted in the *Simcoe Reformer*, 20 February 1973

Tillsonburg,
Tillsonburg,
My back still aches
When I hear that word

– Stompin' Tom Connors, "Tillsonburg," 1971

CONTENTS

TABLE AND FIGURES

ACKNOWLEDGMENTS

In many ways, the origins of this book can be traced to the summers of 2009 and 2010, when, as a labourer-teacher for the literacy organization Frontier College, I worked on two farms in southwestern Ontario (a tree nursery and a broccoli farm) alongside twenty-five or so Mexican migrants, labouring as a farmhand during the day and teaching the occasional English or computer lesson in the evening. Here I made friends with many brilliant, thoughtful, hilarious, and hard-working men, and received a crash course in everything from cutting broccoli, to Canada's migrant farm labour regime, to the gross injustices of the global capitalist order. Everything I've done since has been profoundly shaped by this experience. To my farm-worker friends, *mil gracias por todo, gueyes.* Thank you also to the staff at Frontier College who made the placement possible and who I've since come to count as friends – namely, Janine Wass, Steve Freeman, and Sandra De Lorenzi.

In a more literal sense, the book first took shape as a doctoral dissertation at the University of Toronto, where I was fortunate to encounter some remarkable mentors. Ian Radforth was a model thesis adviser in every respect, generous with his time, thoughtful with his feedback, and always supportive of my interests and vision for the project. Sean Mills has given me so much valuable advice that I feel I should owe him a portion of all future earnings. Sean's brilliance – including his remarkable ability to see through a fog of jumbled ideas and instantly extract the core message – is matched only by his kindness and good humour. Donna Gabaccia pushed me to think globally and is still teaching me how to be a migration historian. Melanie Newton gamely took me on as a comps student despite my being a complete newcomer to Caribbean history, and as a thesis committee member made this project stronger in so many ways. Steve Penfold was another important mentor. Thanks as well to Chris Berkowitz, Brian Gettler, Paula Hastings, Franca Iacovetta, and Jeffrey Pilcher. At Queen's University, where I completed my MA, thank you especially to Barrington Walker (for his belief and support), Ian McKay (for being Ian McKay, and also for pointing me toward tobacco in the first place), and Karen Dubinksy (for introducing me to this thing called transnational history).

After completing my PhD, I took the subway north to York University, where, as a SSHRC post-doctoral fellow, I benefitted immensely from the advice and support of Michele Johnson. Craig Heron has also been a great mentor and friend. At McGill University, colleagues have helped ease my transition, making the task of finishing the book that much easier. Special thank yous to Catherine Desbarats, Suzanne Morton, and Jason Opal. Thanks also to Megan Coulter for her assistance in preparing the manuscript.

Archivists in four countries guided me through their collections. I want to especially thank Kimberly Blackwin of the Jamaica Archives and Records Department in Spanish Town, Jamaica, for going way beyond the call of duty. A special thank-you as well to Judy Livingston and Carene Morrison at the Delhi Tobacco Museum and Heritage Centre. Many people helped me locate oral history interviewees, including Laura Kovacs, Vincenzo Pietropaolo, Chris Ramsaroop, Adaoma Patterson and the Jamaican Canadian Association, Aldaine Hunt, Kim Knowles, and Gilberto Fernandes. And my sincerest gratitude to the twenty-nine current and former workers and farmers who sat down with me for oral history interviews and shared so much of their lives. Their names are listed in the bibliography.

A number of people gave me advice and assistance on my research trip to Jamaica and Barbados, including Sheryl Reid, Godfrey Levy, Knoxwain Reid, Cindy Hahamovitch, Nicole Bourbonnais, Stefanie Kennedy, Julian Cresser, Matthew Smith, Aaron Kamugisha, Aviston Downes, Nichola Cameron-Williams, Andrea Roach, Engrid Griffith, Kay Best, Andrea Miller-Stennett of the Jamaican Ministry of Labour and Social Security, Caileigh McKnight, and Tigana Tulloch and his grandfather.

My biggest thanks from my Caribbean trip are reserved for Devon James, a migrant worker at a canning facility in Ontario whom I met – in a moment of remarkable serendipity – while stopped on a rural highway after flash flooding had submerged the road ahead. By the time the water had subsided enough to keep going, night had fallen. With reports of more flash flooding ahead, Devon took me, a complete stranger, under his wing, guiding me into the next town and, when more flooding made it impossible to continue, putting me up at his sister's place overnight. I have often thought since that day about the stark contrast between how Devon treated me as a visitor in his country, and how he and his colleagues are treated as visitors in mine. I am forever grateful for his generosity and hospitality and am pleased to now call him a friend.

Cindy Hahamovitch was a superb external examiner. Jonathan McQuarrie, Katie Mazer, Emily Reid-Musson, Anelyse Weiler, Dennis Molinaro, Phil Fernandez, Carmela Patrias, and Mark Dance shared research, leads, and insights. Sally and Ian Clarke, Dan Beamish, and Georgina Alonso hosted me in Ottawa. Vic Satzewich, Andrew Downes, Anne Whyte, Kim Knowles, Ann Weston, and Adrienne Petty (with special thanks!) shared unpublished reports and manuscript collections with me. The Social Sciences and Humanities Research Council of Canada provided financial support for my doctoral and post-doctoral work. At McGill-Queen's University Press, Jonathan Crago was unfailingly patient with a first-time author and shepherded the manuscript through the various stages of development with the utmost professionalism. The three anonymous readers provided invaluable critiques and suggestions. Ryan Perks provided a truly outstanding copy edit. My thanks to all.

Fellow-travellers in grad school provided good company, stimulating discussion, and commiseration throughout the twists and turns of life and graduate studies. At U of T, four friends in particular made the journey considerably more pleasant: Sanchia deSouza, Joel Dickau, Zac Smith, and Simon Vickers. And a special shout-out to the Queen's crew, alumni of Ian McKay's grad seminar on the Canadian Left, many of whom have remained friends and colleagues: Kassandra Luciuk, Mikhail Bjørge, Mark Culligan, Katrin MacPhee, Will Langford, Nik Barry-Shaw, and Ryan Targa.

Friends outside of academia (or at least academic history) were also huge supports. Richie Keith was always game to give writing advice, edit, or play a severe examiner in a mock comps oral. Keith Esch, Al Halavrezos, and Adam Saifer have been great friends as well.

Parts of this book were previously published in other venues. Parts of chapter 6 originally appeared as "'Me a Free Man': Resistance and Racialisation in the Canada-Caribbean Seasonal Agricultural Workers Program," *Oral History* 49, no. 1 (Spring 2021): 71–82; selections from chapters 1, 3, and 5 appeared as "Race, Exclusion, and Archival Silences in the Seasonal Migration of Tobacco Workers from the Southern United States to Ontario," *Canadian Historical Review* 99, no. 4 (Dec. 2018): 563–93; and parts of chapter 2 appeared as "Green Gold, Red Threats: Organization and Resistance in Depression-Era Ontario Tobacco," *Labour/Le Travail* 79 (2017): 105–42. My thanks to all three journals for their kind permission to reprint this material here.

It's at this stage of the acknowledgments that words begin to seem hopelessly unequal to the task. Leading by example in their own lives, my parents, Ed and Barbara, have given me a lifetime of encouragement to pursue what I was passionate about and provided limitless support along the way. My sisters and their families (Kate, Darren, Robyn, and Owen; Sally, Mike, Alexander, and Morgan; and Jacqueline, Matt, and Sadie) likewise offered much encouragement and many welcome distractions over the course of writing. So, too, did my parents-in-law, Durvis and Humberto, and the rest of the clan, Humberto, Emily, and Vicente, and Alvaro and Chrissy. My parents and parents-in-law together provided nearly a month of child care at a critical junction toward the end of the process. My love and gratitude to all of you.

The final words of these acknowledgments go to the two brightest lights in my life, Vanessa and Ignacio. Simply put, without Vanessa, none of this would have been possible. As for Iggy, it will be a few years before you can read this, but when that time comes, you can try these words out loud: since the day you were born, my precious boy, you've lit up our world.

HARVESTING LABOUR

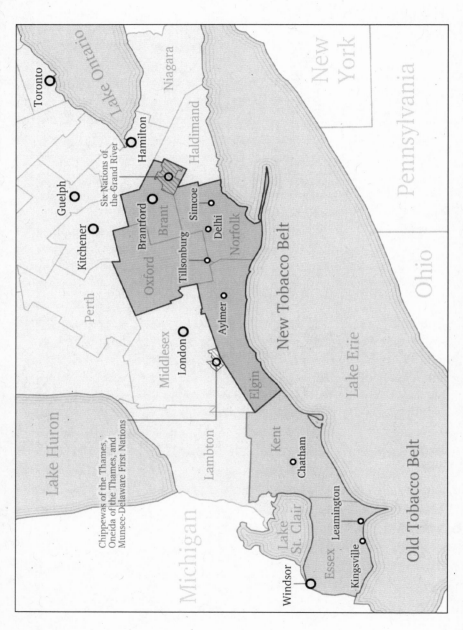

0.1 Ontario's old and new tobacco belts. Map by Nate Wessel.

INTRODUCTION

In the summer of 1966, the tension and tumult of the sixties landed with a thud in the tobacco belt of southwestern Ontario.

On 3 August, a crowd of two hundred young migrant job seekers marched on the village of Delhi (pronounced *Del-high*), the epicentre of the province's tobacco zone. Hailing mostly from Quebec and Ontario, and sporting the long hair, fashions, and politics that provoked such anxiety among their seniors, the young marchers were protesting the meagre provisions and ghastly accommodations at the pre-harvest campsite where they were directed to stay. They didn't get very far into town before being stopped by a blockade of seven shotgun-wielding officers from the local and provincial police forces and ordered to disperse. When nine protestors – all Québécois men between the ages of eighteen and twenty-three – attempted to break through police lines, they were promptly arrested, bringing the demonstration to a dispiriting close. The arrestees spent about a week in jail (where they reported being physically assaulted by guards) before being released with thirty-five-dollar fines, or about two days' wages for a tobacco harvester.[1]

The day after the nine young protestors were released from jail, another controversy involving tobacco workers made headlines when at least twenty-four Black migrant workers from the southern United States, participants in a long-standing guest-worker scheme, were denied employment after arriving at their assigned farms in Ontario, for no apparent reason other than racism. With little money and no local connections, the workers were forced to make their way back across the border to Buffalo, from whence their story made it into the press on both sides of the border. Unbeknownst to reporters covering the story, 1966 was in fact the first year in which Black workers were permitted

to participate in the scheme, a change that came not as a result of a liberalization of immigration policies in Canada in this era, but rather at the behest of
American authorities concerned about contravening new civil rights legislation
in the United States. Unfortunately for the twenty-four workers, their admission into Canada did not result in the high, if hard-earned, wages they had expected, but instead in bitter disappointment.[2]

It wasn't just the social unrest and racism of the 1960s that made headlines
in rural southwestern Ontario that summer. The global dimensions of that
momentous decade were also making themselves felt. That same year, two
new groups of temporary foreign workers made their debut in Ontario's
fields. First were the inaugural participants in what would become known as
the Seasonal Agricultural Workers Program (SAWP): 264 Jamaican farm
workers placed on fruit and vegetable farms and canning facilities in and
around the tobacco district (they would join the tobacco workforce the following year). As far removed from the halls of international diplomacy as a
muddy field or noisy packing plant may seem, the arrival of the Jamaicans –
and the Barbadians and Trinidadians who joined the program in 1967 – was
nonetheless an event of geopolitical and diplomatic significance. Launched
amid the context of decolonization and the Cold War, the SAWP was the
product of a mutual desire on the part of Canada and the newly independent
Caribbean countries to forge closer economic and diplomatic ties. The second
cohort of newly arrived guest workers that year was a very different group
than the West Indians but no less a product of the global 1960s. That summer,
university students from Belgium, France, and Austria joined the tobacco
workforce, riding the wave of work-abroad programs swelling throughout
the Global North in this era, a less altruistic counterpart to the international
volunteer movement, but one that was no less ardent in its rhetorical devo-
tion to the creed of liberal internationalism.

At the very same time that the world-altering dramas of the 1960s were making their mark in the tobacco belt, some less sensational, but no less important,
developments were taking hold in the sector. A wave of technological innova-
tions was making tobacco easier to harvest and process, reducing the number
of required labourers and making the work of those who remained less arduous
– a trend that would only become more pronounced in the years ahead. Meanwhile, after nearly forty years of seldom-interrupted boom, the tobacco sector,
and its small farms in particular, suddenly found itself struggling under the

weight of significant economic stress. With rising costs of inputs and falling prices for their tobacco, small farmers struggled to remain profitable, sparking a wave of farm sell-offs in 1965, the result of which was a greater consolidation of tobacco lands and quota rights into the hands of large operations with the ability to grow at scale. Finally, far away from the sun, dirt, and tar of tobacco farms, a critical mass of scientists, politicians, and public health officials was delivering ever more dire pronouncements about the links between cigarette smoking and lung cancer. While by the early 1950s there was incontrovertible evidence – from myriad studies in multiple scientific disciplines, carried out in many countries – of the culpability of cigarette smoking in the global lung cancer epidemic, it was not until the early 1960s that national governments began to take significant action. In 1963, the Canadian minister of national health and welfare, Judy LaMarsh, declared the smoking-cancer association in a speech to the House of Commons. The following year, the surgeon general of the United States released a report saying the same, and LaMarsh's department launched a public awareness campaign about the dangers of smoking.[3]

Contained within these striking though seemingly disparate events were the seeds of a major transformation, at whose precipice stood the tobacco sector – though no one quite knew it at the time. Within thirty years, a sector that had once featured thousands of profitable small and medium-sized farms, whose high wages and plentiful jobs attracted tens of thousands of migrant job seekers each harvest from sundry parts of Canada and around the globe, had become something entirely different, dominated now by a few hundred highly capitalized, highly mechanized farms whose labour needs were increasingly met by one specific source: temporary foreign workers from the Caribbean and Mexico. And yet, at the same time as they portended something of tobacco's future, the events of 1966 were also firmly rooted in its past. Remarkable though that summer was for its drama and the swirling simultaneity of so many important trends, many of these events were simply the latest manifestations of long-standing attributes of the sector: collective action among its working people; a labour force marked at once by its diversity and by patterns of exclusion; and the pervasive influence of international dynamics, from geopolitics to the vagaries of global capitalism.

This book tells the story of the tobacco sector's workforce over the twentieth century (and extending into the twenty-first) using tobacco as a case study to shed new light on the history of farm labour and temporary foreign worker programs in Canada. For much of the twentieth century, in July and early August of each year, thousands upon thousands of workers streamed into the towns and villages of Norfolk County, Ontario, and its environs, seeking employment in the tobacco harvest. Though the work was famously grueling, it paid high wages, and in some cases even afforded the opportunity for upward social mobility – attractions enough for the motley crew of working people who took jobs in tobacco during these decades. Helping to meet the surging demand for cigarettes in Canada and overseas, the Norfolk area transformed rapidly in the 1920s and '30s into Canada's largest producer of flue-cured tobacco, the type used in cigarettes, and soon became known as Canada's tobacco belt.

As tobacco acreage skyrocketed in Norfolk, so, too, did the demand for workers to plant, nurture, and especially harvest the labour-intensive crop. Within a few years, the emergent sector required upwards of 10,000 workers to bring in its crop each year. By 1944, nearly 32,000 people worked the harvest, and the harvest workforce would remain above 25,000 into the 1980s.[4] Tobacco employed both women and men in significant numbers (the workforce was about 40 per cent female in the sector's early decades), even if the types of jobs women and men performed were rigidly demarcated according to gender. Though many local residents laboured in tobacco, in most years at least 40 per cent of harvest workers were estimated to come from outside the Norfolk region, making tobacco probably the country's primary destination for migrant farm labour.[5] Some tobacco job seekers intended to take up strictly seasonal work, others sought permanent opportunities, and still others began in the former category but ended up in the latter.

From its earliest days, the tobacco sector's workforce was decidedly cosmopolitan, though opportunities within it were by no means open to all. Many tobacco workers were new European immigrants who had settled in other parts of Canada before relocating to the tobacco belt to pursue the new and exciting opportunities afforded by the "green gold": Belgians, Hungarians, ethnic Germans, Poles, Lithuanians, and others. Others came from the southern United States, principally from the tobacco-growing states of North Carolina and Virginia (and later Georgia), in a movement that transitioned over time from an informal migration system to a bilaterally administered guest-worker program. The greatest number of tobacco workers came from within Canada: from nearby parts of Ontario, including First Nations communities; from industrial cities such as London, Brantford, Hamilton, and Toronto, and from across the Quebec-Ontario border, from cities like Montreal; and in some years – particularly during the Great Depression – from even greater distances within the country.

Though Ontario's tobacco workforce was diverse from the start, it was always marked by exclusion as well. While some farm workers were welcomed and even recruited, shifting configurations of employers, government officials, and/or community leaders simultaneously sought to exclude others – sometimes successfully, sometimes not – on the basis of "race," ascribed skill level, or perceived membership in another group deemed undesirable. Nowhere was this more apparent than in the barring of African Americans from participation in the annual US-Ontario migration until 1966, a form of racist exclusion produced in tandem by transnational networks of southern American tobaccomen, Canadian government bureaucracies, and local tobacco belt cultures. Not only was entry to farm labour markets characterized by inclusion and exclusion; so, too, were the terms of incorporation for those workers who were able to secure employment. Workers in the tobacco belt found their access to certain jobs, opportunities for social mobility, freedom of movement, and the warmth of their welcome (or lack thereof) in the region differentiated – in highly uneven and ever-evolving ways – according to race, ethnicity, gender, class, and immigration status.

Over the years, the composition of the tobacco workforce evolved, at times reflecting broader trends, at others as a result of more localized dynamics. In the decades after World War II, new groups of immigrants, including Portuguese and Dutch, found their way to the tobacco belt, and Quebec emerged as the predominant sending region for migrant workers from within Canada. Starting in the mid-1960s, women and girls, long critical parts of the tobacco workforce but limited to certain jobs, began securing positions as "primers" (harvesters) – a job previously reserved exclusively for men and boys. The mid-1960s also saw important changes in the sector's guest-worker schemes, with the desegregation of the US program and the launching of new arrangements that brought European students and West Indians to the district's farms. Eventually, the West Indians (and later Mexicans) labouring in the SAWP would become the dominant labour source, but it would take over two decades for this to come to fruition.

Tobacco was in many respects exceptional within Canadian agriculture, boasting, especially from the 1930s to the 1960s, relatively steady profits, high wages, unusual opportunities for social mobility, and a greater degree of working-class mobilization than other crop sectors. However, as perhaps the country's top destination for migrant farm workers, and as one of its most economically important crop sectors, it was no mere curiosity. Indeed, its transformation has been broadly mirrored by agriculture writ large, which, like tobacco, has over the last few decades become an increasingly consolidated, capital-intensive industry dependent on temporary foreign workers. Ontario's tobacco belt, then, makes an advantageous case study through which to better understand twentieth-century farm labour in Canada: representative and significant enough to stand in for other sectors within the larger industry, yet exceptional enough to cast familiar narratives in a new light. To this end, the central questions animating this book are: How did Canada's agricultural workforce come to look the way it does today? And what can tobacco tell us about this history?

The dominant understanding of this history, on display in seemingly every public commentary on migrant farm labour with any pretense to historical perspective, was concisely articulated in an opinion piece written by Ken Forth, president of the grower-run organization that manages the SAWP, for the *Hamilton Spectator* in January 2018. Responding to an article published in the newspaper nine days earlier, penned by two professors and critical of the SAWP, Forth sought to correct the record on the program's history and purpose. "The program," he writes, "was established in 1966 to respond to a severe shortage of domestic agricultural workers. It continues to serve the same role 52 years later, enabling Ontario farmers to stay in business." This latter statement, Forth assured readers, was no exaggeration. "Ontario's fruit and vegetable industry wouldn't exist without supplemental seasonal labour from Mexico and the Caribbean. The equation is as simple and as stark as that – no outside help to do the seasonal farm work that Canadians refuse to do, then no fresh, local produce on the shelves at your neighbourhood grocery store."[6]

Though they would likely disagree on nearly every point concerning the SAWP – not least the precise ways in which migrant workers allow Ontario farmers to stay in business – scholars like those to whom Forth was responding have not offered a significantly different portrayal of the history of the program, or farm labour in twentieth-century Canada more broadly. While assuredly containing vastly more detail and nuance, historical depictions have still followed the same broad plot points: Canadian farmers struggled to find workers, pressured the government for a guest-worker program, and once they got it, found their problems solved as temporary foreign workers became the dominant source of farm labour – a version of events that I call the "labour shortage narrative."[7]

This book tells a very different story. It disputes the notion that Canadian agriculture was permanently plagued by labour shortages and that growers turned rapidly to guest workers in response to this challenge. Rather than struggling to find workers, Ontario tobacco farms were for decades extremely popular places to work, as high wages and opportunities for social mobility attracted tens of thousands of seasonal workers each summer from Canada and abroad, including guest workers. The addition of Caribbean guest workers to the labour force in 1967 (and Mexicans in the mid-1970s) changed little in and of itself. Tobacco growers were extremely slow to hire West Indians and Mexicans; in fact, the entire SAWP remained quite small across all crop sectors for its first two decades of existence. When tobacco farmers did, belatedly, turn in greater measure to the SAWP, it was not the result of labour shortages or the unwillingness of Canadians to perform agricultural jobs, but thanks to economic restructuring that left the sector dominated by large operations able to afford the higher costs of contracting guest workers, whose primary attraction lay in their unfreedom, as many scholars have pointed out.[8]

Though the ultimate switch to temporary foreign workers sprung from economic forces, tobacco labour's many transformations along the way were the product of more varied factors. As previous accounts have suggested, the relationship between employers and the state was critical in all of this. Indeed, there could have been no switch to guest workers had the state – two states in fact, Canada and Jamaica – not created a guest-worker scheme in the first place. But whereas many studies of guest-worker programs have cast employers and the state in relatively static roles – the former as perpetual petitioners for labour, the latter as gatekeeper – I offer a more dynamic account. Specifically, I demonstrate that government involvement in the tobacco labour market was never guaranteed and advanced in ways that were gradual, uneven, and often vigorously contested by shifting alliances of employers, workers, and various state actors.[9] Rather than supplicating at the feet of the state, tobacco growers spent much of the twentieth century lobbying government to *get out* of the labour picture entirely. By advancing these findings, I aim to historicize the role of the state in this domain, joining an emerging group of historians seeking to do the same in the area of migration control.[10] At the same time, this study also contributes to a wider (and older) literature whose authors have turned the tools of social and cultural history toward the study of politics and the state.[11]

But the drama of twentieth-century farm labour cannot be staged with employers and the Canadian state as the only two lead actors. Working people in the tobacco belt – wage labourers and farming families – made their own history, even if, to paraphrase Karl Marx, they did not do so under circumstances of their own choosing.[12] Workers leveraged their wage labour into farm ownership and other forms of economic security. Migrants made strategic choices about where and when to pursue opportunities; they also evaded and manipulated border controls, bypassing regulations to further their own interests. And working people from across the intersecting hierarchies of class, race, gender, and immigration status acted individually and collectively to resist poor conditions, racism, and other forms of bigotry, and to push for a more equitable sector.

Nor can we adequately tell this story by fixing our gaze solely on the local, or even national, context. Instead, tobacco's labour force was shaped in significant ways by factors and actors beyond Canada's borders. Transnational migrant networks helped determine who would – and who would not – participate in the burgeoning tobacco sector. International political and intellectual currents informed the actions of workers, employers, and state actors alike. And the rise and fall of Ontario's tobacco sector cannot be extricated from the ebbs and flows of global capitalism. In placing Ontario's tobacco workforce in global relief, *Harvesting Labour* joins a concerted effort by scholars over the last two decades or so to write histories that do not take the nation-state as the default frame of study but instead capture the myriad ways in which the human past has been moulded by factors that pierce or lie beyond national boundaries.[13] This scholarly movement, coalescing under the banner of transnationalism, is not, of course, without its own history and lineage. In particular, the present work, as a transnational study of labour in a decidedly capitalist industry, situates itself within a long tradition of authors – from Marx to Eric Williams to Immanuel Wallerstein to Sven Beckert, to name just a few – who, in one way or another, have made the point that to truly understand the history and inner workings of the capitalist system, one must adopt a global perspective.[14] While labour historians in other contexts have increasingly adopted transnational frames of analysis,[15] the Canadian field has been slow to make the "transnational turn" – notwithstanding such notable exceptions as Sarah Jane-Mathieu's work on cross-border Black railway workers or Karen Flynn's on health-care workers in the transatlantic Black diaspora.[16] There has, to be sure, been a greater uptake of *comparative* labour studies, especially between Canada and the United States. Fewer and farther between, however, are *connective* works that follow people and processes across national boundaries.[17] For their part, the torchbearers of transnational history in Canada have demonstrated only passing interest in questions of labour.[18] This, I believe, is to the impoverishment of both fields. This book aims to bring these fields into closer dialogue and to showcase the promise and possibility of transnational labour history in elucidating the historical origins of our increasingly interconnected, globalized, capitalist world.

Harvesting Labour's transnational perspective also speaks to the international scholarship on guest workers and labour migration. The book reveals the important – and up to now, little-understood – roles played by migrant-sending governments in determining the structures and operations of guest-worker programs in Canadian agriculture. It further demonstrates how even guest-worker resistance was transnational in character, directed not only toward workplace conditions in Ontario, but also toward the aspects of the schemes that operated in workers' home countries.

In advancing these findings, *Harvesting Labour* joins a small but growing number of studies that are complicating the conventional narratives of guest-worker schemes as simple expressions of the dominance of Global North over South.[19] Rather than dismissing the very real inequality of the North–South axis along which these programs operate (a move as disingenuous as it would be untenable), my study instead injects a degree of complexity into the formulation, by showing how power in guest-worker schemes operated along multiple axes, and that commonality of interest between actors in sending countries should by no means be assumed. In particular, when government officials from countries such as Jamaica exerted their influence in setting the terms of guest-worker arrangements, their interest often had much less to do with the protection of their citizens than with the protection of the program and its perceived geopolitical and economic benefits to the sending country – not to mention its political benefits to politicians and operatives from the governing party in a local context (in Jamaica at least) where guest worker programs operated within a system of patronage. As such, sending-country representatives and receiving-country employers sitting at the negotiating table often found themselves in complete agreement.[20] It follows then, that when guest workers pushed back against program conditions and agitated for a fairer deal, their resistance was just as likely to occur at home and be directed toward home country government agencies as it was to take place on the job in Canada. Here, too, *Harvesting Labour* contributes to a burgeoning literature, one that is documenting often-hidden guest-worker resistance, including not just workplace actions, but also more ordinary, individual assertions of humanity such as the pursuit of relationships – sexual or otherwise – or participation in leisure activities.[21]

Underpinning these findings is *Harvesting Labour*'s transnational research methodology. Discussed in greater detail below, it is worth highlighting here how conducting research in both migrant-sending and migrant-receiving countries (Jamaica, Barbados, the United States, and Canada) was pivotal for revealing the important roles of sending countries in setting the terms of guest-worker arrangements. It sounds obvious, but to understand a binational guest-worker scheme, one must conduct binational research. Self-evident though this tenet appears, it has been ignored in a large number of historical guest-worker studies, which have either limited their archival research to the receiving country,[22] or, in the case of one prominent scholar, been overly dismissive of the archival holdings of the sending country – in this instance, Jamaica.[23] Fortunately, scholars of migration – and of guest-worker schemes – are increasingly adopting methodologies that include archival research in migrant-sending and migrant-receiving countries alike, allowing them to develop fuller portrayals of human migration – a methodological program that this book enthusiastically joins.[24]

✦✦✦

Relatively little has been written on the history of farm workers in Canada, especially when we consider the size of the agricultural labour force compared to that of other sectors in twentieth-century Canada. In 1941, for example, 179,000 Canadians worked for wages on farms at some point during the year – part of a total agricultural workforce of 1.1 million that included farmers and unpaid family labourers. The number of paid workers in agriculture was greater than those in mining, forestry, fishing, education, health services, food and hospitality, textile manufacturing, food, beverage, and tobacco manufacturing, railway transport, other transport, and government – many of whose workers have received far greater attention from labour historians. Of course, over the subsequent decades the farm labour force decreased and was surpassed – and even dwarfed – by many of those listed above. But even in 1975, there were still 110,000 Canadians who worked for wages in agriculture at some point during the year.[25]

Despite the numerical significance of the agriculture workforce – not to mention the fundamental importance of its work in underpinning the supply of food and other agricultural products in Canada and beyond – the historiographical record on farm labour has been sparse. The historical literature that does exist has been written by two broad groups of scholars: social historians and social scientists. The "new" labour and social historians of the 1970s and '80s, with their field-altering interests in the day-to-day experiences of working people and the dynamic interactions between classes and economic structures and processes, produced some studies on farm workers, as they did for workers in many other sectors.[26] But these articles and chapters – including superb accounts of striking sugar beet workers in 1930s Alberta and Ontario; British and eastern Canadian excursionists to the prairie harvests of the early twentieth century; agricultural wage labour in Ontario from the early nineteenth century to the 1980s; and rural labour in nineteenth-century Ontario – tended to be one-off studies that, with one exception, did not lead to monographs. Thus, the project of giving farm workers their rightful seat at the table of the "new labour history" was never fully realized.[27] In the decades since, historical studies of Canadian farm labour have been few and far between, but those that have come out have infused the topic with the sorts of questions – on racism, gender, colonialism, and culture – that have increasingly informed the work of scholars following in the footsteps of the trailblazing social historians of the 1970s and '80s.[28]

The other major group of scholars who have investigated aspects of Canadian farm labour's past are social scientists. The interests of these scholars differ starkly from those of social historians. Whereas the latter tackled mostly nineteenth- and early twentieth-century farm workers and were animated by the questions of working-class experience at the heart of their discipline, social scientists have been primarily interested in the post–World War II period and in state policy. While a small number of studies examine Canadian farm workers – including internal migrants, as well as racialized and Indigenous workers – these have been dwarfed in the last twenty years by a veritable explosion of scholarship on guest-worker programs.[29] This scholarship, when it has attempted historical inquiry, has been principally animated by one driving question: How and why did guest-worker programs – in particular the SAWP – come into existence? The answers these scholars propose tend to focus on two sets of actors: employers and the state.

Undoubtedly the most important historical work in this vein is sociologist Vic Satzewich's 1991 book *Racism and the Incorporation of Foreign Labour: Farm Labour Migration to Canada since 1945*. The product of detailed research in government archives, Satzewich produced what still stands as the definitive history of the foundation of the Caribbean-Canadian guest-worker program, in which he details the many twists and turns of grower lobbying, international diplomacy, and internal government debates that eventually led to the creation of the SAWP in 1966 – a story shaped at every turn, as Satzewich's title suggests, by racism. Its important findings and unimpeachable empirical research notwithstanding, the book still produces a relatively linear history of postwar farm labour, the broad plotlines of which I outlined earlier: labour shortage, lobbying, guest-worker program. In the three decades since the release of *Racism and the Incorporation of Foreign Labour*, interest in the SAWP and other guest-worker schemes among social scientists has ballooned, particularly in the last ten to fifteen years. For all their insightful contributions to the contemporary study of temporary foreign farm labour, those scholars – even the ones who have conducted some of their own historical research – have largely echoed Satzewich's historical account.[30]

Harvesting Labour takes an approach that differs from both the social historians' and social scientists' treatments of farm labour history – even while building on the findings of scholars in both fields. Its orientation is aptly captured by the fictional journalist Alex Pierce, a character in Marlon James's novel *A Brief History of Seven Killings* (quoted in the epigraph), who argues that "You can't just give [a story] focus, you gotta give it scope."[31] Like the social historians of farm labour, I focus on workers in a particular sector and locale and am interested in the experiences of working people and how those were shaped by the dynamics of class, race, ethnicity, and gender. Like the social scientists, I am interested in the origins of Canada's contemporary farm labour regime and its dependence on temporary foreign workers. But I aim to add significant scope to both approaches. Though anchored in the specific location of southwestern Ontario's tobacco belt, *Harvesting Labour* follows tobacco's workers back to their diverse places of origin and analyzes the sector's transformations in a global frame. It also bucks the pre-war/postwar temporal split, adopting a longer timeline (from the 1920s to the present) in order to better account for longer-term patterns of historical change. Finally, though concerned with the creation and evolution of the SAWP, it places that story within a much broader context, purposely eschewing the tendency of much of the social scientific literature to trace the origins of Canada's contemporary farm labour system to a single policy event – namely, the creation of a tiny pilot guest-worker scheme in 1966. As the following chapters demonstrate, the evolution of Canada's agricultural workforce was anything but straightforward, and it was by no means inevitable – even decades after the SAWP's creation – that it should come to be dominated by temporary foreign workers.

Achieving this long-term, global scope required the adoption of a wide-ranging and transnational research methodology that included oral history, data analysis, digital mapping, and documentary research in archives, newspapers, immigration records, and numerous other textual sources. This research was conducted in four countries: Canada, Barbados, Jamaica, and the United States. Oral history forms a particularly important part of the book's approach. Oral history has been a key methodology for historians of migration and labour for many decades. The "new social historians" of the 1970s and '80s embraced oral history as a means of accessing the day-to-day experiences of ordinary people, details that were often frustratingly absent from government documents and newspaper articles. A core tenet for both social and oral historians has been the recognition of ordinary people – including workers, women, migrants, Indigenous peoples, racialized groups, LGBTQ2+ folk, and others – as important historical actors, and a central preoccupation has been the contextualization of people's day-to-day experiences within broader social, economic, political, and cultural trends.[32] In recent decades, oral historians have adopted a growing concern with "memory," or the particular ways in which interviewees narrate their stories: what they include and exclude, how they sequence and associate events, and how they remember or "misre-member" certain historical or biographical details.[33] A critical engagement with memory affords researchers invaluable insights into how narrators make sense of and derive meaning from their life stories. Following the innovative work of Luisa Passerini, scholars have also paid significant attention to the "subjec-tivity" of interviewees, a concept that not only reveals much about narrators' consciousness and self-identities, but also about the ways in which culture, ideology, and structures of power are manifested in – and sometimes chal-lenged by – individual and collective ways of understanding the world.[34]

While much has been written about the dramatic shifts in oral history – what we might call the "subjectivity turn" – Joan Sangster has cautioned that this linear narrative of the field's development is somewhat reductive. Earlier oral historians weren't so ignorant of subjectivity as has sometimes been sug-gested, nor have contemporary oral historians abandoned themes like experi-ence and agency.[35] Like Sangster, my own approach to oral history draws on both traditions. I utilize interviews to more fully narrate the lives and labour of tobacco workers and growers, and also to learn something about the par-ticular ways in which interviewees remember and make sense of their time working in tobacco – a preoccupation most evident in chapter 6, with its con-sideration of racialization and resistance in the Caribbean program.

Over the course of the research for this project, between 2016 and 2018, I conducted 27 oral history interviews with 29 participants (some were group interviews), including 20 former tobacco workers, 8 tobacco farmers, and the former president of Foreign Agricultural Resource Management Services (or FARMS, the grower-operated agency that has administered the SAWP since 1987). In addition to my own interviews, I drew on interviews conducted in the 1970s and '80s by the Multicultural Historical Society of Ontario with to-bacco belt residents of various European, Canadian, and American back-grounds, and transcripts of interviews by Leonard Rapport, who, as part of a Works Progress Administration project, interviewed dozens of people involved in North Carolina's tobacco sector in the 1930s, including a few participants in the seasonal US-Ontario movement.

In my own interviews, I tried, insofar as possible, to secure participation from a representative cross-section of workers and growers, including both women and men from the many diverse groups who laboured in tobacco throughout the twentieth century, and from different decades within the period of study. Out of 11 interviewed Canadian workers, 8 hailed from Ontario, 2 from Quebec, and 1 from Newfoundland. Of these Canadian workers, 5 were women and 6 were men, and the times of their employment ranged from the early 1960s to the 1990s. I conducted interviews with 9 Caribbean workers, including 2 Jamaicans, 6 Barbadians, and 1 Tobagonian. The most senior of these workers joined the program in 1974, and others' experiences ranged from the late 1970s to the early 2000s. Interviews with Jamaican and Barbadian workers were conducted in those countries, while Tobagonian Hassel Kennedy was interviewed in Ontario. Participation in the SAWP was restricted to men until the mid-1980s, and even after that the workforce has never been more than 4 per cent female. As such, all Caribbean interviewees for this project were men. Out of 8 interviewed growers, there was just a single woman, a sample in keeping with the male gendering of "grower." Some growers came from multi-generational tobacco families and shared either personal or family stories from as far back as the 1930s. All but one of the farmers was retired from growing tobacco, though some were still farming other crops. Growers and local workers traced their backgrounds to many of the European-origin groups predominant in the tobacco sector's history.

Conducting oral history interviews in both Canada and the Caribbean was a critical part of the project's methodology. Given the structuring of the SAWP as an explicitly temporary labour migration program, the vast majority of participants, once they leave the program, remain in their home countries. And although there certainly are SAWP workers in Canada whose experiences date back to the late 1980s or early 1990s, program structures that make it easy for employers to repatriate workers (or not request them in subsequent years) – not to mention the well-documented blacklisting of "troublemaking" workers by sending-country governments[36] – create a strong disincentive for current participants to speak to researchers about their experiences. This is all the more apparent when it comes to experiences of resistance – in the workplace and

elsewhere. *Retired* program participants, however, often have no such com-
punctions, since speaking out about their experiences no longer poses any risk
to their livelihoods. For these reasons, a transnational oral history methodology
involving travel to workers' countries of origin proved critical to the book's
research agenda.

◆◆◆

Almost all cultivated tobacco in the world today comes from a common plant
species, *Nicotiana tabacum*, and almost all of it is destined to be used in the
manufacture of cigarettes, distributed to retailers, purchased by an individual
consumer, and smoked. It was not always so. People have consumed tobacco
– about a dozen different species – for tens of thousands of years. Archaeologi-
cal evidence reveals the ancient presence of tobacco in just two regions of the
world: Australia and the Americas. In Australia, a number of wild species of
Nicotiana were consumed by chewing as far back as 50,000 years ago, but, so
far as archaeologists can tell, it was only in the Americas that tobacco was intentionally cultivated and consumed by smoking. Two species were domesticated in the western hemisphere, both in the Andes Mountains. The first was
Nicotiana rustica, some 7,000 to 10,000 years ago, which was carried north and
south by farmers and travellers and eventually reached the continental extremes of present-day Chile and Canada, the latter over 1,500 years ago. *Nicotiana tabacum*, the species found to this day in cigarettes the world over, was
domesticated a few thousand years after *rustica*, and it remained restricted to
warmer parts of the hemisphere until recent centuries. Tobacco was traded
throughout the Americas, where it also played important religious, ceremonial,
and diplomatic roles in Indigenous societies.[37]

Tobacco smoking among Indigenous peoples was noted in some of the earliest descriptions of the Americas written by Europeans. In spite of declarations
by priests, administrators, and monarchs about the immorality of tobacco use,
it quickly caught on among the newly arrived Europeans and began finding
its way back to their home continent, originally for medicinal uses. It was not
until the late sixteenth and early seventeenth centuries that large-scale colonial
production of tobacco for export took off, but it did so rapidly, in the Caribbean islands occupied by Spain, France, and England, and in the mainland
colonies of Virginia and Brazil, held respectively by the English and the Portuguese. Some of these colonies were established with the express goal of es-

tablishing tobacco production; others adopted the crop upon witnessing its immense potential for profit.

The expansion of tobacco agriculture was fuelled by growing demand for the product in Europe, increasingly for recreational, rather than simply medicinal, use. Some of the earliest export crops of tobacco from the Americas were grown by indentured servants and smallholding settlers from Europe, but in many cases they were soon replaced by enslaved Africans. Indeed, the surging production of tobacco was an instrumental factor in the rapid expansion of the transatlantic slave trade in the seventeenth century. In Brazil, tobacco was never the focal point of agricultural production under slavery, but it still played a special role in the transatlantic traffic in human beings: Brazilian tobacco, produced at a small scale by freeholders and enslaved people alike, was a highly desired item among African slave traders, who often accepted it in exchange for their human captives. Tobacco, then, along with sugar and cotton, formed part of a triumvirate of crops that lay at the crucible of colonization, slavery, and globalized capitalism.[38]

In the lands now known as southwestern Ontario, Indigenous peoples, including the Tionontati, Attawandaron, Wendat, and Haudenosaunee, grew tobacco for well over a thousand years before the arrival of Europeans. Its consumption was even more widely spread, extending to the far northern reaches of the continent and a diverse array of peoples.[39] The combination of European-introduced diseases and warfare with the Haudenosaunee Confederacy in the seventeenth century spelled demographic disaster for many of the region's principal tobacco cultivators, their few surviving members leaving their homelands to form new communities elsewhere or join other pre-existing Indigenous ones. The area was not opened up for significant European settlement until the late eighteenth century, when, in the interest of securing territory to resettle British Loyalists from the newly independent United States, representatives of the British Crown negotiated a series of controversial land-surrender treaties with the various Anishinaabe nations who were by then prevalent in the region. Some of the agreements provided "reserve" land; others did not.[40]

In 1791, a rush of newcomers flooded into what was henceforth known as "Upper Canada," first from the rebel colonies to the south, and later in far greater numbers from across the Atlantic, principally the British Isles. Here, they undertook a project of massive transformation (predicated on the prior dispossession of Indigenous peoples), clearing lands to create cities, towns, roads, and – importantly – farms.[41] A few decades into this transformation, in the 1820s, tobacco began to be cultivated as a commercial crop in the south-western corner of the province, in Essex and Kent Counties. (Small communities of French settlers had raised tobacco in gardens in Essex since the mid-eighteenth century, mostly for local consumption.) This emergent tobacco sector featured not the *Nicotiana rustica*, which had been grown on these same lands for eons, but instead *tabacum*, specifically its Virginian varieties, which some claim was first brought to the region by Blacks fleeing slavery in the American South.[42]

Regardless of its precise origins, both Black and white migrants from the United States cultivated tobacco in Essex and Kent, transporting not only seeds but also the agricultural techniques of the southern US tobacco zone, which depended on the forced labour of enslaved people until the end of the Civil War. Ontario tobacco production remained relatively small-scale for much of the nineteenth century, however. In 1851, for example, the average tobacco crop in Essex was a mere 0.61 acres,[43] and Ontario's total production of tobacco was dwarfed by that of Quebec. Things began to change rapidly around the turn of the twentieth century, when a tariff on imported tobacco leaf (introduced in 1897), combined with the splashy entrance of James Buchanan Duke's American Tobacco Company to the Canadian market, served to spark a surge in tobacco cultivation in Ontario.[44] The latter development was part of a broader story of "corporate imperialism" that saw American Tobacco, and the exclusively white and male southern network within which it and its managerial staff were embedded, come to dominate the global tobacco industry. In the process, historian Nan Enstad explains, this network inserted the "racial hierarchy" of Jim Crow "into the new social and economic structures that came with capitalist expansion."[45]

By 1923, Ontario's tobacco production had permanently surpassed Quebec's, and the Essex-Kent area was well-established as Canada's tobacco belt, producing leaf first for cigars and pipe tobacco, and later for cigarettes.[46] It was amid the worldwide boom in demand for this latter product, which required a type of *tabacum* known as Virginia, bright leaf, or flue-cured tobacco,[47] that growers in the vicinity of Norfolk County began their first forays into large-scale production in the 1920s, soon wresting the title of "tobacco belt" from their neighbours to the west, a story that we will pick up in chapter 1.

✦✦✦

The book is divided into a total of seven chapters, followed by a conclusion. The first three chapters broadly cover the period up to the end of World War II, while the remaining four continue the story down to the present. Chapter 1 describes the rapid development of Ontario's tobacco sector in the 1920s and '30s, as migrants and capital poured into the Norfolk district hoping to strike it rich in the "green gold rush." With workers hailing from Canada, the United States, and many parts of Europe, the nascent tobacco sector was, from day one, utterly dependent on mobile labour to produce its crops. Diverse though the sector was, the welcome mat was not rolled out to all, and the tobacco industry was also characterized by exclusion and discrimination: the outright barring of African Americans, but also the differential treatment of First Nations workers and members of less favoured immigrant groups, Hungarians in particular. Though they did so on different terms, working people drove the stunning transformation of the Norfolk region as it was converted from agricultural "wasteland" into Canada's tobacco belt – and an important node in the global tobacco industry – in just a few short years.

Once these migrants had settled in their new environs, they turned their attention toward building a better life, an objective they pursued through two main avenues: the pursuit of social mobility via farm ownership, and participation in left-wing politics and workplace organization, as I explore in chapter 2. These strategies for improving life courses were not mutually exclusive, though they were at times contradictory. As the chapter reveals, the tobacco sector was decidedly different from the stereotype of conservative, labour-starved agriculture.

While the flood of migrants to the tobacco district was a boon to employers and upwardly mobile working people alike, the tobacco bonanza's sheen began to wear with the onset of the Great Depression in the 1930s, as we see in chapter 3. All of a sudden, the thousands of migrants arriving each summer in search of harvest work began to be seen as a problem. As a result, local, provincial, and federal governments all struggled to exert some form of control over these "influxes," efforts that were contested at nearly every turn by employers and workers alike and that were mostly unsuccessful. It was only under the emergency conditions of World War II that the state's luck in this regard began to turn, as emergency measures enabled authorities to take an unprecedented level of involvement in the tobacco labour market. It was also during the war that the US-Ontario tobacco workers movement first began transitioning to a bilaterally managed guest-worker program. Though labour bureaucrats had more resources at their hands than ever before, controlling the movement of farm labour still posed considerable problems, for authorities in both Canada and the United States.

Chapter 4 details the changes in the tobacco workforce in the three decades following World War II. In these years, the tobacco workforce became younger, saw an increase in migrant workers from Quebec and Atlantic Canada, and began to feature women and girls in jobs that had previously been gendered exclusively male. These changes resulted from a combination of demographic, economic, cultural, and technological trends. The chapter documents the anxieties provoked among the local population by these changes in the workforce, and the continued efforts of the Canadian state to regulate the movements of migrants. It also shows the continuing attraction of tobacco harvest work as a short-term employment option, even in the changing postwar context.

The 1960s witnessed important changes not only in the domestic workforce, but also in tobacco's quotient of foreign workers, the topic of chapter 5. In the late 1960s, tobacco growers enjoyed access to three different guest-worker programs: the long-standing US-Ontario scheme, and two newer arrangements that brought in workers from the British West Indies and western Europe. This chapter explores the creation of the Caribbean and European programs and a major change in the US scheme, in the process demonstrating the fundamental role played by sending countries' governments (and other transnational factors) in the structuring of guest-worker programs. This is most strikingly revealed in the US-Ontario scheme. Previously open to whites only, the program was integrated in 1966 at the request of US officials wary of contravening civil rights legislation at home.

Though guest workers were often extolled by employers as models of reliability and professionalism, they were not always the cure-all that they were made out to be, a story explored in chapter 6. Despite their marginalized status, guest workers still found ways to protest their substandard working and living conditions. They were also significantly more costly to employ. Nor did temporary foreign workers fulfill governments' dreams of an orderly farm labour force, frequently breaking their contracts and causing officials headaches in other ways. Finally, guest workers also sometimes disrupted the goals of their home governments by pushing back against aspects of the program operated by those governments – meaning that their resistance, like the other aspects of their lives, was transnational. Of course, these exceptions to the guest-worker ideal notwithstanding, temporary foreign workers still found themselves severely marginalized by program conditions. The severity of this marginalization – especially in the realm of immigration enforcement – was, like so much else in the guest-worker story, almost certainly shaped by racism.

Chapter 7 opens on a quiet street in downtown Delhi, Ontario, in the summer of 1985. The transient workers who long jammed the village's parks and sidewalks and caused headaches for locals are nowhere to be found. What happened? Despite the claims of growers, Canadian workers did not stop working in tobacco because of an inherent disinterest in agricultural work. They did so because, from the 1960s to the 1980s, the tobacco farm became a decidedly less attractive place to work. Real wages decreased, opportunities for social mobility disappeared, and worker organization shrivelled. These changes happened amid a crisis for tobacco farmers, as declining demand for their product (due primarily to health risks) and increased competition from foreign product precipitated a vast restructuring of the sector. In the transformed tobacco sector, only a small number of large-scale, heavily mechanized operations survived. It was only then, in the changed context of the 1990s and 2000s, that growers began to rely on temporary foreign workers.

The switch to a migrant labour force, then, did not happen because of labour shortages, nor did it spring automatically from the creation of guest-worker programs. Instead, it was primarily a consequence of the economic restructuring of agriculture. Despite all this, the growers who did hire Caribbean and Mexican guest workers in the 1970s and '80s told a very different story, arguing that labour shortages – and the poor quality of Canadian labourers – forced them to hire guest workers. These claims, empirically suspect though they were, helped create the labour shortage narrative that persists to this day, and paved the way for the eventual widespread employment of temporary foreign workers.

The book ends with a conclusion that considers the impact of the Covid-19 pandemic on migrant farm workers, the connections between farm labour

and the climate emergency, and how all of this connects with the arguments
and findings of this book.

✦✦✦

Despite superficial understandings of farming as a "traditional" sector, one
that is rapidly disappearing in the rear-view mirror of our ever-accelerating
high-tech economy, agriculture in fact sits at the very core of capitalist modernity. This is not only because of the obvious fact that everyone – from
workers to CEOs – needs to eat, nor simply because agriculture is every bit as
capitalist and modern as any other sector, nor even because the very existence
of the modern, capitalist world – with its large concentrations of population,
high degree of economic specialization, and never-ending growth – is utterly
dependent on hyper-productive agriculture. Rather, in addition to the sector's
foundational role within the global capitalist order, agriculture and its labour
force also occupy key terrain upon which some of the most pressing questions
of twenty-first-century modernity are, and will continue to be, debated and
struggled over.

As a leading greenhouse gas emitter, agriculture figures prominently in questions about the proper relationship between human beings and the natural
world; about the relative valuing of profit, human life, and ecological well-
being; and about the very structures of society and economy in the face of climate catastrophe. As a sector marked by profound inequalities – between
rapidly vanishing smallholding farmers and rights-poor and hyper-exploited
workers, on the one hand, and an ever more consolidated and powerful agribusiness, on the other – agriculture is also deeply implicated in questions about
what character the response to the climate emergency in the wealthy world
should take (which, given the primacy of the climate crisis in the century to
come, is really to say what character society as a whole should take). Should it
be exclusionary, exploitative, and authoritarian, marked by the barring of the
globe's ever more numerous climate migrants, the continued transfer of wealth
from poor to rich, and rule by emergency decree? Or should it be inclusive,
just, democratic, and internationalist, a social movement–driven response –
in alliance with movements in the Global South – in which the emergency of
climate change is tackled alongside the emergencies of racism, colonialism,
imperialism, poverty, and the exploitation of working people?[48]

To adequately answer these questions – and to develop a political program to make those answers a reality – requires a robust understanding of our history, of how we got to where we are today. This book is a modest contribution toward that project of better knowing our past so that we might craft a radically different future.

1

GREEN GOLD RUSH

Since boyhood, Yates Eaker had heard stories about men going up to Canada to work in the tobacco fields. They returned home to Virginia each fall, flush with cash, regaling friends and family with epic tales about their feats of physical stamina, Saturday night dances, and the many curious cultural differences between Canada and the American South. Some of them even met – and married – Canadian girls. A young man toiling on his family's struggling tobacco farm, it was hard for Eaker to decide which sounded more appealing: the money or the adventure. "It was a rough go" growing tobacco in Virginia, Eaker recalled in a 1985 interview. "You didn't get very much for it ... Sometimes you could sell it. One year you could, the next year you couldn't." In such trying economic circumstances, each member of the family was expected to chip in to keep the family afloat. "I had to quit school to help my father on the farm," he remembered.

In 1923, at the age of fourteen, Eaker decided that the time had come for him to join in the yearly northward expedition – to get off the family farm, earn some pocket money, and have some adventures of his own. His dreams, however, were dashed by that age-old vanquisher of teenage schemes: his parents. "My father wouldn't let me come because he needed me on the farm," Eaker explained. "So I always said, 'When I get big enough and old enough, I would go to Canada.'" Six years later, that day finally came, and Eaker made his way to Ontario's tobacco district for the very first time.

Eaker and three male companions from Chase City, Virginia – ranging in age from eighteen to twenty-nine – piled into a car and headed north, crossing into Canada at Niagara Falls on the newly opened Peace Bridge on 18 August 1929. The officer at the immigration checkpoint glanced only briefly at their paperwork before waving them through. Southern tobacco workers, provided

they were white, were permitted to enter Canada for temporary work on tobacco farms, and Eaker was the ninety-ninth such traveller to enter Canada
through the same checkpoint that month. Cleared for entry, Eaker and his
companions continued on to Delhi, Ontario, where it didn't take them long
to find work.

In Delhi, Eaker found a tobacco sector that contrasted greatly with the one
he had left behind in Virginia. "This was a big boom here," he explained. "[It
was] a gold mine." Eaker was employed as a harvester by a farmer named Bird,
paid twenty-five dollars per week plus room, board, and round-trip travel costs
from Virginia – excellent wages compared to back home. Eaker did not just
find work in Ontario. He also found love. The young southerner hit it off with
Nina Jeanne Harper, a seventeen-year-old local girl employed in the farmhouse
kitchen, where she helped Mrs. Bird provide three square meals a day for the
ravenous harvest crew. Eaker went home at the end of the season but returned
to Canada in May 1930 after a fruitless search for winter work. This time, he
had come for good. In August of that year, he and Nina tied the knot in a simple
ceremony at the United Church in Woodstock. The couple eventually settled
in Delhi, where they would remain involved in the tobacco sector for decades
to come.[1]

Yates Eaker was one of tens of thousands of migrants, from diverse parts of
the world and all social stations, who streamed into the Norfolk region in the
1920s and '30s to participate in the "green gold rush" as the district was rapidly
remade into the heartland of Canadian tobacco production. Not ten years prior
to Eaker's arrival, much of the county had been regarded as an agricultural
wasteland, its soil unable, after decades of clear-cutting and unsustainable land
use, to support most food crops or even livestock. That changed in the early
1920s, when a series of experimental crops revealed those same light, sandy,
nutrient-depleted soils to be ideally suited to flue-cured tobacco, the type predominantly used in cigarettes.[2] Unproductive as they had been, the farms on
Norfolk's sand plain were available for bottom dollar, while flue-cured tobacco
was among the hottest of global commodities. Together, these factors sparked
a "crop boom" in Norfolk, as everyone from itinerant labourers to big-city capitalists sought to cash in on the golden leaf.[3]

"A great new life is pulsating through the agricultural activity of South Norfolk," exclaimed the *Simcoe Reformer* in 1928 in reference to the changes taking
hold in the area. "Formerly a land of comparative quiet, the district is now

alive and teeming with industry. Delivery trucks of business men in Simcoe, Delhi and Tillsonburg; great loads of lumber being hurried to the farms where tobacco kilns are in course of construction; ... hundreds of men working in the fields, and almost as many more making ready for the curing process."[4] The formerly struggling region took quickly to tobacco. In just one year, between 1927 and 1928, Norfolk's acreage of flue-cured tobacco nearly quadrupled, from 1,300 to 5,000 acres. By 1941, flue-cured covered 26,500 acres in Norfolk, with sale of the crop accounting for 67 per cent of the county's total farm revenues.[5] The crop reinvented Norfolk's economy, becoming the dominant commercial activity and bringing unprecedented wealth to the region. Stories abounded of the fabulous profits to be made in the new tobacco district, even as the crisis of the Great Depression wreaked havoc in the world around it. "$30,000 to start 100-Acre Tobacco Farm – But One Year's Return May Be $50,000," proclaimed a 1939 headline in the *Toronto Star*.[6]

Norfolk was the newest frontier in the global corporate empire of tobacco, whose rapid growth in recent decades had been fuelled by soaring demand for cigarettes. Mass-produced, cheap, stylish, and extremely addictive, cigarettes were the ultimate modern consumer product, and over the previous few decades had become the dominant form of tobacco consumption in the industrialized Global North, a trend that only became more pronounced in the interwar years.[7] Between 1922 and 1936, total annual consumption of cigarettes in Canada almost tripled, from about 2 million cigarettes to 5.6 million, and the story was similar in the United States and the United Kingdom. Multinational tobacco corporations, craving new sources of tobacco leaf, eagerly supported the development of the Norfolk sector and purchased its produce. Cigarette manufacturers in Canada (Montreal mostly) and the United Kingdom were especially thrilled to gain access to raw product that carried no or low tariffs – as opposed to the American tobacco that had dominated raw leaf imports up to then.[8]

Trade policies, commodity markets, environmental factors, and land prices may have provided the perfect preconditions for the green gold rush, but it was people who carried it out. And a significant majority were, like Eaker, newcomers to the region. From the very beginning, Norfolk's flue-cured tobacco sector was utterly dependent on migrants, new settlers and seasonal workers alike. Despite the new tobacco belt's need for labour, however, not all prospective tobacco workers and growers were equally welcome to partake in the green gold rush. Indeed, access to the tobacco labour market – and opportunities within it – were highly differentiated along lines of gender, "race," ethnicity, and class. Still, during the interwar years, a diverse range of working people joined the green gold rush, with some becoming lifelong Norfolk residents and participants in the tobacco sector. Over the next half-century, the industry they built would become one of the country's most profitable agricultural sectors and, with its high seasonal labour requirements, the epicentre of migrant farm labour in Canada.

Owners, Workers, and Production

The scores of working people flooding into the Norfolk region did not arrive, for the most part, as farm owners. Instead, they came to fill positions – as wage labourers and sharecroppers – opened up by wealthy landowners who had purchased farms in order to convert them to tobacco production. Unlike monocrop agriculture in some other contexts that featured massive, centrally controlled operations, Ontario tobacco was organized around the relatively small production unit of the farm: large landholdings were divided up into multiple farms, each operated by a sharecropper.[9] A typical farm was between 100 and 150 acres, which allowed for the planting of 30 acres of tobacco each year, accounting for land needed for rotation crops and buildings, as well as non-productive terrain.[10]

Farm buyers participating in the green gold rush ran the gamut from small businessmen purchasing one or two farms to publicly traded corporations acquiring thousands of acres, holdings they unselfconsciously dubbed "plantations." On the smaller end of that spectrum, many farm-purchasing investors hailed from the old tobacco belt in Essex and Kent Counties, in the most southwestern corner of Ontario, where they had been involved in the sector as farmers and managerial staff. On the larger end, the first such company on the scene was Ontario Tobacco Plantations (OTP), founded in 1926. Headed by investment bankers from Toronto and Montreal, by 1929 OTP controlled 1,900 acres of tobacco land. Its public stock offerings gave potential investors "an opportunity to share in unusual farm profits," with advertisements boasting that "farm lands sold a few years ago for less than $100 an acre are changing hands at from $600 to $1,000 an acre ... as a result of profits from tobacco." Prospective shareholders wanting more information could request a copy of a booklet entitled *The Weed that Brings Wealth to Canada*.[11] OTP was hardly the only, or even the biggest, of the corporate plantations. Windham Plantations, whose directors hailed from the agribusiness centre of Guelph, Ontario, and the industrial city of Troy, New York, ballooned from 5,300 acres in 1931 to 10,000 in 1939, when it acquired three other plantations, boosting the total number of farms in its possession to ninety.[12]

Corporations controlled a significant proportion of tobacco production, especially in the sector's early years. In 1928, seven companies grew 33 per cent of Norfolk's tobacco, and in 1929 ten companies grew 40 per cent of the crop. Together, corporations' and investors' farms produced an estimated 65 per cent of the total flue-cured crop in 1937. The remaining 35 per cent was grown by smallholders who owned and operated their own farms. Many had farms of similar size to the units owned by investors and corporations, with approximately 30 acres of tobacco, though a fair number also produced smaller amounts. In 1939, for example, 403 out of the region's 2,026 tobacco growers (about 20 per cent) planted fewer than 13 acres.[13]

In order to produce their crops, the vast majority of corporations and investors contracted "sharegrowers," as sharecroppers were more commonly known in Ontario's tobacco belt. The exact details of this cost- and profit-sharing arrangement varied, but generally speaking, the landowner provided the land, equipment, and physical structures such as greenhouses and kilns, while the sharegrower and his family contributed their own labour, and also covered most of the costs of wage labour, with other expenditures divided on a contract-by-contract basis. Profits were shared evenly, or close to it.[14]

Tobacco belt sharegrowing was not simply an import from the United States. Though the American investors purchasing tobacco farms may have drawn inspiration from southern sharecropping, Ontario boasted its own long history of tenant farming and related production arrangements.[15] Furthermore, sharegrowing in Ontario tobacco was far less exploitative than its US counterpart and provided ample opportunities for social mobility, as will be explored in more detail in chapter 2.[16] While investors managed sharegrowers directly, corporations typically hired a plantation manager to oversee operations on all of their farms.[17] Only one of the major plantations chose to forego the sharegrowing system by directly employing workers to produce its crop: the Lake Erie Tobacco Company, which hired 125 labourers to work its 420 acres.[18]

For their part, sharegrowers and smallholders utilized a combination of family and waged labour to bring in their crops. The typical tobacco farm of about 30 planted acres required a harvest crew (often called a "gang") of about a dozen people. (Farms with smaller acreages employed "half gangs" or "three-quarter gangs.") According to prevailing gender- and age-related norms, on a 30-acre farm, at least six of the harvest jobs could only be done by adult men, or by older teenage boys at the youngest, meaning that even the largest of families would struggle to furnish an adequate workforce without turning to supplemental wage labour. Indeed, whether operated by sharegrowers or smallholders, nearly every farm hired workers, not only at harvest time, but for pre- and post-harvest jobs as well, though these periods generally required no more than three paid hands. At harvest time, most farmers turned to workers from outside the region to complete their crews, arrangements that included the provision of room and board.[19] For most farms, labour was far and away the greatest expense, accounting for more than half of all expenditures.[20] The rapid expansion of the industry – combined with changes in work processes that amplified labour requirements on each farm – resulted in an explosion in the overall size of the annual harvest workforce. In 1931, estimates of the total harvest workforce ranged from 4,000 to 5,000. Four years later, in 1935, an estimated 16,000 were required to bring in the crop, a number that by 1944 had ballooned to almost 32,000.[21]

Farmers had little trouble finding harvest workers, since high crop prices allowed them to pay wages that were significantly better than those in other crop sectors – and sometimes even outstripped rates for industrial jobs. Whereas a hired hand on a general farm in Norfolk County earned less than a dollar per day (plus board) in the late 1930s, a tobacco harvest worker could make up to four times as much, with wages averaging between three and four dollars per day plus board.[22] As George V. Haythorne and Leonard C. Marsh observed in their 1941 book on the central Canadian farm labour market, "tobacco workers who perform highly seasonal labour are among the highest paid agricultural wage-earners in Canada." Of course, as Haythorne and Marsh hinted, these high wages were only paid during the limited time period of the six-week harvest. Paying higher wages was not an act of generosity on the part of employers, but simply allowed growers to ensure a steady supply of qualified workers, a crucial consideration when dealing with a perishable crop at harvest time.[23]

The tobacco raised on farms in the Norfolk region was ultimately destined for manufacture into cigarettes, but it took years and many stages of production for leaf to travel from the fields of southern Ontario to the lips of smokers. The tobacco-growing season began in March, with the planting of seeds in greenhouses and ploughing of land. Around the last week of May, seedlings were taken out of greenhouses and transplanted in farmers' fields. The delicate job of "pulling" plants from greenhouse seedbeds was gendered as women's work and was often performed either by women farmers or female wage labourers. These same women often transplanted as well, though this job was also done by men. The freshly planted rows of tobacco represented a significant investment for farmers, who went to great lengths to ensure that each plant reached its full potential. As a leading expert told the *Toronto Star Weekly* in 1931, "A tobacco plant requires as much attention as a race horse." Tobacco fields required irrigation and were hoed to keep weeds from stealing nutrients. As the harvest approached, plants needed to be "topped" (removing the flower at the head of the plant) and "suckered" (removing plant growth underneath tobacco leaves). Hoeing, topping, and suckering were gendered as male tasks. Since these jobs only needed to be done occasionally, farmers sometimes hired crews of workers via a labour contractor rather than entering multiple agreements with individual workers.[24]

Finally, after months of preparation and careful nurturing of the plants, came the harvest, usually beginning in late July or early August. Here, in the early years of Norfolk's tobacco boom, the methods of production were undergoing significant changes. The first crops of flue-cured tobacco in the new tobacco belt were harvested by cutting down entire tobacco plants, called "stalk-cutting." By 1930, some farmers were beginning to switch to a different harvest method, "priming," which had been widespread in the United States since the late nineteenth century. Rather than cutting down the entire plant, workers picked ("primed") three leaves at a time, starting at the bottom of the plant; they returned repeatedly to the same field over the course of a few weeks, gradually working their way up the plants' stalks. Though harvesting by priming added significantly to farm owners' labour costs (by one estimate, it increased the average harvest crew from six to twelve workers), it boasted many

1.1 Harvesting tobacco by stalk cutting, Norfolk Plantation, ca 1927. RG 16-274, vol. D011465, I0033981, AO.

advantages, increasing quality and yields while providing insurance against adverse weather events by allowing farmers to start harvesting earlier in the year, before the topmost leaves were ripe. By 1932, about 90 per cent of growers were harvesting by the new method. The final push toward priming came that winter in the form of economic compulsion, when the sector's biggest buyer, the Imperial Tobacco Company of Canada, refused to purchase the crops of the few remaining stalk-cutting farmers. In 1933, "practically every grower" primed their crops.[25]

Priming was dirty, difficult, dangerous, and physically exhausting work. Novelist and one-time primer Hugh Garner described the work in a short story inspired by his experiences in the fields: "Without a word we walked to our rows and crouched between them, tearing off the sand leaves like destructive ants, and cradling them in the crook of our other arm. We shuffled ahead on our haunches through a world suddenly turned to jungle, along a sandy aisle that promised an ephemeral salvation at the other end of the field."[26] Folk

1.2   Priming tobacco: piling leaves into a horse-drawn "boat," Delhi, Ontario, 1959. *The Back-Breaking Leaf*, 1959, National Film Board of Canada.

singer Stompin' Tom Connors was more direct when he crooned, "Tillsonburg / Tillsonburg / My back still aches when I hear that word."[27] Primers experienced the full range of climatic extremes: cold and wet in the early morning dew-soaked fields, and oppressive heat in the afternoon sun. They often contracted a skin condition, called green tobacco sickness or tobacco poisoning, brought on by contact with the dissolved nicotine on wet tobacco leaves that could also have more serious side effects.[28] The combination of heat and physical exertion could sometimes be even more dangerous, and numerous workers were reported to have died from heat stroke and related conditions.[29] Due to its strenuous nature and prevalent ideas about work, gender, and exertion, priming was limited exclusively to men until technological changes starting in the 1960s made the job significantly easier to perform.[30]

Not only did priming add to labour requirements in the field, but it also created a new set of jobs for handling leaves after being harvested. Whereas before, entire plants were hung in kilns for curing, now individual leaves had to be affixed to wooden slats in order to be cured. This work happened at the

1.3 Working at the tying table, Delhi, Ontario, 1959. *The Back-Breaking Leaf*, 1959, National Film Board of Canada.

"tying table" and was gendered almost exclusively female. Once primed, to-bacco leaves were piled into a "boat" that, when full, was taken by horse to the tying table, stationed outside the kiln being filled that day. There, a crew of six women was typically employed, working in two groups of three. Two "handers" passed handfuls of leaves to the "tier," who, with remarkable speed and dex-terity, affixed them to laths. A reporter described the work of Mary Werner, a "champion" tier from Teeterville: "She worked like a shuttle in a loom, weaving handfuls of leaves alternately on either side of a four-foot lath resting on notches [on] a wooden horse. With one hand she took the leaves from a helper, with the other she twisted the string about them, and fastened them securely without ever making a knot."[31] Sticks affixed with tobacco leaves were then hung in the kiln by a "kilnhanger," invariably a man, who nimbly (and dan-gerously) climbed from beam to beam inside the kiln and packed it full of to-bacco. Farms with a full "gang" filled one kiln per day; most farms had six or seven kilns that were filled and emptied on a rotating basis.[32] Tying did not pose the same occupational hazards as priming or kilnhanging, but women

1.4 The scene at the kiln, Delhi, Ontario, 1959. *The Back-Breaking Leaf*, 1959, National Film Board of Canada

workers in tobacco – as in many other sectors, agricultural and otherwise – all too often faced the threat of sexual violence.[33]

Since workers were paid by piece rate – with a daily quota of filling one kiln – they were incentivized to work quickly rather than extend their day unnecessarily. This frequently sparked tensions within harvest gangs, in particular between tiers and primers, but also within each group. A slow crew of primers meant that the tying table would have to wait idly for the next batch of tobacco leaves to come in, while slow tiers could delay the delivery of an empty "boat" to the field. Olive Elm of the Oneida Nation of the Thames reported that slow primers could sometimes force tiers to stay after dark to finish the day's work. But "if they were fast, then sometimes by two o'clock we were done. If it was a good group. But it has to be a good group, only then would it get done fast. You couldn't be resting every little while."[34]

To keep the day short, slower workers would often be exhorted to speed up, something that frequently played out along generational lines, with older, more experienced workers schooling younger ones – in some cases constructively, in others, less so. Though such criticism could be difficult for young workers to take, they often quickly came to understand that working fast was indeed

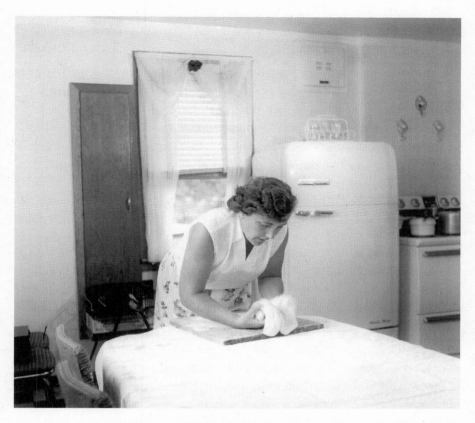

1.5 Making bread for the harvest crew, Delhi, Ontario, 1959. *The Back-Breaking Leaf*, 1959, National Film Board of Canada.

to the benefit of all. As Joanne Passmore recalled in an oral history interview about her time working in tobacco in the 1960s, "When you're doing that kind of work, … everything is so connected … If I wasn't fast enough unloading boats, well, yeah, the ladies at the table would … not yell at me, but [tell me to speed up]. But that was okay. It made you more efficient."[35]

The necessity for larger harvest workforces – and an increased incidence of boarding migrant workers – added significantly to the duties of women members of tobacco farming families. Farm women cooked meals and kept house for their families and employees, an enormous task with serious repercussions: the quality of the food was often an important factor in determining where the most-skilled harvesters would choose to work for the season.[36] The *Canadian Tobacco Grower* magazine regularly published a column sharing farm women's recipes for feeding harvest crews and strategies for handling the immense amount of labour that entailed.[37] Farm women's work during the harvest was so intense that multiple growers interviewed for this book mentioned that one of the biggest benefits of hiring Caribbean guest workers (in the 1960s or later) was that they prepared their own meals, thereby drastically reducing women's workload.[38] In some cases where farmers hired family groups rather than individual wage labourers, family groups provided their own meals. Oneida woman Mercy Doxtator, for example, reported working with her family at a farm in Walsingham as a young girl and being responsible – along with the daughter of another working family – for preparing snacks and lunch for the older, wage-earning members of the families.[39] This sort of arrangement, however, appears to have been extremely uncommon compared to the near-universal practice of grower-provided meals in the tobacco sector's early decades.

After being primed, tied, and hung in the kiln, tobacco was ready to be cured. To oversee this process, most farmers hired a curer (always a man), who was tasked with meticulously managing the kiln's temperature and humidity over the seven days of curing. Curing was considered the tobacco job requiring the most skill, and a good curer was absolutely crucial to producing a profitable crop; a single spoiled kiln would take a sizeable chunk out of a farmer's earnings. As such, not just anyone was entrusted to perform this job, and the majority of farms hired (white) curers from the tobacco-producing regions of the southern United States, who were considered experts in the task.[40] Curing was spoken of in reverential terms by many observers. "The curer is regarded as a high-priced man, but it seemed to me that he earns his money," wrote one reporter. "His nearest parallel is the Roman sentry at Herculaneum, who remained at his post until the ashes buried him. The curer never takes off his clothes in the whole five weeks of his sentry go. He has a sort of kennel near the kilns and the most important tool in his trade is the alarm clock. He can never take more than two hours sleep at a stretch."[41] Curing a kiln of tobacco typically took three to five days, after which the cured leaf was removed and stored in barns, where, once the harvest was completed, it would be removed from the wooden sticks, sorted into groups based on colour and

1.6 A full table at harvest time: French-Canadian workers, Langton, Ontario, 1961.
London Free Press Collection of Photographic Negatives, 2 September 1961,
Western University Archives and Special Collections, London, Ontario.

quality, and stacked into bales – work that was performed by both women and
men. At this point, the crop was ready to be sold.[42]

Corporate plantations, smaller investors, and individual farm owners alike
sold their crops to a small number of companies. Some of these were vertically
integrated firms (such as the Imperial Tobacco Company of Canada), which
controlled every aspect of the post-farm production process, while others purchased tobacco in order to later resell it to manufacturing firms. After being
acquired from farms, but before moving on to cigarette factories, tobacco leaf

1.7 Tobacco curer in the kiln, Delhi, Ontario, 1960. London Free Press Collection
of Photographic Negatives, 14 September 1960, Western University Archives and
Special Collections, London, Ontario.

required additional stages of preparation, including weighing, sorting, and
drying. Next, it was stored in barrels and warehoused for two to three years
(important for the development of the desired flavour) before being shipped
to a manufacturing plant. Local tobacco factories – whether owned by vertically
integrated firms or by reselling companies – handled these intermediate stages
of production; cigarette manufacturers, on the other hand, were usually located
in industrial cities, Montreal in particular.

Like on the farm, work in tobacco factories was rigidly divided along gender lines. The Imperial Tobacco Company of Canada was by far the most important tobacco-buying company; it purchased the largest share of Ontario leaf (53 per cent in 1932, for example) and wielded immense power in the sector's operation. Along with other buying companies, it invested significant capital in the Norfolk region, most strikingly via its erection of a $750,000 tobacco plant in Delhi in 1930. Part of an 8-acre compound in the village's south end, the Imperial plant was hailed as a monument to modernity and industry, its opening billed as the "climax" of Norfolk's rapid conversion into the heartland of Canadian tobacco production. Other major tobacco buyers included Canadian Leaf, with a plant in Tillsonburg, and British Leaf, with one in Chatham.[43]

Delhi's Imperial plant was a bricks-and-mortar confirmation of the new tobacco belt's importance within the international tobacco business, one of the most thoroughly globalized industries of the pre–World War II period. Imperial was (and remains) a subsidiary of British American Tobacco (BAT), founded by a group of capitalists from both countries in 1902 as a market-sharing venture aimed at ensuring mutual profits from tobacco production and sales in the world beyond the United States and the United Kingdom. Though BAT's initial focus was on securing global markets for its products (most famously, Lucky Strike), it soon also became involved in extending tobacco agriculture and manufacturing into new regions in order to augment and diversify its supply of raw leaf. By the start of World War II, it boasted operations in China, Japan, Rhodesia (later Zimbabwe), South Africa, Australia, Germany, and Canada. According to historian Howard Cox, "between the two world wars, [BAT] was the world's most geographically extensive multinational company, pioneering techniques of international marketing and human resource management."[44] Norfolk, Ontario, represented another wing of this empire, though it was far from the first foray of a tobacco mega-corporation into Ontario agriculture: one of BAT's co-founders, the American Tobacco Company (ATC), had been present in Essex County since the 1890s. With the formation of BAT in 1902, it was reorganized under Imperial's banner. Though most of Norfolk's flue-cured tobacco was destined for Canadian cigarette manufacturers, about one-fifth of crops were exported in the 1930s, with more than 90 per cent of exports going to the United Kingdom.[45]

Green Gold Rushers

Just as the cigarette business was global, so, too, was the workforce that produced its raw materials in Ontario. While long-standing Norfolk residents
certainly participated in the tobacco sector, there can be little doubt that the
green gold rush was driven primarily by migrants. "Tobacco ... has added
3,000 to the county's population and has made it cosmopolitan," observed
one reporter. "On one field I saw Germans, Hollanders, Belgians, Hungarians,
Canadians, and southerners working together." On Saturday night, Delhi became a "southern or Belgian town full of soft drawling voices and loud clat-
tering wooden shoes."[46]

Though the correspondent's description of Belgian footwear as a ubiquitous
presence on the streets of Delhi might have been somewhat exaggerated, his
take on the district's newfound cosmopolitanism was not. Indeed, a motley
crew descended upon Norfolk and its environs in the 1920s and '30s. Seasonal
migrants and permanent settlers alike, they hailed from as close as Hamilton
and as far as eastern Europe. Perhaps the biggest group of new settlers in Norfolk were immigrants – Americans, Belgians, Hungarians, and other Europeans
– who had first settled elsewhere in Canada but jumped at the chance to try
their luck on the tobacco frontier, a type of migration that historian Yukari
Takai labels "transmigration."[47] Transmigrants came in large numbers from
Ontario's prior tobacco hub in Essex and Kent Counties, where immigrants
from the southern United States and Belgium – specifically Flemings from the
latter country – had figured prominently (the Belgians had also worked ex-
tensively in sugar beets). So important was Belgian migration from Essex-Kent
to Norfolk that the Flemish newspaper *Gazette van Detroit*, which served the
community in both Michigan and southwestern Ontario, began running a
regular column about Belgians in Norfolk called "Our People from the East."[48]

Transmigrant Europeans also came to the Norfolk district from western
Canada and central Canadian industrial cities such as Montreal, Toronto, and
Hamilton. Many had come to Canada under the 1925–30 Railway Agreements,
in which the federal government, in an effort to provide agricultural labour
to western Canada, contracted transportation companies to recruit and transport immigrants from continental Europe, resulting in the entrance of over
370,000 newcomers during this period. Upon arrival, many of these immigrants realized that the prospects of farm ownership and prosperity in the

Prairie West were not quite so attainable as company agents had led them to believe, and promptly moved on to jobs in resource-extraction industries or industrial cities.[49] High wages and opportunities for social mobility made Norfolk's burgeoning tobacco sector another attractive destination for the Hungarians, Czechs, Slovaks, ethnic Germans, Ukrainians, Poles, Lithuanians, and others who found themselves in similar situations.

For a sizeable chunk of these immigrants, the tobacco belt represented the final destination of a multi-year itinerary, featuring stops in the West, industrial cities, resource-extraction regions, and other agricultural zones. Two examples drawn from life history surveys conducted with Norfolk-area residents in 1977 will illustrate the point, but hundreds more green gold rushers had comparable trajectories. Born in Lithuania, Mrs K. Simutis immigrated to Canada in 1929 at the age of twenty-one. She settled first in Saskatchewan, but after just six months as a domestic worker there relocated to Montreal, where she also performed domestic labour until 1933. In that year, Simutis began working in a men's clothing factory, where she stayed for eleven years before coming with her husband to Norfolk to work as a harvest labourer. After three years they were able to purchase a farm in the area, and they henceforth remained permanently.[50] John Mayer, an ethnic German born in Romania, also immigrated to Canada in 1929, when he was twenty-three. While his original destination was Winnipeg, he stayed there for only three days before heading back east to Hamilton. There, he found six months' work at a shipyard, followed by two and half years at the Dominion Steel Foundry. During the 1930s, Mayer went back and forth between working in Norfolk tobacco and industrial jobs in Hamilton at Dominion Steel and Canadian Canners (a food processing plant). After years of trying, in 1938 he finally got a contract to grow tobacco on shares, and he settled permanently in the Norfolk region, eventually becoming the owner of two farms.[51]

Not all migrants to the tobacco belt came to stay. Many were seasonal workers, attracted by tobacco's relatively high wages who responded to employers' large periodic labour requirements, particularly at harvest time, but also during planting season. They came from industrial cities such as Hamilton, London, Toronto, and Montreal, and from nearby agricultural districts and Indigenous communities. Many tobacco workers came from farming families who raised crops other than tobacco or kept livestock. It was particularly common for the children and wives of male farmers to work for wages in tobacco at times when their labour was not required on the home farm.[52] Short-distance migrants came to the tobacco belt not only for farm work, but also for winter jobs in tobacco factories, especially at Imperial. About half of these latter jobs were filled by women from proximate farming communities, who nevertheless boarded in Norfolk for the duration of their contracts.[53]

First Nations workers represented a steady – if numerically very small – component of the tobacco workforce for much of the twentieth century, hailing principally from Six Nations (just east of the tobacco belt), Saugeen First Nation (on the Bruce Peninsula, two hundred kilometres north of London, and working on the much smaller number of tobacco farms in that region), and three communities just outside of London: Munsee-Delaware, Chippewa of the Thames, and Oneida Nation of the Thames.[54] While precise statistics prove elusive, it appears likely that the number of Indigenous workers each harvest fell somewhere under or around a thousand.[55] It was particularly common for Indigenous labourers to work in family groups, sometimes with as many as three generations working side by side on the same farm. Mercy Doxtator of Oneida Nation, for example, reported travelling with her family to work on various farms in Norfolk, including a farm in Walsingham, where she worked alongside her siblings, parents, and grandfather.[56] Sometimes Indigenous families worked for the same farmers year after year, with employment even being passed down through generations. In an oral history interview, Bill Byer, member of a long-time tobacco-farming family, reported that his grandfather hired members of three families from Six Nations for many years – and three generations of at least one family.[57] Not all tobacco farmers were willing to hire First Nations workers, however, with some refusing employment on racist grounds.[58] Other patterns of Indigenous employment differed little from non-Indigenous ones – for example, occupational mobility. Clifford Cornelius of Oneida Nation, who began working in tobacco around the 1940s, had an employment record very similar to those of the tobacco belt's European immigrants, moving frequently between jobs in construction, canning, and agriculture throughout southwestern Ontario and Detroit.[59]

The attraction of the tobacco belt to migrant workers only grew as the Great Depression took hold around it, and each summer during the 1930s, in late July and early August, job seekers from across North America flocked to Delhi, Simcoe, and Tillsonburg, eager for some short-term, well-paid work. Labelled "transients," and their arrivals dubbed "influxes," some of these mi-

1.8 Jean Kewageshig, Christine Wesley, and Audrey Roote of Saugeen First Nation pull tobacco plants in greenhouse, southeast of Southampton, Ontario, 1963. London Free Press Collection of Photographic Negatives, 1 June 1963, Western University Archives and Special Collections, London, Ontario.

grants travelled alone, others with groups of family members or friends. Most had made no prior arrangements for work or accommodations – instead, they spent their days hanging around town, hoping to be hired onto a farm. At night, they slept wherever they could – in barns, boxcars, or simply on benches or in parks. The *Reformer* described the scene in 1937 as follows: "At every crossroad there is a labor fair, for each area of 25 tobacco acres needs a dozen pickers. Growers come in with a truck, bargain and make their pick and drive away with an exultant load. The workers who are left on the shelf roll over for another snooze or put a tomato tin on an open fire for a cup of solacing tea."[60] As the 1930s wore on, transient workers were increasingly deemed a "problem" by local populations and officials from all levels in government, as we will see in subsequent chapters. Not only did they jam up sidewalks and parks, but they also had a pesky tendency to organize for better conditions within the sector.

Rounding out the new tobacco belt's workforce were migrants, such as Yates Eaker, from the southern United States. Hailing largely from the historic epicentre of flue-cured tobacco agriculture, North Carolina and Virginia's "Old Bright Belt," southerners filled all roles within the Norfolk tobacco sector, from farm to factory, but they were especially coveted for the highly skilled role of curer. Most came first to Ontario as seasonal workers, but like Eaker, some chose to settle permanently in the Norfolk region.[61] Farm owners in Ontario had little trouble locating willing workers in the Old Bright Belt, where the tobacco economy had faced years of stagnation and – during the Great Depression – outright crisis, as tobacco prices plummeted, banks and other systems of credit collapsed, and tenant farmers and sharecroppers were cut out of contracts and pushed off the land.[62] In the 1930s, about 1,000 seasonal workers participated in this annual migration, increasing in later decades to about 1,500 per year, though in peak years as many as 4,000 southerners came north to work in Ontario tobacco.[63]

The Virginians and North Carolinians travelling to Ontario were part of a global network of southern tobaccomen that extended into Ontario. As James Buchanan Duke's ATC (and then its successor, the BAT), expanded its operations around the world, it drew on experienced farmers, managers, and technicians from the tobacco heartland to guide the establishment of tobacco farming and manufacturing concerns from Georgia to Germany to China.[64] Historian Pete Daniel has noted that Granville County, North Carolina, served as an especially important source of these globe-trotting experts, and hence the worldwide diffusion of flue-cured tobacco culture, a phenomenon he has labelled, "Granville County Imperialism."[65] Granville imperialism was no less evident in Ontario's tobacco sector, some of whose biggest players traced their origins to that very county.

Participation in this network, however, was not open to all tobacco-savvy southerners. As historian Nan Enstad explains, "to be part of the transnational

1.9 A young tobacco worker, Granville, North Carolina, 1939. Dorothea Lange, LC-DIG-fsa-8b34080, July 1939, Prints and Photographs Division, Library of Congress.

network, one had to be white and male and to have some connection to farming, curing, auctioning, or manufacturing bright leaf tobacco." This meant that African Americans, critical participants – from farm to factory – in the Old Bright Belt tobacco industry and a significant segment of the area's total population, played no part in the more gilded project of Granville imperialism. The network, Enstad continues, was "a product and expression of Jim Crow" that served to reproduce "segregation's hierarchies" on the global, corporate stage.[66]

The US-Ontario movement was no exception, and until the 1960s participation in this seasonal labour migration was open exclusively to whites, due
not only to the racist structure of southern tobacco networks, but also to
Canada's unofficial colour bar in this period, and likely as well to some Ontario
growers' anti-Black prejudice and concerns about sparking racial tensions
on their farms, ideological tendencies that would be revealed in a series of
incidents in the 1960s. Regardless of the precise division of responsibility for
the movement's whites-only status, Blacks from the southern tobacco zone
appear to have gotten the message loud and clear: they were not welcome in
Canada.[67] An examination of 2,053 border-crossing records for farm workers
(mostly in tobacco) entering at Fort Erie from 1928 to 1935 turned up a grand
total of one migrant whose "race or people" was listed as "colored" – though
he was headed not to the tobacco belt, but instead to Manitoba.[68]

For workers who were able to secure entry to Ontario and the tobacco labour
market, migration to the Norfolk region – particularly in the early years of the
sector's development – was often organized by the investors and managers of
corporate plantations who had scooped up tobacco farms. This was especially
apparent in the transmigration of sharegrowers and workers from Essex-Kent.
Such "elite brokers" of migration to the tobacco belt often fell within the classic
role of facilitating the migration of members of their ethnic group, but this
was not always the case.[69] Notably, a number of American investors, firmly entrenched in the exclusive, whites-only global network of tobacco experts, played
important roles in encouraging Europeans – as well as some of their white
compatriots – to relocate from Essex-Kent to the Norfolk area.[70]

Perhaps the most important of these businessmen was Francis R. Gregory,
widely considered one of the foremost "pioneers" of the so-called New Belt
and of the Canadian tobacco industry more broadly. Born in 1881 to a tobacco
plantation–owning family in Granville County, North Carolina, Gregory
moved to Leamington, Ontario, in 1901, at the age of twenty, to take up a
managerial position with the Canadian branch of the ATC, eventually progressing to plant manager – a telling example of Granville imperialism. In
1926, Gregory joined in the green gold rush and purchased a farm in Norfolk,
eventually amassing a fortune from tobacco farms (by 1950, he owned fifty)
and other ventures that by the time of his death in 1959 was estimated at $10
million. Gregory was also instrumental in the founding of the Flue-Cured
Tobacco Marketing Association of Ontario in the 1930s (established in 1934

THE BRIGHT LEAF

CANADA'S PREMIER TOBACCO MAGAZINE

JUNE
1960

Limit To Water
Supply, What
Science Can Do
Page 11

THREE-QUARTERS OF TOBACCO
FARMS HAVE IRRIGATION
Page 23

THE LIFE STORY OF FRANCIS GREGORY — Page 10

1.10 Francis Gregory on the cover of *Bright Leaf*, June 1960. Courtesy of Delhi Tobacco Museum and Heritage Centre. George Demeyere Library, Delhi Tobacco Museum and Heritage Centre.

under a different name before being reconstituted in 1936), and he served as a director in that organization in every year but one until 1957, including eight years as chairman. A cantankerous man who throughout his career fought many pitched battles with any government official or tobacco farmer with the temerity to disagree with him, Gregory's presence in the sector was so all-encompassing that he was given the nickname "Mr. Tobacco." In addition to facilitating the migration of southerners and Belgians from Essex-Kent to Norfolk, Gregory – and other American investors – encouraged the travel of migrant workers from North Carolina and Virginia.[71]

Like migrants from Essex-Kent, some of the early relocations of European immigrants from elsewhere in Canada were facilitated by elite brokers, often within ethnic communities. Hungarian Paul Rapai, for example, after purchasing a tobacco farm in 1933, placed notices in two Hungarian newspapers in order to alert his countrymen to the bounty to be made in the tobacco belt (and, of course, to secure his own workforce). According to Rapai, a thousand Hungarians responded to the ads and came to work in the tobacco harvest, with many staying on permanently. In addition to facilitating migration, Rapai for decades fulfilled many of the other roles often associated with elite brokers, representing the community in meetings with government officials and organizing the establishment of the Delhi and Tobacco District Hungarian House in 1947.[72]

Over time, however, the importance of elite brokers like Rapai and Gregory in facilitating migration waned, eclipsed by informal networks organized along lines of kinship or ethnicity, as newcomers to the Norfolk area relayed information to family members, friends, and acquaintances about the opportunities available in the tobacco sector, and helped new arrivals secure employment and housing.[73] Europeans coming through these channels tended, like their established contacts in Norfolk, to be transmigrants rather than direct transatlantic immigrants, which is unsurprising given the stringent immigration restrictions in place after 1931.[74] Only with the relaxation of immigration rules after World War II would Norfolk begin to receive a significant number of immigrants directly from Europe. In their new home, Norfolk's immigrants forged ethnic communities, settling close to fellow community members, building ethnic halls (by mid-century, Delhi boasted Hungarian, Belgian, German, and Polish halls), establishing political organizations and growers' associations, opening businesses catering to each community, and developing informal social ties.[75]

As the tobacco belt's new residents built community networks and institutions in Ontario, they maintained transnational ties with their home communities. These lines of communication served to maintain cultural links, transmit knowledge about the tobacco industry and other economic matters, and encourage future migration. The *Reformer*'s social pages frequently mentioned southerners returning home to visit for a month or two, often during the winter, and big events affecting Norfolk's American community were reported on in an Oxford, North Carolina, newspaper.[76] Like their American counterparts, Belgian families also returned home for winter visits, sometimes proudly displaying evidence of their Canadian prosperity to relatives in Europe, and reported back on happenings in Europe. Transnational ties also helped preserve Belgian cultural traditions. The musician M. Victor Van Geyseghem, a master of the Flemish-origin instrument called the carillon, performed a show in Simcoe while in Canada for the Congress of Carilloneurs.[77]

The flurry of mobility that supplied the emergent tobacco sector with its labour force came with its own sets of risks to workers, in addition to those encountered on the farm – namely, traffic accidents. Agriculture's diffuse rural geography meant – and still means – that workers spent a lot of time on the road, both to find work and, while employed, to move between farm and town. As Frank Bardacke writes in his history of the United Farm Workers, cars are "perhaps the most essential agricultural implements in California."[78] Job seekers travelling to the tobacco belt by car sometimes did not make it to their destination. In 1936, a Belgian immigrant family of four – mother Sidonia, father Acheele, and daughters Georgette and Marlette, aged seventeen and twelve, respectively – along with family friend Maurice Vandenhende, were driving from Bleinheim, Ontario, to Delhi in search of work when their car failed to brake at a rail crossing just outside of Delhi and was struck by an on-coming train, killing all five.[79] Tobacco workers walking or stopped along rural roads were also at risk. In 1942, First Nations tobacco worker Alex Porter (likely from Munsee-Delaware Nation) was struck by a passing car in a hit-and-run while changing a flat tire on his car, just east of Tillsonburg. A newspaper report listed him as in "critical condition," but it is unclear what became of him.[80]

Though newcomers led the tobacco rush, locals also participated at all levels of the emergent flue-cured economy. At the farm level, they worked as wage labourers, grew tobacco on shares, and owned their own farms. It was estimated in 1931 that 32 per cent of Norfolk's tobacco crop was grown on farms owned by long-time Norfolk residents, though a proportion of these were held by wealthy Norfolkians who hired sharegrowers – likely newcomers – to produce their crops. Beyond the farm gate, locals found other ways to cash in on the green gold rush. The rapid establishment of new tobacco farms sparked a con-struction boom, as farms required kilns, greenhouses, and other structures. Builders, hardware and lumber merchants, as well as other local storeowners, all benefitted from the increase in economic activity. The wives of local general farmers also got involved, growing tobacco plants in hotbeds to sell to tobacco farmers when the latter's plants failed or were killed by early frost. Finally, a number of locals were able to find jobs in the region's new tobacco processing and storage facilities.[81]

Norfolk Remade

The green gold rush left Norfolk County and its environs utterly transformed. After a generation of economic and demographic decline – marked by Norfolk's 21 per cent drop in population from 1881 to 1921 – the region was resuscitated by tobacco, which quickly became its most important industry. As tobacco migrants flocked to Norfolk, its population recovered, growing by 35 per cent between 1921 and 1941, with even more dramatic increases in Simcoe and Delhi (see table 1.1).[82]

The rapid switch to tobacco brought massive change to patterns of land ownership and use. In a 1928 report, Norfolk's agricultural representative for the provincial Ministry of Agriculture described the upheaval then afoot: "Much land has changed hands; many farmers who were operating their places as mixed farms have sold out to tobacco growers, other farmers who are continuing to operate their own farms are beginning to grow tobacco. So the development of tobacco growing in the County is rapidly changing the type of agriculture practiced on many of our farms."[83] The sudden interest in Norfolk farmland sparked a surge in land prices. In early 1927, the *Reformer* reported that land prices in Lynedoch had tripled over the past three years, and Delhi, too, had seen a rapid increase.[84] There was no shortage of stories about farms purchased in the early years of the boom selling for vastly higher prices just a few years later.

In subsequent decades, the local landowners who had decided to sell their farms rather than invest in tobacco would be remembered as having been too risk-adverse and as having missed out on a golden economic opportunity. This phenomenon was sometimes chalked up to what were deemed to be inherent differences in work ethic and entrepreneurialism between Anglo-Canadians and the mainland European immigrants who were so prominent in the tobacco belt.[85] Such analyses of course ignore the fact that for many struggling general farmers who could not afford the capital outlay required to grow tobacco, selling their farms was their one chance to profit from the crop boom. Furthermore, as we have seen, locals were significantly involved at all stages of tobacco production, even if they were outnumbered by newcomers.

As the district's total population and patterns of land ownership changed, so, too, did its ethnic composition, as Norfolk became decreasingly Anglo-Canadian and increasingly European and American. To be sure, the county

Table 1.1 Total population, 1921–41

Location	1921	1931	1941	% Change, 1921–41
Delhi	733	1,121	2,062	181.3%
Simcoe	3,953	5,226	6,037	52.7%
Norfolk	26,366	31,359	35,611	35.1%
Ontario	2,933,662	3,431,683	3,787,655	29.1%
Canada	8,787,900	10,376,800	11,506,700	30.9%

remained majority Anglo-Canadian, but immigrant populations saw a rapid increase. From 1921 to 1941, Norfolk's foreign-born population rose by a factor of six, from 834 to 5,072, despite the post-1931 immigration restrictions (as we have seen, most immigrants who settled in Norfolk had arrived earlier and first lived elsewhere in Canada). Whereas 96.8 per cent of county residents were Canadian-born in 1921, that proportion dipped to 85.8 per cent in 1941. Individual immigrant communities grew rapidly with the tobacco boom (see figure 1.11). "Many of the mail-boxes in front of the farms that used to have names like 'McCall,' 'Johnson,' or 'Smith,'" observed Robert Burnett Hall in his 1952 doctoral dissertation on Norfolk tobacco, "now have 'Degroote,' 'Vander-haege,' or 'Rapchak,' printed on them. The older inhabitants of the county say that most of the farms had been in the same families for generations before tobacco was introduced."[86]

As Hall's observations suggest, the rapid changes in Norfolk's demographics provoked various anxieties among locals. They fretted about losing the "traditional" makeup of the county, and paradoxically about immigrants not integrating into local society. They worried, too, about immigrant criminality, drinking cultures, and radical politics.[87] Suspicion was not doled out equally among Norfolk's immigrant communities, however, and Hungarians were singled out for particular scorn. As a police officer explained in an anonymous survey conducted in the early 1950s, "the Belgian element cause very little trouble however I am unable to say the same for the Hungarians."[88] Of course, not all reactions to Norfolk's newcomers were negative. Local organizations like the Rotary Club made efforts to welcome new immigrants, and civic celebrations sometimes recognized the contributions of immigrant groups to the

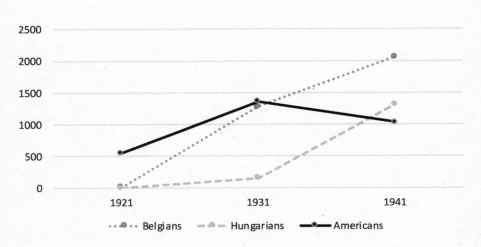

1.11 Number of Belgians, Hungarians, and Americans in Norfolk County, 1921–41.
Source: Census of Canada, 1921–41.

region's prosperity.[89] As with the police officer's comment, praise of certain
ethnic communities often came at the expense of others. "We know what the
Belgians and the Dutch are capable of in the way of developing agricultural
projects to which they set their hand," wrote a *Reformer* columnist in 1928. "We
only wish that we could secure many more like them rather than many types
of Southern European immigrants, lacking any sufficient knowledge of farming methods, who are flocking to Canada's shores."[90]

Tobacco remade not only Norfolk's demographics and economy, but also
its elite society, though here the changes were somewhat more subtle and gradual. Many members of Norfolk's long-standing elite, most of whose ancestors
had profited off Norfolk's earlier (and rapidly exhausted) timber trade, were
enthusiastic participants in the tobacco boom. Some became farm owners –
such as Albert Wilbur, Delhi resident since the 1870s and owner of four tobacco
farms, who became the village's reeve (equivalent to mayor) in 1938. Others,
such as Max MacPherson, found different ways to benefit. Wilbur's predecessor in the reeve's office, and secretary of both the Board of Trade and Masonic
Lodge in Delhi, MacPherson profited handsomely from tobacco real estate.
As the examples of Wilbur and MacPherson suggest, the tobacco sector quickly
became a central concern for Norfolk's elites and their associations, signalled,

for example, by the 1927 creation of a "Tobacco Committee" within Norfolk's Chamber of Commerce. Tobacco-specific organizations such as the Marketing Association became important players in the region's political sphere. Newcomers to the region also began to break into the district's halls of power, though wealthy Anglo participants in the tobacco boom had a distinct advantage in this respect. For example, H.M. Fair, who had relocated from Kingston to oversee his Norfolk Tobacco Plantations, Ltd, was "honorary" vice-president of the Business Men's Association of Delhi in the 1930s, while one of the early pioneers of flue-cured in Norfolk, William Pelton of Wisconsin, became the reeve of Charlotteville in 1944.[91] It would take a generation or more for the tobacco belt's more conspicuous (and, at the outset, decidedly less wealthy) newcomers to make the same inroads, a process that was marked by constant struggle.[92]

+ + +

As the case of Norfolk during its rapid transformation into Canada's tobacco belt demonstrates, there is nothing particularly new about the reliance of Canadian farmers on migrant labour. Though the character of farm labour mobility has changed in important ways since the green gold rush, the sector's utter dependence on migrant labour has not – a condition it shares with all but the most mechanized corners of capitalist agriculture. A diverse lot of newcomers streamed into the tobacco district in the 1920s and '30s, but participation within the sector was marked not only by inclusion, but also by exclusion and differentiation. The most obviously excluded group were African Americans from the tobacco-producing areas of the southern United States, barred from participating in the seasonal labour migration that their white neighbours could engage in by simply hopping in a car and heading north. But even those who did gain access to Norfolk's tobacco labour market found opportunities within the sector, and the warmth of their welcome, highly differentiated according to gender, race, ethnicity, and class. As Norfolk's new residents settled into their lives in the tobacco belt – and many seasonal migrants became accustomed to yearly forays in the golden leaf – they turned their attention to how they might improve their conditions within a sector that so thoroughly depended on their labour.

2

MOVING UP AND FIGHTING BACK

Out they piled from cars and trucks – children, men, and women, clutching picnic baskets, blankets, and bottles of wine. As they ambled from the roadside to the field located just outside of Delhi, neighbours and old friends greeted each other, making plenty of new introductions along the way. Young families snatched up the shaded areas under trees, unfurling blankets as their children darted off to play. The voices carrying through the air spoke mostly in Hungarian, though snippets of Flemish, German, and Slovak could also be heard, with English serving as the lingua franca for cross-cultural communication. It was the first Sunday of August 1939, thirty degrees and sunny, the perfect day for a picnic.[1]

The picnic was organized by Delhi's Canadian Hungarian Mutual Benefit Federation, one of many Hungarian Communist organizations in the region. Though unmistakably a political outfit, the Benefit Federation was also a linchpin of social life within the Hungarian community. So while a good number of those mingling in the park that day were undoubtedly committed Communists, many more came simply to socialize with friends and neighbours over cabbage rolls and wine.[2]

They had plenty to talk about. Over the preceding week, as many as ten thousand migrants had descended on Delhi and the surrounding areas in desperate search of work. Hailing from as far east as Nova Scotia and as far west as Alberta, they had been drawn to the region by handbills and newspaper advertisements, of unknown provenance, proclaiming the availability of thousands of harvest jobs in Norfolk. They arrived to find that fellow job seekers were in far greater supply than actual jobs, and, to make matters worse, the harvest was a week late. The village of Delhi found its population quintupled over the span of a few days and strained under the burden of the arrivals. Many residents fretted over the petty crimes committed by "transients" (mostly pilfering food from porches or gardens), reserving special concern for the alleged threat posed by the largely male crowds to the district's women and girls. Local police were stretched to the limit as they tried in vain to exert some control over the masses. One Catholic church, led by a progressive priest, made a spectacular effort to provide meals for the job seekers. All the while, newspaper headlines blared the latest developments in Norfolk's *Grapes of Wrath* moment (Steinbeck's Depression-era classic had been released earlier that very year). Adding to the drama, a cohort of Communists and others launched an effort to unionize tobacco workers, founding the United Tobacco Workers, Local 1, and urging job seekers to hold out for higher wages.[3]

The picnickers weren't merely talking about the excitement of the last few days – they were living it. Among the attendees were tobacco farmers, farm workers, job seekers, and many of the leaders of the United Tobacco Workers. So when it came time for the speeches (and at a Communist picnic, there were always speeches), it was only natural that the unionization efforts were the focus of discussion. A succession of multilingual speakers – József Müller in Hungarian, J. Bracska in Slovak, Bader Mihály in German, and lead organizer of the United Tobacco Workers, Jack Scott, in English – stressed that the key to improving conditions in the tobacco sector lay not simply in worker militancy, but in collaboration between workers, job seekers, and small farmers. Only by working together could the labouring classes of the tobacco belt confront the large landowners and multinational tobacco companies who were the industry's true profiteers. In addition to the loftier goals of cross-class alliance, organizers hoped the picnic would facilitate a much more immediate form of collaboration, by matching job seekers with farmers to fill the latter's labour needs – in essence, a job fair.[4]

The combination of Communist rally with job fair was not as odd as it might have been in some other time and place. What Norfolk's radicals readily recognized was that any strategy that unequivocally pitted all workers against all employers was bound to fail, and fail miserably. This was because, in the tobacco belt, wage labourers and owners of small farms, who hailed from the same families and communities, were set apart by little more than a few years' experience and accrual of capital. Indeed, the booming tobacco sector provided working people with remarkable opportunities for upward social mobility, advancing from wage labourers to sharegrowers to farm owners even in the deepest throes of the Great Depression – in spite of the fact that, by the 1920s, such opportunities had all but disappeared elsewhere in Canadian agriculture.[5]

But the fact that Norfolk's working people, by a combination of hard work, co-operation, and good fortune, could attain a level of economic security within the tobacco sector did not mean that they simply accepted it the way it was. To the contrary, many working people had a keen understanding that the hard-earned benefits they wrested from the golden leaf were mere table scraps compared to the fabulous feast of profit being enjoyed by large land-owners and especially tobacco manufacturing companies. Seeking to transform the sector to better meet their interests, many turned to radical analyses and collective action, making events like the Benefit Federation picnic a common occurrence in the tobacco belt of the 1930s. Given the connections between workers and small growers in terms of both community membership and social mobility, forging alliances between the two groups became a key part of radicals' strategies. In practice, however, this proved to be fraught with difficulty and contradiction.

The picnic's tandem goals of job placement and unionization, then, were not so incongruous as they might appear on their face and were indicative of two key strategies by which working people in the tobacco belt sought to improve their life outcomes: social mobility and working-class organization. Despite their inherent contradictions, the two strategies were not mutually exclusive, nor did they fit neatly into an individual versus collective binary. Not only did collective efforts recognize and support the interest of working families in progressing financially, but the actual process of social mobility was anything but an individual undertaking. Instead, advancing from wage labour to farm ownership required contributions from the whole family (with women's capital and labour standing out as particularly important) – and often community support as well.

Moving Up

The economic factors facilitating social mobility in the tobacco belt were many of the same that had attracted newcomers to the region in the first place: high wages, relatively affordable land prices, and the insatiable demand for tobacco in domestic and global markets. A critical additional factor was the easy access to credit enjoyed by aspiring tobacco farmers. In the sector's early decades, banks were eager to invest in tobacco farms and offered growers a unique form of mortgage called a "quarter-crop" loan. Under this arrangement, prospective growers were able to secure a bank mortgage on a farm with a down payment as small as 10 per cent. Their subsequent payments each year were fixed at one-quarter of the revenue of the crop, which, barring calamity, would cover both interest and some of the principal, a practice that mitigated growers' risk of being unable to make payments during down years. In addition to quarter-crop loans, other important sources of credit included government programs and family and community networks.[6]

As the land rush of the 1920s and '30s gave way to a more stable – but still very profitable – sector, two trends helped ensure the continuation of pathways to farm ownership. The first was the selling off of farms by the plantations that had dominated the sector in the early phase of the boom. As production costs and corporate tax rates rose in the waning months of World War II, corporate plantations found their profit margins shrinking. Meanwhile, tobacco lands were in demand and selling for high prices. One after another, starting with St Williams and Windham in 1944–45, plantations began to sell off their farms, and almost all of them were completely dissolved by the 1950s.[7] The second trend was the spread of tobacco production into the neighbouring counties of Oxford, Elgin, and Brant (and to a lesser extent other areas in southern Ontario), especially in the 1940s and '50s. Accounting for 5,748 acres of tobacco in 1931 (less than a third of Norfolk's total), by 1956 the three counties' combined production had surged sevenfold to 41,787 acres, just 24 per cent less than Norfolk.[8] Both developments served to significantly increase the number of viable tobacco farms on the real estate market and allow more working people to make the leap to farm ownership.[9] In short, then, beginning in the sector's early years and extending well into the 1950s (and to a lesser extent the 1960s), opportunities for upward social mobility were very much available to working people.

Patterns of agrarian socio-economic advancement such as those that existed in Norfolk's tobacco sector have often been conceptualized as the "agricultural ladder," a term that describes the process by which a farm worker climbs, rung by rung, from wage labour to tenancy to proprietorship. But a close examination of social mobility in the tobacco belt finds this metaphor lacking.[10] While many working people did indeed progress from farm worker to owner, their trajectories are not accurately encapsulated by the metaphor's evocation of a frictionless climb by an individual male. Instead, social mobility was very much a family and community affair – one in which women played an especially critical role through their capital and labour. And moving up in the sector was never so easy as simply stepping onto the next rung of the ladder, but instead was fraught with pitfalls and coloured by conflict.

Standing in stark contrast to the masculinist leanings of the agricultural ladder was the fact that, in Norfolk's tobacco belt, one of the most important milestones on the journey from farm worker to owner was marriage. One source where this is revealed with particular clarity is the Delhi Tobacco Belt Project Papers, a collection of hundreds of life history surveys conducted with Norfolk-area residents from the district's major immigrant communities, in 1977. The survey was itself moulded within a masculinist purview. Most interviews were conducted with men, and those completed with married couples typically described the man's employment history in much greater detail than the woman's, if the latter was mentioned at all. Furthermore, women participants were rarely identified by anything more than a "Mrs" prefixing their husbands' names – even when they were the ones answering the questions.[11] Despite these limitations, women's work and contributions to social mobility are visible within the survey responses, if one scrapes a little beneath the patriarchal veneer.

It is particularly telling that, in response to a survey question about employment history ("After you emigrated to Canada, what sort of jobs did you have and where were they?"), respondent after respondent mentioned marriage, specifically linking it with the transition from wage labour to sharegrowing. The Brinkers, immigrants from Holland: "Got married 1938. Sharegrow tobacco South Middleton. 1946 home farm bought." Peter and Helen Sterczer from Hungary and Czechoslovakia, respectively: "In 1948 was a hired man until 1950 – then worked with father on farm for 1 year – then married and sharegrew one year and bought present farm where [we] still reside." The Van De Walles of Belgium: "1928 hired man on tobacco farm La Salette. 1933 got married share grown tobacco La Salette-Langton. 1939 bought own tobacco farm Delhi area."[12] As these examples suggest, the trend of marriage as a bridge to sharegrowing was sustained in the survey responses from the 1930s through the 1950s and was seemingly consistent across all the district's immigrant groups. (The Tobacco Belt Project conducted surveys solely with members of immigrant communities and thus the records do not provide much of a window into social mobility, or its absence, among longer-standing residents, including First Na-tions people, none of whom were interviewed for that project.) Similarly, John Kosa's 1957 study of Hungarian immigrants to Canada, which drew signifi-cantly on the life stories of tobacco belt residents, concluded that "marriage ... is a great help in improving financial position." This finding, he explained, "seems to corroborate the common saying of immigrants that bachelors 'make no good.'"[13]

One of the main reasons why marriage was so important to social mobility was that women frequently contributed capital toward taking up sharegrowing or purchasing a farm. Often these savings were accrued via various types of wage labour. For example, when Lithuanians Ona Aleksandravicius and Julius Strodomskis married in 1936, "he had about $700 or $800, she twice that much from working for several years in a sweatshop in nearby London, Ontario," ac-cording to historian Milda Danys. In fact, over the previous two years, Julius had launched a failed bid to sharegrow and been forced to return to wage la-bour. By marrying, the couple could combine their savings, and this roughly $2,000 in capital allowed them to become sharegrowers immediately after mar-riage. Two years later, they were able to secure credit and buy a farm.[14] Another Lithuanian, Mrs K. Simutis, combined her savings from wage labour in Mon-treal and Simcoe with her husband's in order to buy a tobacco farm in 1947.[15] Helen and Peter Sterczer, whose survey answer was quoted above, reported that money received as wedding gifts covered a significant proportion of the down payment for their first farm.[16]

Women's essential and multi-faceted contributions to farm work also helped facilitate upward mobility. Beyond tasks such as meal preparation and tying tobacco, women also at times played important parts in managing farm op-erations. Never was this clearer than during World War II, when the wives of enlisted male farmers often took up managerial duties. (Enlisted men appear, however, to have been in the minority among tobacco growers, since farmers were exempt from conscription). One such woman was Mary Huffman, a Sim-coe-area tobacco farmer who, with her husband Clair at war, took the reins of their operation. When Clair returned in May 1945, the couple was photo-graphed by the National Film Board of Canada, with the resulting images dem-onstrating the importance of women's managerial work in this period. In one photograph, Mary demonstrates the amount of seed needed to plant twenty acres of tobacco, along with the amount of money required to purchase it.

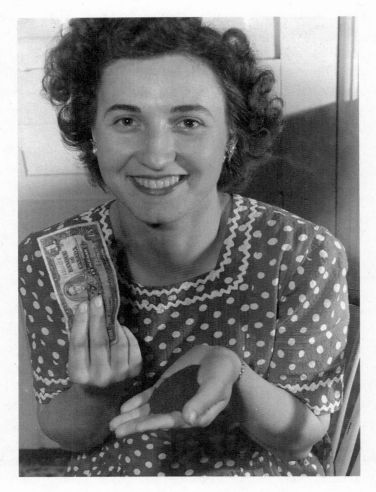

2.1 "The cost and amount of seed necessary to plant twenty acres of
tobacco is illustrated here by Mrs Mary Huffman, wife of a Simcoe
tobacco grower," 1945. Photographer: John Mailer. Item 13531,
R1196-14-7-E, acc. 1971-271 NPC, LAC.

Another depicts Mary and Clair on a tractor she purchased while Clair was
away. According to the caption, Mary "explains their tractor to her repatriated
husband." In both images, Mary appears quite comfortable in her role as primary farmer. Though Mary's experience was likely something of an exception
to the overall rule of patriarchal control, it was not a total outlier. In the postwar

2.2 "Mrs Mary Huffman, who kept a small Norfolk County tobacco farm producing while her husband Clair was overseas, explains their tractor to her repatriated husband," 1945. Photographer: John Mailer. Item 13557, R1196-14-7-E, acc. 1971-271 NPC, LAC.

period, women owner-operators became increasingly common, and women often took charge of administrative duties such as accounting and payroll.[17]

Sometimes, wages earned by women off the farm helped to support farming operations. North Carolinian immigrant Laura Snow, for example, boarded workers from a nearby farm while she and her husband were sharegrowing tobacco in the 1940s. Pauline Cook and her husband Erland were sharegrowers near Simcoe at around the same time. Their farm met with various challenges over the years, particularly as a result of frost and other weather incidents, and

Pauline worked as a waitress and a cook at a local restaurant to help keep the family business afloat.[18]

Children's labour also contributed to social mobility in the tobacco belt. Many authors have made similar observations about how the patriarchal structure of the immigrant family allowed for the substitution of hired hands with unpaid family labour and the rapid accumulation of wealth. For example, in explaining the success of Belgian tobacco growers, Cornelius Jaenen pointed to the "efficiency" of the "traditional patriarchal family working unit."[19] Indeed, children did often pitch in on family farms, but not only on those of European immigrants. Various newspaper reports indicate that tobacco farmers from the American South and those with deeper roots in the region utilized their children's labour too.[20] Children also sometimes worked as wage labourers, putting their earnings toward family savings. In his response to the Tobacco Belt Project survey, Lithuanian P. Vindasius explained his family's economic trajectory after immigrating in 1951 as follows: "Came to the Eden district on a tobacco farm as a hired man for 75 dol. per month, worked for 3 years. Wife and children worked for 50 cents per hour. With 1800 dol. saved sharegrow tobacco in Delhi district. Sharegrow tobacco for 20 years."[21]

Kinship and ethnic ties also played an important role in facilitating social mobility in the tobacco belt. Danys, considering the question of why postwar Lithuanian "DPs" (or displaced persons) in the tobacco belt were more successful than most other refugees (including Lithuanians in other regions), concludes that the presence of an already-established Lithuanian community in the Norfolk area was crucial to the newcomers' success. "In all the accounts given by Lithuanian tobacco farmers, the importance of aid, both practical and psychological, given by fellow Lithuanians is paramount."[22] People of the same ethnicity frequently partnered to start tobacco farms.[23] Established tobacco growers would help family members start their own farms, often following a period of working on the already-established farm. Especially common was for sons of tobacco growers to be assisted in setting up their own farms once they became adults. McQuarrie notes that out of fifty Belgian tobacco farm proprietors surveyed for the Tobacco Belt Project, forty had children who owned their own farms. Credit was often advanced within ethnic communities as well.[24]

Another complication to the agricultural ladder model is that social mobility is rarely as straightforward a process as simply stepping onto the next rung.

While a remarkable degree of social mobility did occur in the tobacco belt, tobacco workers and growers were still enmeshed in a world of class relations, even if class was fluid. Productive relations in the tobacco belt were rife with conflict along class lines: between wage earners and their employers; between sharegrowers and landlords; and between farmers (of all classes) and tobacco companies. Particularly common were disputes over control of the work process and wages, which sometimes erupted into physical violence. One example took place on the farm of Joe Poche in in September 1936. With no further tasks to assign his employee, Joe Myore, Poche attempted to rent Myore – who was presumably under contract – out to another farm. Myore objected to this arrangement and the two men got into a physical altercation. Poche claimed Myore stabbed him in the eye, a claim Myore disputed. Neither man was charged with any crime.[25] The incident between Myore and Poche, who were both Hungarian, was not the only time when physical violence along class lines occurred between members of the same ethnic group, a reminder of the limits of ethnic affinity.[26]

Working people's efforts to progress socio-economically could also be derailed by sickness, crop failures, and bad luck. Cyriel Rabaey's life story demonstrates how unforeseen circumstances such as an illness could derail plans for economic advancement. Rabaey, a Belgian immigrant, started off on a familiar path to farm ownership. After sharegrowing tobacco for three years with his parents, he got married and began to raise tobacco on shares with his wife in 1931. In 1950, he moved to Delhi but got sick with an illness that lasted five years. In 1957, he began working as a hired hand on tobacco farms. At the time of his interview in 1977, he was propertyless, and it is not clear from his survey whether he was still working.[27] Stanley Tokarz made even more progress toward farm ownership before running into trouble, also due to health issues. After immigrating from Poland in 1947, Tokarz worked in a Brantford foundry and on tobacco farms before becoming a sharegrower in 1949. In 1955, he was able to purchase a mixed crop farm, but was forced to sell it in 1969. To the question of "present occupation" on the survey, Tokarz's answer was "seasonal worker due to health."[28]

Making matters worse for working people in such situations was the fact that, in many of the tobacco belt's immigrant communities, newcomers who did not attain farm ownership (or some equally esteemed station), were regarded as failures.[29] While Tokarz's and Rabaey's deferred dreams take on a tragic tone, it is important to point out that for many thousands of tobacco labourers, work in the sector was nothing more than a temporary job, not something that they intended to make a career out of.[30] Many who worked in tobacco used their wages to fund unrelated business pursuits, pay for education, or even to support family farms that produced crops other than tobacco. A 1946 report of the Indian Affairs Branch, for example, stated that "the seasonal demand for workers at high wages in the tobacco growing sections of Ontario ... has greatly increased the incomes of many Indian families whose men and women operate small farms on reserves and are able to take advantage of this work."[31] Non-Indigenous workers from nearby farming districts often had similar goals of supporting their family farms.[32] For many of those who did desire a life growing tobacco, farm proprietorship proved to be an attainable goal, potential obstacles notwithstanding. But even as they worked their way to greater economic stability, working people in the region fought to create a more equitable sector – with more of its many fruits going to workers, sharegrowers, and small farmers, and fewer to plantations and manufacturing companies.

Fighting Back: The Infrastructure of Dissent

The seemingly surprising moment of farm-worker revolt that was the talk of the picnic on that hot Sunday in August 1939 was not the first time that Ontario tobacco workers had engaged in collective action to improve their conditions, nor would it be the last. Instead, it was in many ways simply the latest manifestation of what sociologist Alan Sears calls the "infrastructure of dissent." The concept comes out of Sears's attempt to understand "the specific circumstances that are conducive to working-class self-activity, movement activism and the development of critical consciousness." Examining Windsor's Drouillard Road, site of a massive, community-supported auto workers' strike in 1945, as his key case study, Sears argues that working-class collective action is never truly "spontaneous" but instead emerges from a foundation of community, political culture, and collective learning. "Working-class mobilization [is] founded on an infrastructure of dissent," writes Sears, which he defines as "the means through which activists develop political communities capable of learning, communicating and mobilizing together. This process of collective capacity-building takes a variety of forms, ranging from informal neighbourhood and workplace networks to formal organizations and structured learning settings. The infrastructure of dissent is a crucial feature of popular mobilization, providing the basic connections that underlie even apparently spontaneous protest actions." As in the case of Drouillard Road, the collective action of workers, sharegrowers, and smallholders in the tobacco belt was built atop an infrastructure of dissent comprised of a constellation of formal organizations and informal networks that allowed for the development of radical ideas and provided a platform from which to launch oppositional efforts, both coordinated and spontaneous.[33] During the 1930s in particular, working-class Norfolkians participated in left-wing organizations, read Communist newspapers, and organized for better conditions, wages, crop prices, and for a more democratic, producer-driven tobacco industry.

As a result of their efforts, labour relations in tobacco became perhaps the most contentious in Ontario agriculture, a sector not typically associated with working-class mobilization or radicalism. Out of eighteen strikes and "disturbances" reported in Ontario agriculture during the 1930s by the federal Department of Labour, the highest tally was in tobacco, with four.[34] Many more instances of tobacco-worker dissent did not make it into the official government record. Aiding the work of organizers and radicals was what, following Andrew Herod and others, we might call the region's "labour geography."[35] The packing of job seekers into the public parks and downtown streets of Delhi, Simcoe, and Tillsonburg before each year's harvest was not just convenient for employers looking to quickly round out their harvest crews. It also made the work of collective organization possible, and these points of congregation became the perfect places at which to overcome the geographic diffusion that has historically inhibited much farm labour organizing.[36]

Though women were unquestionably important contributors to the tobacco belt's infrastructure of dissent, only rarely were they part of its public face, and locating women's contributions in archival records proves even more challenging than uncovering their role in social mobility. (In the few instances where it is possible, the names of women radicals are mentioned in the remainder of this chapter.) But we can be confident that, in addition to their seldommentioned role in formal labour politics, women bolstered the infrastructure of dissent in myriad other, unmentioned ways, including by performing the essential labour of nourishing and caring for their families and communities. As Linda Kealey has observed, "women in [left-wing] movements experienced a gendered division of labour much as they did in the labour market."[37]

While working people from many tobacco belt communities participated in collective efforts to improve their conditions, there can be little doubt that the most important builders of the district's infrastructure of dissent were Hungarian Canadians. As detailed by Carmela Patrias, Canada's pre-war Hungarian communities were often sharply divided along political lines between "patriots" and "proletarians." The latter's Communist politics could be traced back to Europe, but they were also reshaped by experiences in their new home. In the tobacco belt, Hungarian Communists founded Hungarian Workers' Clubs in Delhi and Tillsonburg and a branch of the Benefit Federation in Vanessa.[38] The Hungarian-language Communist newspaper published in Toronto, *Kanadai Magyar Munkás*, gained a healthy readership in the district (a 1935 RCMP Security Bulletin noted a highly successful subscription drive in Delhi, spearheaded by Mariska Szakolcai). In turn, *Munkás* afforded extensive coverage to the goings-on in the tobacco sector.[39] Hungarians in the tobacco belt also practised Communist politics in informal gatherings, such as in 1934, when *Munkás* reported that 250 workers met in the Delhi area, raised a red hammer-and-sickle flag on a tree, and heard a speech by a worker named Sproha, who advised the assembled that, "to get out of the economic crisis, we have to organize." He also urged them to join with the "one-sixth of the world" already united under the Communist flag. (A few days later, an agent from the village council asked the workers to take down the banner. In response, a compromise was reached in which the workers were permitted to leave the flag up so long as they raised the Canadian red ensign next to it. According to the *Munkás* writer, this was evidence that "the capitalists are afraid of us ... They are afraid of the workers," and were especially spooked to see workers organizing under the hammer and sickle.[40])

But Hungarians were by no means the only contributors to the tobacco belt's infrastructure of dissent. Belgians, for example, participated in Hungarian Communist events such as Benefit Federation picnics, and they were a significant force in the 1937 small-grower campaign to raise tobacco prices.[41] Belgians and Hungarians also launched parallel campaigns in 1938 to achieve greater ethnic representation for farmers in the Marketing Association.[42] It is quite possible that some Belgians were carrying on a tradition of left-wing politics carried over from the Low Countries. One fleeting but suggestive example comes from historian Joan Magee, who reports that at a 1929 singing competition at the Belgian dance parlour in Delhi, Edmond Cartier won second place with a song about a 1907 strike in Wetteren, Belgium, in which the socialist-led mill workers were victorious.[43] Like the Belgians, many other ethnocultural groups attended events organized by the Hungarian Communists – with "13 or 14 different races" reported in attendance at the August 1939 picnic, for example.[44]

As the internationalist speeches and songs suggest, the infrastructure of dissent in the tobacco belt did not develop in isolation but was formed in the context of a growing radical politics at the local, national, and international levels, taking shape as people became increasingly critical of the capitalist order that had produced the poverty and instability of the Great Depression. Of special note, the 1930s and '40s – beginning particularly in the late 1930s – represented the high-water mark of Communism in Canada and of its most important party, the Communist Party of Canada, or CPC (as was also the case for Communist parties in the United States and much of western Europe). The critical junction here was the strategic about-face of the Communist International, or Comintern, in 1935, when it switched from the highly sectarian, revolutionary strategy of the "Third Period," in which the party line proscribed collaboration with non-Communist parties and unions, to the much more open "Popular Front" strategy that encouraged Communists to join in a broad coalition of revolutionary and reformist organizations in order to confront the menace of fascism. CPC membership soared in the aftermath of the Popular Front's adoption, tripling between 1934 and 1937 and reaching 16,000 by 1939, with tens of thousands more involved with affiliated organizations.[45]

Though the Hungarian Communist organizations in the tobacco belt fell under the banner of the CPC, by all appearances party leaders had little involvement in Communist activism in the district. Farm labour organizing was decidedly *not* a priority of the CPC after the end of the Third Period, during which the Workers' Unity League (WUL) had formed unions among farm workers (sugar beet workers in particular) in Ontario and Alberta.[46] But the dissolution of the WUL brought a close to these efforts. Though source limitations make it difficult to declare definitively, it appears that Communist activism in the tobacco belt was by and large the product of local actors directing their efforts toward local concerns, even as those actors were obviously informed by the broader direction of the party and connected to national and international networks.[47] Such links were especially common within immigrant diasporas. Hungarian Communists in Ontario, for example, likely followed with keen interest the dramatic unionization drive and strikes of sugar beet workers in Alberta (many Hungarians among them) in the mid-1930s, which received extensive coverage in *Munkás*.[48] And at the 1936 National Convention of the Hungarian Workers' Clubs, held in nearby Hamilton, organizing farmers in western Canada was named as a key priority. Considering as well that many of Norfolk's Hungarians had moved east from Alberta – where a fair number worked in sugar beets – it is reasonable to infer that Hungarians organizing in tobacco would have seen themselves not as engaging in an isolated struggle confined to a single crop, but rather as part of a broader network of Hungarians and other proletarians fighting for better conditions not only in agriculture, but in all corners of the capitalist economy, across Canada and around the world.[49]

Political action in the tobacco belt, while shaped by transnational leftist thought and diasporic ethnic identities, was generally concerned with the day-to-day existence of workers and small growers at the point of production, on the farm. Tobacco workers often gathered informally to discuss their conditions and find ways to improve them. This type of conversation was an important part of the infrastructure of dissent, which, as Sears writes, "provides spaces for activist learning, analysis that challenges dominant ideas, [and] collective memory to draw resources from past struggles."[50] In 1933, a tobacco worker, identified only by the initials S.M., penned an article in *Munkás* that described the precarious conditions faced by labourers over the winter, but also the collective solutions that down-on-their-luck workers employed to try to better their lot. Three months after the end of the harvest, the author wrote, many tobacco workers were struggling to make ends meet. S.M. was part of a group of five or six families living in the same area; some had resorted to building a mud hut for shelter. "Nobody knows what will happen to us, how we will survive the winter," he wrote. Some members of the group had found winter work on tobacco farms for a mere ten dollars a month plus board, but most were not so lucky and had to turn to begging or asking the local authorities for assistance. But despite the hardship, the residents were organizing a Workers' Club, which, evoking Sears, provided a space for both "activist learning" and organization. According to S.M., in the Workers' Club, "the workers are studying while having fun." The author also called for the organization of tobacco workers into unions.[51]

While engaged on harvest crews, tobacco workers faced with conditions or wages they deemed unacceptable often joined together to demand improvements via unplanned acts of worker self-activity. A typical example occurred in 1937, when six tobacco primers, after emptying the morning's kiln and eating breakfast, returned to their hay-beds in the barn, with the message "Wake me if you will pay $3.50 a day" written on their shoes. The farmer woke them up and agreed to the 50-cent increase.[52]

A final, critical feature of the tobacco belt's infrastructure of dissent was the commitment to forming alliances between workers, sharegrowers, and small farmers. This was not limited to Ontario tobacco, but instead was a core principle within Communist rural organizing during the 1930s – during the Third Period and Popular Front phases alike.[53] In this era, historians John Herd Thompson and Allen Seager explain, the CPC "considered the bulk of the farming population" – workers as well as farmers – "to be a potentially revolutionary class."[54] Thus, not only in the tobacco belt, but also in organizing efforts among sugar beet workers in Ontario and Alberta, uniting all agriculturalists against the large corporations profiting from their labour became a core objective of activists. It was not, however, a very successful undertaking, in tobacco or sugar beets.[55] In Ontario's tobacco belt, workers tended to contribute significantly to growers' campaigns, but when the situation was reversed, the favours went all but unreturned.

The 1937 Wage Campaign

Working people in tobacco also undertook more formal efforts to form organizations and push for better wages and conditions, both for workers and small growers. The first major attempt to organize tobacco labour across the sector was in 1937, when in the days leading up to the harvest, a "small group of Hungarians" passed out handbills urging job seekers to hold out for between $3.50 and $4.00 per day instead of the going wage rate of $3.00. The group appears to have had some initial successes. Two growers reported being unable to contract workers with offered wages of $3.00 and $3.50. Workers on at least one farm struck, securing a 50 cent pay hike from the grower, who preferred to increase wages rather than risk losing part of his crop. The organizers were helped in their cause by a short labour supply, thought to be caused in part by increased industrial production in Hamilton, which cut into the usual number of workers from that city who would seek work in the harvest.[56] The early yet seemingly minor gains were apparently enough to scare tobacco farmers, and a swift, coordinated, and hard-fisted reaction by growers, the provincial government, and the mainstream press ensued.

Farmers immediately sought to dampen any hopes workers might have had of achieving higher wages. E.C. Scythes, president of the twenty-three-farm Vittoria Plantations, told the *Simcoe Reformer* that "if those men who are holding out for exorbitant wages continue to do so, they are most likely to be left without work, and their places filled by young Canadians." For its part, the Marketing Association let it be known that they were engaged in meetings with US officials to arrange for additional labour to come north.[57]

Premier Mitch Hepburn and the provincial government also did their part to contain the threat before it could gain momentum. After meeting with the chairman of the Marketing Association, Archie Leitch, and a consortium of growers, Hepburn took to the press to decry the work of "foreign agitators." The premier threatened to quash any tobacco strikes with the provincial police and import replacement workers from western Canada, where drought had dried up harvest work. True to his word, a few days later, Hepburn spoke at a conference of the provincial ministers of agriculture from across the country, asking them to help supply four thousand extra workers to the tobacco belt, even as local police and employment officials stressed to reporters that no extra workers were needed, since the mass arrivals of transients over the preceding days had ended the labour shortage. If anything, officials cautioned, there was already an oversupply of labour in the district. Hepburn also assigned additional provincial police to the area.[58]

The mainstream press was firmly on the side of growers and the provincial government. Editorials and letters to the editor used the events as evidence that the jobless did not in fact want to work, blaming them for their own plight. They also repeated Hepburn's labelling of organizers as "foreign agitators."[59] A *Globe and Mail* editorial provides a typical example of these sentiments: "Surely it cannot be that Ontario is short of farm labor. If so it is a sad reflection of hundreds of able-bodied men on relief who profess eagerness to work, and a further indication that abuse of relief funds is far from ended ... Jeopardizing the harvesting of any crop would be an act of vandalism. Still, agitators are

prepared to take advantage of any condition, no matter what the cost to inno-
cent sufferers."[60]

The workers behind the organizational efforts and their closest ally in the
press, *Munkás*, were appalled by the crackdown. *Munkás* blasted Hepburn for
his "reckless statements" about the need for labour in the district while "thousands" of job seekers slept outside, hoping to be hired on to harvest crews. The
paper also disagreed with the portrayal of the organizing campaign in the mainstream press, reserving special ire for the suggestion that activists were working
against the best interests of growers. In fact, *Munkás* claimed, the $3.50 wage
rate had actually been set in consultation with growers, the amount representing a mutually beneficial arrangement for workers and farmers. The article
alleged that a rogue group of workers had created a second flyer demanding
$4.50 a day. *Munkás* was upset at the premier and the press for driving a wedge
between workers and growers, but it also slammed the organizers who it accused of creating this second flyer. The paper frequently called upon workers
and growers to band together, and it expected both sides to compromise on
their interests for the sake of greater solidarity and strength. It is impossible to
determine the accuracy of *Munkás*'s reporting, but the political imperative of
worker-grower co-operation could not be clearer.[61] The righteous rage of *Munkás*
and fellow radicals notwithstanding, the end of the labour shortage and Hepburn's strongman efforts served to take away what little leverage the organizing
workers had enjoyed, and the campaign fizzled out by early August.

The Small Growers' Campaign of 1937

Later in 1937, it was the turn of small growers to push for better conditions
within the sector, and they launched a campaign demanding higher prices for
their crops than those offered by the Flue-Cured Tobacco Marketing Association of Ontario. The Marketing Association was founded in 1934 in response
to the instability of tobacco prices during the Great Depression.[62] The association issued voluntary acreage allotments to growers and set standardized
price scales each year for harvested tobacco. It's 23-member board of directors
included 16 growers, elected by members, and 7 representatives of tobacco-
buying companies.[63]

Though the Marketing Association – also referred to as the Simcoe organization, for its base of operations – was unmistakeably successful in ensuring

the continuing boom of flue-cured tobacco, it was also a controversial organization, accused of supporting the interests of the tobacco companies and large
landowners at the expense of smaller farmers. *Munkás* regularly made such
allegations, contending that the democratic appearance of the organization's
price-setting was nothing more than a curtain shielding from view the true
puppet master: the Imperial Tobacco Company of Canada.[64] But it was not
just the fiery Communist newspaper that slammed the association. Growers
shared *Munkás*'s critiques, and in fact often went further in their denunci-
ations. Some examples can be found in a batch of letters sent by growers to
the provincial minister of agriculture, Patrick M. Dewan, in 1939. Though
written after the campaigns of 1937, the correspondence reflects concerns that
were common among farmers throughout the 1930s and subsequent decades.
The letters alleged that the association withheld membership from small
farmers in order to push them into selling their farms and that board directors
and their friends were given preferential acreage allotment, allowing them to
buy non-tobacco farms, receive tobacco acreage allotments, and resell the farms
for a substantial profit. Growers also claimed that banks and insurance companies were reluctant to extend the same services and rates to non-members,
further extending the association's monopolistic reach. Some complained that
it scared growers into agreeing to sell them their surplus crop, and then paid
below the market rate per pound.

Dewan's response to growers is telling in that, instead of dismissing their
claims, he appears sympathetic, writing in a 1939 letter to a small grower, "Certainly it has been a monopoly, and the question in my mind is whether or not
it has been pretty much a combine." In a 1940 letter to another grower regarding
the association's coercive tactics, he wrote that, while he had still not seen con-
clusive evidence, he was "of the opinion that the growers were very strongly
encouraged to have their tobacco processed under the direction of the Marketing Association."[65] Alternative co-operatives to the Simcoe organization
existed – for example, the Intercounty Tobacco Growers Limited – and these
were touted during times of dissatisfaction with the association, but leaving
for a rival group was not necessarily an attractive option for growers, since
they did not have the same close-knit ties with the tobacco companies and
banks as the Marketing Association. In fact, the Simcoe organization was often
quite aggressive in pressuring Intercounty growers to come into the mainstream fold.[66]

The decade's biggest moment of conflict between the board of the Marketing Association and its smallholding members took place in 1937, when growers, dissatisfied with the prices being offered for their crops, launched a protest movement and refused to sell their crops until a higher price was extended. The campaign seems to have been at least in part an outgrowth of the workers' organizational efforts earlier in the year, and, from the beginning, workers were deeply involved in the farmers' efforts. A series of growers' meetings were held beginning in August of that year, just two weeks after the workers' campaign had fizzled out. At the initial meeting, workers and growers discussed the need to work together for higher crop prices for farmers, allowing for higher wages for workers. The group resolved to form a joint committee to pursue the issue. E. Holwell, of the United Farmers of Ontario, was invited to speak at the meeting, and pointed out that low prices from Imperial hurt both growers and workers, repeating the message of co-operation.[67]

By mid-September, it had become clear that farmers were going to be offered significantly lower prices than had been expected – between 23 and 26 cents per pound instead of the anticipated 35 to 40 cents.[68] The meeting organizers placed an ad in the *Reformer* – "Good Crops Merit Good Prices" – and on 15 September, about two hundred and fifty growers and workers convened in Delhi. Both the meeting's chair, Nerky (a Hungarian whose first name was not printed), and its main speaker, Carl Hichin, were tobacco workers. In his remarks, Hichin, a Communist activist who had been involved in various campaigns in the Norfolk region in previous years,[69] again repeated the need for worker-farmer co-operation. The assembly agreed to demand 40 to 45 cents per pound for their crop.[70] Over the next month and a half, growers and workers continued to meet, and Holwell led a joint delegation to present their concerns to Norfolk's member of provincial parliament, Eric Cross. Cross was sympathetic to the group but promised only to have parliament "study the issue."[71]

When the Marketing Association finally announced the crop price in late October, it did not even come close to meeting the assembly's demands, setting the rate per pound at 24.5 cents. This sparked a flurry of four mass meetings between 3 and 10 November, and participation skyrocketed. From 250 attendees at the September and October meetings, attendance jumped to 1,200 at the 3 November meeting in Simcoe. According to the *Reformer*, a majority of attendees were "foreign born," and a number of angry speeches were made in Eng-

lish, Hungarian, and "Belgian" (presumably Flemish). Holwell chaired the
meeting and by this time was firmly established as a key leader in the movement, being named to a five-person committee to interview members of the
association and a fifteen-member delegation to meet with the provincial minister of agriculture, Patrick M. Dewan, which also included a woman worker
with a Hungarian surname, Elizabeth Csiszar. The growers again lowered their
price demand, however, this time to 34.5 cents.[72]

The next meeting, on 6 November, was "again principally foreign" in attendance. Hichin, according to the *Reformer*, "assured the growers that the tobacco
labourers are behind the movement one hundred per cent," while Holwell
claimed that 90 per cent of farmers were on board and that the association
was starting to weaken. Despite the signs of strength, the meeting witnessed
the first real indications of a fissure among the group. A fierce debate erupted
over whether sharegrowers should be included in the group meeting with
Dewan, or whether only farm owners should be allowed to attend. Farmer
Martin Stirtzinger led the owners-only argument, but by meeting's end had
lost his bid, and it was agreed that the entire committee of fifteen owners,
sharegrowers, workers, and Holwell would meet with Dewan.[73] The owners,
however, did not honour the outcome of the vote, and the next day refused to
allow the sharegrowers and workers a place at the meeting table, cutting the
committee from fifteen to six.

Over the next two mass meetings, on 9 and 10 November, this undemocratic
decision was the cause of great uproar, and the crowd booed Stirtzinger off
the stage when he tried to give his report of the meeting with Dewan, telling
the assembly that there was nothing more they could do. After the room had
quieted down, Stirtzinger stepped back to the podium to tender his resignation
from the committee. Holwell, ever the consensus-builder, attempted to patch
up the differences, saying that he harboured no ill will toward the new, smaller
committee, and told the gathering that they, too, should throw their support
behind the delegation, no matter what form it took. He also tried to boost the
strikers' morale: "The Imperial Tobacco Co. controls 70 per cent of the tobacco
industry in Canada and they say there is a market for the tobacco, that is, if
the growers knuckle down to them. But what are they going to do if you do
not sell your tobacco? ... If you people are as determined as ever in your stand
there is no doubt that the increase in the price will be forthcoming."[74]

Despite Holwell's optimism, the growers' movement had already reached its limits. Dissension in the ranks was one problem; another was the campaign of fear led by the Imperial Tobacco Company and the Marketing Association, with the *Reformer* happily serving as mouthpiece. The paper often printed the viewpoints of both entities, even allotting front-page space for extended statements, and these served to assure growers that resistance was futile: prices were determined by processes far out of their control, and the best they could do was to accept the offered rates and not rock the boat. Chairman Leitch issued a statement in the *Reformer* notable for its condescension and xenophobic overtones: "Because of the great increase in numbers, and profound change in racial and language origins of the flue-cured tobacco growers of the Norfolk area in the [last] four years ... it is understandable that the nervous, jittery atmosphere inevitable at the actual time of marketing this year's crop, should produce misunderstandings and misconceptions of the purposes and powers of the Marketing Association." Leitch took care to explain the complex evaluation of market factors that went into setting the average tobacco price, concluding that "lack of knowledge and understanding of these important matters leads to absurd and fantastic conclusions and decisions which cause irreparable disaster for growers." Continuing, he declared that "the intelligence of a child would grasp" that the offer of 24.5 cents per pound was to the farmers' ultimate benefit, all things considered.[75]

In the next issue of the *Reformer*, Imperial president Gray Miller waded into the conversation, with a statement that was also read on radio stations in Brantford, Chatham, and London two days prior. The article's front-page headline is telling: "Strike is Threat to Industry, Head of Imperial Tobacco Company Broadcasts; Stocks Ample." Miller informed growers that Imperial had sufficient stocks of tobacco, as well as access to American product, assuring the holdouts that they needed Imperial more than Imperial needed them. Like Leitch, Miller took a paternalistic tone, combining a call for quasi-familial unity with a thinly veiled threat of discipline: "I, personally, have always taken the greatest interest in the development of the raising of flue-cured tobacco in Ontario, and cannot help but feel that the present situation, if continued, will give your industry a setback."[76]

Whether due to fearmongering or fatigue, the industry representatives got their wish. Almost immediately after the 10 November meeting of growers, when Stirtzinger was shouted down, farmers were offered a slightly higher price and began selling their crop in droves. By 13 November, only ten crops remained unsold. Though the movement dried up quickly, the holdouts did get a higher price for their crop – with many receiving between 1 and 6 cents more per pound than the price originally offered. The dispute prompted reflections on both sides about its meaning and legacy. Holwell, in a letter published in *Munkás* on behalf of the leadership committee, tried to raise growers' spirits, declaring that the efforts hadn't been a total failure since a modest price increase had been attained. He criticized the lack of power afforded to small growers under the Marketing Association, arguing that "we need a new tobacco growers' association, an association which elects its own representatives democratically." Such an organization would be able to compel government to take action to curtail the unchecked powers of the tobacco companies and large plantations.[77] An editorial in *Munkás* echoed the call for a new, more democratic association, stressing the need for such a body to incorporate the interests of both farmers and workers. Co-operation between the two groups had in fact been one of the bright spots of the movement: "Workers ... were a huge help in the war fought against the common enemy." They helped promote meetings, "and did everything for the growers' success. They also knew that if the growers are going to win, it's a win for the workers as well."[78]

On the establishment side, Marketing Association secretary J.K. Perrett, when asked about the strike about a week after its collapse, "laid the blame for this at the door of outside agitators ... The dispute, he said, had for a time threatened amicable relations between growers and buyers as well as jeopardizing a promising export market."[79] Perrett, of course, was partially correct. The leadership of Holwell, an outsider, was crucial to the movement's modest gains. But the efforts of smallholders, sharegrowers, and workers to increase their share of tobacco profits was not simply a case of a doe-eyed community being whipped into a frenzy by a mysterious, magnetic outsider. Instead, the 1937 campaign was built atop the tobacco belt's infrastructure of dissent. Perrett's second point was much more accurate – the dispute did indeed threaten "amicable relations," as growers and their worker allies became increasingly aware of, and rejected, a system that exploited them to the benefit of the tobacco companies and large landholders.

In the years after 1937, growers continued agitating for a fairer deal from tobacco companies and for a more democratic Marketing Association. In 1938, for example, Belgian and Hungarian growers successfully lobbied for increased representation for members of their respective ethnic groups on the association's board of directors.[80] The big breakthrough finally came in 1957, when small growers campaigning on a program of stricter supply management and fairer and more transparent crop sale practices won a plebiscite that resulted in the replacement of the old Marketing Association with a new organization, the Ontario Flue-Cured Tobacco Growers' Marketing Board.[81]

1939: The Summer of Dissent

If 1937 represented the peak of small-grower mobilization during the 1930s, then the decade's greatest moment of worker resistance came during the harvest of 1939, when the region's proletarian political culture linked up with the "politics of indignation" of the Depression-era unemployed, who arrived by the thousands late that summer with no grander expectation than to make a hard-earned buck in the harvest, only to encounter a shortage of work and a chilly reception.[82] Organizational efforts began in the early days of the influx when a combination of local and migrant activists – including Communists – founded the United Tobacco Workers (UTW), Local 1. The "provisional committee" of the union was made up of six men, including four from the tobacco belt: Nick Kuchinsky, Frank Pastor, Bill Koracz, and Marvin Burke, the last of whom frequently served as chairman at Communist Party meetings in Delhi. The other two were party members from Toronto: Steve Hill, who had come out of the Hungarian Workers' Clubs, and Jack Scott, who had occupied various prominent roles within the party and was seen as the central leader of the union.

While the UTW had strong Communist participation among its leadership, it appears to have been a grassroots creation of job seekers rather than the product of Communist Party directives.[83] The union's first tasks were to set wage demands and then spread the word. With the harvest days away and hiring already beginning, there wasn't a moment to lose. Activists fanned out across the district, handing out flyers printed with the wage demands: $3.50 to $4.00 per day for skilled tiers and primers, and $2.75 to $3.00 for lower-skilled handers. The Hungarian Workers' Club coordinated flyering efforts in Tillsonburg, while the union worked Delhi, where members also picketed farms that had hired workers at below the union rate.[84]

2.3 United Tobacco Workers meeting, Delhi, Ontario, 2 August 1939. London Free Press
Collection of Photographic Negatives, 3 August 1939, Western University Archives and
Special Collections, London, Ontario.

The first reported meeting of the UTW took place in a park beside Delhi's
Baptist church on the night of 2 August, with five hundred in attendance (see
figure 2.3). Marvin Burke chaired the assembly, and speeches were delivered
from a tree stump in Hungarian, English, Slovakian, and Ukrainian. Jack Scott
pushed back against the oft-repeated accusations that the unemployed did not
want to work, suggesting that the presence of thousands of job seekers in Delhi
was ample evidence to the contrary. "We came here to work, we are staying
here to work, and we are going to fight to get fair wages when we do work."
The union leaders reminded attendees of the wage demands and urged them
to fill out a union card and join up – they could wait until they secured jobs
before paying dues. Organizers also repeated the common refrain of tobacco
belt radicals: that workers and growers should co-operate and together reap
greater rewards from their labour. Unfortunately for the workers, these efforts

produced minimal results. Whereas in the small growers' movement of 1937, workers undertook a large leadership role, the gesture was not reciprocated two years later, when growers did not appear on union committees, speak at meetings, or support the workers in the press.[85]

UTW organizers rejected the idea that they were "troublemakers" or "agitators" and instead characterized themselves as respectable citizens simply trying to make an honest living. As Scott said in his 2 August speech, "We want to keep order, but we want work. I myself walked 20 miles to find a job. Others have walked still further." Transients, too, fought for recognition of their respectable status as they expressed indignation at their rotten treatment in the tobacco belt: some invoked their belonging in the Canadian polity, while others rejected the labels of "Communists" and "radicals," demonstrating the ideological heterogeneity among the job seekers, even as they expressed a common refusal of their situation. "This isn't Regina of 1933 and 1934," said one job seeker, likely referencing the clash between On-to-Ottawa Trek participants (mostly unemployed men travelling from Vancouver to the capital to demand better conditions) and the RCMP that took place in Regina in 1935. "We came here to spend our money looking for jobs, and we're not looking for any trouble."[86] Frank Kubasky, a Czech Canadian who had lived in Canada for fifteen years, told a reporter, "It cost me $8 to become a Canadian. How is it that I am not as good a Canadian as the people who became citizens merely by being born here? ... We're workers, not bums ... We're not a bunch of Communists either."[87] But the refusal of the Communist label did not mean that job seekers were simply defending the tobacco belt's ruling order. As Kubasky was quoted in a different article, "There have been reports that we are Communists. We are not Communists. But if authorities want to force us out we are ready."[88]

Workers and job seekers looking to organize were generally harassed and thwarted by police with the support of local and provincial authorities. Organizers passing out handbills were taken in by the police for questioning and had their flyers confiscated.[89] The police not only helped to quash dissent, but also assisted growers in the hiring process by helping them find labourers, including for the purpose of replacing strikers.[90] Local and provincial governments alike were clearly committed to protecting the interests of farmers. Queen's Park dispatched additional provincial police officers to the region to deal with the influx.[91] For their part, the reeves of Delhi and Walsingham were much more explicit in their condemnation of the attempts at organizing and advocated threatening striking workers with jail time and running them out of town. Such policies, Walsingham's reeve explained, would quell the spread of unrest elsewhere in the district and have a "sobering effect" on worker militancy.[92] Police ousted not only strikers and organizers, but also job seekers who refused to take offered wages.[93] Such coordinated repression on the part of police and local government were experiences common for Depression-era rural dissidents across North America, and they represented serious obstacles to successful organization.[94]

Despite these difficulties, the union does appear to have had some measure of success. Scott recalled in his memoir that "out of more than twenty thousand people there weren't more than a hundred that went to work," and that growers soon caved to the pressure and raised wages to within 50 cents of the union's demands.[95] Given the lack of corroboration in the press (including *Munkás*), it is likely that Scott's account was hyperbolic, but certainly some workers did indeed hold out. Two such individuals were Mrs Vincent Dorton (whose first name was unfortunately not published) and her husband, who decided to move on to London rather than work for below the union rate. Mrs Dorton explained that they were offered a combined $6.00 per day. "We didn't take it. The union officials told us we had better not start to work unless we were being paid $8 a day."[96] In late August there were reports of job seekers in nearby Langton refusing to work for below the $3.50 rate the union had set.[97]

As a formal institution, the UTW petered out almost as soon as it had gotten going. Certainly, state repression made its work more difficult, but the more important reason for the union's decline was the dissipation of job seekers from Delhi. Despite the panicked cries in the press, the transient situation worked itself out within about a week. As the harvest approached its starting point, farmers took on their usual numbers of employees. Many job seekers who did not get hired on in Delhi moved on to other parts of the tobacco belt, or left the region entirely. By the time the Delhi Village Council voted on 8 August to evict transients within a week, most of them had already left of their own accord. The net result was an end to the massive congregations in downtown Delhi, and with them went the union. Neither the UTW nor its leaders were mentioned in the press again after the Benefit Association picnic.[98]

But the abrupt decline of union activity by no means spelled the end of the tobacco belt's summer of dissent, as a number of spontaneous strikes and other worker actions continued on farms throughout the month of August. Rather than ending with the UTW's demise, the sites of struggle simply shifted locations, from the parks and streets of Delhi to the individual points of production. At least four strikes or work disruptions took place during the harvest. On the morning of 11 August, nine wage labourers on a farm in Langton refused to work unless the grower upped their pay from $3.50 to $4.00 per day. The sharegrower who operated the farm refused the pay increase and summoned the local police constable, James Pepper, who escorted the strikers – hailing from Brantford, Toronto, and Saskatchewan – out of town. They were easily replaced with job seekers in the area.[99] Two days later, Pepper took to the press to warn of ongoing agitation in the region, citing calls from two growers asking for replacement workers. Pepper warned, "If there is any attempt to strike, the men are here in the village to replace the strikers who will be escorted out of the district immediately."[100] On 14 August, the *Brantford Expositor* reported on the militancy spreading throughout the region: "Miniature strikes and threats of bigger strikes on the part of tobacco laborers have been causing some uneasiness, but the authorities stated they are fully capable of dealing with it."[101] The last reported strike, on 25 August, was actually successful, as workers at a farm near Delhi refused to work unless their $3.00 wage was upped to $3.50. The grower complied within an hour.[102]

The tobacco workers' revolt of 1939 did not produce a lasting union presence in the sector, and the UTW was never heard from again. The transient nature of tobacco's workforce would have made it difficult enough to sustain the momentum of that summer, but well before such challenges could arise, events across the Atlantic spelled the end of the summer of dissent. With the start of World War II in early September, many tobacco workers enlisted, and the wartime economic boom quickly ended the mass migrations of unemployed in search of work. While labour strife continued in the tobacco sector well into the postwar era, it never again reached the tenor of the late 1930s. A picnic organized by the Canadian Hungarian Mutual Benefit Federation in Delhi on 3 September, the day before Labour Day, provides a telling indication of the war's instant usurping of centre stage from the strike wave. On this important weekend on the left and labour calendars, the picnic organizers had succeeded in

booking the general secretary of the Communist Party, Tim Buck, to speak to
attendees on "The Tobacco Situation."

It is not hard to imagine tobacco activists interpreting the speech as a confirmation of the importance and successes of their struggle and of the gathering
momentum of their movement. As a *Reformer* editorial complained, "Mass
meetings of foreigners, addressed by Communists, have become altogether too
frequent in the tobacco area in recent months."[103] However, the commencement
of hostilities on 1 September prompted Buck to instead speak about the war
and what it meant for Communists in Canada.[104] Clearly, tobacco's summer
of dissent was over, as the struggles in the fields were quickly overshadowed
by the start of a new global war. Though manifestations of the tobacco belt's
infrastructure of dissent would continue into the war and beyond, never again
would they reach the intensity of the 1930s or the decade's peak moment of
protest in 1939.[105]

◆◆◆

In the years following the green gold rush, working people in the tobacco sector found more than one way to improve their conditions and social station.
Benefitting from market conditions and easy access to credit, and drawing on
the labour and resources of the whole family (women especially), a remarkable
number of working families were able to progress from wage labour to sharegrowing to farm ownership. That ordinary folk could, with the right blend of
hard work and circumstance, secure a decent living within the capitalist tobacco sector did not mean that they acquiesced to its mode of operation. To
the contrary, workers, sharegrowers, and small growers frequently challenged
employers, tobacco companies, and the Marketing Association to demand a
greater share of tobacco's rich rewards. To be sure, these were efforts that had
significant limits – topmost, perhaps, was the difficulty of forging alliances
between workers and small growers. While workers were often willing to support small growers in their campaigns, the reverse was seldom true. By the
postwar period, worker-grower solidarity was no longer even a topic of discussion. Both groups continued to agitate for better conditions within the
sector, but they did so in isolation (and indeed, when it came to workers' campaigns, in opposition).

The elusiveness of such alliances was far from the only challenge faced by
working people in tobacco in the interwar and mid-century period. Life within

the sector was rife with conflict, and the road to farm ownership was littered with pitfalls and obstacles. And those excluded from participation in the sector – most notably African Americans from the southern United States – were by extension excluded from its economic opportunities.

For those who could access the tobacco labour market in this period, three important features of working life – freedom of movement, social mobility, and working-class organization – together left ordinary people well-poised to secure better livelihoods within the tobacco belt. But these conditions would not remain static. As early as the 1930s, the first of these, freedom of movement, came increasingly under fire, as governments sought desperately to exert some control over the movement of migrant job seekers during the Great Depression.

3

CONTROLLING MIGRANTS

The crisis of 1939 represented the coming to fruition of many powerholders' worst fears about the tobacco belt's migrant labour situation. Over the preceding decade, local officials, civic leaders, and journalists had become increasingly concerned about the mass arrivals of migrant workers to the Norfolk district each harvest. In the early years of the tobacco boom, authorities had been happy to permit the flurry of mobility underpinning the sector's success to continue unperturbed, but the onset of the Great Depression rapidly changed the equation. Now, the ever-growing numbers of job seekers arriving in Norfolk each July and August threatened to disrupt the region's fragile prosperity amidst the economic crisis, by causing social unrest, putting locals out of work, and swelling its relief rolls. Migrant arrivals were frequently portrayed as "influxes" or "invasions," especially when they featured members of the region's more vilified ethnic groups – Hungarians in particular – and by 1935, Norfolk authorities were talking about "waging war" on transients.[1] In early August of 1939, as ten thousand migrants jammed the tobacco district and militant labour action reached its peak, the worst doomsday predictions seemed to be coming true.

Officials from multiple levels of government – but particularly at the local level – had certainly tried to avoid such a situation, making desperate attempts over the course of the 1930s to exert some control over the yearly entrance of transients to the Norfolk region. But order was not so easily attained. In the case of workers moving within Canada's borders, the problem was left largely to local authorities who, try as they might, could do little to stem the tide. When it came to migrant workers from the United States, federal authorities proved more willing to step in, and indeed in this domain they had a much more powerful tool at their disposal: the border. Even here, however, officials' efforts were perpetually frustrated by rule-defying migrants and logistical challenges.

Only a second global crisis, World War II, provided governments in Canada and the United States with the opportunity to secure firmer control over the movement of farm workers, both within and across their national boundaries. Yet again, however, regulatory efforts were frustrated by familiar challenges, as well as by fierce opposition from tobacco growers and their allies, who bristled at officials' efforts to stem the unregulated movement of workers into high-paying tobacco harvest jobs each summer. At issue was not simply government intervention in the labour market, but also the very question of just how important tobacco was to the war effort. In the case of the US-Ontario movement, the wartime emergency precipitated the transformation of that previously informal seasonal migration system into a more formalized, bilaterally managed guest-worker program, while still maintaining its whites-only composition. State involvement in the tobacco labour market, then, was neither natural nor inevitable, nor did it represent a clean break from previous practices, but instead came about through gradual, uneven, and hotly contested processes.[2]

Furthermore, the story of government intervention in the tobacco labour scene during the Depression and war contrasts starkly with the conventional representation of the state's role in agriculture, where it is typically cast as either provider or denier of workers to labour-starved farmers. In the booming tobacco belt of the 1930s and '40s, the growing presence of the state was aimed not at alleviating labour shortages – at least not those of tobacco growers – but instead at securing greater control over the movement of workers *into* the attractive sector.

The Transient Problem

Despite widespread agreement that mass migrant arrivals were a problem, local officials and journalists struggled to identify their cause. Yes, there were jobs in the Norfolk area at a time when jobs were scarce, but not nearly enough to employ all the thousands who jammed the region each year. Why did so many transients choose to come to such small places as Delhi, Simcoe, and Tillsonburg? Theories abounded, some based in fact, others of murkier reasoning.

Sometimes blame was pinned on nearby cities, such as in 1932, when Simcoe and Norfolk officials alleged that Windsor was "loading its foreign unemployed on trucks" and sending them east on Highway 3, a claim that Windsor politicians vehemently denied. At other times, critics pointed to boosterish job advertisements that told of the thousands of jobs available in the tobacco harvest.[3] Unlike the allegations against Windsor and other cities, this claim was easier to substantiate. In 1939, for example, such advertisements were broadcast in newspapers across the country, prompting many desperate job seekers to pull up stakes and head for Delhi. There was much speculation and disagreement over who might have been behind such publicity, but no definitive answer was ever established.[4]

While the source of the 1939 advertisements remained a mystery, it is clear from this and other instances that such promotion did indeed have the power to move large numbers of jobless men to the tobacco belt. In 1935, when Leamington growers placed a newspaper ad for jobs suckering tobacco, so many job seekers showed up – even from as far away as Toronto, 350 kilometres to the east – that local police converted their station into a "transient hotel."[5] The publication of job availability was used at least once to dampen organizing efforts: in 1937, Ontario premier Mitch Hepburn, in response to efforts by Hungarian Communists to raise harvest wages, publicly called on provincial ministers of agriculture from across Canada to help supply four thousand additional workers to the tobacco belt, despite the fact that local officials were actively trying to *dissuade* job seekers from coming to an already flush labour market.[6]

The tobacco belt's transient problem connected to a broader set of conflicts in Depression-era Canada over the provision of relief to the unemployed. Debates about which level of government (federal, provincial, or municipal) should be responsible for the unemployed dated back to at least the 1910s, but became particularly acute during the 1930s as swelling relief rolls drove many municipalities and the four western provinces toward insolvency. Meanwhile, growing numbers of out-of-work men traversed the country in search of jobs, each indignity pushing them further in the direction of collective, militant solutions to their plight. In this turbo-charged climate, an ever-increasing contingent of politicians, experts, activists, and others called on the foot-dragging federal government to take more decisive action (and dramatically increase expenditures) in response to the crisis.

3.1 Transient family, Delhi, Ontario, 1939. The London Free Press Collection of Photographic Negatives, 3 August 1939, Western University Archives and Special Collections, London, Canada.

These debates also played out in Norfolk, where the arrival of thousands of transient workers seeking tobacco work each summer added a local flavour to the question. For one, observers in the region placed part of the blame for Norfolk's unemployment on migrant workers, who they reasoned were keeping some locals out of work. Indeed, when plans for a relief work camp in the county were announced in 1933, it was specified that the two hundred jobs at the camp would not be open to "outsiders or transients." Conditions in the tobacco sector also prompted local authorities and the press to lobby higher levels of government for assistance. For example, during the summer of 1939, editorials in the *Reformer* called on the federal government to take bolder action to confront the crisis of unemployment. "Surely the acute situation created at Delhi will arouse the federal government to the imperative need of providing some scheme of employment for these thousands who otherwise will inevitably

end up in the clutches of Communist propagandists," reasoned the paper. Norfolk's pleas for assistance, however, like those of many municipalities across
the country, went largely unanswered. In confronting the problem of transient
workers, government officials in the tobacco belt were left almost entirely to
their own devices.[7]

Norfolk officials concentrated their efforts on attempts to manage the entrance of transients into the region and to control their activities once present.
Their principal tool for achieving these ends was the local police, whose ranks
were sometimes bolstered at harvest time by provincial officers. Local authorities often talked tough about exerting control over the movement of transient workers, in part to discourage prospective job seekers from setting out
for Norfolk. Simcoe reeve J.C. Austin told the *Reformer* in 1935, "There is not
enough work to absorb our own citizens here in the county and we are certainly
not going to allow a lot of outsiders to come in here during the summer months
and keep our own taxpayers out of work." He claimed that the previous year,
trucks bringing workers in from other parts of Canada (including from as far
away as Montreal), were escorted by police back outside county lines.

Police often told arriving transients to return to where they came from.
Local authorities also dreamed of more thorough controls over transient mobility. In 1939, Delhi's chief of police met with a corporal of the RCMP to discuss
implementing a registration system for transients, such as existed in France,
where "a foreigner ... must carry with him a registration card to be presented
to the authorities of each municipality as he moves about the country." Despite
the tough talk, local attempts to control the entrance of job seekers to the
region were by and large a failure, as thousands of transient workers continued
to enter the tobacco towns year after year. A handful of local and provincial
police officers patrolling all of Norfolk stood no real chance of preventing job
seekers from crossing county lines – and this is to say nothing about the legality
of banning free subjects from moving about the country.[8]

While transients were in the tobacco towns, looking for work, they were
subject to constant police surveillance and harassment. When they were on
sidewalks, they were told by police to keep moving. Activists attempting to organize tobacco workers were routinely arrested and dropped outside of the
tobacco belt, with an unlucky few receiving beatings in the process. The increased incidence of petty crimes during each harvest season meant that every
transient was seen as an actual or potential criminal. Newspapers reported,

3.2 Typical harvest-time scene, Delhi, Ontario, 1953. London Free Press Collection
of Photographic Negatives, 6 August 1953, Western University Archives and Special
Collections, London, Ontario.

somewhat ironically, on vegetables being stolen from gardens, milk bottles
being swiped from front porches, and other (mostly) small-time thefts like the
one described in the following headline: "Pet Bunny, Corn, and Spuds Go;
Probably Stew." Law enforcement essentially enjoyed free reign to detain and
investigate transients. For example, when George Pinnion of Brantford was
arrested for unclear reasons in August 1936, he was found to have $146 on him.
According to police, he was unable to give a "satisfactory explanation" for his
stash, so officials decided to dig deeper and investigate his record. It is unclear
what, if anything, was found.[9]

During the crisis-level rush of job seekers in 1939, local officials sought to
control transient mobility through an additional measure – evicting transients
en masse from town. The Delhi Village Council voted on 8 August 1939 to clear

transients from the area, and soon police were rounding up migrants every night and depositing them outside the village limits. By this point the harvest had already started, so remaining job seekers had diminishing chances of finding work. For many, being removed by police might have been simply another factor encouraging them to move on. Indeed, newspapers reported a general movement of transients from Delhi to nearby Langton, where rumour held that more jobs were available. But while economic and police coercion appear to have had some success in dispersing transients from Delhi, local authorities remained limited in their powers to govern migrant mobility: many transients who were removed by police at night simply walked back into Delhi the following day.[10] When it came to managing the movement of transient tobacco workers within Canada, then, state intervention remained mostly a local endeavour and therefore was limited in its success. While able to frustrate the efforts of labour organizers and make it difficult for transients to remain in the region unperturbed for long periods of time, when it came to establishing any widespread control over the movement of migrant job seekers, local officials were hopelessly impotent.

Southerners and the Border

Whereas the control of Canadian transient workers in the tobacco belt was left largely to municipal authorities, the federal government took much more decisive action when it came to seasonal workers from the United States, a movement all but untouched by authorities before 1931. "There is no red tape surrounding their entry into Canada," declared the *Reformer* about southern workers in 1930.[11] In a similar vein, tobacco executive R.A. Parham, who worked in Leamington's Imperial plant as a low-level manager in the 1920s, wrote in his autobiography,

It has been interesting to recall that when I first entered Canada there was no red tape at all. The officer merely asked, "Where are you from? Where are you going? What are you going to do?," and that was all. He wished me God Speed, and hoped we could get the tobacco grown before the frosts came in the fall. How different from to-day's world, when each little part of the world wants to set up its own bureaucratic machinery and impede travel with forms to be filled out every time you move a few hundred miles and cross a border.[12]

With the onset of the Great Depression, however, migrant workers from the South, like their Canadian counterparts, came increasingly to be perceived as a problem. In 1930, newspapers started publishing reports of "influxes" of southerners and others camping out in tobacco towns in search of work. An article describing Simcoe's application to the province for its share of relief funds explained that the town's unemployment situation was worsened by the arrival of Americans who took jobs that otherwise would have been filled by local men. Highly regarded for their valuable expertise as tobacco curers, southerners began to attract suspicion that perhaps they weren't all the highly skilled, elite migrants they were made out to be. Norfolk County agricultural representative F.C. Paterson warned that "Norfolk is quite attractive to a certain type of Virginia or Carolina citizen that we don't want. There are a great many of these Southerners that we do want, however, but we have had a lot of men come to this county who aren't worth anything to us. They claim they know the tobacco business, but they don't." The solution, Paterson and many other government officials reasoned, was to limit the entrance of US tobacco migrants to Canada. "In regard to this matter," he explained, "steps have already been taken to call the attention of the immigration department to the influx of worthless labor each year, without jeopardizing the position of the better class of men which Norfolk desires and needs to help in the tobacco fields."[13]

Norfolk wasn't the only place in Canada where there were concerns about foreigners stealing jobs during the Great Depression. In fact, Canadian authorities had already started taking action to restrict immigration, with farm workers as a particular target. Order-in-Council PC 1957, signed by Prime Minister R.B. Bennett on 14 August 1930, removed farm labourers and domestic servants from the list of admissible classes. The policy was confirmed in the sweeping changes made to immigration policy a few months later in PC 695 (signed on 21 March 1931), which limited immigration to four categories: subjects of the British Empire from its white settler colonies; US citizens (a migrant in one of these first two groups needed to have "sufficient means to maintain himself until employment is secured"); wives and children of legal residents of Canada; and "agriculturalist[s] having sufficient means to farm in Canada."[14]

The category "agriculturalist" denoted farmers rather than farm workers. Canada's use of immigration restriction in order to protect domestic jobs was part of a global trend during the late nineteenth and mid-twentieth centuries, and during the interwar period in particular, when international migrants – racialized ones especially – had become frequent scapegoats in times of economic downturn and depression, and the closure of borders emerged as a well-trodden populist response to such conditions.[15] The practice was also part of a long homegrown tradition of using the state apparatus to exclude or deport foreigners deemed threatening to the economy, political order, or social fabric of the nation.[16]

The supposedly ironclad Canadian immigration rules of the early 1930s, however, required some repurposing in the tobacco belt: while government officials were happy to utilize them to keep out unskilled harvesters, they had no intention of curtailing the entry of curers, on whom the young tobacco sector – a rare economic bright spot in the bleak world of the Depression – depended. In June 1931, F.C. Paterson and J.K. Perrett, from the local office of the provincial Department of Agriculture, announced how the changes would affect tobacco growers. Starting that year, a tobacco farm owner wishing to hire a southern curer was required to submit an application to the Department of Agriculture office in Simcoe. If approved, the form was forwarded on to the Department of Immigration and then the port of entry where the curer planned to cross the border. The farmer also had to send a "letter of identification" to his curer, to be presented to immigration officers at the border and matched with the grower's application. Prior to the June announcement, reports had circulated that only sharegrowers, curers, and growers from the South would be allowed in under the new rules, and that unskilled harvesters would be barred. Officials backed down from this hard line in the final announcement, though it was clear that the entry of unskilled workers was to be limited and closely scrutinized. Paterson and Perrett explained, "A limited number of cutters or primers will be admitted under the same regulations, only in cases where farm owners show that such help is necessary."[17]

The sudden change in procedures for the US-Ontario movement was remarkable, considering how unregulated the movement had been before 1931. As North Carolinian curer Sid Williams recalled in a 1939 interview, "When I first went up there anybody could go; now they have to send you a pass. I used to carry a couple cousins to help prime but the law done cut that out."[18] Gov-

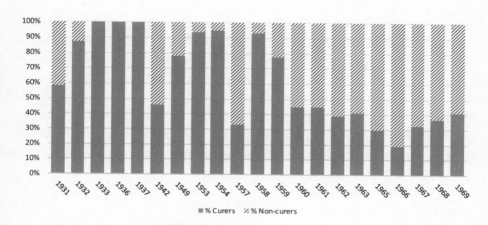

3.3 Per cent curers and non-curers in US-Ontario tobacco worker movement, select years, 1931–69. Sources: Satzewich, *Racism and the Incorporation of Foreign Labour*, 108; Agricultural Representatives' Field Reports, Norfolk, 1931–37, RG 16-66, AO; Department of Labour (RG 27, vols 667–8), Immigration Branch (RG 76, vols 853, 1112), and Manpower and Immigration (RG 118, acc. 1985–86/071, vol. 84), LAC.

ernment control over the entry of tobacco workers would only increase in the years following the first regulations. Starting in 1932, quotas were issued dictating the number of US tobacco workers permitted entry to Canada, jointly determined by the provincial Ministries of Agriculture and Labour, federal Departments of Labour and Immigration, and tobacco growers' representatives.[19] The next year, immigration authorities took a harder line regarding unskilled workers, and at least officially, only curers and sharegrowers were allowed in (the latter category included a small number of women and children). The movement would remain officially barred to unskilled workers into the late 1930s (see figure 3.3).[20] Beyond immigration reforms aimed at regulating the supply of curers, officials from various levels of government also sought to reduce the demand for southerners by launching a training program to teach Canadians the delicate art of curing.[21]

While the Depression-era changes profoundly transformed the functioning of the US-Ontario movement, there were discrepancies between official regulations and what actually happened on the ground. From the very first year of the new policy, migrants found ways to skirt the rules and get into Canada.

Really, it was often not all that difficult. In 1931, the *Reformer* reported that many southerners were travelling to Buffalo and buying bus tickets to Detroit. The route went across southwestern Ontario and made stops along the way, making it easy for job seekers to simply get off and make their way into the tobacco belt. Others entered Canada as visitors, then proceeded to work in tobacco anyway. Officials also reported instances of primers pretending to be curers in order to gain entry. These forms of resistance to border controls were often on the minds of officials in charge of the program, as they sought to perfect state control.[22]

There were also inconsistencies in the ways in which the new border controls were applied. The story of one migrant family, drawn from border crossing records, is instructive in this regard. On 2 March 1933, Florence Randolph Lacks and her six children, all from Halifax County, Virginia, arrived at the Niagara Falls border crossing, en route to join Florence's husband, Littleton Lacks, in Vittoria. It is unclear if Littleton was living permanently in Canada, or if he was there temporarily as a sharegrower. Florence and five of her six children – those who were under eighteen years of age – were granted admission into Canada, but her eldest child, twenty-five-year-old Richard Lacks, was not so lucky, and was rejected. A border agent with the surname Rigg listed PC 695 as the reason for Richard's rejection.

Two aspects of Richard's case might have cost him entry – his age and his listed occupation. Whereas Florence and her other children qualified for admittance under PC 695 as dependents of a legal resident of Canada, Richard, being over eighteen, did not. Furthermore, Richard's occupation was recorded as "tobacco farm labourer," and it was noted that he intended to undertake the same work in Canada. Under PC 695, Richard could have qualified for entry either as an "agriculturalist having sufficient means to farm in Canada" or as an American possessing "sufficient means to maintain himself until employment is secured." But contradicting these rules were the tobacco-specific regulations, which limited migration to curers and sharegrowers. We cannot know how these competing directives sorted themselves out in the mind of the immigration agent on that day in March, but despite Richard having twenty-five dollars in his possession (which presumably would have been more than enough to support himself until finding a job), he was denied entry.[23] Florence and her five youngest children proceeded into Canada, while Richard was forced to head back into the United States.

The story, however, did not end there. Almost two weeks later, on 15 March 1933, Richard came back to the border. We don't know if he returned home to Virginia in the intervening period, or secured lodging in western New York, or what contact he might have had with his family in Canada. What is knowable from the border crossing records is that this time, Richard listed his occupation as "tobacco farmer" instead of "tobacco farm labourer," and stated that he planned to work as a farmer in Canada. And even though he now had just $7.50 on him (perhaps he gave some of the $25.00 to his mother before parting ways, and perhaps some was spent on travel and lodging during his two-week limbo), Richard was allowed in.[24]

We are left to speculate on whether or not Richard, perhaps in consultation with southerners like his father who had successfully entered Canada, consciously decided to represent himself as being part of a different occupational category, and therefore eligible for entry. If he did so, he would have been partaking in a migrant practice as old as state controls over borders: the manipulation of state-defined categories to produce more favourable outcomes for migrants.[25] Or perhaps the story of his admittance is much more banal and Officer Cupole, who granted him entry on 15 March, was simply more lenient than Rigg, who had turned him away thirteen days earlier. Regardless, the Lacks family's story – along with the more definitive instances of migrant resistance to border controls – demonstrate that the new restrictions placed on the entry of tobacco workers were far from absolute. Not only did migrants find ways to evade border controls, but state officials also struggled with how to interpret and apply the rules.

Of course, the uneven application of the new rules did not always work in migrants' favour; sometimes it had the opposite effect. In at least one case, immigration agents assigned themselves much greater discretionary power than afforded by either PC 695 or the tobacco-specific rules. Two southern curers travelling to an East Elgin farm in 1932, despite having made the proper arrangements with their employer, were subjected to a literacy test at the border, and when it was discovered that they could not read or write, were denied entry. The grower who was expecting them took to the press in an effort to contest the decision, but it is unclear if he was successful.[26]

The enforcement of controls over the US-Ontario movement did not only take place at the border: migrants who had entered illicitly were subsequently subject to arrest and deportation. A major push to locate and deport such migrants took place in 1935, when an investigation by provincial and federal agriculture officials reported that a "considerable number of Americans are coming in as tourists and are engaging in harvesting operations, and thus displacing Canadian labour." After being notified of this practice, the Department of Immigration sent its own representative to tour the tobacco belt, who confirmed the allegations and took action: "Our officer located thirteen aliens who appeared to be in Canada illegally. The deportation of three of these men has been ordered and they will be promptly returned to the United States." For the other ten workers, "Boards of Inquiry are under way and these will finally be disposed of just as quickly as possible." Immigration officials sometimes had trouble obtaining information from US workers on the whereabouts of their unauthorized co-nationals. "As in previous investigations," one letter noted, "it was found difficult to obtain co-operation or information from southern growers in the district, but the local officials extended every co-operation possible." US tobacco migrants who had entered Canada clandestinely would continue to be subject to investigation, arrest, and deportation in the years ahead.[27]

World War II: Emergency Order

The border was the state's most effective tool for managing the movement of tobacco workers during the Great Depression, but the crisis of World War II afforded it much greater powers to control not only the entrance of migrants from abroad, but also the movement of workers within Canada's boundaries.

Canada's participation in World War II created massive labour shortages. In addition to the more than one million Canadians who would join the armed forces by war's end, ramped-up production in support of the war effort required the labour of hundreds of thousands more. The country and its businesses were compelled to draw on every available reserve of labour; most famously, by bringing an unprecedented number of women into the workplace. Canada's economy reached "full employment" during the war, and employers were often desperate to find and retain workers. This situation, combined with a wave of labour militancy, resulted in dramatic increases in both wages and worker power.[28]

While bombers and bullets are perhaps more dramatic examples of war production, farming was no less crucial to the war effort: industrial workers and soldiers alike needed to eat. Agriculture, however, faced even greater labour challenges than industry during the war. The low pay and unappealing conditions of agricultural labour meant that farmers were losing workers not only to the armed forces, but also to industry, which after years of depression now offered a seemingly limitless number of jobs and astronomical wages. The economic prosperity brought about by the war, then, posed serious problems for the state, which needed the labour market to align itself closely with war aims. Instead, high wages prompted workers to move from job to job, seizing better opportunities, and agriculture in particular struggled to find sufficient workers to maintain food production.[29]

In response to these problems, the Canadian state undertook an unprecedented level of involvement in the labour market. In 1942, the government created the National Selective Service (NSS) within the Department of Labour, which it tasked with regulating and rationalizing the labour market. Agriculture was at the core of these plans: from the earliest stages of the NSS's creation, one of its three main initiatives was the "freezing" of farm workers in place, meaning that they were forbidden from leaving their jobs in agriculture without permission from an NSS official.[30] To further encourage the maintenance of the agricultural workforce, farmers, their sons, and farm workers were able to postpone military service under the 1940 National Resources Mobilization Act if they could demonstrate that they were required in agriculture. Toward the end of the war, soldiers from farming families were also permitted to receive "farm leave" from military service in order to help on the farm.[31]

Simultaneous to the implementation of NSS regulations were a number of government programs – at both the federal and provincial levels – aimed at mobilizing labour for farm work. At the provincial level, no such scheme was as ambitious as Ontario's, whose Farm Service Force formed eight brigades – of children, women (the "Farmerettes" and "Women's Land Army"), and other groups of untapped labour – to help produce crops. To support the Ontario Farm Service Force and efforts in other provinces, the federal Department of Labour created the Dominion-Provincial Farm Labour Program in 1943 and entered into agreements with provincial governments to assist with the costs of running such schemes.[32] Government efforts to mobilize and rationally manage the labour force were deeply informed by a state-interventionist school of thought that had made major inroads among academics and civil servants over the preceding decade, as leading promoters such as John Maynard Keynes (a Briton whose ideas were most famously taken up in the United States under Franklin D. Roosevelt), William Beveridge (United Kingdom), and Leonard Marsh (Canada) encouraged an active state response to the Great Depression.[33] This ascendant political and economic philosophy also found favour within the NSS's farm labour staff. George V. Haythorne, perhaps the single most important farm labour bureaucrat of the 1940s, co-authored a 1941 book with Leonard Marsh himself that argued for greater state involvement in the agricultural labour market.[34]

The wartime labour squeeze was also felt in tobacco, where growers adapted by hiring more women (a common occurrence in many wartime sectors), sharing harvest crews, and raising wages – quite significantly in some years.[35] Between 1937 and 1943, for example, the highest reported wages for an adult male tobacco worker doubled from four to eight dollars a day (see figure 3.4). In their ability to raise wages, tobacco growers differed significantly from other agricultural employers, whose thinner profit margins did not allow for such strategies. Where most farmers were losing workers to industry, during the harvest tobacco in fact lured workers away from other farms and even from industrial jobs. Because of this, state intervention took on a different character in tobacco than it did in other crops. The Ontario Farm Service Force, for example, did not send Farmerettes or the Children's Brigade to the tobacco fields; they weren't needed. In most agricultural sectors, state intervention was directed at getting workers to the farm and keeping them there, but tobacco, with its high wages and its production of (arguably) non-essential goods, was deemed by NSS officials to be part of the problem.

Early warnings about tobacco's disruption of wartime production came from local NSS staffers stationed in southwestern Ontario. In 1942, "thousands left industries from Windsor to Kingston without our being able to control it due to the fact that permits were not required," stressed E. Poste of the NSS's Woodstock office, imploring the Ontario regional superintendent to do something about it. "The labour situation in Woodstock could not be much more serious [than] it is at the present time," Poste continued. "Every war plant here is desperately in need of both men and women and we have no source of supply locally … This situation would be greatly aggravated by a migration of workers from the industries to the tobacco farms."[36] Employers in other sectors, particularly in agriculture and canning, also complained repeatedly about tobacco siphoning workers from them.[37]

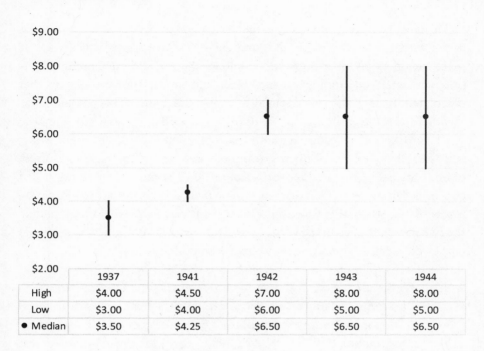

	1937	1941	1942	1943	1944
High	$4.00	$4.50	$7.00	$8.00	$8.00
Low	$3.00	$4.00	$6.00	$5.00	$5.00
● Median	$3.50	$4.25	$6.50	$6.50	$6.50

3.4 High, low, and median reported daily wages for adult male harvest workers, 1937, 1941–44. Sources: Agricultural Representatives' field report, Norfolk, 1938, RG 16-66, AO; Department of Agriculture (RG 17, vol. 3130), LAC; *Simcoe Reformer*, 17 August 1942, 19 August 1943, 10 August 1944; *Globe and Mail*, 16 August 1943.

But there was no easy fix for the NSS. Within the labour priority classification system initiated in 1942, tobacco had been given the lowest possibly rating, "D." However, tobacco's status as an agricultural sector superseded its rating, meaning that the NSS could do little to prevent workers in high-priority agricultural or industrial occupations from leaving those jobs for high-paying work in the tobacco fields.[38] NSS officials determined that the best way to correct this issue, and to excise tobacco from the broader agricultural sector, was via an order-in-council, which, after wending its way through the bureaucracy, was finally passed on 6 August 1943.[39] The order prohibited men between the ages of sixteen and sixty-five from taking a job – or remaining in a job – on a flue-cured tobacco farm between 15 July and 15 October without having first secured a permit from an NSS officer. It also banned growers from employing or continuing to employ permitless men who fit this description.[40]

The task of enforcing the order would be led by Arthur MacNamara, director of the NSS since the fall of 1942. Nicknamed the "Master Conciliator," MacNamara's leadership style was grounded in consultation and open communication with staffers, employers, and other stakeholders, a philosophy that percolated through the NSS during his time at the helm.[41] This tendency was revealed from the earliest stages of drafting the Order-in-Council, when the NSS heeded tobacco growers' requests that women be excluded from the order, reasoning that such requirements would be disruptive of the highly localized, often informal labour market for women. While some civil servants raised concerns that not requiring women to get permits could jeopardize the workforces of Niagara agriculture and certain industries in the region, ultimately the NSS decided to "meet the views of the local Association," since most female employees were not being removed from essential industry.[42]

The order was initially well-received by growers, who worked in partnership with government to design a system of controls that suited their interests. As NSS civil servant T.B. Pickersgill reported about a meeting with tobacco growers, "The tobacco growers welcomed this whole proposal. They frankly expressed the opinion that they realized that it was not in the national interest for them to employ labour essential on food producing farms or vital war industries." Growers were looking out not only for the national interest, but also for their own. Specifically, they hoped that labour market management would bring wildly soaring tobacco wages under control by reducing competition between farmers for workers, a benefit noted as well by the provincial Ministry of Agriculture and the local press. Though formal wage controls were never enacted (mostly due to infeasibility), growers did informally agree to certain wage ceilings, and one NSS official promised that if a worker requested outlandish compensation, his tobacco work permit could be cancelled. It does not appear that this in fact happened to any significant extent. The one worker whose opinion on the subject is available in the sources unsurprisingly did not support wage ceilings, reasoning to the editor of the *Reformer*, "Control the wages, yes, leave them alone!"[43]

While the promise of wage controls initially encouraged growers to support the order, they were eventually repelled by the slow pace with which it crawled through the federal bureaucracy. By the time the order passed on 6 August 1943, the harvest was beginning, thousands of job seekers were already in the tobacco belt, and many had been hired on to farms. So late in the game, the regulations were basically unenforceable. To make matters worse for growers, in 1943 job seekers again seized on the tight labour market to demand high wages (as high as ten dollars a day) – exactly the problem that growers had hoped the NSS would help with. The NSS's failure to deliver an order-in-council with enough advance notice to make a difference soured many growers to the agency moving forward. Delhi reeve Harry Collins told a Department of Labour bureaucrat in August that "the goodwill of the farmers has been entirely lost by the dilatory action in not putting the original arrangements into effect." Given these challenges, the NSS decided in mid-August to put a hold on enforcing the order until 1944.[44] MacNamara and his staff would have to expend considerable energy over the next year as they attempted to bring growers back on side. Some, however, were simply not to be appeased.

Indeed, when the NSS – now with an already passed order in hand – began planning for the implementation of regulations in 1944, they met with opposition from many quarters – from workers, growers, local press, and politicians, but also from elements within the federal public service. Critics balked at the hardship on growers, who were already struggling to meet high demand for tobacco while navigating new restraints on their labour supply. They also worried that NSS regulations would keep away workers who feared that registering with the NSS would cancel the postponement of their draft status or force them into conscription – in particular farmers and farmers' sons for the former outcome, and Indigenous workers for the latter.[45] Francis Gregory wrote to MacNamara to make his case. "This class of people, especially farmers, farmers' sons, farm labourers and Indians very often prefer to stay away, rather than to register," wrote Gregory, adding an anecdote to support his point. "One of my [share]growers had an Indian, who had worked for him all year, but when told that he had to register, refused to do so, and went back to the Reservation." Workers' fears may be "ill-founded," conceded Gregory, but "the effect is the same."[46]

Indigenous reluctance to register with the NSS was part of a broader conflict between First Nations and Canada's wartime mobilization program. First Nations across the country, including nearby Six Nations, had been vigorously protesting the government's efforts to conscript Indigenous men into non-combat duty under the National Resources Mobilization Act (NRMA) since the law came into effect in 1940. It would not be surprising if Indigenous people were wary of registering with another federal mobilization initiative, whether for fear of being conscripted under the NRMA or simply out of a desire to preclude even further involvement of government agents in their day-to-day lives.[47] Conflict also brewed between Six Nations and the federal government on the growing income tax burden on working people during the war.[48]

The battle over the order requiring tobacco workers to register with the NSS was perhaps most pitched, however, over the question of just how important tobacco was to the war effort. Tobacco growers were dumbfounded that their product had been given the lowest priority rating and deemed of "no essentiality." Not only did such a designation ignore tobacco's massive economic contributions – generating $125 million in federal tax revenue in 1943, for example. Perhaps more insultingly, it dismissed tobacco's significance to the war effort – namely, to the morale of troops and workers. "The demand for tobacco by men in the armed forces is unlimited," declared four prominent representatives of the tobacco industry in an indignant memorandum sent to MacNamara in October 1943, opposing tobacco's low priority rating. "As a matter of fact, we know almost without exception [that] our boys and girls over there who write home, invariably complain about the shortage of cigarettes and smoking tobacco." In fact, tobacco was immensely popular not only among soldiers, but also among the industrial workers so critical to the war effort. "One has only to stand outside any large war industry and watch the employees leaving work. The first thing they do when they get outside is to light a cigarette or a pipe." In sum, the memo argued, "the tobacco industry makes a real contribution to the war effort as a whole."[49]

Growers were joined in their spirited defence of tobacco's importance by a surprising ally: the office of the administrator of tobacco in the Wartime Prices and Trade Board (WPTB), whose staffers broke ranks with their colleagues in the NSS to argue the growers' case. "I can not but express my surprise over the apparent low labour priority rating given tobacco," wrote technical advisor N.A. MacRae to senior NSS staffer George Haythorne in 1943, expressing particular befuddlement that crops such as spinach and asparagus received "B" ratings, compared to a "D" for tobacco. "The members of our armed forces and the workers in our war industries are not likely to subscribe to this classification." MacRae's boss, Administrator of Tobacco David Sim, wrote Mac-Namara repeatedly to advocate for growers. In April of 1944 he reported to the NSS head that farmers were considering planting smaller crops in order to adjust to the new regulations, and he cautioned MacNamara against provoking such an outcome. "It is very much in the national interest that we should endeavour to secure a large crop this year," wrote Sim.[50] Local press and politicians also took up the cause. Harry J. Collins, reeve of Delhi and frequent contributor to local newspapers, hammered the issue repeatedly in his columns. "The National Selective Service claim[s] that tobacco is non-essential but considering the wounded on the battle fields of the world in their intense suffering, I maintain that tobacco is secondary only to medical service," Collins railed in one article.[51]

By any measure, a majority of growers were unhappy with the enforcement of NSS regulations. The Marketing Association and individual growers repeatedly lobbied the NSS to scrap the implementation of the order, to delay it another year, or at the very least to make some modifications that would render it more palatable.[52] Despite the nearly universal disapproval, once it became clear that, like it or not, the order was going to be enforced, two main camps of growers emerged. In the larger group were those who decided to co-operate with the NSS in the hopes of arriving at a mutually agreeable system within the framework of the order. Some of the most prominent of these growers found their way onto the Tobacco Advisory Committee, named by MacNamara in June 1944, which liaised with the NSS on the implementation of the regulations. The smaller camp of growers comprised the intransigents, led by prominent North Carolinian tobacco farming magnate Francis Gregory, who would quickly emerge as the most vocal opponent of the regulations. The positions of the two groups of growers are nicely summed up in the minutes of a meeting between NSS officials and growers. Marketing Association president Archie Leitch, while still protesting aspects of the order, "agreed that he would try to adhere to it, at which point Mr. Gregory said he would break it readily if 'he wasn't caught at it' because he thought the order to be silly and nonsensical."[53]

The abrasive and hyperbolic Gregory represented a perfect foil for the ever-cool MacNamara. Gregory did not limit his objections to meetings, but rather launched a multi-pronged and spirited campaign against the order, writing frequent letters to MacNamara, David Sim, Norfolk's member of Parliament, and other representatives, in addition to getting his views published in newspapers such as the *Globe and Mail* and *Simcoe Reformer*. He also, on at least one occasion, pressured other growers to write letters of protest to government representatives.[54] Gregory's opposition became increasingly hyperbolic as the harvest of 1944 approached, warning that the tobacco crop might be lost due to the regulations. A July letter to MacNamara (which was also published in the *Reformer*) is representative of the tone of much of Gregory's writing: "I think your information and advice has been ill-advised, and I suggest that you delegate an impartial authority to investigate the matter in the tobacco growing Counties. One who is not a Government employee. Instruct him to interview the real tobacco grower, Bank Managers, merchants and others. If my views are proven to be wrong, so much the better, otherwise we ask that the regulation be repealed."[55] Of course, Gregory was not behind all opposition to the order, and the government also received plenty of complaints from growers and local politicians with no apparent connection to the man known as Mr. Tobacco.[56]

True to his nickname, "Master Conciliator" MacNamara handled this onslaught with tact and strategy. He engaged in frank but polite dialogue with dissenters, even the belligerent Gregory, and was willing to occasionally compromise, such as in 1944, when he allowed the relaxing of regulations for men on postponement. MacNamara was no pushover, however, and remained steadfast in his commitment to bringing the tobacco labour market under NSS regulations.[57] He also rejected the suggestion that the NSS policy underestimated tobacco's importance to the economy and war effort. "I fully appreciate the importance of obtaining sufficient labour for harvesting the tobacco crop," MacNamara wrote in April 1944 to the secretary of the Marketing Association. The intention of the regulations, he explained, was not to "reduce [the] movement of workers required to harvest the tobacco crop, but only to exercise some control of the movement of labour into the tobacco fields."[58] MacNamara's comments were not empty promises, and he and his staff devoted considerable resources to ensuring an ample labour supply for tobacco growers during the harvest, committing their "full recruiting service" to the matter. The mounting pressure from growers seems to have gotten through to MacNamara. "We are in a position where we will have to take this crop off or there will be a terrible row," he wrote to Haythorne in May 1944. In a follow-up letter, MacNamara stressed the importance of the file: "I don't want to fall down on the job. Do not let me forget about it."[59]

MacNamara and his staff did not fall down on the job and, contrary to the apocalyptic scenarios predicted by Gregory and his fellow intransigents (who launched one final letter-writing offensive as the 1944 harvest arrived, including a telegram to Prime Minister Mackenzie King),[60] the execution of the order-in-council proceeded smoothly and successfully. Early reports from the region indicated a remarkable level of success in getting workers to register with the NSS. A 10 August report from the Tobacco Advisory Committee tallied 5,577 permits issued for tobacco workers, and a shortage of just 406 primers. The supervisor of the tobacco belt's NSS offices confirmed this, saying that while 3,000 to 5,000 more men would eventually be needed, they were definitely "over the hump." For women workers, more tiers were required, but other female-gendered jobs were already filled.[61]

A week later, the good news continued to flow in, with the number of issued permits now up to 8,000, and another 1,500 southerners and 400 NRMA soldiers (non-active troops) from the Régiment de Joliette also working in the harvest. (The placement of the soldiers was the result of co-operation between the NSS and the Department of Defence, part of the NSS's efforts to ensure an adequate workforce.) NSS staffer T.W. Wells reported that "there is now very little opposition to NSS permit regulations," and that "many Indians and others, whom it was rumoured would not register with NSS, have registered."[62] By the end of the harvest, 10,962 permits had been issued, and an additional 4,500 male workers who did not require permits (such as American migrants, boys under sixteen, and men over sixty-five) also helped bring in the crop. Spot checks of 2,907 tobacco workers in September found that only 3 per cent were working without permits, and another NSS report estimated the non-compliance rate to be no higher than 5 per cent.[63]

The success in getting workers to register appealed more to civil servants' goals than to growers', but farmers had their own reasons for celebration after the 1944 harvest. For all the panicked frenzy about lost crops and millions of dollars being poured down the drain, the 1944 crop was in fact the most successful the region had ever had. The crop was the biggest acreage ever planted and resulted in the second-greatest tonnage ever produced. The total value of the crop, $25.7 million, outperformed the previous high-water mark of $17.9 million (set in 1942) by 44 per cent.[64] So successful was the harvest and the use of NSS regulations that many growers ended up thanking Mac-Namara and the agency for their efforts. The Marketing Association passed a resolution of thanks in March 1945. E.C. Scythes, president of Vittoria Tobacco Plantations and member of the Tobacco Advisory Committee, commented at a post-harvest meeting that "without [the] National Selective Service, the harvest would have been impossible." David Sim of the WPTB, who had repeatedly questioned the NSS's approach, also wrote MacNamara to offer his compliments on a job well done. To no one's surprise, Francis Gregory was not among the well-wishers, and he continued to oppose NSS regulations into the next year. True to form, however, MacNamara did send a letter or thanks to Gregory in which he expressed appreciation for "the views you were generous enough to write me about." One wonders if MacNamara did not also take some pleasure in telling Gregory that most growers had expressed "satisfaction in the manner in which the tobacco crop was handled."[65]

In 1945, as the war wound down and eventually ended in August, NSS regulations were again applied to tobacco, this time with almost no resistance from growers, who in fact now mostly welcomed the controls. To be sure, some employers hired workers outside of the regulatory framework, but those who did were taken to task by the Marketing Association, which, just one year removed from passing resolutions against the order, had become its loyal defender. The 1945 crop was another success, producing $26.1 million of tobacco, slightly more than in 1944.[66]

World War II and the US-Ontario Movement

The war not only transformed state involvement in the Canadian farm labour market, it also produced significant changes in the operation of the US-Ontario movement, which for the first time came under bilateral state control. Farm labour shortages in both Canada and the United States prompted increased co-operation between the two countries in order to facilitate the movement of workers across the border and ensure maximum agricultural production in support of the war effort.[67] For the United States, this was just one of many international farm worker accords struck with regional allies during the war. The most famous was the Bracero program, a bilateral agreement between Mexico and the United States that between 1942 and 1964 brought more than 4.5 million Mexicans north to work on American farms.[68]

No Bracero-level program developed between Canada and the United States, but the war sparked a formalization of pre-existing movements of farm workers across the forty-ninth parallel. In February 1942, as an outgrowth from the Hyde Park talks, the two nations' Joint Economic Committee agreed to a resolution "for facilitating the movement of agricultural machinery and farm labour across the international boundary." Unlike American arrangements with the Caribbean and Mexico, the Canada-US agreement covered the movement of workers across the border in both directions. Primarily directed toward the two countries' western grain harvests, the agreement also applied to other pre-existing movements of workers such as the seasonal migration of Québécois and New Brunswickers to Maine's potato fields and, of course, the southern tobacco workers, enabling farm workers and machinery in all these exchanges to move across the border "with a minimum of restrictions."[69]

Discussions between Canadian and American officials about farm worker mobility also opened the door for an explicit conversation about the composition of these movements, their racial makeup in particular. The US-Ontario tobacco worker movement had excluded Black workers by informal means since its beginnings in the 1920s, but the wartime resolution prompted a broader discussion about who exactly would be able to participate in all such exchanges. One bureaucrat in particular, Immigration Branch director A.L. Jolliffe, was adamant that African Americans should not be admitted to Canada as temporary labourers.[70] As representatives from the two countries worked out details of the agreement in June and July of 1942, Jolliffe proposed the exclusion of Blacks via "unofficial discussion" (in order to avoid a public-relations fallout) and used a US request for the barring of persons born in enemy countries (even if now British subjects) as a negotiating chip to secure his exclusionary ends. Given that the United States was granted this request and that no further known mention was made about African Americans' participation, it seems likely that Jolliffe got his way.[71]

Regardless of whether this was the case for all cross-border exchanges, it is clear that as the tobacco worker movement formalized, its whites-only status was simply absorbed into its new bilateral structure. Always wary of a scandal, officials on either side of the border seldom put this feature of the program into writing, but they did occasionally slip up. Fred Sloan, of North Carolina's Extension Farm Labor Program, noted in 1946, for example, that "we issued 1,993 passports to *white* workers for entry into Canada to assist with their tobacco harvest." And a similar report from Virginia the following year commented that "the tobacco workers sent to Canada were all white men." Correspondence among Canadian immigration officials in 1960 was particularly revealing of both the program's racist structure and government attempts to keep it quiet. "There were no coloured workers included in those selected by the state officials for work in the tobacco fields of Ontario, but [a Department of Labour official] was not prepared to put this statement in writing for various obvious reasons."[72]

Though the Canada-US resolution was signed in 1942, it was not until 1944 that US authorities began attempting to exert more control over the northward migration of tobacco workers. In 1944, an ever-tightening labour market in the United States prompted officials to institute clearer regulations for the to-bacco program, in the interest of ensuring that workers who were needed at home did not leave for the Ontario harvest. The new rules allowed growers to continue making private arrangements with workers but stamped out the un-regulated private recruitment that had previously predominated.[73]

While the new procedures looked good on paper, in practice, establishing state control over the sending side of the tobacco movement offered challenges reminiscent of those experienced by Canadian officials in Ontario's tobacco belt. In addition to various mundane yet troublesome bureaucratic hurdles, the regulations were subverted by growers and recruiters operating outside of the approved channels. One of the prime offenders was none other than Francis Gregory, who was chided by NSS director Arthur MacNamara in 1945 for breaking the new program rules by hiring a private recruiter in North Carolina, though Gregory insisted that it was all a simple misunderstanding. In the same year, a Tillsonburg insurance agent was also discovered to be op-erating a clandestine recruitment scheme, providing curers to tobacco farmers who insured their crops with him.[74] Confusion was also caused when some workers making private arrangements with employers received multiple per-mits in the mail, allowing them to become small-scale recruiters themselves and dole out the extra permits, a situation one North Carolina official de-scribed as "rather embarrassing to us."[75] While American civil servants had ample experience in managing domestic farm labour and the importation of foreign guest workers (including to the tobacco fields), exerting state control over a guest-worker program that sent workers *out* of the country clearly posed some new challenges.

Neither US federal and state civil servants nor their Canadian counterparts were pleased with how the movements of 1944 and 1945 unfolded, and they made changes in advance of the 1946 season that required all workers going to Canada to attend a recruitment meeting in order to receive their entry per-mit directly from a Canadian representative.[76] The intended outcome of this fix was made null and void when the sanctioned recruiters gave out far more permits than there were jobs for southerners – five hundred too many by one count. This created a difficult situation for job seekers and a diplomatic and public relations headache for bureaucrats. Two American workers, Garland Speed and Carl F. Burm of Durham, North Carolina, described the chaotic situation in an angry letter to the Canadian Embassy in Washington, which was forwarded on to the Department of Labour in Ottawa. The men had received their entry permits via the proper channels and had been led to believe that if no work was available in Ontario, their transportation costs (fifty dollars) would be reimbursed. When they arrived in the tobacco belt and found this not to be the case, they were understandably incensed: "No such thing Sir, leaving me and several hundred men to hold the bag. To get back the best way we could." After arriving in Tillsonburg at four in the morning, "we found absolutely no beds, very little hospitality of any description – I would call it a (Kill Joy)." To add insult to injury, when the men eventually tried to get some rest outdoors, they experienced the same cold treatment that tobacco belt transients had been subject to since at least the Great Depression: "Here came the law to make you stand on your feet keep moving after traveling nearly 1200 miles. Every time we set down to rest after traveling so long – (Keep Moving) Don't set down – (The Law would move you on) I call it unfare, after we were willing to sacrifice to help your farmers out. To make a long story short the farmers Tob would rot in the field when, where theres no help given us." The story also received coverage in the press.[77]

While Canadian officials absolved themselves of responsibility for the matter – insisting that they had warned job seekers of potential shortages of employment and that they had made no guarantees of work – their American counterparts were not impressed. Looking back on the Canadian movement of the previous few years, North Carolina's Extension Service noted in its 1947 report that, after the bungling of 1946, "we in North Carolina took the position that we could not participate in such an undertaking again unless proper steps were taken to guard against a similar situation in the future." At bilateral meetings in early 1947, other state officials echoed the concerns of the Carolinians.[78] The result of this pressure was a renegotiation of the terms of the agreement.

As the largest sending state and prime agitator for improving the program, North Carolina took the lead on this endeavour. The supervisor of the state's Extension Service, Fred Sloan, travelled to Simcoe in July 1947 to meet with representatives from the Department of Labour, the provincial Ministry of

Agriculture, and the Marketing Association. While some growers wanted to revert to the old system of sending permits directly to workers (something they would repeatedly lobby for in years to come), this was out of the question as far as US and federal Canadian officials were concerned. The trend was toward more state involvement, not less. The resulting 1947 agreement doubled down on the 1946 procedures, but also included provisions to prevent against the kind of situation that had taken place the previous year. This time, the guarantees that the jilted workers Speed and Burm had understood to be part of the arrangement were in fact formally agreed to. If prospective workers arrived in Ontario only to find that no job was available, their costs of transportation would be reimbursed. And migrants who did obtain work were guaranteed a minimum of sixty dollars per week plus room and board, and would also have their transportation covered by employers. The arrangements also formalized employers' ability to request particular workers by name, something that would remain an important feature of agricultural guest-worker programs in Canada moving forward. While the agreement was negotiated with North Carolina, the same terms were readily adopted by the other sending states as well.[79]

By now, the US-Ontario tobacco workers' movement was taking on many of the familiar characteristics of twentieth-century guest-worker programs: bilateral government negotiation of terms; structured, state-managed recruitment and job placement; minimum guarantees of wages and conditions; and mechanisms to ensure repatriation upon completion of work periods. To be sure, all these features were gradually and unevenly adopted, but by the late 1940s, the previously unregulated migration system was rapidly fading from view as a formal guest-worker program replaced it. The new version of the program was met with approval from all parties: "The whole procedure of 1947 was a decided improvement over that of the previous years," North Carolina's Extension Service reported.[80] This general set-up was continued through to the 1960s, and while periodic problems cropped up, authorities on both sides of the border were generally content with the overall structure.[81]

◆◆◆

The wartime controls on the tobacco labour market were in many ways exceptional; never again would it be so closely managed by state agencies. But the genie of state control was never put entirely back in the bottle. While 1944

3.5 Tobacco workers from North Carolina, Delhi, Ontario, 1958. London Free Press Collection of Photographic Negatives, 15 August 1958, Western University Archives and Special Collections, London, Ontario.

and 1945 represented extremes in the degree of state participation, government agencies would remain involved in the farm labour market (including in tobacco) in subsequent decades to a far greater extent than they had been beforehand. The character of state involvement did, of course, change in the years following the war – from enforced management during the conflict to a postwar role that was largely advisory and facilitative, consisting of voluntary labour placement services, education, and incentivization programs aimed at improving working and living conditions on farms. Like government involvement in the domestic labour market, the conversion of the US-Ontario movement into a bilaterally managed guest-worker program, precipitated by the wartime emergency and solidified in its immediate aftermath, proved to be a lasting change.

The development of government intervention in Ontario's tobacco farm labour market undermines many assumptions about the Canadian state and farm labour, in particular the idea that the state's primary purpose in this domain has been to provide a workforce to farm owners. Instead, in Ontario's tobacco belt, the state first became involved in the labour market not to alleviate a shortage of farm workers, but to limit the entrance of foreign migrants seeking to take up harvest jobs during the Great Depression. The expansion of state intervention during World War II was also about control rather than labour provision – in this case the primary goal was limiting the movement of workers out of essential industry and other agricultural sectors into lucrative tobacco jobs.

State efforts to exert control over tobacco labour were anything but straight-forward and were obstructed in various ways by workers, growers, and others. Indeed, farm labour systems – even supposedly "state-managed" guest-worker programs – are never so neatly and completely in the hands of state agents as the bureaucracies (and much academic literature) would lead us to believe, a fact that would continue to prove true in the decades following World War II.

4

HIPPIES, FRENCHIES, AND GIRLS

It was the early 1970s, and eighteen-year-old Patricia was ready for a change. Fresh off a stint overseas with Canada World Youth, Patricia found herself back on the farm near Trois-Rivières, Quebec, where her mother had moved a few years earlier from Quebec City to do "the back-to-the-land thing." An exit opportunity presented itself when three male acquaintances – "hippie types" – announced they were headed to Ontario to work the tobacco harvest. "I jumped in the car and went along," she recalled. "I had no idea." The four of them made their way to Delhi, where they presented themselves at the Canada Farm Labour Pool (CFLP). After Patricia and her companions had done a bit of pre-harvest suckering work, the CFLP office found them jobs on two farms, so they split into pairs and went their separate ways.

Patricia enjoyed the physical challenge of tobacco work. Even "being covered in ... the black tar that you had to get off your arms at the end of the day" had its charm. "It was not a resort-type setting," of course, but she loved "roughing it ... having a pump to clean up, and bunk beds, ... and shacks. It was for me a very romantic thing to do, but to realize at the same time that there [were] real people [and] that this was their lives, this was what they did ... It definitely shaped how I look at the world from there on." After the completion of her first season in tobacco, Patricia and her companions moved on to the apple harvest. In other years, they also worked in tomatoes, cucumbers, and grapes.

Though overall Patricia "loved the experience" of farm work, there were aspects of working in tobacco that were decidedly less appealing. Both sets of tobacco farmers she worked for were young couples who had "a lot riding" on their harvests and were "incredibly stressed out," she remembered. "You could really feel the tension ... It always seemed like there was lots of yelling going on in the tobacco fields ... So they weren't particularly fun to work for."

As a young, educated woman from a radically different cultural background than many farmers and residents of the tobacco belt, Patricia was often made to feel uncomfortable. "I was quite disturbing to them," she recalled of the first farmers for whom she worked. "I think they were quite traditional ... I was a hippie kid travelling with a guy, [and] we weren't boyfriend-girlfriend. That just, kind of, really muddled them." Things weren't much better in local communities, where Patricia and her fellow-travellers constantly felt the disapproving gaze of residents. "They didn't like hippie kids ... My friends all had long hair at that point. They didn't like us."

Patricia also clashed with her employers over a variety of gendered expectations concerning work and living arrangements. "She [the woman employer] expected me to do the cleaning up after meals ... I was put in a quite traditional woman role." Patricia was also required to live in the growers' house rather than in the bunkhouse with her male travelling companion. "I never got out of the house, but I wasn't very happy about being under there," she explained. She was successful, however, in getting off the tying table and into the fields, where she worked as a primer, despite prevailing gender norms that made that an unusual occurrence in the early 1970s. "I didn't want to be on the tying machine. The pay wasn't as good, and I just didn't want to be working with the women that seemed very disapproving that I was there at all." Priming suited her much better. "I would've been one of the earlier [female primers]. And I was very skinny at the time so I guess they didn't think I could do it ... But you know, you don't have to be that strong. You just need to have a lot of stamina."

Patricia's first season working in tobacco came to a bitter end. With the harvest nearly complete, her employer attempted to increase the crew's daily workload by 50 per cent, with no raise in pay. "We squawked, [and] we got fired," Patricia recalled. Patricia suspected that the farmers got exactly the result they desired, since letting go of their workers before the end of the harvest meant that they would not have to pay the ten dollars per day bonus paid to workers upon completion of the season. Her suspicions were probably correct: such wage-stealing chicanery was a common trick among growers in this period.[1]

Patricia's participation in the tobacco harvest was reflective of three major demographic changes that occurred in the sector's workforce in the postwar era, especially in the 1960s and '70s: it got younger, saw a gradual but significant realignment of women's roles, and witnessed a major shakeup in its ethnic and

4.1 Young job seekers, Delhi, Ontario, 1974. London Free Press Collection of Photographic Negatives, 13 August 1974, Western University Archives and Special Collections, London, Ontario.

place-of-origin composition, with Quebec emerging as the major sending region of migrant workers. These transformations were deeply intertwined with other phenomena, both local and broader, including technological advances, socio-economic developments, and evolving cultural and gender norms.

As Patricia's recollections reveal, the new constituents of the tobacco workforce were not always welcomed with open arms. Local leaders and residents often viewed "hippie" job seekers with suspicion – doubly so when they spoke in French – and many of the long-standing tropes about transients were repurposed and applied to these new groups of "problem" migrants. Not ones to disappoint, the young people working in tobacco in the 1960s and '70s frequently did take up the role of troublemakers, continuing the sector's long tradition of working-class resistance and organization, though in this realm, too, important transformations were afoot. All the while, officials at all levels of governments continued their efforts to bring the yearly harvest migrations under control, a project whose successes were limited but whose frustrations were seemingly infinite.

Technological, Demographic, and Economic Changes

In the 1950s and '60s, a number of important technological advances were made in the farm-level production of tobacco. The improvements began in the kiln and emanated outward, in the process transforming the labour of curing, tying, and priming. First, the transition to oil-heated kilns and the development of more sophisticated thermostatic controls made the formerly quasi-mystical art of curing suddenly much more accessible to the average Canadian tobacco farmer, and in the 1950s and early 1960s many growers began curing their own crops instead of bringing curers up from the United States.[2] Next, at the tying table, the development of a tying machine – in essence a large sewing machine that attached tobacco leaves to sticks – served to gradually replace the old hand-tying method, starting in the early 1960s. This reduced the number of people required at the tying table from six to three.[3] Finally, "mechanical priming aids," increasingly used over the course of the 1960s, represented a major technological innovation in the fields. These motorized devices allowed primers to be carried through fields on adjustable seats, priming leaves and placing them into baskets in front of them, making the job of priming significantly less strenuous. Most priming machines pulled five primers through the fields with one operator, though a range of variations existed.[4]

The adoption of these new technologies did not happen all at once – for example, difficulties with tying machines were reported to have slowed their uptake in the early 1960s[5] – but by the end of that decade, the trend was clear. In 1967, 59 per cent of growers were using tying machines and 32 per cent priming aids.[6] Two years later, in 1969, those figures had jumped to 93 and 68 per cent, respectively.[7] Technological developments were heartily encouraged by the federal Department of Agriculture's experimental farm in Delhi as well as the Marketing Board.[8] Mechanization was also good business for manufacturers and sellers of agricultural equipment, who tirelessly promoted the latest and greatest in labour-saving technologies.[9]

Technological changes played an important role in two major transformations in the workforce of the 1960s and '70s, helping it to become younger and

4.2 Cindy Matthews of Port Burwell priming tobacco, Elgin County, 1973. Courtesy of Elgin County Archives. "Tobacco Farming in Elgin County – Harvest Begins," 25 July 1973, St Thomas Times-Journal fonds, C8 Sh2 B2 F5 29, Elgin County Archives.

redefining the role of women within the harvest. A federal labour official explained the first change in 1969 noting that, while most farms were now using priming aids, "these machines do not replace workers, but rather take the great exertion once required, out of the priming job. This is a reason why both the older and younger worker, whether experienced or not, are able to perform

satisfactorily in jobs they were once incapable of handling. The average age of
the transient worker group is under 20 years."[10] Though his estimate was likely
hyperbolic, the bureaucrat was not alone in noting the youth movement taking
place in the harvest workforce and its connections with technological developments. In 1967, for example, the *Globe and Mail* noted that the "face of the
harvest" was changing, with fewer "winos" and more younger workers in the
district. "The automated priming machine, which eliminates the backbreaking
labor of picking tobacco by hand, has attracted thousands of local university
and high school students to the tobacco fields," the article continued.[11] The in-
tersection of technological change and downward trends in age was also clear
in the US movement, where the advances in curing technology cut out many
curers, paving the way for greater participation from primers who were significantly younger on average. In 1959, 78 per cent of US migrants were curers,
but the next year this dropped to 45 per cent, and it did not climb back above
that level again before the entire movement petered out over the next decade
or so (see figure 3.3 in the previous chapter).

The changes in tobacco production also redefined the role of women and
girls within the harvest workforce. At first, mechanization was bad news for
female workers. Whereas priming aids simply made jobs easier without eliminating them, the same was not true for tying machines, which cut female-
gendered jobs at the tying table by half. The changes appeared to hit migrant
women the hardest, as the surviving jobs were reserved for local women and
girls, many of whom were part of growers' season-long workforce, hired at
planting, harvest, and for post-harvest market preparation. As the manager of
Simcoe's Canada Manpower Centre reported in describing the transient workforce in 1967, "there was very little demand for females as tobacco tiers and leaf
handers this year as the farm family and friends do this work in the majority
of cases as they find the tying machine quite easy to operate."[12] While statistical
evidence on the changing composition of the overall workforce is not available,
figures from the seasonal US movement reveal a stark decline in the number
of tiers travelling within that program. In 1958 and 1959, tiers represented 7
and 14 per cent, respectively, of the total US workers. As the tying machine
caught on in the early 1960s, those numbers dropped rapidly, and by the last
five years of the decade an average of just 1.7 per cent of workers in the US program were tiers (see figure 4.3).

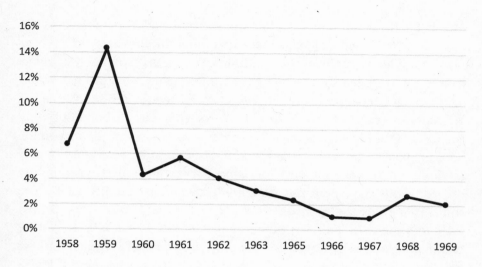

4.3 Per cent tiers in US-Ontario tobacco worker movement, select years, 1958–69.
Sources: Satzewich, *Racism and the Incorporation of Foreign Labour*, 108; Immigration
Branch (RG 76, vols 853, 1112, LAC); Department of Manpower and Immigration (RG 118,
acc. 1985–86/071, vol. 84, LAC); Ministry of Agriculture and Food (RG 16-102, AO).

The new technology not only served to eliminate women's positions; it also
significantly de-skilled the formerly difficult jobs at the tying table, allowing
growers to pay even less per worker to the half-size crew that remained at the
station. As a Manpower staffer glibly explained in 1969, "One of the effects of
this mechanization has been that the occupation of tobacco tier has practically
been eliminated. This is quite a benefit to the farmer, as this occupation normally was paid at least $2 a day above that of the primers, and in many instances
when these workers were in short supply wages went much higher than that.
In effect, these workers could control the whole flow and production of the
crop."[13] The official's comment about tiers previously being paid more than
primers might have been exaggerated, but he was correct in noting the trend.
Assembled wage data reveal that, while before the 1960s tiers could sometimes
earn the same as primers, after the adoption of the tying machine the wages
of field and table workers diverged, with the latter earning about 10 per cent
less than their mostly male co-workers.[14] Of course, this was hardly the first

time in the history of capitalism that women's jobs and income were cut out by a male-dominated, state-encouraged process of mechanization.[15]

But the effect of mechanization on women's roles was not purely negative: conversely, it opened up new opportunities for women and girls to work as primers. The development of ride-on priming devices allowed prevailing gender norms to bend slightly. Just as the less strenuous method of priming encouraged the hiring of younger and older workers, so, too, did it open the door to female primers, an idea that would have been inconceivable to most in the era of on-foot harvesting.[16] Newspaper headlines reflected the novelty of the situation and the paternalistic attitudes that framed the discussion. "Five Ladies Prime Tobacco," gushed the *Delhi News-Record*; "Debbie Takes Tobacco Road to Beauty Field," declared the *Toronto Star*; "Five Female Primers Have Just the Right Touch," the *Reformer* chimed in.[17] Growers profiled in these articles were typically thrilled with their female crews, who they said were easier to work with and more respectful – both of their employers and the all-important tobacco leaves. As one grower remarked, "Normally the girls have quicker hands than the guys, but their biggest asset is that they are more reliable. They don't go out and get drunk at night and they don't seem to come up with as many excuses to sleep late in the morning."[18]

But though priming jobs were no longer 100 per cent male, they still remained overwhelmingly so. In 1969, the only year in which a detailed census of the workforce was conducted, a mere 147 out of the 22,071 primers – or less than 1 per cent – registered in the harvest were female.[19] That percentage almost certainly climbed in the coming years; a 1977 *Toronto Star* article estimated that 20 per cent of primers were female, though it was not clear where that figure came from.[20] Still, there is little doubt that the small number of priming jobs that opened up for women did not come close to making up for the slashing of half the jobs at the tying table. The opening of priming opportunities to women appears to have been limited mostly to local tobacco workers, a further blow to migrant women, who were disproportionately hit by the curtailing of tying jobs. Tobacco's migrant workforce remained exceedingly male, at least until 1969, the last year for which detailed information is available. In that year, while 27 per cent of the total labour force were women or girls, a mere 3.5 per cent of non-local workers were female, and just 20 of the 147 female primers were non-locals.[21]

The slow pace of change in women's participation as primers – and the limited opportunities for migrant women – can in large part be explained by persistent gender norms having to do with women's alleged incapacity for strenuous physical labour and concerns about housing both male and female migrants on the same farms, ideas that Patricia would find herself having to face in her time as a tobacco worker.[22] Another instructive example of both roadblocks took place in 1974–75, when Manpower and Immigration officials – in honour of the United Nations–declared International Women's Year of 1975 – asked the Marketing Board to reserve 25 per cent of the spots in the European student program for women. Marketing Board officials responded with incredulity and mockery. "What year isn't women's year?" chortled tobacco grower and Marketing Board director Earl Johnson.[23] Board chairman Ted Raytrowsky, meanwhile, voiced growers' objections in a letter to Manpower: "We are not male chauvenists [sic] but certainly do not feel that the priming in the tobacco harvest is suitable for women." The small number of farms that employed women primers in 1974, he explained, by and large used a particular type of priming machine, one that demanded less heavy lifting from its labourers. Furthermore, wrote Raytrowsky, "Our farmers do not have suitable housing to accommodate female help, [and] the expense of building another bunkhouse is just too expensive for such a short period of time."[24] Raytrowsky elaborated on both concerns in comments made to the *Reformer* two months later: "How are we going to accommodate them on the farm? We're not going to have women and men on a priming machine and have them working well together."[25] This reluctance to have women and men work closely together – let alone live together – was also revealed in the tendency of priming crews to be either all-female or all-male. Indeed, one solution proposed to the Marketing Board's "problem" of fulfilling the quota for women within the student program was that growers interested in having all-women harvest crews might consider asking for female European students to fill those roles.[26]

Of course, these two demographic shifts in the tobacco workforce weren't solely the result of mechanization. Canada's workforce as a whole got younger during the 1960s.[27] And perhaps more importantly, in the years following World War II, the era of seasonal migrant labour for adult men (within Canada) largely drew to a close. In addition to higher incomes across the board, various sectors evolved to offer workers employment on a year-round rather than seasonal basis. In some industries dependent on seasonal labour, such as logging, this led to serious labour shortages.[28] While no such shortages occurred in tobacco, the shift away from "single unemployed men" and family groups toward students and other young people seeking summer employment was clear.[29] Women's shrinking participation in the tobacco harvest was out of step with the broader trends of growing female participation in the Canadian labour force, but the opening of priming jobs did mirror the limited re-gendering of jobs in other sectors in the postwar period. And the efforts of women such as Patricia to demand inclusion in male-dominated jobs and to resist gender segregation happened within a broader context of feminist politics and activism in the 1970s.[30]

The demographic shifts also partly reflected economic developments taking hold in the tobacco sector. After over three decades of seldom-interrupted boom in the sector, tobacco farmers, particularly those with smaller land holdings, began to face a series of mounting economic challenges in the 1960s. In the early years of the decade, the costs of inputs were on the rise, while tobacco prices declined – a situation made worse by small production quotas that made it difficult for small farmers to make mortgage payments and remain profitable. This sparked a reversal in the social mobility trends witnessed between the 1920s and the 1950s. Whereas many new farmers had purchased land between 1957 and 1962, the above-mentioned challenges sparked a wave of sell-offs in 1965 – at a per-acre price much lower than it had been a few years prior. The trend in these real estate transactions was clear: small farmers were increasingly being priced out of the business as larger outfits snatched up their land and tobacco rights.[31] (The technological developments discussed above played a role in this story too, since it was larger, more heavily capitalized farms who could afford new machinery and thus transition to more efficient production – a connection discussed at greater length in chapter 7.) Unsurprisingly, the most vulnerable of farmers – sharegrowers – found themselves under the most pressure. A concerned letter writer aptly described these challenges in a letter to the *Tillsonburg News* in 1964:

> I think it is terrible the way tobacco sharegrowers are used [now]. There is absolutely no way of them making a decent living now. Wages keep going up steadily and so is everything else, but the tobacco is going down. They are selling the tobacco for less now than they did a couple of years

ago. Is there no way to give them a break? ... One more year like this and
the smaller tobacco farmers will be all finished. This only leads to a very
bad thing ... The big guy has everything while the rest of the people live
in poverty. Is this what we want in Canada? Surely not.[32]

The increasing difficulty of advancing from wage labourer to sharegrower
to farm owner within the tobacco sector also played a role in shifting the demographics of the harvest labour force. While wages were still high enough to attract young job seekers, the sector no longer held the same allure for newly
arrived immigrants, though of course this was a gradual transition.

Another reflection of the decline of opportunities for social mobility was
the emergence of a conspicuous community of working poor in Norfolk,
whose members were the recipients of a rush of media attention in 1965 after
a federal Agricultural Rehabilitation and Development Association report cited
Norfolk as one of the ten most "poverty-ridden" counties in Ontario, in spite
of the immense wealth brought in by the region's tobacco industry.[33] Social re-
alist investigations into the lives of residents of "the Colony" revealed that many
earned their meagre livings through a combination of seasonal tobacco work,
social assistance payments, and various forms of informal employment, from
collecting and selling scrap metal to sex work.[34]

Harvest Youth: Adventure, Romance, and Fun

For the legions of young people trooping into the tobacco belt each summer
during the 1960s and '70s, the declining opportunities for social mobility mattered little. While tobacco's high wages were obviously a major attraction,
young people's motivations in pursuing tobacco work cannot simply be reduced to economics. As Patricia's story suggests, a summer working in the tobacco harvest also provided an opportunity for adventure. Marc Chaussé of
Rouyn-Noranda, Quebec, first travelled to the tobacco belt for harvest work
in the early 1970s at the age of sixteen, after hearing about it from "some older
guy who used to go every summer." Chaussé was intrigued by the high wages.
"So I gave it a shot. I decided to take a chance. I hitchhiked down there with
one of my friends ... We didn't know what we were [getting into]." The wages
weren't the only thing that appealed to Chaussé; so, too, did the excitement.
"At the age of sixteen, when you're hitchhiking to a town that you've never

been [to]," it was exciting. "You could be away from home for a month or two. For me, it was an experience, and I enjoyed that a lot. Not that I had some problem at home. But me, I like the adventure."[35]

Part of the adventure of working in tobacco was the excitement of meeting new people, especially young people, from all over the world and from a wide array of backgrounds. Many former workers I interviewed spoke about the friendships they formed on the farm. Kimberlie Ladell, who grew up in the tobacco belt and worked on her uncle's farm in the 1970s and '80s, commented on the bonds that developed among harvest crews based on shared experiences: "People who've never worked in tobacco really don't get the sense of camaraderie that you have with other people who are working in tobacco." Ladell recalled "meeting at the beach after [work], covered in tar; you look like crap, [but] you don't care, you go in the water. Because it is such physically demanding work, and it can be long hours, and some of the characters are definitely sketchy [*laughs*] ... [people whom] you wouldn't normally be exposed to. It's just this little unit."[36] Craig Berggold, who worked in tobacco as a teenager in the late 1970s, provided a particularly beautiful assessment of life in a harvest gang:

You're working with a group of people, and they all come from different backgrounds ... Having a First Nations guy from the Mohawk [community], having an itinerant hobo, having a northern Ontario miner's kid, having artists' child like myself all mix together and form camaraderie, you realize that you share so much more in common than your differences ... When you've been working all day, and the end of the week comes, and you're [a] gang of five or six people, and you all jump in that car together, and you're driving down the country road, speeding as fast as you can because you want to get as far away as possible, and all of your lives are bound together, and you can die together in that moment in that car, the differences between myself and my co-workers are less important. The camaraderie, the feeling of togetherness – what used to be called brotherhood or sisterhood. That's what the tobacco experience taught me ... In that time that we're working together on the priming machine, during that time that we're cleaning the kiln out and each of our lives is dependent on each other, for fear of falling and breaking our neck, or that moment when we step away from the job and enjoy our camaraderie to escape that common condition – during that time, we experienced something together. And that's what I learned from picking tobacco, how important that feeling is.

Just as the tobacco harvest fostered new friendships, so, too, did it provide opportunities for the formation of sexual or romantic relationships. "The summer I was eighteen I fell in love with the kiln hanger," recalled Joanne Passmore, who worked in tobacco in the 1960s. "We dated that summer and throughout my first year of university. He introduced me to chugging straight whiskey with a chaser of Coke, my first cigarette, and the only time I was ever drunk in my life."[37] Passmore was far from unusual in this experience; one other interviewee also recounted falling in love during the tobacco harvest, though they preferred not to put it on record. Other such harvest romances undoubtedly bloomed throughout the region each summer. The pursuit of relationships – or even simple flirting – could sometimes spark tension between migrant workers and locals as boys and young men competed for the attention of girls and young women. Marc Chaussé recalled a dance at the Belgian Hall at which there were "some nice girls" accompanied by some guys who were "probably their boyfriends." Chaussé and his friends were "inviting the girls for dancing … [and] they were not saying 'no,' and that was causing some … testosterone stuff," he recounted with a laugh.[38]

As Chaussé's story suggests, young people working in tobacco also found plenty of ways to have fun during the harvest, not only in town but also on the job. A couple interviewees recalled pranks being played between tying and priming crews – fun that took on some gendered dimensions given the frequent female-male divide between the two different jobs. The most common prank was to sneak a surprise passenger into the tobacco baskets that travelled back and forth between the crews – a mouse, snake, or toad, for example. For many interviewees, a highlight of every harvest was the end-of-harvest party, where growers often put on a lavish celebration for their workers, with food, drink, and fun aplenty.[39]

The fun, romance, and adventure of tobacco work notwithstanding, the money still mattered, of course. Young tobacco workers were often shocked at how much money they received on their first payday. "The first time I got paid, gosh I was really surprised," recalled Norma Kennedy of Oneida Nation. "I had a lot of money." A major benefit of those high wages for young people was the ability it afforded them to purchase consumer goods, whether for immediate consumption – drinks, food, or entertainment – or more substantial items like the always popular post-harvest purchase of a new car. Kennedy recalled buying a radio with her first paycheque that enabled her and her father to listen together to the broadcasts of their favourite team, the Cleveland Indians.[40]

Such purchases were also wrapped up with the youthful quests for fun, experience, and independence. When Willie Moran of Quebec was asked in 1954 about saving the money he earned in the harvest, he told the *Reformer*, "We can, but we don't. Not us guys anyway. We're young. We've got to have fun, and some beer. But it's a good time."[41] For his part, Marc Chaussé recalled, "Doing the tobacco harvest was ... big money in a very short period of time. And when I [would] go back to my hometown, as a student, I had that money from the harvest ... [to buy] things that usually you cannot afford as a student." Using his harvest savings, Chaussé was able to buy his first car, a 1965 Ford. "I enjoyed [the] independence" of being able to afford more things, he said.[42] Of course, young people also put their harvest earnings toward less fun – if certainly sensible – ends, such as post-secondary tuition, school books, and other school supplies.[43] Such investments in education could be said to be a way in which tobacco harvest wages continued to foster upward social mobility *outside* of the sector – although in a decidedly more muted fashion than the crop's earlier bounty.

New Migrants, New (and Not-So-New) Anxieties

A final important set of changes in the tobacco workforce's postwar demographics had little to do with technological or economic developments within the sector: shifts in the make-up of the labour force by ethnicity and place of origin, and changes in workers' patterns of arrival. After the war, European immigrants continued to find their way to the tobacco belt in pursuit of high wages and the opportunity for farm ownership. Whereas most European participants in the green gold rush of the 1920s and '30s had relocated to Norfolk from elsewhere in Canada, those arriving after 1945 increasingly immigrated directly to the tobacco belt, often joining pre-existing communities of co-nationals or those from the same ethnic backgrounds. Hungarians, ethnic Germans, Lithuanians, Poles, Ukrainians, Czechs, Slovaks, and Dutch, many displaced by the war and its aftermath, arrived in large numbers in the 1940s and '50s, with the population of each group in the tobacco belt's three principal counties doubling between 1941 and 1961 (with the possible exception of Lithuanians, who were not separately recorded in the census). European immigrants were thus decreasingly in the position of seasonal migrant labour, and instead became, by and large, part of the local workforce, from which they hoped to advance to sharegrowing and farm proprietorship.[44]

Indeed, tobacco's postwar *migrant* labour force became ever more detached from networks of kinship and ethnicity, and the ranks of non-local workers travelling from elsewhere in Canada came to be dominated by migrants without ethnic ties to local communities. The chief source was Quebec. Migrants had long travelled from Quebec to work in the tobacco harvest, but many earlier sojourners – from Montreal especially – had been members of ethnic groups with large participation in the sector – Hungarians or Lithuanians, for example.[45] After the war, their numbers came to be dominated instead by francophone Québécois.[46] Reports of Québécois migrants working in the tobacco harvest date back to the late 1930s, but this seems to have attracted greater attention – and statistical prominence – beginning in 1944. First came the attention, following a newspaper report that nine men and one woman, all from Montreal and most with French names, had attacked a police constable in Delhi.[47] This news was quickly followed by reports that six hundred soldiers from Quebec's Régiment de Joliette on non-combat duty (under the National Resources Mobilization Act, or NRMA) were to be placed in Simcoe to assist with the harvest of various crops. Tobacco farmers received about a hundred of these workers. Local observers greeted these twin developments with suspicion, beginning what would become a long regional tradition of discrimination against and dislike of migrants from Quebec. A column in the *Reformer* captured the sentiment of the moment, which was also linked with disdain for NRMA soldiers, or "Zombies," as they were often disparagingly referred to:

It is hoped that the 600 French-Canadian soldiers coming into the tobacco area this week will conduct themselves more becomingly than some of their compatriots have done. The question is asked why English-speaking soldiers from military camps in this district ... many of whom are experienced tobacco workers, are not released for work instead of importing the French-Canadians. The answer seems to be that the English-speaking boys are being trained for overseas service as soon as possible and cannot be spared from their training. Presumably the French-Canadians are Zombies who are not going anywhere in particular.[48]

After the war, by all appearances, the number of workers coming from Quebec increased, though exact statistical comparisons of multiple years are not possible. One imperfect indication: in 1944, out of 4,683 civilian male tobacco workers placed by the NSS with a listed "office of origin," 416 (just under 9 per cent) were from Quebec. By 1969, Québécois workers represented 20 per cent (7,686) of the total workforce of 38,181, and over half (53 per cent) of the migrant workforce.[49] Observations by government officials and reporters suggest that this trend had already taken hold by the 1950s. Delhi, Tillsonburg, and Simcoe are "crowded with workers from all parts of Canada, especially Quebec," noted federal labour bureaucrat W. Davison in August 1954.[50] It is not clear if there was a link between the Joliette regiment's stationing in Norfolk and the later migrations of Québécois. Joliette was the hometown of at least some tobacco migrants, but it also happened to be the centre of Quebec's own small tobacco district (and in fact received some transmigrant tobacco growers from Ontario who moved east to purchase farms at cheaper prices).[51]

Behind Quebec, two other Canadian regions emerged as important senders of tobacco migrants: northern Ontario and the Maritimes, each of which accounted for about 7 per cent of non-locals in the harvest.[52] The three major sending regions of Canadian migrant workers had something in common: all were characterized by high unemployment[53] and were the targets of a variety of government development initiatives in this period, including in the realm of "manpower mobility," as will be discussed later in this chapter.[54] Within Quebec, large numbers of workers travelled from Montreal but also from the agroforestry and aluminum-producing region of Saguenay–Lac-Saint-Jean, which was plagued in this era by particularly high levels of unemployment.[55]

A final, much smaller, and fleeting group of workers who joined the tobacco workforce in this period were Indigenous workers from the James Bay region of northern Ontario and Quebec. In 1965 and 1966, a hundred or so seasonal workers from such places as Moose Factory, Fort Albany, Attawapiskat, Ghost River (all in Ontario), and Fort George, Quebec, joined the tobacco workforce each year as part of a federal scheme to transport northern Indigenous workers to jobs in southern Canadian agriculture. The program, a collaborative effort between the Federal-Provincial Farm Labour Committee and the Department

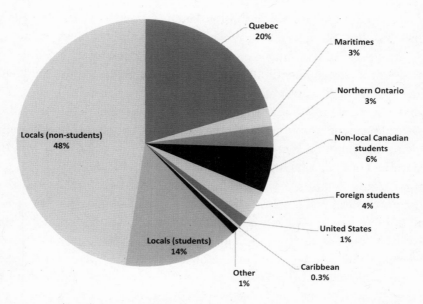

4.4 Origins of tobacco harvest workers, 1969. Sources: OFCTGMB Annual Report, 1970, RG 16-250, box B388334, file "Tobacco Plan: Regulations & Annual Report, 1970," AO.

of Indian Affairs was most extensive in western Canada, where by 1962 over 2,100 Indigenous workers from northern communities were working on sugar beet farms in southern Alberta. By comparison, the Ontario movement was quite small, comprising 549 workers in 1965 and 361 in 1966, with tobacco's share smaller still at 90 workers in 1965 and an estimated 100 the next year.[56] Ostensibly aimed at alleviating poverty on northern reserves, the labour mobilization scheme – at least in western Canada – had a more pernicious side, with state officials cutting off social assistance payments during sugar beet season in order to coerce First Nations people into participation, as detailed by Ron Laliberte and Vic Satzewich and documented in reports written in the 1960s.

Given the paucity of information available on the Ontario movement, it is not possible to say whether similar practices occurred with those workers who headed to the tobacco belt. Nor is it possible to say anything about workers' individual experiences. In any event, northern Indigenous workers – at least through this official channel – seem to have worked in the tobacco sector for just two years. Not coincidentally, those were two years in which tobacco growers and government officials worried about labour shortages. In 1966 especially, no effort was spared to secure the maximum number of labour sources for the tobacco harvest, after a big increase in the planted acreage during a time of low unemployment.[57] In 1967, however, the movement was suddenly halted – while workers from the James Bay area were placed in Quebec, they were not brought back to southern Ontario. The coincidence of the curtailing of this movement, combined with the launching of the Caribbean guest-worker program in 1966, raised the eyebrows of at least one official with the Department of Indian Affairs, R. Biddle, who wrote to his Manpower counterpart J. LeBlanc: "I must ask whether the advent of the West Indian workers in Southern Ontario had any bearing on the fact that Indians from James Bay were not required." LeBlanc was evasive in his response, writing simply that the answer "can not be determined at this time."[58]

The changing demographics of the tobacco workforce were also reflected in the evolving nature of anxieties about so-called transients. While many of the long-standing tropes employed by local residents, civic leaders, and politicians from all levels of government to describe the "problem" of transients persisted into the postwar period, these deficiencies were increasingly projected onto two particular, and in some cases overlapping, categories of worker: "hippies" and Québécois.[59] Local reactions to each group fit comfortably within prevalent Anglo-Canadian attitudes of the day. The "hippie" and "countercultural" youth of the 1960s and '70s attracted an inordinate amount of scrutiny from contemporary observers and authorities across North America, Europe, and beyond. Not only were the perceived characteristics of this emergent "youth culture" – including drug use, sexual permissiveness, and "antisocial behaviour" – deemed beyond the pale of respectability, but the growing radicalism and militancy among young people – students and workers alike – were seen as a threat to the Cold War–era liberal order.[60]

In the mass arrivals each summer of young people seeking harvest jobs, the spirit of the sixties made its way to the tobacco belt, with the decade's attendant anxieties following close behind. Unsurprisingly, relations between locals and job-seeking young people were anything but a love-in. "Hippies" with "long hair" and "big mouths" were criticized for causing trouble and for not truly wanting to work, a trope about job seekers dating to at least the Great Depression.[61] Employers and residents worried too about drug use, a fear that was not exactly eased by a 1970 Department of Health and Welfare study that

4.5 Sign in tobacco belt park, 1961. London Free Press Collection of Photographic Negatives, 2 September 1961, Western University Archives and Special Collections, London, Ontario.

found that 90 per cent of "young transients" that year had used drugs, mostly cannabis, amphetamines, and hallucinogens such as LSD.[62] Sometimes portrayals of hippies tended more toward mockery than fearmongering. A 1968 cartoon in the *Delhi News-Record*, for example, featured a gaunt, long-haired, bearded young man, chest hair spouting out of his army jacket, sporting a medallion that read, "Yorkville Type," referring to the popular hippie neighbourhood in Toronto. The man attempts to explain how to prime tobacco:

"Well, first ya grab a bunch of these whatchamacallits – and put em in the thin-gamabob – and then ya take it to these whatevertheyare – y'know – and then ya put em on the – uh – the – uh …"[63]

Young job seekers from Quebec were marked as doubly suspicious, guilty of all the same questionable characteristics of their English-speaking peers but with the additional distinction of coming from a province with a surging sovereignty movement, a development that provoked great anxieties among Anglo-Canadians.[64] Locals' worst fears seemed to be coming true when "separatists" were blamed for instigating labour unrest, and when, on another occasion, Québécois migrants gathered in a Simcoe park and chanted "Vive le Québec libre!" before being dispersed by police. Like job seekers from elsewhere, Québécois, too, were accused of not really being interested in finding work.[65]

Dislike of Canadian transients – Québécois in particular – did not only play itself out discursively, but also in much more physically dangerous ways. Migrants were frequently subjected to random vigilante acts of violence while in the tobacco towns. Some locals – almost always young men – enjoyed passing the time by driving around and hurling insults like "frog" or "Frenchie" at migrant workers. Sometimes they hurled projectiles as well. Even more frightening were physical beatings, such as the one that occurred in 1975, when four local men in their twenties went on a drunken, late-night spree of violence and assaulted four migrant workers, two from Quebec, one from British Columbia, and the fourth from France. Two of the victims were attacked while asleep in their tents. This was far from an isolated incident.[66] It was also common for job seekers who had set up camp on private property to be aggressively removed, something that happened to Patricia and her companions in the 1970s when the owner of a fallow field where they had pitched their tents chased them off with a shotgun.[67]

Evolving Patterns of Dissent

Perhaps the biggest concern about tobacco's evolving workforce was its perceived penchant and potential for causing trouble – namely, through collective labour action. Though the tobacco belt had long been a site of working-class organization and resistance, the local infrastructure of dissent that had helped produce the dramatic campaigns of workers and small growers during the

4.6 Pierre Lafranche, of Rimouski, Quebec, looking for work, Aylmer, Ontario, 1974. Courtesy of Elgin County Archives. "Tobacco Farming in Elgin County – Transient Workers," 13 August 1974, St Thomas Times-Journal fonds, C8 Sh2 B2 F5 33, Elgin County Archives.

Great Depression underwent some significant transformations in the decades following World War II. For one, in the years following the war, Communism rapidly waned as an ideological force in the tobacco belt. A major factor here were immigration patterns that brought in scores of newcomers from Hungary, Ukraine, Lithuania, Poland, and Czechoslovakia. Many had lived under Soviet occupation during the war, and others (such as the famous Hungarian fifty-sixers) were fleeing political repression in Soviet-controlled satellite states, experiences that gave them a very different political orientation than, say, the radical Hungarians who preceded them in the Norfolk district. Robust screening measures by the Department of Citizenship and Immigration further ensured that newcomers' loyalties would lie on the right side of the Iron Curtain.[68]

Of course, the retreat from radical leftist politics in the tobacco belt and beyond was not solely due to changing demographics. News of Soviet repression of political dissidents – particularly in the wake of the 1956 Hungarian Revolution and Khrushchev's speech in the same year revealing the purges and abuses perpetrated under Joseph Stalin – proved highly damaging for Communist parties around the world, leading not only to a decline in party memberships but also to a general turning away from the USSR's brand of socialism.[69] The sum of these factors, in both the Norfolk area and Canada as a whole, was a decisive rightward turn within a number of immigrant communities, particularly those whose homelands fell within the Soviet orbit.[70] These political changes were particularly apparent in the Hungarian Canadian community, where formerly influential Communist organizations found themselves increasingly sidelined over the course of the 1950s.[71] The trend was observed early on in a 1952 *Financial Post* article about Communist meetings in the tobacco belt: "Southwestern Ontario has always been a Communist rural stronghold. They used to claim about 500 members. Now they're down to about 300."[72]

The fading of Communist politics did not, however, mean that tobacco belt residents stopped pursuing collective strategies to improve their conditions. Tobacco growers continued to agitate for better prices and more democratic representation through the 1940s and '50s, securing a major victory in 1957 with the disbandment of the old Marketing Association and the creation of the Ontario Flue-Cured Tobacco Growers' Marketing Board in its stead. In later decades, tobacco growers would continue to organize collectively, in particular taking on provincial and federal governments over tobacco policy.[73] But as these examples suggest, as the tobacco belt communities' politics shifted rightward, they became exclusively concerned with the interests of growers, rather than workers.

With locals checking out, collective action among workers became almost the sole domain of migrants, signalling the loss of the combination between tobacco belt radicals and indignant transients that had produced such a potent reaction in 1939. In spite of these developments, tobacco's migrant workers continued to use their pre-harvest congregations to orchestrate annual wage rate demands. Long-time seasonal tobacco worker Archie Larson explained how it worked to a *Toronto Telegram* reporter in 1961: "You just sit around and the word is passed around that we hold out for $13. If the good primers stick together, the growers have to meet the price."[74] Such tactics were still in place in 1974, when about eighty transients "congregated and began to make demands" (the specifics of which were not reported), before being dispersed by fifteen police officers.[75]

Even after the waning of the infrastructure of dissent, workers sometimes made demands in more organized and audacious campaigns, none more dramatic than the labour unrest that took place in 1966. In that year, for the fifth consecutive summer, transient workers entering the tobacco belt were encouraged to stay in camps organized and funded by a committee comprised of representatives from local and provincial governments, area churches, and growers. As geographer Emily Reid-Musson has explained, the camps, which were established in or on the outskirts of some of the major tobacco towns, were intended to keep migrants out of the downtowns and parks, in the process creating a more orderly labour-recruitment system and answering the long-standing complaints of local residents about the yearly influxes.[76] As a woman farmer explained even more pointedly, "the camps where workers stay until harvest begins are set up in the first place to keep them away from our homes."[77] Job seekers staying in the camps were given two meals a day, access to bathroom facilities, and space to sleep inside a large "circus tent." The accommodations were far from glamorous. "We never started out to give them more than bare subsistence," explained the chairman of the camps committee, Catholic priest Father R.J. Langan.[78] This much was clear to residents of the Delhi camp. Already fed up with their meagre twice daily meals of bologna sandwiches and coffee, they were pushed over the edge after enduring a couple chilly nights without enough firewood or blankets to keep warm. Unable to obtain firewood from the committee, the transients resorted to tearing down an outhouse for fuel.[79]

Soon, camp residents decided to progress from mere survival tactics to a more coordinated effort. On 2 August, they delivered a list of demands to the camp administrator in which they asked for three meals a day of varied fare (with at least two meals served hot), tent heaters, blankets, and beds. The petitioners made it clear that if they were not provided with more food, they would march on the town and take it.[80] The petition drew immediate concern from

local police, who quickly responded by supplying two hundred and fifty ham-
burgers and cups of coffee to the camp dwellers. It was too little, too late, however, and workers were incensed when the menu reverted to bologna sandwiches
the next morning. Residents began demonstrating, claiming the sandwiches
they were being fed weren't "fit for pigs." Said one worker, "If we can't get enough
to eat the right way I will steal food." After about forty minutes of airing grievances at the camp, the group, guided by a few leaders, took their protest to
downtown Delhi.

The authorities jumped quickly into action. Every on- and off-duty officer
in town was summoned, and before the workers had even reached the town,
they were stopped at the top of a hill by a blockade of seven shotgun-wielding
police officers from the Delhi and provincial squads. The Delhi mayor himself
soon arrived and took the unusual measure of reading the Riot Act. The act,
which stated that anyone who did not disperse from the "riot" would be subject
to a penalty of up to life in prison, was read in both English and French, and
was met with derisive jeers from the assembled protestors. The marchers
turned around and went back down the hill, where they continued their protest
for about thirty minutes. When a few attempted to climb back up the hill and
break through police lines, the officers took action, arresting nine (all men)
and prompting the dispersal of the remaining protestors. The detained men
claimed that Delhi police officers assaulted them in their cells on the day of
their arrest. They spent a total of nine days in jail before being released with
fines of thirty-five dollars each, or about two days' wages for a tobacco primer.[81]

The march produced some modest short-term gains: greater variety was introduced to the camp menus, and the portion size was increased slightly.[82] But
its most important outcome was decidedly less favourable for migrants: the
protest helped guarantee the permanent closure of sanctioned transient camps,
which were never again provided for incoming job seekers after 1966. Instead,
migrants were forced to return to the familiar patterns of pre-harvest subsistence if they did not come through a government-approved mobility program.[83] While the closure of the camps was motivated by a desire to ward off
"troublemaking," this goal proved unattainable so long as transients still con-
gregated in central areas, and groups of migrant workers continued to cause
headaches for local authorities in the years after 1966.[84] There can be little
doubt, however, that the waning of the infrastructure of dissent hurt tobacco
workers' chances of securing gains from collective efforts. No longer able to

4.7 Arrested workers exit courthouse, Delhi, Ontario, 1966. London Free Press Collection of Photographic Negatives, 5 August 1966, Western University Archives and Special Collections, London, Ontario.

link up with local networks of radicals, transient job seekers were unable to create (or benefit from) any year-to-year continuity in organizing efforts.

The final significant attempt at sector-wide organization came in 1981–82 when the Canadian Farmworkers' Union (CFU) launched an organizing drive in the tobacco belt – and it, too, suffered for the lack of a local infrastructure of dissent. The CFU campaign was unusual in tobacco's history of organization and resistance for a couple of reasons. For one, it marked the first and only time during the twentieth century that an established union sought to organize – or even meaningfully engage with – workers in tobacco, an endeavour that would not be repeated until the 2000s when the United Food and Commercial Workers launched outreach efforts with agricultural guest workers from the Global South. And second, unlike previous high points of worker organization (such as 1939 or 1966), the efforts were not the result of grassroots organization among workers and job seekers but instead were led by paid and volunteer organizers from outside the district.

The CFU originated in British Columbia, officially founded in April 1980 by a group of mostly South Asian farm-worker activists and allies who had been organizing agricultural workers in the Fraser Valley since the fall of 1978. Within months of its founding, the union won certification on three farms, while expanding organizing drives to include the Okanagan Valley. Support committees for the CFU were founded across British Columbia and in Ontario and Quebec, comprised mainly of members of the labour movement and progressive churches, mirroring the types of committees that had sprung up across the continent in support of the United Farm Workers of America's various boycott campaigns since the 1960s.[85] In early 1981, the CFU's national office decided to capitalize on the support for the Ontario committee by launching an organizing drive in that province. After a few months of investigations into the farm labour picture, union officials decided to concentrate their efforts on the tobacco sector. Two full-time CFU staff members were assigned the job, assisted by the existing support committee and a small number of volunteers.[86]

The campaign was launched in May and focused first on information gathering, especially concerning health and safety issues faced by tobacco workers. Since farm workers in Ontario were barred from legal unionization under the province's Labour Relations Act, organizers did not attempt to get workers to sign union cards. Instead, the union hoped to launch a legal challenge against this exclusion and potentially to encourage workers to engage in recognition strikes to force the hands of government and employers, though both these possibilities were long-term considerations that were not pursued during the CFU's time in the tobacco district. While a full-on union drive was on hold, CFU organizers turned to gradually building the profile of the union by introducing themselves to workers and distributing educational material about the (limited) rights of farm workers. Here, activists made use of the tobacco belt's labour geography, setting up a trailer in a park in Simcoe that was a popular gathering place for transients, where they hung a banner offering "medical and legal support" free of charge. CFU organizers also capitalized on transients' practices of mobility while in the region. As job seekers walked and hitchhiked between farms and towns, looking for work or going on after-work outings, organizers picked them up in their cars, using the ride as an opportunity to discuss the union and exchange contact information.

Despite the best efforts of organizers, however, the CFU's tobacco campaign very quickly ran up against a number of daunting challenges. The two full-time staff representatives – who were in fact based in Toronto and therefore had to drive two hours to the tobacco belt for any on-the-ground work – were not nearly sufficient to cover the massive task of organizing 35,000 workers at 4,500 workplaces spread over 750 square miles. There were also various tensions and breakdowns in communication and trust between the organizers, the pre-existing members of the CFU's Ontario support committee, the CFU's national office, and certain allies within the labour movement. While the union made some inroads among transient workers, they struggled with the more conservative local workforce, a crucial component of the organizing drive since these were the workers who were actively engaged in the sector year in, year out for more than a few weeks at a time. In other words, they found no local infrastructure of dissent to link up with. As volunteer organizer Craig Berggold recalled, "The problem for the union was trying to build a base that could be sustained, because of course the migrants come and go." Part of the issue, he reasoned, was that the organizers were all outsiders to the region, and only one of them – Berggold himself – had ever worked in tobacco.[87]

Organizers had not predicted that the path would be easy; indeed, they estimated that it would be a matter of years before they would be able to win any certifications on tobacco farms or set up a hiring hall in the sector.[88] Still, the difficulties weighed on union staff and hampered their efforts, particularly the ever-looming reality that even if large numbers of farm workers were interested in unionizing, they would have to secure a difficult legal or legislative victory for this to go forward. As a report on the union's efforts in tobacco noted, "The CFU moved into Ontario very cautiously ... There was no mandate for organizing which became the point of frustration for everyone involved."[89] When the CFU suspended operations in Ontario in April 1983, however, the primary motivator was not the myriad obstacles, but instead the development of a crisis situation for the union in British Columbia that compelled the union to redirect all its resources toward protecting the tenuous gains it had made out west.[90] Just as abruptly as it had begun, the union's brief foray into Ontario's tobacco belt came to a close.

The diminishing returns for large-scale organizational efforts within the tobacco belt – both formal and informal – did not signal the end of resistance in the sector. Instead, the locus of tobacco workers' protest shifted to individual farms, where they engaged in the types of impromptu workplace actions that had been a feature of the sector since its earliest days. Small-scale resistance took many forms. At the most basic level, individual farm workers faced with sub-par pay or conditions often simply switched employers or quit altogether, opting to embrace what Reid-Musson has called "informal mobility agency."[91] Labourers also continued to engage in wage negotiations while already employed on farms. As CFU organizer Berggold explained, this was most successfully done partway through the harvest, when workers' skills had improved and fewer replacements were available, making the existing crew more difficult to dispatch. Of course, they also needed to stick together. "If the primers are tight and all friends – and the farmer is unjustly treating them, they can confront the farmer on wages," Berggold noted.[92]

Disputes emerged between workers and employers not only over the daily rate of pay, but also over the payment of bonuses. This employer practice appears to have begun sometime in the 1960s or '70s and was a technique for keeping workers on the farm until the end of the harvest. Harvest workers received their base daily wage no matter how long they stayed on the farm, but for each day of work the farmer would put away a smaller bonus, payable upon completion of the harvest. If a worker quit or was fired before the end of the harvest, they forfeited their entire bonus. In 1973, for example, primers were paid an average of twenty-five dollars per day, plus a three dollar daily bonus.[93] Not only did the bonus system help farmers retain labour, it also could serve as a disciplinary tool since workers – especially as the end of harvest approached – were understandably wary about being prematurely dismissed and cut off from the sizeable payment.[94] Though bonus payments had been contrived by growers to bolster their interests, they sometimes abused the system they had created by firing a crew shortly before the end of the harvest and hiring new workers to complete the crop, thus freeing themselves from paying the supplemental wages.[95] Of course, workers fired in this manner often pushed back. CFU organizer Craig Berggold described one such case, when a crew was fired ten days before the end of the harvest: "They all sat in the bunkhouse – said no way are we going to hit the road until we get all our money." The workers proceeded to call the Ontario Provincial Police, "who came by, listened to both sides, and awarded the farmworkers their bonus." In another case, when a local woman was fired without receiving her bonus, her husband confronted the grower and threatened his life, securing the unpaid funds.[96]

A great deal of conflict arose on the farm over control of production, as had been the case since the sector's early years. Wage labourers disputed productive practices on the farm, particularly when farmers attempted to extract more labour from workers for no additional pay. This type of conflict most commonly occurred over the amount of tobacco harvested per day. Workers were expected to harvest enough tobacco each day to fill a kiln and were paid at a daily rate for this work. A standard kiln was filled with exactly 1,250 sticks of tobacco, but often, toward the end of the harvest as the threat of frost loomed, farmers rushed to get as much of their crop harvested as possible and instructed workers to fill the kilns with even more tobacco. This created more work for workers, both on harvest days and also in the mornings when they were required to empty a kiln of cured tobacco before breakfast.[97] Workers often pushed back on the matter, but they weren't always successful. Québécoise migrant worker Patricia, whose story opened this chapter, recalled one such incident when she and her co-workers – including three student workers from Germany – were asked to prime more tobacco toward the end of the harvest. "They wanted us to do a day and a half in a day, but they weren't going to pay us for a day and a half," she recalled. "We squawked, [and] we got fired, which is probably what they wanted anyway because you lost your ten-dollar-a-day bonus that you only got if you stayed to the end."[98] Another example comes from grower Paul Donohue, whose workers confronted him one year complaining that too many leaves were being tied onto the sticks. "They come up and they yanked a couple sticks off [the kiln]. I says, 'Okay. You gonna count 'em? ... If there's more than a hundred [leaves] on 'em, I'll pay ya. But if there isn't a hundred on there, I'm going to deduct money off you. So they put the sticks back up in the kiln and went back to work," recalled Donohue with a chuckle.[99] Sometimes workers were able to turn the tables on kiln conflict by under-filling kilns, hanging tobacco around the visible edges but leaving the inside empty, thus shortening their workday.[100]

State Efforts to Control Postwar Labour Migration

Just as concerns about transients continued into the postwar period, so, too, did efforts on the part of civil society and the state (at all levels) to exert some control over this "problematic" workforce. At the local level, police continued to form a central part of the state's handling of migrant workers. As has been suggested elsewhere, relations between police and job seekers remained at best testy; at worst, they resulted in violence. Police continued their long-standing practice of disrupting "loitering" migrants during the day, exhorting them to keep moving. Transients also often reported being roughed up by police.[101] Without a doubt, the most shockingly violent police action against transients in this period came in Tillsonburg in 1960 when, two weeks after the start of harvest, police entered a campsite housing twenty-five migrants yet to find work, doused their makeshift dwellings in gasoline, and set the site ablaze. The act was met with criticism from a number of newspapers and observers in the region, but the town's mayor stood by his police officers, declaring that "We in Tillsonburg have no intention of allowing anyone to panhandle, erect tar-paper shacks and carry on drinking bouts in the centre of our town."[102]

Meanwhile, some political and civic leaders in the region began to pursue decidedly more proactive strategies for dealing with yearly arrivals of transients, most importantly through efforts to provide temporary accommodations for pre-harvest job seekers. Three main initiatives were launched in this period by shifting coalitions of local clergy, civic leaders, and politicians from all three levels of government: a hostel at the Norfolk Fair Grounds in Simcoe (1950–56), a series of camps in Delhi and other locations (1962–66), and hostels in Tillsonburg and Aylmer (ca 1970–75).[103]

Despite their considerable success in certain years (particularly with the hostels in the early 1950s and the camps in the following decade), efforts to provide pre-harvest accommodations to job seekers faced a number of challenges, which help explain the limited scope and duration of those initiatives.[104] Locals residing close to proposed or actual camp or hostel sites often protested at the prospect of hundreds or thousands of transients bedding down in their neighbourhoods. As one Courtland resident explained after a proposed camp was successfully squashed by protesting locals, "I just don't want the transients here. Why bring vandalism into the village when we don't have it now? We are a small village and don't have a police force and will have to keep a shotgun near the bed."[105]

Staffing and funding were also persistent challenges. All three initiatives relied on volunteers, largely drawn from church groups, who were often overtaxed and burned out. While the federal Department of Labour funded hostels in the early 1950s, they resisted committing long-term dollars, arguing that the hostels should be locally funded.[106] An obvious potential source of funding was tobacco growers themselves, an observation made countless times by newspaper editorials, government officials, and others, but aside from its foiled attempts to build a hostel in 1967, the Marketing Board and its members displayed little interest in supporting the initiatives (and the same was true of the board's precursor, the Marketing Association, in operation until 1956). The growers' organization donated an uninspiring $400 to the hostel in 1956, $500 to the camps in 1962, and a paltry $293 to two Tillsonburg hostels in 1972. It became slightly more generous in 1973, contributing $3,000 out of the $8,900 received for the Tillsonburg hostel, but by 1975 it refused to make any further contributions.[107] Reverend McCann of St Paul's United Church, which operated the hostels in Tillsonburg in the 1970s, summed up years of frustration on the part of local community and religious leaders when he complained that "I can't understand their arrogant attitude. It's their industry that's causing the problem and they should take some responsibility."[108] In the earlier hostel period, the Marketing Association was not merely stingy but actively obstructionist, wary of any meddling in their annual steady supply of labour. When representatives from the federal and provincial governments were supporting community efforts to establish a hostel in 1950, long-time Marketing Association representative J.K. Perrett "strode into [the provincial agricultural representative's] office, and asked him what the hell he meant by being involved in such an affair, and told him to keep out of that business as they weren't going to tolerate any interference."[109]

At the federal and provincial levels, state efforts to manage the annual migration of tobacco workers exhibited some continuity from the war years. Civil servants remained convinced of the necessity of state involvement to produce a more orderly, rational system of farm labour provision. If anything, this conviction only grew stronger. As historian Tina Loo details, the postwar era saw federal agencies take an increasingly active role in attempting to improve citizens' social and economic conditions, efforts that were informed by a fierce belief on the part of state agents in the "power of social scientific expertise to understand and transform the world."[110] Less a distinct political philosophy and more a general disposition toward the appropriate role of the state in society, the tendency labelled as "high modernism" by anthropologist James C. Scott came to form a governmental "common sense" in many parts of the globe from the 1930s and into the postwar period.[111] In Canada, state efforts to create a "good life" for citizens were particularly focused on inequality between provinces and regions, a problem that labour mobility programs – including those in agriculture – sought to address by placing workers from areas of high unemployment in sectors with high labour demand, such as tobacco.[112] It was unsurprising, then, that the cost-sharing Dominion-Provincial (later Federal-Provincial) Farm Labour Committees, which facilitated the migration between and within provinces, continued into the postwar years, even if federal contributions did decline over time.[113]

For all the continuity, however, farm labour policy took on some new dimensions in the postwar years. For one, the interventions of state agencies were now aimed at more than just the management of labour mobility. Instead, officials believed that the key to creating a more rational and stable farm labour market – and to alleviating (non-tobacco) farmers' problems with labour recruitment and retention – was to help farmers transition to more "modern" business models, with more efficient, evidence-based production practices, and more attractive wages and working conditions. This was the farm labour bureaucracy's version of "high modernism." Bringing the vision to reality, however, would require a different approach than that pursued during the war. Having lost their wartime powers to compel employers and workers to cooperate with state labour initiatives, government agencies were now forced to turn to the art of persuasion. This took two principal forms: education and incentive programs. Educational efforts, promoting modern business practices and urging both workers and employers to follow government guidelines on the employment of migrant labour, took many forms: public events, radio broadcasts, published booklets, and even a film produced by the National Film Board, *Workers on the Land*.[114] Farm labour bureaucrats also used incentive programs to encourage agricultural employers to follow the high-modernist agenda, notably by offering farmers subsidies for building or improving accommodations for workers, a program that many tobacco growers took advantage of.[115]

The postwar decades witnessed a number of administrative changes in the federal labour bureaucracy and, by extension, the farm labour portfolio. Immediately after the war, the NSS, which had taken charge of the wartime labour mobilization efforts, was replaced by the National Employment Service (NES), with many of the same officials continuing on the farm labour file (both agencies were housed under the Department of Labour).[116] In 1966, the Department of Labour and the Immigration Branch of the Department of Citizenship and Immigration were brought together into the newly minted Department of Manpower and Immigration. Employment offices were rebranded as Canada Manpower Centres (CMCs), which expanded their scope of operations beyond job placement to include counselling and training as well. Then, in 1974, in response to exposés on the proliferation of undocumented, underage, and poorly paid workers in Ontario agriculture, Minister of Manpower and Immigration Robert Andras embarked on a series of initiatives to improve labour mobility programs and bring a greater percentage of the agricultural workforce under their supervision. Andras's response to the legitimacy crisis facing his department resulted in the creation of a number of programs aimed at Canadian migrants – most notably for tobacco, the Canada Farm Labour Pools (CFLPS).[117] CFLPS continued the work previously done by NES and CMC offices in placing workers on farms, but also added an important component by becoming in essence a labour contractor: employers utilizing their service paid the CFLP, which in turn paid out workers' wages and made all necessary deductions from their paycheques.[118]

As was the case before 1945, bureaucrats' dreams of a rational system of farm labour mobility were not so easily brought to fruition. Officials consistently struggled to get farmers to report their labour needs with sufficient notice, and they were frequently barraged with requests at the start of harvest. (One such instance occurred during the harvest of 1959, after which a deflated NES staffer remarked, "We try to educate the farmer to place his order early. Last season he didn't leave us in a very good spot to determine what he would need.")[119] A parallel challenge was getting workers from other parts of Canada to seek employment only through approved channels – or at minimum to not travel to the tobacco belt in advance of the harvest, to avoid creating the sorts of scenes witnessed most dramatically in 1966. Though in some years, officials reported that close to one-third of the tobacco workforce had been placed by government agencies (for example, through the Federal-Provincial Farm Labour Committee in 1962, or the CMCs in 1973), these successes were always fleeting; within a year or two, officials invariably seemed to be back where . they started.[120] Such limited returns will come as little surprise to students of Canadian "high modernism," whose projects often produced results somewhat more modest than the audacious goals of rationalism and efficiency that they had set out to accomplish.

+ + +

In the decades following World War II, tobacco continued to be an attractive place for thousands of migrant workers from many parts of the country, though the makeup of the workforce changed in important ways under the influence of technological developments in tobacco farming, evolving gender norms, and shifting national employment patterns. Emerging from this flurry of changes was a workforce that was younger, had fewer connections to local communities, and in which the role of women in tobacco work was rapidly changing. The hippies, Québécois, and young women who were the face of a changing workforce prompted various anxieties among local leaders and residents. Though some of these were particular to the era (especially worries about long-haired, drug-using, Quebec-separating reprobates), in a broader sense, such concerns about transient workers echoed ones raised since the 1930s. In two other important domains, the postwar tobacco labour scene also witnessed a broad continuation of factors from the 1930s through to the 1940s that nevertheless underwent important, if subtle, processes of evolution: working-class organization and state involvement.

While the tobacco sector remained an important site of working-class struggle, in the decades following the war the interests of workers and growers – always aligned far more in leftist rhetoric than in organizational practice – diverged along two separate paths. As local residents became almost exclusively preoccupied with the position of growers, labour politics became, in essence, the sole domain of migrants. Efforts by wage labourers to secure higher pay and better conditions persisted throughout this period, but they were undoubtedly hampered by the severance of ties between migrant workers and the local infrastructure of dissent.

Also continuing into the postwar period were state efforts to more rationally and efficiently control the movements of workers into the tobacco belt each harvest. Here the story was first one of decline, in which government agencies lost forever the more coercive powers they enjoyed during the war, and second one of continued frustration, with only intermittent, mild successes to boost civil servants' spirits. What it certainly was not was the grand march toward rational labour mobility that high-modernist bureaucrats had so lustily envisioned.

The transformations discussed in this chapter all relate to tobacco's domestic workforce. But in the mid- to late 1960s, important changes were also taking place in the sector's international migrant workforce, ones that would serve to radically transform the makeup of the long-standing US movement, as well as introduce two new groups of foreign migrant workers to the tobacco belt – in the process planting the seeds for the drastic overhaul of the workforce that would take hold by century's end.

5

GLOBAL GUEST WORKERS

When Gladston Williams returned home to Jamaica each fall after a season working in the tobacco fields of southwestern Ontario, it was cause for celebration. In the days after his plane touched down, Williams and his family would host friends and relatives for a big dinner, at the centre of which was always a freshly slaughtered goat from the Williamses' small herd. After about two months away from family and a season of difficult work in tobacco, it was a relief to return home. "It was good," Williams recalled, "for you have a few dollars, and you're glad to see your family again. And you can buy [some] things, which your family ... appreciate." At the homecoming feast, "we come and eat and give God thanks." Describing what, exactly, he and his family were thankful for, Williams explained, "We go and come back."

Williams "went and came back" between his home in Clarendon Parish, Jamaica, and a tobacco farm in Langton, Ontario, for about five years in the late 1980s and early 1990s as a participant in the Seasonal Agricultural Workers Program (SAWP). Williams's lifetime of experience working in agriculture had prepared him well for the back-breaking leaf. At the age of fifteen, he left school and began labouring on one of the largest sugar cane estates in the parish. Later on, as a young man, he worked for two seasons in the US farm-worker program, picking apples in New Hampshire and cutting cane in Florida. Back home, he and his family raised a small number of crops and animals on their one-acre plot. Even with all this experience, harvesting tobacco in Canada still proved difficult; particularly challenging was priming dew-soaked tobacco leaves bare-handed on frigid fall mornings. But, Williams confessed, "the cane harder."

Returning home also called for celebration because Williams's participation in the Canadian farm-worker scheme was considered in his home community

5.1 Vincenzo Pietropaolo (photographer), Joseph Arthur of Saint Lucia priming tobacco, Otterville, Ontario, 1984.

a great privilege. Indeed, getting into one of Jamaica's foreign guest-worker programs was no easy feat and required a combination of luck and agricultural credentials. Williams had both. Luck came in the form of living in a district represented by a member of Parliament from the governing Jamaica Labour Party. Through the patronage system under which the farm-worker program operated, local functionaries selected Williams for the pool of applicants from which final spots in the overseas programs would be selected. But patronage could only get you so far. To advance into the program itself, you needed to prove your chops: for the Canadian program, this was done through interviews and a review of candidates' work history; for the US scheme, where Williams first worked, this depended on a "hand test," in which Jamaican Ministry of Labour officials examined applicants' hands for evidence of manual labour. Williams remembers many hopefuls rubbing their hands in dirt and scuffing them up in order to fool the bureaucrats. Williams himself needed no such gimmicks. "I never have to do that. I was cutting cane at that time … so my hand did rough. When they look at it, they go, 'Woah!' …. That's the hand they were looking for."[1]

By the time Gladston Williams first arrived in Canada in the late 1980s, guest-worker schemes such as the SAWP were well-established in the Norfolk tobacco zone. The SAWP – which first supplied workers to tobacco growers in 1967 – was, in fact, the sector's third guest-worker program, joining the long-lasting US movement and a new scheme, launched in 1966, that brought in university students from western and central Europe. Just as they had been for the sector's domestic workforce, the 1960s were a time of important transformation for tobacco's foreign labour component, and 1966 and 1967 were particularly busy years. Not only were two new guest-worker schemes launched, but the sector's oldest foreign worker arrangement, with the United States, saw a major shake-up when, in 1966, African Americans were allowed to participate for the first time in what had up to then been a whites-only movement.

In many ways, each of tobacco's three guest-worker schemes differed starkly from the next. The US program, as we have seen, did not start out as a *program* at all, but instead as an organic migration system that was only brought under bilateral state control via a gradual and often messy process. Before that happened, many US migrants ended up making rural Ontario their permanent home. Conversely, the SAWP, now a lynchpin of Canada's agricultural workforce, was in many ways the quintessential guest-worker program. Governed from its outset by bilateral agreements between Canada and the various sending countries, it was construed as strictly temporary, ensuring the departure of participants upon the completion of their contracts – the "go and come back" recalled by Williams that was a hallmark of guest-worker programs the world over.[2] The outlier of tobacco's three foreign worker schemes was undoubtedly the European Student Tobacco Worker Program, whose relatively privileged, white student-participants cut a vastly different profile than the tobacco migrants who hailed from struggling agricultural regions of the Global South and the southern United States.

For all their differences, the three guest-worker programs also shared some important similarities. All three were overwhelmingly male, in most years exclusively so.[3] Workers in each were valued by employers for their "reliability" – a euphemism for the high degree of employer control that program structures enabled (something that will be explored in more detail in the next chapter). And each program would have its turn as tobacco's top supplier of guest workers: the US movement until the late 1960s, the European scheme in the early 1970s, and the SAWP from 1974 onward.

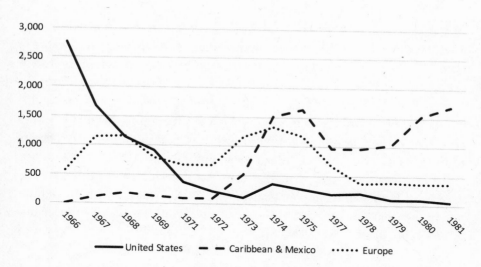

5.2 Tobacco guest workers by origin, 1966–81. Sources: Whyte, *The Experience of New Immigrants and Seasonal Farmworkers*, 4.5; Satzewich, *Racism and the Incorporation of Foreign Labour*, 108; Immigration Branch (RG 76, vol. 1112), and Department of Manpower and Immigration (RG 118, vols. 244, 246, 273, acc. 1989–90/039, vol. 76), LAC; OFCTGMB Annual Report, 1970, AO.

The three schemes shared another similarity: the design, operation, and evolution of each was shaped in critical ways by forces beyond Canada's borders. Most important in this regard were government officials from migrant-sending countries, who wielded considerable influence when it came to moulding the programs in which their citizens participated. But other transnational factors also played their part: sending countries' political, economic, and social contexts; transnational intellectual and political currents; and geopolitics and diplomacy, to name a few.

The creation of two new guest-worker programs, and the racial integration of a third, happened during a time of profound transformation in Canadian immigration policy. Under the twin pressures of domestic human rights activism and international diplomatic considerations, the federal government removed national origin and "race" as legitimate admission criteria for prospective immigrants via a pair of orders-in-council passed in 1962 and 1967. The second of these introduced the meritocratic and widely praised points system that, in modified form, remains the cornerstone of Canadian immigration policy to this day.[4] Curiously, however, these measures had virtually no bearing on the changes in the country's guest-worker programs that were occurring at precisely the same time. The addition of Black workers from the United States and the Caribbean resulted not from any sweeping trend of liberalization, but instead from more pragmatic considerations that in many ways represented the *continuation* of racism as an influence on migration policy rather than its banishment. The European program, with its overwhelmingly white and wealthy participating nations, cast this fact into stark relief. The speed and facility of its implementation contrasted sharply with the tedium and tumult that characterized the long wait and belated inclusion of Black migrants in the tobacco workforce.

The Integration of the US-Ontario Program

In April 1966, a delegation of Canadian government and employer representatives embarked on a ten-day tour of the United States, stopping in seven states and Washington, DC, for meetings with federal and state officials about the US-Ontario tobacco workers program. The trip was occasioned by the Marketing Board's plans to increase tobacco acreage by 40 per cent that year, a feat that would require a commensurate increase in harvest workers – at a time when employment levels in Canada were particularly high. To help meet the need, growers and federal officials turned to that long-time stalwart of Ontario's tobacco migrant labour force, the southern United States.

The Canadian party, consisting of Marketing Board representative James Leathong and federal labour bureaucrats W. Davison and G.H. Kidd, was met with "a fine spirit of co-operation and friendly interest" by their American counterparts, who were happy to help boost the number of participating workers. But they had one major condition: Black workers could no longer be excluded from the movement. "Ontario growers must be prepared to accept a certain number of coloured workers," Davison stated in a hand-written report on the trip. "Anti-segregation legislation in the U.S. precludes the possibility of State Employment Services denying the opportunity of employment to qualified workers of coloured origin and no new recruitment can be undertaken without this qualification."[5] Presumably, the legislation in question was the 1964 Civil Rights Act, parts of which prohibited discrimination by government agencies receiving federal funds and banned discrimination in employment.[6] Indeed, in 1966, the same year as the Canadian delegation's US tour, the federal Bureau of Employment Security (BES) sent out a number of directives to its state employment agencies reminding them not only that discrimination by their own offices was prohibited, but also that referring clients to discriminatory employers was contrary to the BES's policies.[7] It stands to reason, then, that US bureaucrats no longer found it advisable to place American workers in a whites-only guest-worker scheme.

The Canadian delegation appears to have accepted the integration of the program with little resistance, but one aspect did cause some concern: the mixing of white and Black workers on farms. US officials allayed these concerns: "In every state we were given assurance that no trouble need be anticipated if white workers from the States found themselves working with coloured workers," Davison wrote. "It is usual for them to work together in their own localities without any antagonism. There might be instances where objections could be raised if they were expected to share the same sleeping quarters but this was not expected to be of frequent occurrence." This assurance in hand, the Canadians – in no place to bargain given the pressing labour needs of that season – assented to the inclusion of Black workers, along with the Americans' requests for various procedural modifications.[8]

The way officials chose to integrate the program, however, also discriminated against African Americans. Under the new structure, quotas were issued for the percentage of each sending state's workers who were to be Black (it is unclear if the percentages were to apply to the total number of participants or merely to new recruits in the program). In North Carolina, 10 per cent of workers (whether total or new recruits) were to be Black; the corresponding figures were 5 per cent in Virginia; 33 per cent in South Carolina; 10 per cent in Georgia; and 33 per cent in Florida.[9] No evidence is available on whether or not these quotas were followed, and Davison in fact noted that they were to be considered "elastic" rather than exact figures.[10] Neither is it clear how the figures were determined. They did not, for example, match any discernible demographic data for the sending regions: in all states but Florida, the percentages of Black workers to be included in the movement were vastly lower than African Americans' share of the population in the major sending counties. Two examples: in 1970, African Americans made up 44 per cent of the population of Granville County, North Carolina, the biggest sending county in the

Ontario program, but North Carolina's quota of Black workers was just 10 per cent. Meanwhile, the three major sending counties of Virginia – Pittsylvania, Halifax, and Mecklenburg – were all over 33 per cent Black, but Virginia's quota was a mere 5 per cent.[11]

Conscious of the burgeoning civil rights movement in the United States and growing public outcry over racism on both sides of the border, the Marketing Board hoped to avoid negative attention in connection with the arrival of Black workers.[12] They were not successful. When migrants actually began arriving in the tobacco belt for the 1966 harvest, at least twenty-six Blacks were refused employment at their assigned farms, a story picked up by newspapers on both sides of the border.[13] The first migrants to suffer these indignities were a group of twenty-four men from North Carolina and Georgia who, upon being dismissed, returned to the border and crossed back into Buffalo. There, with insufficient funds to return home to the South, they turned to the Traveller's Aid Society, whose staff person Muriel Currier alerted the press to the migrants' plight.[14] "Different ones were told they were not needed because they were colored," Currier told the London Free Press. "I phoned one farmer in the Scotland area [in Norfolk County] and he told me outright that mixing white and coloured would lead to trouble on the farm, and trouble was one thing he could do without." Racist hiring preferences in the sector came as no surprise to Currier: "I toured the tobacco area there a few years back and was told Negro help wasn't preferred." The workers were unable to re-enter Canada because their visas had expired, compelling many to turn to the New York State Employment Service to find farm work in that state in order to pay their way home.[15] The story was repeated a few days later when at least two more Black migrants were refused work and trudged back across the border to Buffalo. This time workers reported being told that the "work wasn't ready for them yet," or that they were "too slow," suggesting that some might have begun working before being dismissed.[16] Officials of the NES and the Marketing Board responded to the reports by denying that there was any "colour bar" in the tobacco fields and refusing to offer any compensation or apology to the affected workers.[17]

Remarkably, at no point during the discussion of the movement's integration nor during its bumpy first year was any mention made – either by government officials or by the press – of Canada's supposedly de-racialized immigration policies, which had come into force by an order-in-council in 1962. Perhaps because it facilitated temporary labour migration rather than permanent immigration, the US scheme – and indeed tobacco's other guest-worker programs – did not register with officials as being in violation of the new rules. And its eventual, if flawed and incomplete, inclusion of Black workers derived not from the changes taking place in Canada, but rather from the changing legal and civil rights landscape in the United States.

In any event, the integration of the US-Ontario movement did not actually facilitate the participation of very many Blacks. A confluence of factors on both sides of the border resulted in a rapid decline of the movement in the years after 1966. (In fact, the decline had begun in the early 1960s, with 1966 standing as something of a "last hurrah" for the movement, occasioned by Ontario growers' desperate labour needs that year). In Canada, technological improvements resulted in fewer growers relying on wage labourers to cure their crops; they increasingly did it themselves. In the United States, two things happened. First, guest-worker arrangements with Mexico and the Caribbean either ceased to exist (in the case of the Mexican Bracero program, in 1964) or removed tobacco farmers as eligible employers (in the Caribbean H-2 program, in 1966), generating increased demand for local labourers. Second, the sharp decline of tobacco agriculture in North Carolina – accompanied by rapid industrial development – took thousands out of tobacco growing and into year-round industrial work, making seasonal migrant labour a decidedly less appealing pursuit.[18] By the late 1970s, the US-Ontario movement had dwindled to little more than a legacy program, with fewer than two hundred tobacco workers – mostly long-serving veterans with close ties to their employers – crossing the border annually (see figure 5.3).

Guest Workers from the Caribbean

The program that would come to be known as the SAWP was founded in 1966,[19] the exact same year as the integration of the US scheme. In that first year, 264 Jamaican men travelled to Canada to work on fruit and vegetable farms and in processing plants. Tobacco growers began employing Caribbean workers the following year, when the sending countries expanded to include Barbados and Trinidad and Tobago. Mexico would join the program in 1974, followed by eight eastern Caribbean states in 1976. (Mexican workers did not work in significant numbers in tobacco for their first decade or two in the SAWP, and

5.3 Workers in the US-Ontario movement, 1931–81. Sources: Satzewich, *Racism and the Incorporation of Foreign Labour*, 108; Agricultural Representatives' Field Reports, Norfolk, 1931–37, RG 16-66, AO; Department of Labour (RG 27, vols 667–8), Immigration Branch (RG 76, vols 853, 1112), and Manpower and Immigration (RG 118, acc. 1985–86/071, vol. 84), LAC.

hence are not discussed in great detail here.[20]) Though the SAWP would come to form the backbone of Canada's horticultural labour force, it took decades of growth, in fits and starts, for it to reach this status. As late as 1985, for example, the SAWP brought just 5,005 workers to Canada, with 1,089 of those working in tobacco, a small percentage of tobacco's roughly 20,000-person harvest workforce (see figure 5.4).

The founding of the SAWP and the particular ways in which it was structured emerged from a complex web of factors in Canada and the Caribbean, as well as on the international plane. In Canada, complaints by farmers about labour shortages and the poor quality of available workers, while they had been commonplace for decades, became particularly acute in the 1950s and '60s as non-agricultural wages rose, making farm work even less attractive to job seekers. While federal agencies sought to organize domestic labour markets to supply

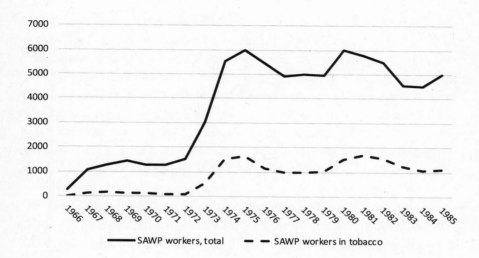

5.4 SAWP workers, total and in tobacco, 1966–85. Sources: Whyte, *The Experience of New Immigrants and Seasonal Farmworkers*, 4.5; Satzewich, *Racism and the Incorporation of Foreign Labour*, 108; Immigration Branch (RG 76, vol. 1112), and Department of Manpower and Immigration (RG 118, vols 244, 246, 273, acc. 1989–90/039, vol. 76), LAC; OFCTGMB Annual Report, 1970, AO.

farms with Canadian workers, many growers were increasingly dissatisfied with these efforts and began lobbying for the creation of a guest-worker scheme with the Caribbean. It is important to note that such lobbying did not come from growers in all agricultural sectors, but was instead confined to certain segments – specifically, Ontario fruit, vegetable, and sugar beet growers and their associations, with sugar beet interests' lobbying efforts occurring largely in the 1950s, and those of fruit and vegetable farmers in the 1960s.[21] Tobacco growers, replete with numerous sources of domestic and foreign labour, played essentially no role in advocating for a Caribbean program, and were quite slow to make significant use of it, as will be discussed later in this chapter.

In asking for Caribbean labour, Canadian growers joined a chorus of West Indian officials who had been lobbying Ottawa for such a program since the 1940s, part of a broader diplomatic agenda aimed at securing opportunities for migration. Emigration (and migrant labour) was seen by colonial – and later independent – governments in the Caribbean as a viable solution for two interrelated problems: poverty and "overpopulation." Historians such as Nicole

Bourbonnais and Karl Ittman have described how the two problems became firmly linked in official discourse in the 1930s, particularly after the pan-Caribbean labour uprisings of that decade, which prompted a Royal Commission on the socio-economic problems of the British West Indies. Under the influence of neo-Malthusian ideas, local elites, the press, and colonial authorities came to see overpopulation as a significant problem and a primary cause of poverty, which contributed to the sort of social unrest witnessed during the 1930s. These conclusions were deeply infused with ideas about race and class: elites were specifically concerned with population growth among "coloured" people and the "lower classes." Curtailing poverty and unemployment would require exerting some control over population growth, and emigration emerged as an important tool for accomplishing this goal (alongside the even more prominent strategy of state-sponsored birth control programs).[22]

There was, of course, nothing new about emigration from the Caribbean. Faced with limited economic opportunities at home, West Indians had been travelling in search of both temporary and permanent employment since the end of slavery throughout the British West Indies in the 1830s – to labour on plantations throughout the circum-Caribbean region, on megaprojects such as the Panama Canal, in metropolises such as New York City and London, and in formal guest-worker programs in the United States and Canada. Labour migration became so central to household economic strategies that historian Bonham C. Richardson has labelled it "a traditional process."[23] In the mid- to late twentieth century, however, Caribbean states became increasingly involved in encouraging emigration as a remedy to overpopulation, both at home and on the diplomatic front,[24] where Caribbean officials repeatedly lobbied the United Kingdom, United States, and Canada to accept more West Indian migrants and to create and expand guest-worker programs. While the temporary exit of migrant workers did not result in a drop in population, it still – in theory at least – served to reduce competition for jobs and direct foreign currency into circulation at home. Alongside programs for domestic (household) workers, agricultural guest-worker schemes emerged as one of the primary vehicles through which Caribbean officials aimed to secure foreign jobs for their constituents.[25] This desire for foreign agricultural jobs dovetailed nicely with a key economic policy prerogative in the newly independent Commonwealth Caribbean: rural development.[26]

When officials from the British West Indies and Canada discussed agricultural guest-worker programs, it occurred within the context of long-standing diplomatic relations on a broad range of portfolios including defence, trade, agriculture, aid, migration, and labour.[27] Caribbean and Canadian officials had even negotiated a pre-existing migrant labour arrangement, the West Indian Domestic Scheme (1955–73), which by the 1960s placed over 250 women per year (from Jamaica, Barbados, Trinidad and Tobago, Guyana, and the eastern Caribbean) in Canadian homes, where they cooked, cleaned, and cared for children and other members of the household.[28] It was within this framework of ongoing, multi-faceted diplomatic relations that West Indian officials repeatedly approached Canada for a farm-worker scheme, with Jamaica and Barbados making requests through various channels in 1947, 1952, and 1954. Each time, they were unsuccessful, in part due to the racist concerns of Canadian officials, who fretted about Black West Indians staying on permanently in Canada and about the mixing of Black men with white Canadian women in rural workplaces, as Vic Satzewich detailed in his 1991 book *Racism and the Incorporation of Foreign Labour.*[29]

Discouraged but not defeated, the West Indians played the long game, strategically planning the timing of their next requests. In the 1960s, things began to turn in their favour. In 1962, Canada officially removed racial and national origin preferences from its immigration policy, with a few exceptions – a change owed in no small part to the lobbying of countries such as Jamaica and Barbados. As these and dozens of other countries around the world gained independence in this era of decolonization, securing positive diplomatic relations with them became an imperative for Canada and other "First World" nations, particularly in the context of the Cold War.[30] Though "deracialization" in reality was a gradual process (many, including the Jamaican high commissioner, accused the Canadian government of clandestinely continuing to discriminate against Jamaicans after 1962), the announcement still represented a monumental shift in policy and was widely hailed in the Caribbean and elsewhere.[31]

Within a few years, Caribbean officials would also get their farm-worker program. As Satzewich explains, years of lobbying by growers' organizations and Caribbean countries received an extra push when labour officials began to issue dire predictions about farm labour shortages in the lead-up to the 1966 harvest season. On 31 March 1966, the federal cabinet finally approved the Canada-West Indies agricultural guest-worker scheme. Jamaica was the sole participant in the first year, though Canada promised to consider extending the program to Barbados and Trinidad and Tobago should the pilot be a success. Canada's relenting in the creation of a farm-worker program cannot simply be chalked up to the trend toward de-racialization of immigration regulations or a liberal awakening among officials; instead, as Satzewich demonstrates, one of the attractions of the program to Immigration bureaucrats was that it would alleviate some of the pressure from Caribbean countries to accept more permanent immigrants.[32] Truly, one of the important concerns of Manpower and Immigration officials as they considered and eventually approved the scheme was that it remain a strictly *seasonal* movement that ensured the departure of participants at season's end.[33] The diplomatic context also mattered: commenting on the approval of the farm-worker program, Jamaica's minister of labour, Lynden Newland, opined that the success of the Domestic Scheme had paved the way for the SAWP.[34]

Interestingly, the SAWP's strictly temporary nature was not explicitly mentioned in communiqués about the program, nor was it outlined in the official agreements between Canada and the sending countries, or in workers' contracts, which strictly covered aspects of the employment relationship and was silent on immigration regulations.[35] This provoked some surprise and consternation among some farmers who, after a satisfactory first year in the program in 1966, wished to offer year-round employment to their Caribbean guest workers but were told that no such provisions existed. The matter was brought before Parliament by Harold Warren Danforth, Progressive Conservative member for Kent, in October 1966, who emphasized the confusion among farmers and workers on the topic of permanent settlement:

> Mr. Speaker ... I posed a question some days ago to the Minister of Manpower and Immigration concerning the provisions under which the workers were brought into this country from Jamaica to assist in the agricultural industry ... The calibre of worker who came into this area ... was very high and their conduct was beyond repute. They did their work very skilfully and to the satisfaction of their employers. My question arises because of the uncertain future of these men who came into Canada

under certain provisions and conditions which were not clearly understood. Certain arrangements apparently were made under which these people must leave this country on completion of their work here. I felt it would be of vital interest to all parties concerned if the provisions under which they entered Canada were placed on the record. I have received many representations, like many other honourable members, from people who are interested in procuring their further services here. Representations have been made in an effort to see that these young men are allowed to stay in this country, particularly those who possess skills which can be employed to the advantage of the areas to which they gave service this summer. My question to the minister is a simple one. Under what provisions did these people come and will the minister place those provisions on the record so that interested parties can become aware of the terms of their transportation in and out of this country? If this can be done, these prospective employers will know the proper channels through which they can obtain the services of these men, and the men in turn will know how to obtain immigrant status as workers here.

Responding to Danforth, Liberal John Carr Munro, parliamentary secretary of manpower and immigration, disputed the alleged lack of clarity on the question, saying that the temporary nature of the program had been clearly articulated and was widely understood. "If any of these workers should decide in the future that they would like to become immigrants, and if they have the necessary qualifications," Munro concluded, "then they would at that time be admissible in the ordinary way. They cannot be accorded special treatment because they came for seasonal work, on conditions strictly defined as temporary."[36] Munro's claims of clarity notwithstanding, internal communications at the Department of Manpower and Immigration suggests a tacit admission that the messaging around permanent residency could have been much clearer, with official R.M. Mackie emphasizing in a letter that, in the second year of the program, Jamaican workers should be clearly informed that if they desire to stay permanently in Canada, they will have to return home to Jamaica after the completion of their contract and apply "through the proper channels."[37]

The SAWP and the North American Guest-Worker Complex

One element of the founding of the Caribbean-Canada scheme that has been underemphasized in the literature is the all-important role played by already-existing guest-worker arrangements – in particular the United States–West Indian farm-worker program – both in helping to connect bureaucrats from Canada and the Caribbean, and in serving as a model for the Canadian program. It is essential to understand that the SAWP emerged not only from a long history of connections between Canada and the Caribbean (and years of pressure from those countries and employer groups), but also from what we might think of as the North American guest-worker complex. This complex featured a wide array of guest-worker programs, agricultural schemes in particular, which sent workers back and forth between a number of countries and territories. It was also characterized by linkages between the labour bureaucracies of the sundry nations that participated in such schemes. These networks, and the meetings, conferences, and correspondence that took place within them, provided opportunities for transnational learning and the forging of new connections, ultimately facilitating the creation of new guest-worker programs. The core of this system was undoubtedly the United States, and by far the dominant dynamic was the movement of workers from other North American and Caribbean countries (including Canada) to the United States, but periphery-to-periphery movements like the SAWP also developed.

The United States' long-standing migrant labour arrangements with both Canada and various Caribbean countries meant that officials from both places usually attended the annual National Farm Labor Conference and other similar meetings organized by the US Department of Labor. While Caribbean delegates attended to discuss the arrangements that sent West Indian workers to the United States (in place since 1942), Canadian representatives were in the unusual position of discussing movements of labourers in both directions. To be sure, in most years a larger number of seasonal workers went from Canada to the United States than the other way around. Grain harvesters from the prairies, and woods workers, apple pickers, and potato harvesters from Quebec and New Brunswick were especially important here. In 1960, for example, about 8,000 Canadian farm workers worked in the northeastern United States, the vast majority in Maine's potato harvest, and another six thousand or more worked in logging operations. The only significant movement in the other direction were the tobacco workers, who, though fewer in number than south-bound Canadian migrants (3,400 Americans tobacco workers came to Canada in 1960), still represented an important item on the agenda at the annual meetings.[38] If it appears paradoxical for guest workers to have been travelling in both directions across the border, it is worth pointing out that labour markets rarely conform to national boundaries. Workers participating in cross-border movements typically did not come from regions that were simultaneously recipients of migrant labour from the other country. In other words, these are – in an economic if not administrative sense – much more accurately characterized as transregional movements rather than binational ones.

The annual Farm Labor Conference not only provided Caribbean and Canadian officials with an opportunity to meet with their American counterparts; it also gave them a chance to discuss potential guest-worker agreements between their own countries. At meetings in 1960, for example, Harry F. Edwards,[39] the chief liaison officer for the British West Indies Central Labour Organisation (the body that supervised the United States–Caribbean program, sponsored by the various participating West Indian governments), spoke with representatives from Canada's Department of Labour and Ontario's Ministry of Agriculture about "Canadian prospects." The Canadians were at the meetings primarily to discuss the US tobacco worker movement, and Edwards immediately recognized the potential for West Indians to undertake the same work, explaining in a report that "workers of this category make an annual trek to Ontario and return home after several months employment in doing work which is extremely simple and is done by West Indian workers both in their homelands and in Connecticut – that is, looking after the growing and harvesting of leaf or field tobacco as opposed to shade tobacco grown in Connecticut." Well aware of previous efforts on the matter, Edwards took the opportunity to lobby once again for the inclusion of Caribbean guest workers in Canada, and he was apparently supported by US officials on the matter. As he later wrote, "the Canadians were hard put to justify to the Americans the use of American nationals and the prohibition of BWIS [British West Indians]."[40] What Edwards likely did not know, of course, was that the "American nationals" working in Canada included no Blacks.[41]

The US–West Indies guest-worker program also served as a model for the SAWP; indeed, it was cited as a prime example of a successful scheme by Caribbean officials and Canadian employers alike as they lobbied the Canadian government for a similar program.[42] Their arguments did not fall on deaf ears: a key part of Canadian officials' research into the feasibility of the proposals involved investigations of the US model, including visits to West Indian–employing sugar cane plantations in Florida, where everything from working conditions to menus were studied in detail.[43]

When Canada finally acceded to the years of pressure from Caribbean governments and employer organizations in 1966, much of the program's structure and regulations were essentially cut and pasted from the US–West Indies scheme. As Jamaica's minister of labour and national insurance explained in a submission to cabinet, "The proposals agreed to are largely on the basis of the current United States Farm Labour Programme, with similar provisions for the protection of workers."[44] As in the US program, workers would be recruited by Jamaican government officials and assigned to a pre-designated employer in the receiving country, and government-appointed liaison officers would oversee the program's operations while workers were on contract. Just like the US labourers, a significant proportion of the wages of Canada-bound workers (20 per cent initially; 25 per cent in later years) would be deducted and remitted directly to the Jamaican Ministry of Labour: the bulk of which as part of a compulsory savings plan, only accessible upon return home, the remainder retained to pay for program costs. Insurance coverage for participants was arranged simply by extending the existing plan for US workers to the new (and by comparison tiny) program. Procedures for medical examinations were also copied.[45] Even the worker identification cards were lifted from the US scheme. As a Canadian government memo explained, "A Jamaican identification card for the Canadian worker movement was made up merely by using the United States card as a basis and substituting all reference to u.s.a. with Canada."[46]

State officials in both Canada and the Caribbean repeatedly considered borrowing yet another feature from the US program: a regional body to organize program recruitment and oversight. The participating British West Indian colonies in the US scheme had formed the Regional Labour Board (RLB) in 1951 to collectively negotiate contract terms with American employers and allocate program spots among sending islands. A subsidiary organization, the British West Indian Central Labour Organisation, was formed to handle liaison services, which had previously been conducted by each colony in isolation.[47] Jamaican and Canadian authorities expressed interest at various points in extending the RLB to manage the SAWP (or creating a parallel regional organization), but Jamaica's dominance of the board made this a decidedly less appealing option to Barbados and Trinidad and Tobago. A regional organizing body never did come into effect, with each sending country instead maintaining their own bilateral agreements with Canada.[48] Still, the US program and the RLB continued to play a role in the SAWP. In 1968 in Jamaica, the administration of the Canadian program was simply added to the responsibilities of the committee in charge of the US scheme. And the RLB's country-by-country allocations of spots in the US program served as points of reference for Canada's SAWP.[49]

Worker Selection and Sending-Country Interests

In embarking on this new guest-worker arrangement, few matters were as important to sending countries as worker selection. Structures and regulations were one thing, but it was people who would make the program work – or not. Given governments' lofty aspirations for the scheme, which was counted on to contribute to rural development, alleviate unemployment, and foster closer diplomatic ties with Canada, selecting the right sort of worker became a top priority. "Much depends on the initial selection," wrote Jamaica's minister of labour, Lynden G. Newland, in a 1966 submission to the Jamaican cabinet outlining the scheme. Newland's ministry determined that the ideal participant was a single man aged twenty to thirty with at least two years of agricultural experience and "of medium build, energetic, nimble and not colour-blind." Curiously for a guest-worker program, they also preferred that workers be literate. "Only by rigidly adhering to the selection requirements will the venture stand a chance of succeeding," Newland wrote.

The measure of success would be easily determined: the continued existence of the program, along with an "enlargement of the numbers engaged on Canadian farms each year." Newland also held out hope that the "satisfactory performance" of farm workers could lead to employment and immigration opportunities for Jamaicans in other sectors in "the expanding Canadian economy," a desire that helps to explain the literacy requirement.[50] It also represents a bitter irony around the founding of the SAWP. Not only was Newland's hope for more permanent immigration never reciprocated by his Canadian counterparts; they were in fact motivated by exactly the opposite logic, hoping that the granting of a farm-worker scheme would alleviate pressure to accept more permanent immigrants from the West Indies.

Newland's adamance when it came to selection criteria was also closely bound up with the role of patronage in the recruitment of guest workers. The US scheme was plainly operated within a system of patronage: potential participants were recommended by district committees appointed by members of Parliament in their electoral districts – the pathway taken by Gladston Williams, whose story opened this chapter. Unsurprisingly, this set-up posed problems for meritocratic worker selection, and it was frequently criticized by whichever party happened to be in opposition (for obvious reasons), but also by Newland himself while serving as minister of labour. Rising above partisan considerations, Newland voiced concerns that patronage-driven selection resulted in workers who were more likely to breach their contracts, thus damaging the program's reputation. Despite these critiques, patronage remained the organizing logic of the US scheme.[51] The new Canadian program, however, offered an opportunity to turn over a new leaf, and Newland proposed establishing civil servant–run recruitment centres in rural areas whose staff would be able to conduct non-partisan recruitment. "This departure from the Committee system of the United States Farm Labour Programme is thought to be necessary to make certain that the right types of workers are selected," he explained to cabinet.[52]

But much like his desire for the Canadian farm-worker program to lead to expanded opportunities for Jamaicans in Canada, Newland's dreams of patronage-free recruitment did not come true. In the end, applicants selected for the participant pool were chosen by MPs' parish representatives in much the same way as participants in the US program.[53] In 1985, a Canadian High Commission staffer described in detail how the allocation of new spots in the program was distributed among government ministers: 150 "tickets" were reserved for the minister of labour to hand out; 50 for the prime minister; 30–50 each for the deputy prime minister and minister of agriculture; 30 for all other cabinet ministers; and 25 for all other government MPs. Patronage shaped not just participation in the program, but also the staffing of ancillary services such as medical examinations, a fact that, the Canadian official remarked, "may account for the relatively low calibre of medical documentation."[54] Patronage appeared to play little if any role in recruitment in Barbados and Trinidad and Tobago.[55]

The selection process was not a point of priority only for sending countries. It also attracted the attention of Canadian employers and civil servants, specifically at times when they perceived problems with the quality of workers being recruited. This was particularly salient during the first few years of the program. After a problem-filled first year in the scheme for Trinidad and Tobago, that country's permanent secretary of labour "admitted that some selections were unfortunate and might have been avoided." Some of the recruits weren't farm workers, and others should have been denied on medical grounds. To remedy selection issues, Trinidad assigned worker selection for the following year to the Department of Agriculture and planned to conduct more "counselling" of workers prior to departure.[56] Similarly, after Jamaica's first year in the program, a Manpower official called for a "more discerning" selection of workers in Jamaica. A spot check of twenty identification cards found that seven lived not in the countryside but in Kingston, and that other participants worked regularly as "tailors, mechanics, barbers and electricians" rather than as farmers or farm workers.[57] While officials appeared mostly content with the evolution of selection procedures after the program's first few years, they would continue to periodically encourage Caribbean governments to improve their selection procedures in the coming years.[58]

Caribbean Officials and the Evolution of the SAWP

The SAWP, rather than a fixed entity, was in a constant state of evolution. Just as they did in the program's founding, officials from Caribbean governments played critical roles in securing changes to the SAWP's protocols. Indeed, two of the hallmark features of the SAWP – both among those that have received the sharpest critiques from academics and worker advocates – were added to the scheme after 1966, not at the behest of power-hungry employers or conniving Canadian bureaucrats, but instead as a result of lobbying by Caribbean envoys. The first of these, the "naming" mechanism, allowed farmers to request specific workers to return to their employ each year. The naming system has been marked by scholars as an important bolster to employer control: since named workers receive priority for re-entering the program each year, there is a strong disincentive against complaining about work conditions.[59] The idea of having "nominated workers" was pitched to Manpower and Immigration by representatives of all three participating countries – Jamaica, Barbados, and

Trinidad and Tobago – during meetings in 1967. Presumably, their interest lay in protecting their countries' existing positions within the program. As we have seen, for countries such as Jamaica, guarding and increasing the number of spots in the program was imperative if the SAWP were to play its part in the nation's bold program of economic development. Domestic political considerations were also undoubtedly a factor. The loss of program spots would have been politically damaging in any sending country, patronage-dominated or not. Indeed, guest-worker programs, and the number of positions within them, became signature policy items and campaign planks for political parties in sending countries – and remain so to this day.[60] The three participating West Indian nations met no opposition in their proposal of the naming procedure. Canadian representatives "recognized that the practice was both acceptable and desirable," and employers liked it too; it soon formed part of the program.[61]

The second much-critiqued aspect of the SAWP that was instituted in part at the behest of sending countries was the ability of employers to select workers by country of origin. This feature has been accurately described as a curious exception to the end of race- and origin-based immigrant selection criteria in Canada in the 1960s.[62] Country-based selection was first proposed by Jamaican Labour officials during a 1973 visit to Canada. Their rationale was that if farmers were free to do so, they would surely choose Jamaicans over Barbadians or Trinidadians. As Minister of Labour Ernest G. Peart recounted in a report to cabinet on the trip, "It was recommended by the Jamaican delegation that farmers should be allowed to request and obtain workers from a specific participating country. It was argued that some farmers reduce or hold down the size of their migrant work force because they cannot recruit from a particular country. Because of this the Programme suffers and Jamaica is denied an increase in the number of workers she provides."[63] Peart's reasoning is supported by the recollections of a Canadian farmer who joined the program in the early 1970s. The grower recalled being miffed when he was assigned Barbadian workers, who had a reputation for standing up for themselves, and insisted on receiving Jamaicans instead, threatening to go directly to Ottawa if he didn't get his way.[64]

Despite the alignment of employer and Jamaican interests, the Jamaican representatives were not immediately successful in securing this change to program protocols. Canadian officials resisted the initiative in part because it would disrupt the quota allocations between the three participating countries.

But they also prefigured a critique that would be raised by future scholars of the sawp. The Canadians explained to their Jamaican counterparts that "free choice on the part of farmers ... would be contrary to the Canadian legislation."[65] But Canadian hesitancy around this issue appears to have been short-lived. By the time the end-of-year report on the program was penned a few months later, Manpower officials were considering two proposed changes for how employers would request workers: under "proposal A," employers would be allowed to specify a particular country from which they did *not* want workers; or, under "proposal B," they would be able to "indicate which Island they preferred."[66] While it is not clear which – if any – of these options were immediately chosen, we do know that sometime before 1987, "proposal B" came into effect.[67] Other procedural aspects of the program, such as extending workers' maximum length of stay in Canada, were also modified at the request of Caribbean representatives, with the support of employers.[68]

The SAWP and West Indian Diplomacy

The program was also shaped by the diplomatic agendas of West Indian countries. Scholars of the sawp have emphasized the competition between the Caribbean and Mexico, among both government agents and workers, for spots in the program and in securing a reputation as the most attractive sending region.[69] While Caribbean-Mexican competition has indeed been important in the history of the sawp, by flattening the Caribbean participants into one unit, researchers have largely missed the intense competition that existed between West Indian countries, particularly in the program's early years. Jamaica, having done the heavy lifting to negotiate the initial Canadian agreement, was not thrilled to see the program expand to new countries in only its second year. The Kingston *Daily Gleaner* reported that Newland "hoped that when this matter was being considered the part played by Jamaica in taking the scheme off the ground would be reflected in the quota allocation to Jamaica."[70] The addition of Trinidad and Tobago and Barbados also prompted concern among Jamaican officials about maintaining their position in the program. In a 1967 submission to cabinet, Newland worried especially about the "incidence of workers going a.w.o.l.," which was bestowing "considerable hardship on small employers." With the "Eastern Caribbean territories ... now offering competition to the Jamaican workers in the Canadian Scheme," reducing the frequency of workers' breaking contracts as well as the wait times for furnishing replacement workers became a matter of utmost importance. Citing one case in which there had been complications in supplying an employer with a replacement, Newland anxiously wrote, "The fact that to date no replacement has been made is being increasingly known to employers in Canada and is militating against the Jamaica Scheme in favour of Barbados and Trinidad."[71]

All three participating countries kept close watch on the number of workers selected from the other two, and when they felt their citizens were being underrepresented, did not hesitate to complain. In August 1968, for example, Trinidadian authorities protested that more Barbadians than Trinidadians were travelling to Canada to work in the program. A telegram from Canada's immigration officer in Port of Spain explained that "[Trinidad and Tobago's] govt is concerned about this trend since they feel that based on population they should send twice as many workers on the program as Barbados."[72] The target allocations were in fact 50 per cent to Jamaica, 30 per cent to Trinidad and Tobago, and 20 per cent to Barbados.[73]

The battles within the program were also waged on the ground in Canada, where at least one government report noted that Jamaican liaison officer Noel Heron was instructing employers of Trinidadians on how to repatriate their workers in order to hire Jamaicans instead.[74] It was not until Mexico was added in 1974 that a degree of regional solidarity entered into Caribbean representatives' approach to the program. Faced with a new competitor whose population and historic participation in guest-worker programs dwarfed those of the Commonwealth Caribbean, representatives of the three West Indian participants orchestrated a coordinated response to their Canadian counterparts in an attempt to secure guarantees for their countries' position within the program.[75] This effort did not bear much fruit. In fact, the reduction of bargaining power on the part of Caribbean governments was precisely one of the reasons for adding Mexico to the program. As a Manpower staffer wrote in 1974, "The signing of the Mexican arrangement not only gives us an alternative source of supply of agricultural workers but it also acts as a balancing force to the Caribbean supply. The latter is especially important, for we have noted in the last two years, at least, a 'take-it-or-leave-it' attitude with the Caribbean liaison officers almost in direct proportion to the increased use of the Caribbean program."[76]

Social Mobility for SAWP Workers?

If rural development and reducing unemployment were two key goals of guest-worker programs for sending countries, how successful were participants in achieving these aims? In other words, did the SAWP, even amid the vanishing opportunities for social mobility *within* the tobacco sector, enable Mexican and Caribbean workers to advance socio-economically outside of it, in their home countries, in a sort of transnational social mobility? While there can be little doubt that SAWP workers found the wages earned in Canada to be beneficial and that some were indeed able to progress socio-economically, the social mobility record for SAWP workers was decidedly more muted than the rising-tide abundance that characterized the tobacco sector in its early decades.

There is some debate in the literature about just how economically beneficial migrant labour was for participants in North American guest-worker schemes. Most scholars have agreed that a large portion of wages earned on guest-worker stints in the United States and Canada go toward fulfilling familial consumption needs, but there is some disagreement over how often participants have been able to extend their earnings further and consolidate any tangible form of social mobility. A few studies have been overwhelmingly positive in their findings. For example, Amani Ishemo and colleagues, in an in-depth study of rural communities in Jamaica's Rio Grande Valley, found significant differences in the agricultural operations of families with members who participated in temporary foreign labour programs versus families without guest workers. Temporary labour migrants owned farms averaging more than twice the acreage of non-participants (5.4 acres compared to 2). Guest workers were also more likely to engage in export agriculture, in part because they could afford the capital outlay required to enter into such enterprises. In sum, the authors conclude that "temporary overseas migration had a profound positive impact on the survival of farming in the Rio Grande Valley."[77]

Most studies of migrant West Indian and Mexican farm workers' economic outcomes, however, have been somewhat less bullish, finding that while foreign earnings help marginally improve workers' standards of living, these workers typically have to continue in the programs in order to maintain their elevated status.[78] Anne V. Whyte, in a 1984 study of farm workers from Barbados and the eastern Caribbean, produced some statistics that tend to support the latter interpretation. Whyte found that while most remittances were used for day-to-day expenses, "repair and upgrading of the house structure is the single most common objective that the farmworkers have for their earnings." A decent percentage were successful in this regard: 38 per cent of Whyte's survey respondents had purchased a home since joining the Canadian program, while 54 per cent were saving toward this end. Twenty per cent had purchased a car. Land was a trickier proposition, with just 8 per cent using Canadian earnings to obtain it.[79] Another very popular usage of SAWP earnings is to fund children's education, fostering intergenerational social mobility. The former SAWP workers I interviewed for this book echoed these findings, with workers reporting using wages earned in Canada for basic consumption needs, home construction or improvement, and children's school costs.[80] Interviewees also tended to be fairly lukewarm in their assessments of just how far Canadian wages could go back home. Barbadian Victor Bovell, for example, qualified that the benefit of Canadian wages depended a lot on the fluctuating exchange rate.[81]

In sum, what we find are impressive efforts by Caribbean and Mexican SAWP workers to use their earnings to secure improved living standards that are hampered by the extreme difficulty of doing so on a few months' work at Canadian minimum wage rates, all while maintaining extensive responsibilities in their home countries. In other words, important though home construction and repairs, the expansion of entrepreneurial activities, and the funding of children's education undoubtedly are for individual guest workers from the Global South, the promises of rural development or social mobility that justify the existence of these programs for sending countries cannot be said to have come to fruition in any comprehensive way.

Work-Abroad University Students from Europe

Tobacco's third guest-worker scheme, the European Student Tobacco Worker Program,[82] was also launched in the busy year of 1966, and brought university students from western and central Europe to work the golden leaf. The European program consisted of a patchwork of arrangements with civil society groups and private firms in the various sending countries, which were approved and monitored, but not administered, by the Department of Manpower and Immigration – in contrast to the more tightly regulated, bilateral US and Caribbean schemes.

The European program was part of an international wave of work- and volunteer-abroad initiatives that, beginning in the 1950s, facilitated the temporary migration of educated, typically middle-class, white young people from the Global North to work (whether for pay or not) in other countries – a wave that has yet to abate. While the histories of overseas volunteer initiatives such as the Peace Corps, British Voluntary Service Overseas, and Canadian University Service Overseas have been well-documented,[83] comparatively little historiographical attention has been paid to the work-abroad programs that cropped up in many wealthy countries in the same era. The two types of movements bore some important resemblances. Both made similar claims about the benefits to participants, who by gaining international experience would broaden their horizons, gain confidence and independence, and make themselves more attractive candidates to top-tier universities and future employers – trading in what some scholars have labelled "the economy of experience."[84] Furthermore, both volunteer- and work-abroad schemes were situated within a broad ideology of liberal internationalism, concerned as it was with making transnational connections and breaking down the barriers of distance and prejudice separating countries – while remaining firmly ensconced in the liberal order of the Western bloc. There were also crucial differences: an added benefit for working-holiday programs was the attraction of wages, and they did not make the same claims about spreading development and democracy as did volunteer organizations, whose mandates were deeply shaped by Cold War geopolitical prerogatives.[85]

Working-holiday programs were (and are) typically structured as bilateral agreements between countries that allow for the temporary (usually one to two years) employment of qualifying nationals from one country in the other, with placements in either direction permitted. Canada has participated in such arrangements since at least the early 1960s, when various agreements allowed for the temporary movement of young people – often university students studying agriculture – to work on Canadian farms.[86] Quebec and France established their own exchange arrangements for both education and work in the late 1960s, under the Office franco-québécois pour la jeunesse, part of the establishment and fortification of direct diplomatic ties between the two francophone polities in this era (often to the frustration of Ottawa).[87] These programs have frequently been framed as primarily cultural exchanges, but in fact many economic sectors have become dependent on this form of labour.[88] While working-holiday programs should be understood as part of the larger constellation of temporary foreign labour programs, there are of course important differences between these and other schemes that bring largely racialized migrants to labour in sectors such as agriculture and domestic work. Most notably, working-holiday schemes have generally been arranged only between wealthy, often predominantly white, countries (with some exceptions). For example, as of 2017, Canada held such "mobility agreements" with 32 countries: 24 were members of the Organisation for Economic Co-operation and Development, and another 24 (though not an identical group) were European. These temporary migrants have also generally enjoyed better working conditions and have found it easier to access permanent residency.[89]

The Ontario tobacco belt might seem an unusual destination for student workers in such a program, and perhaps it was, but the original connection was made by way of the district's diasporic European communities, in particular the Belgians.[90] The seeds of the scheme were first planted during a trip taken by members of Delhi's Belgium Club to Belgium in 1965, when the visitors crossed paths with representatives of the organization Belgium in the World (in Dutch called Vlamingen in de Wereld – literally "Flemings in the World"). Founded by a Catholic priest, Father Arthur Verthé, Belgium in the World was dedicated to strengthening connections between global diasporic Belgian (specifically Flemish) communities and the mother country, accomplishing its goal in part through student exchanges. In conversations between the two groups, the idea was hatched to arrange a movement of Belgian students to travel to Ontario and work in the tobacco harvest. They had little trouble securing assent from the Department of Manpower and Immigration, who approved the entrance of 340 Belgian students for the harvest of 1966. The venture was framed as part work-abroad opportunity, part cultural exchange. In addition to a summer job, students would learn first-hand about a diasporic Belgian community, develop experience in agriculture, and see a new country.[91]

The news that the tobacco sector's Belgian farmers would be receiving workers from their home country created interest among other tobacco belt communities to start similar movements of their own, and in the coming

5.5 Austrian university students working in tobacco, Straffordville, Ontario, 1968.
Courtesy of Elgin County Archives. "British And Austrian Students Aid in Harvest,"
1 August 1968, St Thomas Times-Journal fonds, c8 sh2 b2 f4 33, Elgin County Archives.

months and years arrangements were made to bring over students from Austria
(1966), West Germany (1967), and the Netherlands (1971). Exchanges with
European countries without significant ethnic communities in the tobacco
belt were also initiated, modelling the example of Belgium in the World. These
included France (1966), the United Kingdom (1968), and Ireland (1978).[92] Some
movements were operated on a purely private basis, others by student organizations, and still others by civil society groups – though these did not always
eschew profit.

While the schemes were justified using the lofty ideals of internationalism
and cultural exchange – with one Manpower official going so far as to say
that the Belgian movement was "primarily a cultural arrangement in which

employment is really incidental"[93] – they could also be money-making opportunities for organizers. This was particularly true for the initial Belgian
program in 1966, when the arrangement was structured so that workers' wages
(sixteen dollars a day) were paid directly to Belgium in the World, which then
released a dollar a day back to workers. This was ostensibly done to recoup the
costs of travel, administration, and a one-week sightseeing tour planned for
the end of harvest. In reality, the set-up lined the pockets of the "benevolent"
society, which Canadian officials reported made $50,000 in profit off the 340
Belgian students who participated in 1966. The findings prompted a serious
review of the program and forced the group to bring its practices in line with
those of the other movements.[94]

From 1967 onwards, the various schemes coalesced around the same basic
financial structure (which the Austrian and French movements had utilized
from the beginning). Students who signed up for the program were given a
seat on a charter flight to Toronto, transported to the tobacco belt, and placed
on a farm. They agreed to pay a flat fee from their wages to reimburse the organizing body for their travel and other expenses (including insurance and
occasional sightseeing tours programmed for after the harvest). Student
workers were to be paid the prevailing harvest wage rates.[95] Of course, profits
were surely still made off the schemes – one doubts that the Canadian National
Railway, contracted by a benevolent society to operate the French movement,
was involved purely out of goodwill, for example – but the structure implemented after 1966 ensured that those profits would be somewhat limited. Organizers also appear to have been motivated at times by the prestige associated
with managing the programs: archival records contain multiple stories of competition between different groups and actors in Europe for the official blessing
of the Marketing Board and Manpower to organize a particular country's
movement.[96] Like the US and Caribbean programs, the European program
eventually allowed growers to request workers by name.[97] The program's peak
years were 1973 to 1975, when it supplied between 1,100 and 1,400 migrant
workers to the tobacco harvest each year. It declined relatively quickly soon
after, dropping to under 400 workers per year by the late 1970s, largely due to
the government's desire to limit the program amid high rates of Canadian unemployment. It remained popular with participating growers, however, and
as late as 1991, it still brought about 200 workers across the Atlantic to work
the harvest.[98]

Racism and the European-West Indian Double Standard

The speed and ease with which the European schemes were developed and approved by Canadian authorities contrasted sharply with the long ordeal required to institute a guest-worker program with the West Indies. An examination of the founding of the Austrian scheme illustrates the point. Inspired by the Belgian arrangement, a tobacco farmer in Langton, Nick Horvath Jr, wrote to a university student friend in Austria describing the Belgian scheme and suggesting that he explore the possibilities of organizing something similar with Austrian students. (Though the tobacco belt did not have an Austrian community, many of its large quotient of ethnic German growers were keen to hire German-speaking students.) Horvath's friend, Paul Pflamitzer, found sixty-six students willing to make the trek, signed them up, and booked travel arrangements for them to fly to New York City and then make their way to Ontario by bus or rail. All of this was done without any consultation with Canadian immigration authorities. The Department of Manpower and Immigration was first alerted to the plan on 11 May 1966, less than three months from the start of harvest, in a letter from the visa office at the Canadian Embassy in Vienna. Ottawa was not impressed. "We cannot approve this plan ... Private arrangements of this type are unacceptable," responded a Manpower official. Any proposed temporary labour scheme would have to go through the appropriate channels and receive approval well ahead of time, just as had been done for the new Caribbean program – or for that matter, the Belgian student movement.[99]

But the winds of diplomacy were blowing in Pflamitzer's favour. The Canadian Embassy in Vienna urged Manpower to reconsider, given the contributions that such a movement could make to "our Austrian promotional effort." Specifically, the diplomats reasoned that the work-abroad scheme could serve as "an effective promotional campaign" for skilled Austrian immigration to Canada. They also argued that refusing the movement "will have an unfavourable effect on Canada's image" (a somewhat perplexing statement considering the circumstances). Pressure also came from the Tobacco Growers' Marketing Board, whose fears of labour shortage had prompted the special trip to the United States that spring that had resulted in the US movement's integration. After receiving assurances from the Marketing Board that they would guarantee jobs and lodging for the Austrian students, Manpower and

Immigration agreed in late June – if somewhat begrudgingly – to approve the plan.[100] The French movement was likewise organized without prior government approval.[101]

Compared with the quixotic, decades-long quest of West Indian diplomats and Ontario growers to secure a Caribbean guest-worker program, the slapdash, cart-before-horse manner in which the Austrian and French work-abroad schemes were organized and approved was nothing short of astounding. Even the Belgian arrangement, which went through the proper channels, was launched at breakneck speed: first proposed to Immigration authorities on 9 November 1965, the scheme was approved a mere six weeks later, on 22 December.

What explanation could there be for such a discrepancy, other than racism? Considering especially the well-documented racist reasoning for Canadian officials' foot-dragging on a Caribbean farm-worker program, it would be either naive or extremely charitable to conclude otherwise. Even Immigration bureaucrats were aware of the hypocrisy of their position. "I have been getting increasingly concerned at the possibility of embarrassment to this Department in connection with our policies regarding the admission of seasonal farm labour," wrote the assistant deputy minister for immigration to his deputy minister in March 1966, alerting him to a request from the *Globe and Mail* for comment on the Belgian student arrangement. "On the one hand," he explained, "we have for several years been resisting pressure from growers' associations and the West Indians for a seasonal farm worker movement." On the other, however, European students were being permitted to enter Canada as seasonal workers – not only the Belgians destined to come later that year, but also Norwegian and Danish students who had been taking harvest jobs in western Canada for the past few years, numbering 190 in 1965. The assistant deputy minister worried that this discrepancy could be "brought up as evidence of inconsistency and possibly even discrimination in our position." In the event that this line of questioning was brought forward by the *Globe* reporter, he advised his superior to "emphasize ... that the movements from Europe are restricted to students or trainees and that they are largely designed to promote cultural exchanges and provide experience for the students in question." Of course, even this dodge sustained the double standard between farm labour migration from Europe and from the Caribbean, implying that "students and trainees" and "cultural exchanges" were categories that could be applied to Europeans but not to Black West Indians.[102]

A final mid-1960s scheme for importing European farm labour drives home even further the double standard between such initiatives and the West Indian program. In 1965, the Ontario Department of Agriculture, with the support of the Immigration Branch, launched a scheme to recruit permanent immigrants from the United Kingdom to perform year-round work on farms – principally on dairy and mixed-crop farms. By 1967, a reported 175 immigrant farm labourers had crossed the Atlantic. In contrast to the bulk placements of the West Indian program, participants in the UK scheme were hand-picked by representatives of the Ontario government after individual interviews, and civil servants kept close tabs on the satisfaction of workers and employers alike after the placement began.[103]

Overlapping nearly perfectly with the beginning of the SAWP, the difference in the official language describing the two schemes could not be more stark. Whereas the temporary nature of the Caribbean program had been a matter of common sense for federal officials – even to the extent, as we saw earlier, that that characteristic was not always explicitly stated and thus not always clear to all parties – a very different logic was advanced by Ontario bureaucrats in explaining the UK scheme. "We are acutely short of skilled and experienced farm labour," Department of Agriculture representative Gordon Skinner told a local publication while on a recruiting trip to Scotland. "We need married men who are not seeking part-time employment. They must be men who want year-round work and will settle with their families." Boasting of the program's success, Skinner added, "We have been raising the status of farmworkers in Ontario by this scheme. Other farmers, who are not in the scheme, will learn the lesson."[104] It is unclear exactly what lesson farmers were supposed to learn, but perhaps it was that if they wanted to recruit permanent immigrants as farm labourers, then they had better be white.

The Incorporation of Guest Workers in Tobacco

It is often assumed that foreign workers – specifically those in the SAWP – rapidly replaced Canadian farm workers after 1966. But this is not what happened – not in any crop, and especially not in tobacco. In tobacco, the total number of guest workers remained fairly steady after the introduction of the Caribbean and European programs, fluctuating between 1,000 and 3,500 from the mid-1960s to the mid-1980s. In fact, this represented a slight decline from the mid-1950s, when the arrivals of US workers, then tobacco's only guest workers, topped 4,000 in two consecutive years (1956 and 1957). Far from radically changing tobacco farmers' labour practices, the new guest workers from the Caribbean and Europe simply replaced the long-standing US movement as it rapidly declined. Guest workers continued to account for less than 10 per cent of the overall workforce, which remained overwhelmingly comprised of locals and Canadian migrant workers into the 1980s. Even in the broader agricultural workforce, SAWP workers remained a small minority: in 1981, for example, the SAWP brought in about 5,700 workers (the third-highest total in its sixteen-year history up to that point), accounting for fewer than 10 per cent of the estimated 70,000 wage labourers on Ontario farms that year.[105]

Out of the two new additions to the guest-worker menu, tobacco growers were especially slow to select SAWP workers, hiring European students in greater numbers than West Indians in each of the first seven years (1967–73) in which they had access to both. It was not until 1973 that more than 200 Caribbean guest workers were placed on tobacco farms, and not until the late 1980s or so that SAWP workers (now including Mexicans) in tobacco surpassed 1,700.[106] In its dealings with Manpower and Immigration, the Marketing Board consistently expressed greater interest in securing Europeans rather than SAWP workers. In 1973, for example, when Marketing Board chairman George Demeyere wrote to Manpower officials to plan for the larger 1973 workforce, his main lobbying objective was a doubling of the quota for European students – a goal in which he was successful. He mentioned the West Indian program but explained, "Our farmers have never used the Caribbean Seasonal Workers to a large extent."[107] In later years, growers' requests for more European students would be denied, and soon federal officials were placing ever-tighter limits on the work-abroad program, wary as they were of potential negative press about the importation of student workers while young Canadians were unemployed. In fact, officials repeatedly tried to nudge tobacco growers away from the European scheme and toward the Caribbean.[108]

The main reason tobacco growers did not turn wholesale to temporary foreign workers was, quite simply, that they already had sufficient sources of labour. Though they occasionally grumbled about labour turnover and

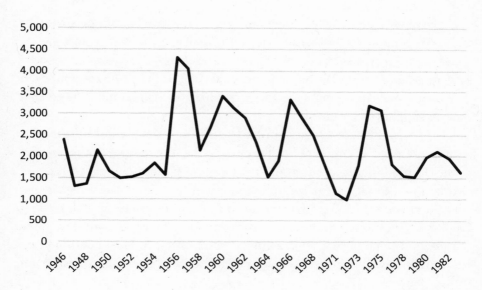

5.6 Total guest workers in Ontario tobacco, 1946–83. Sources: Whyte, *The Experience of New Immigrants and Seasonal Farmworkers*, 4.5; Satzewich, *Racism and the Incorporation of Foreign Labour*, 108; Immigration Branch (RG 76, vol. 1112), and Department of Manpower and Immigration (RG 118, vols 244, 246, 273, acc. 1989–90/039, vol. 76), LAC; OFCTGMB Annual Report, 1970, AO.

unsatisfactory workers, unlike among fruit and vegetable farmers, there was little talk about crops rotting in the fields and no crisis of labour shortage, perceived or otherwise. In fact, in many years, down to the early 1980s, as in the past, the tobacco belt experienced the exact opposite problem: a surplus of labourers that left crowds of unlucky job seekers stranded in tobacco towns after the start of harvest, unemployed and unsure of their next move.[109]

Indeed, tobacco's persistently high wages continued to make it an attractive temporary employment option for workers. It is not all that surprising, then, that tobacco growers played essentially no role in lobbying for a guest-worker scheme with the Caribbean. Reviewing archival files full of letters from growers and grower organizations demanding guest workers (principally in fruit and vegetables in the immediate lead-up to 1966, and also in sugar beets in a slightly earlier period), the utter absence of the tobacco sector – perhaps Ontario's top employer of seasonal farm workers – is striking. Based on available evidence, neither individual tobacco farmers nor the Marketing Board nor any other tobacco agency made any requests for Caribbean guest workers before 1966.[110] It was only once the agreement with Jamaica was falling into place that tobacco growers expressed any interest in participating in the program, and even then it was principally about securing a contingency plan should their existing labour supplies be curtailed.[111]

As to why tobacco growers in particular were slow to hire Caribbean workers, especially compared to Europeans, the most important factor was cost. Despite popular understandings of guest workers as "cheap labour," workers in the SAWP actually came to employers at a significantly higher cost than locals, or even European students. The bilateral agreements with sending countries in the SAWP put employers on the hook for the full share of workers' airfare from 1966 to 1971. In subsequent years, employers were permitted to recoup some costs through paycheque deductions, but they still typically paid 65–90 per cent of travel costs, depending on the year and length of workers' contracts. European students, on the other hand, paid their own way to Ontario.[112] Housing SAWP workers was also pricier, since accommodations had to be outfitted with kitchens and indoor bathrooms, accoutrements that were far from typical in the tobacco belt, where harvest workers often slept in multipurpose barns, bathed in jury-rigged showers in the greenhouse, and relied on outhouses for their other bathroom needs. Growers hiring SAWP workers usually had to build entirely new accommodations to meet program requirements, a significant capital expenditure, and something they had little incentive to do so long as other sources of labour were plentiful.[113] Indeed, government officials repeatedly underscored that the SAWP was a "premium" program, designed merely to complement local labour rather than supplant it. One Manpower staffer explained the logic to Minister Robert Andras: "The result [of the program's guaranteed wages and living conditions] is a premium movement at a cost which exceeds local labour costs, thus providing a constant incentive to employers to try to upgrade their employment's attractiveness to Canadian labour."[114] Even as late as 1988, the memoranda of understanding between Canada and the various sending countries specified, in the second "guiding principle," that "workers are to be employed at a premium cost to employers," though in reality growers had already succeeded in shifting some of their financial burden onto the shoulders of workers, as we will see in more detail in chapter 7.[115]

Another factor delaying the employment of SAWP workers in tobacco was the hesitancy of federal officials to extend the program to that sector. A major reason tobacco growers were not permitted to participate in the program in its first year was federal bureaucrats' concerns about what amounted to "race mixing," specifically the bringing together of Black West Indians and white American southerners on tobacco farms and the threat this could pose to the continued existence of the US program. Just as Canadian officials on the 1966 US tour had worried about how white southerners might react to sharing their workplaces and bunkhouses with African Americans, so, too, did they fret about their potential reactions to Black West Indians. In deciding against allowing Jamaicans to work in tobacco in 1966, Immigration staff mused that "it might be dangerous to mix the racially sensitive West Indians with the Southern United States workers now entering. The result could be to ruin the existing U.S. movement."[116] (A classic bit of victim-blaming, it should be noted, given the identification of the "racially sensitive" West Indians as the problem, rather than the racist southerners.) Similarly, when the Jamaican high commissioner asked about including tobacco in the 1966 program, he was told "that we normally rely on key workers from the Southern United States in our tobacco harvest, and that we might have serious problems if we mixed these people with Jamaicans without adequate planning; that we would therefore not consider the admission of Jamaicans for this purpose in 1966."[117]

The officials weren't wrong about white southerners' perception of Black West Indians – one oral history interviewee recalled the disgust of southern tobacco workers when they encountered their Caribbean counterparts in a tobacco belt store in the early 1970s.[118] Of course, the racism of one group of workers is a difficult justification for the exclusion of another, and perhaps this came to be understood by officials, for the issue was not mentioned again after 1966, and Caribbean workers did join the tobacco workforce in 1967. It is also worth considering that after the integration of the US movement in 1966 – and the negative press attention garnered by the denial of jobs to African Americans at some tobacco farms – officials realized that any form of state-sponsored segregation in tobacco was no longer tenable. But as with so much of the story of racism and tobacco labour, we can only speculate: there is no evidence linking the integration of the US program with the acceptance of Caribbean workers. Beyond concerns about racial mixing and tensions, federal officials were also wary of extending the program to tobacco growers unless they could demonstrate real need for additional workers. Throughout the program's first decade and a half, program administrators consistently treated flue-cured growers as a separate category of employer, and even flirted multiple times with the idea of cutting tobacco from the scheme altogether.[119]

Growers' perceptions of Caribbean workers – some racist in character – were likely a final reason for West Indians' slow incorporation into the tobacco workforce. The refusal of employment to at least twenty-six African American migrant workers by farmers in 1966 revealed the prevalence of racist bigotry among at least some tobacco growers, so it is very possible that this reason alone would have dissuaded some from hiring workers through the SAWP. But given the eventual hiring of Caribbean workers in the mid-1970s in comparable numbers to the US scheme a decade earlier, it seems likely that, when it came to hiring, racism was a decisive factor for only a minority of growers. More important than racism in tempering tobacco growers' perceptions of Caribbean workers was these workers' surprising penchant for resistance – a story we will pick up next chapter.

◆ ◆ ◆

In a cartoon advertisement in the June 1973 edition of the *Canadian Tobacco Grower*, nine tobacco workers are falling from the sky, dangling from parachutes and floating down into a field of ripe tobacco, having jumped moments before from the hold of an airplane marked "Canada Manpower." In the field below stands a farmer who, desperate for labourers, had spelled out the letters "s.o.s." with the smoke from his cigarette, and was presumably delighted to have his distress signal answered before the smoke had even dissipated. The ad, commissioned by the Department of Manpower and Immigration and drawn by artist Irene Anderson of Langton, Ontario (incidentally the same town where Gladston Williams, with whom we opened this chapter, worked), was intended to encourage farmers to "get the jump on the harvest" by submitting their requests for workers early. It also provides a snapshot of the diversity of the tobacco workforce of the late 1960s and '70s – including its three guest-worker programs. Each one of the nine parachutists represents a major – or at least noteworthy – group of workers in Ontario's tobacco harvest, here indicated by the stenciled letters on the canopies of their chutes. A young man whose parachute is labelled "Local Help" was the first to land, the top of his head barely poking out from behind the row of tall tobacco plants. Close behind him are representatives of "Caribbeans," "Women Primers," "Americans," and "European Students." Floating higher up are workers from Quebec and eastern Ontario, as well as university and high school students.[120]

While the cartoon demonstrates the tobacco workforce's cosmopolitan composition, it also contains some hints of the unequal terms by which these various groups of workers were incorporated. Most of the workers depicted in the ad are stereotyped in one way or another, which is unsurprising given the conventions of the genre: bright lipstick and a Rosie the Riveter–style bandana for the woman primer, and long hair, facial scruff, and bell-bottoms for the university students, for example. Alongside these more benign representations, the rendering of the Caribbean worker stands out: drawn with jet-black skin, white eyes that pop against his complexion, and enormous white lips, the image evokes many of the racist tropes of minstrelsy and other dehumanizing historic depictions of Black people.[121] And while the West Indian's fellow cartoon guest workers clutch national flags – the Stars and Stripes for the American and three European flags in the hand of the foreign student – he has none. Nor is he bestowed with any identifiable articles of clothing or props, as many of the other worker-parachutists are. Simply put, for the artist, there was only one important identifier for the Caribbean guest worker: race.

The cartoon's clear differentiation between white and Black guest workers echoed the very different receptions of each group by government officials and, in some cases, employers. In short, guest-worker programs – in terms of both their exclusions and their criteria for inclusion – were intimately shaped by racism. The US scheme – appropriately represented in Anderson's drawing by a white man – for decades barred Black workers from participating. When African Americans were finally admitted, it was on an artificially limited basis, and at least some of the workers who actually arrived in Ontario were refused employment by racist growers. Prospective Black farm workers from the British West Indies were also excluded from Ontario farms for decades, in large part due to the racism of federal officials. The two-decade-long campaign for their inclusion stood in stark juxtaposition to the European Student Tobacco Worker Scheme, which went from proposal to functioning program in a matter of weeks.

But Anderson's cartoon is instructive not only for its reflection of the role of racism in the making of the tobacco workforce of the 1960s and '70s. It also neatly encapsulates the conventional thinking about how guest-worker

5.7 "Get the Jump on Harvest," Irene Anderson, Department of Manpower and Immigration advertisement, 1973. Courtesy of Delhi Tobacco Museum and Heritage Centre. Irene S. Anderson scrapbook, George Demeyere Library, Delhi Tobacco Museum and Heritage Centre.

programs come about and are managed. In the ad, a Canadian government plane drops workers into the field of a labour-hungry employer. The roles could not be clearer: the state as supplier of labour, the farmer as consumer, and workers as commodified labour, even if a zany and diverse version of it. As we have seen in this chapter, however, this assignment of roles – broadly repeated in much of the academic literature (albeit in more sophisticated guise) – leaves out one critically important player: the governments of sending countries. In the US and Caribbean schemes alike, fundamental program features (and changes to them) derived not from Canadian officials or employers, but instead from lobbying by sending countries' envoys: the integration of the American movement, for example, or the selection criteria and mechanisms for employers' requests of workers in the SAWP. The European student scheme, though lacking involvement from sending governments, was no less shaped by organizing bodies in participants' home countries – they just happened to emerge from civil society rather than from the state.

In a broader sense, we have observed that a whole range of factors in sending countries and on the international plane – from legislative changes to economic policy to diplomatic considerations – played a part in determining the makeup of guest-worker programs in Ontario tobacco and, by extension, in Canada. The next two chapters will extend this critique of the conventional view of guest-worker programs even further, and we'll see that employers were not so desperate for foreign workers as Anderson's comic, and other commentary, suggests. Nor were guest workers – or any other workers for that matter – mere commodities, with inherent and predictable characteristics. Though employers and government agents, like Anderson, essentialized tobacco's various groups of labourers in search of the most compliant and productive, workers often refused to play the part, and instead stubbornly pursued their own interests in an evolving sector.

6

BOYS LIKE THESE

It was Winston Bovell's first season in Canada, in the late 1980s, and things were not going well. When payday rolled around on the third Saturday of the tobacco harvest, Bovell and his co-workers, all Barbadians, were not paid like they had been the two Saturdays past, and the boss offered no explanation. At first, hoping it was just a minor delay, they carried on working. "We work from the Sunday to the Friday, looking for money," Bovell later recalled. "We saw him [the farmer] come out and go back in the [house], and we say 'Okay, we might get we money Saturday.'" But when the next Saturday came and they still had not been paid or given any reason for the holdup, they confronted the employer, saying, "We are not working. We want money. 'Cause if we can't eat, we can't work. We need food." The farmer did not take kindly to his Barbadian crew demanding their pay and began berating the men with racist insults. Bovell and his co-workers, however, were not intimidated, and they persisted in their work stoppage, remaining in their bunkhouse for three days. On the third day, to their surprise, two police cars pulled up to the farm; they had been summoned by the employer to remove the men from the property. Luckily for the striking workers, the police took their side, telling the farmer that they had not breached their contracts and that there were no grounds to remove them from the farm. The officers advised the grower to call the liaison officer, the official representative of Barbados's Ministry of Labour, whose job it was to oversee program operations in Canada and resolve any issues encountered by Barbadian workers while on the contract.

"The liaison officer took I think about two days to come," Bovell recalled with frustration. In the meantime, the farmer again verbally assaulted the men when he "came by we bunkhouse and start cursing and saying he want us 'n——s' out of his bunkhouse." When the liaison officer finally did appear, he mediated a long and spirited back-and-forth between the workers and the farmer. Eventually, the employer relented and agreed to pay the men their back wages. He also offered them the option of resuming work. Bovell and his colleagues took their pay but had no interest in returning to the fields, reasoning that if they did, "he gon' treat us cruel, you know what I mean? We are not going to feel comfortable." When the liaison officer asked if they wanted to be reassigned to other farms, the men responded, "No, we going home."[1]

Bovell's narrative differs starkly from the typical portrayals and perceptions of guest workers. For employers, Canadian bureaucrats, and sending-country governments, guest workers are usually cast as something of an ideal labour force, perfectly fulfilling distinct needs for each group. For employers, they are "reliable," unlikely to cause trouble or quit before the end of harvest. For Canadian officials, guest-worker schemes held out the promise of a legal, rationally managed alternative to unregulated and sometimes illegal labour migration. Sending-country governments, particularly in the case of the Caribbean, also idealized guest workers, whom they cast as ambassadors, forging closer ties with the rich Commonwealth nation of Canada, and nation-builders, injecting much-needed foreign capital into their home countries and contributing to developmental goals. The appeal of guest workers was summed up neatly by one tobacco grower speaking about his crew of Belgian university students in 1966, in terms very similar to those often applied to Caribbean workers: "It's good to have boys like this with us. They are so polite and well-mannered, a real nice bunch. They are so different and so much nicer than most of those we have had in the past."[2]

Bold though Bovell and his co-workers were, they were not so unusual as these more common portrayals of guest workers might lead us to think. In myriad ways, participants in all three of tobacco's temporary foreign worker programs refused to stick to the script of guest-worker obedience and orderliness, eschewing the label of "boys like this." They resisted substandard workplace conditions, posed sometimes surprising challenges to state control, and frustrated their home governments' agendas. For Caribbean workers – who are the primary focus of this chapter – resistance was often deeply intertwined with the assertion of dignified personhood against racist, essentializing understandings of guest workers' poverty and subservience. Scholars of guest-worker programs have, with good reason, tended to emphasize the high degrees of exploitation and marginalization that typically characterize these

6.1 Vincenzo Pietropaolo (photographer), Lawrence Ernest and Robinson Girard
of Saint Lucia in a tobacco field, Otterville, Ontario, 1984.

schemes, the SAWP included. The evidence presented in this chapter, however, joins recent studies that have begun to complicate this narrative by examining the ways in which guest workers, even in the face of daunting barriers, have managed to resist their conditions of oppression and exercise agency, not only via workplace actions but also through more personalized, quotidian assertions of humanity.[3]

Challenges to State Control

Guest-worker schemes offered Canadian government officials the opportunity for "managed migration," an ideal that became all the more attractive at times when unregulated and clandestine foreign labour migration caused political complications and public relations headaches for authorities. (Such an instance took place in 1973, when new immigration regulations were protested by tomato and other farmers in southwestern Ontario, who found their twenty-year access to Mexican Mennonite workers suddenly threatened, and a resulting investigation by Manpower and Immigration revealed widespread child labour and abject conditions on Ontario's fruit and vegetable farms. One of the results of this affair was the addition of Mexico as a sending country in the SAWP, intended in part to give growers the option to regularize their Mexican migrant labour force.[4]) Planned by government officials in accordance with labour market needs and with rigid standards in place, guest-worker programs were less likely to attract controversy, and indeed were seen as an important – if limited – part of the state's overall goal of fostering an orderly, rational farm labour market.

But as was always the case with such dreams of control, the reality was somewhat messier.[5] For example, all three of tobacco's guest-worker schemes had the ironic effect of encouraging the emergence of unauthorized labour placement schemes that attempted to piggyback on the legal programs, either by misrepresenting themselves or by offering employers access to a similar workforce with fewer bureaucratic obligations and potentially at a lower cost.

This problem was perhaps most acute in the US program for two reasons. First, its unusual transition from unregulated migration system to bilateral guest-worker program meant that state efforts to control the entire movement entailed breaking the existing habits of both workers and growers, as we have seen in a number of examples. Second, the fact of the US-Canada land border made crossing into Canada quite easy for prospective tobacco workers (with the exception of African Americans before the 1960s), whether or not they were authorized to work in the harvest. Such conditions made illicit labour contracting – parallel to the legal program – relatively commonplace. One example took place in 1967, when Canadian officials received reports that George Dennis of Valdosta, Georgia – a silver-tongued operator who drove a white Cadillac – was matching Georgian workers with Canadian growers, proposing to take a cut of a dollar a day from each. Authorities found out about the scheme in June, giving them enough time to send Dennis "cease and desist" letters (from both Canadian and Georgian state officials), and to warn ports of entry to be on the lookout. Despite these efforts, Dennis managed to get into the country along with nine workers, and he was found on 11 August at a farm in Tillsonburg, where he had been working as a curer. However, he "had been fired the previous evening as he was not much of a curer. He is a smooth talker, flashy dresser and a habitual liar."

The nine recruits Dennis brought north had been placed on two farms. While Dennis claimed to government investigators that he had only asked the men to reimburse the cost of transportation, "in talking to the workers, who were reluctant to say too much, it was found that they were expected to pay Dennis $100 a piece." The growers who had hired them planned to give Dennis a bonus upon completion of the harvest. Dennis was not charged with any crime or issued a fine – he said he was willing to leave Canada, and officials permitted him to do so, though, remarkably, he was not escorted to the border.[6] The other nine workers were apparently allowed to stay, a decision that would have been in keeping with general protocols for undocumented farm workers in Canada in this period – with the exception of SAWP workers, as we'll see below.[7] The European student program also inspired attempts at parallel schemes, particularly in its early years.[8]

Perhaps unsurprisingly, such parallel placement schemes were least common with the Caribbean program, which was bilaterally state managed from day one, and where officials were even more keenly intent on ensuring program compliance. And, of course, since race- and origins-based admissions criteria were only (largely) removed from Canadian immigration policy in 1962, there were no pre-existing West Indian communities in rural areas, and thus the opportunities for launching clandestine recruitment schemes were more limited. Even still, in 1967 a broadly similar scheme to the smooth-talking Georgian's was hatched; it aimed to supply Jamaican workers to Ontario tobacco farms, though it was quashed long before the harvest. In March 1967, the Marketing Board informed Canadian officials that Joseph Hayles of the Canadian-Jamaican Employment Agency in Toronto had been contacting growers and offering them Jamaican workers in return for a placement fee of fifty dollars per worker. (Presumably, Hayles was planning to charge workers for their airfare, though no information is available on this.) The matter was quickly addressed by Manpower officials, who informed Hayles that Jamaican workers would only be permitted to come through the sanctioned guest-worker program.[9]

Guest-worker program regulations were skirted not only by the schemes of unscrupulous businessmen, but also in less organized ways via the practices of individual migrants, employers, and sometimes state officials. In all three schemes, participants often left their assigned employers – or never reached them at all. In the US program, these problems – described in chapter 3's discussion of the pre-1945 period – continued after the war, even as the program became more rigidly managed by state authorities. Officials sometimes re-ported anxiously about "piracy" among growers who met buses of southern migrants before their arrival in the tobacco belt and offered higher wages than what they had agreed to with their pre-arranged employer. Workers frequently took the pirate growers up on their offers.[10]

Europeans and West Indians alike often left their assigned employers, thus breaching the terms of their employment. For European students, the most common practice was simply to work for another tobacco farmer before re-joining their group for the return trip home.[11] In the Caribbean program, workers referred to this as "running off," evoking – intentionally or not – the long histories of slavery, indenture, and other forms of unfree, mobile labour in whose historical lineage the SAWP lies. Though growers employed strategies such as listening in on phone calls and monitoring workers during grocery shopping outings, in reality there was little they could do to stop a worker from leaving if he wanted to. Workers "running off" would often join family or friends in Toronto and live without legal immigration status.[12]

In the SAWP, employers and liaison officers found illicit ways to secure profits supplemental to those afforded by the normal functioning of the scheme. As a Manpower official reported in 1973, "At least one farmer is oc-cupying the place of broker for workers from [the] Caribbean, i.e. he requests a number of workers and then farms them out to other farmers."[13] Caribbean liaison officers also bent the rules, sometimes in cahoots with employers, such as when reports surfaced that officers were taking "kickbacks" from growers in exchange for granting approval to substandard worker housing. This was a key reason why housing inspections were transferred to provincial authorities.[14] Trinidad's liaison officers were known to sometimes avoid sending repatriated workers home, and instead simply swap them with workers from another farm.[15] The most spectacular instance of government corruption was revealed in 1990, when Jamaica's former minister of labour, J.A.G. Smith, was convicted of defrauding the Canadian and US farm labour programs, siphoning money from the workers' compulsory savings fund to purchase luxury vehicles and architectural plans, and even to travel on a Concorde jet.[16]

It was also commonplace for West Indian migrants to secure additional work with employers other than the ones to whom they were contracted. Such under-the-table labour was often arranged by growers themselves, who "loaned out" workers during slack periods, sometimes for a fee and sometimes simply as a neighbourly favour. Workers were paid by their secondary employer in cash. While Canadian state officials worked hard to stamp out the more egregious violations of program rules, they were surprisingly unperturbed by these more casual instances of labour mobility. "There will be cases," a Manpower staffer conceded to an Essex County growers' organization in 1974, "where a man sees a chance to make a little extra money by working a few hours a week, and we see no reason why he should be unreasonably prevented from doing so as long as his performance with the original employer is not impaired."[17]

While state officials were willing to give some leeway to employers and workers operating slightly outside of program bounds, that flexibility came to a screeching halt when guest workers broke their contracts and went "AWOL," to borrow the program's military parlance. Indeed, a major difference between the Caribbean program and its US and European counterparts was the Canadian state's absolute intolerance for workers leaving their assigned employer, and the much stricter regime of repatriation for workers deemed unsatisfactory by growers – a clear indication of the continued role of racism in structuring Canadian immigration policy, even after its liberalization in the 1960s. The disproportionate concern with Caribbean workers who had gone AWOL is reflected in part in the existence of entire files on "crimes and irregularities" and repatriations in the Caribbean program.[18] While officials were at times concerned with irregular immigration and labour practices among US and European tobacco migrants, and occasionally deported rule-breaking members of both groups, the issue was never so big as to warrant the creation of entire files.[19]

The tone of Canadian officials' letters about AWOL West Indians reflects a degree of anxiety that was present from the earliest years of the program – though there was debate within the civil service about the seriousness of the problem. One Manpower official reported that 20 of the 1,077 Caribbean guest workers in 1967 "disappeared while in Canada," exclaiming that "this is a rather alarming increase from the five workers in the 1966 movement who disappeared." The bureaucrat worried about the cost of such breaches of contract, and even called into question the viability of the program under these circumstances: "The Canadian Government will expend a great deal of money in searching for these delinquents ... If the movement is to continue, it may be necessary to consider certain safeguards such as the bonding of workers and/or a more complete identification of them (photographs, and possibly fingerprints, as well as physical descriptions) to facilitate the apprehension of delinquents."[20]

Assistant Deputy Minister for Immigration R.B. Curry picked up the torch a few months later when he drafted letters to the high commissioners of the three participating West Indian countries, suggesting that Canada was considering requiring the posting of a bond for each guest worker in order to guarantee their exit upon completion of the contract. "I am sure you will appreciate that the failure of these workers to take their scheduled departures from Canada has caused us grave concern and the question of more effective control over such future workers is now the subject of serious study by this Department," wrote Curry.[21] The letters appear to never have been sent. Curry's counterpart at Manpower, J.P. Francis, responded to the draft by pointing out that 20 workers out of 1,000 amounted to just 2 per cent, arguing that this was a "strong reaction" to a relatively minor problem.[22] Francis's call for calm aside, program officials continued to closely monitor the AWOL issue. Statistics on contract breaches and repatriations were included in annual program reports, which often included longer commentary on the issue. One such report noted Jamaica's high rate of AWOLs: out of 32 total AWOLs in 1969, 27 were Jamaican.[23] And while Curry's letters were not posted, representatives of West Indian governments were frequently reminded of the importance of selecting workers who would not leave their assigned employers (how, exactly, they were supposed to determine this was never made clear).[24]

Such statistics were not kept for the European student or US programs, nor were immigration-related breaches among these workers a major subject within government correspondence. And in the early years of the European program, as in the above-discussed incident with American migrants, irregular migrants were occasionally "regularized" and allowed to continue working in tobacco, something that did not happen with unauthorized Caribbean workers.[25] The concern about Caribbean contract-breakers – and Jamaicans in particular – fit into broader concerns among Canadian immigration policymakers about "illegal" immigration by Jamaicans. A 1977 report, for example, indicated that Jamaicans accounted for one of the highest shares of deportations from Canada, though the rate per 1,000 entries was tenth highest.[26] Government documents, of course, never explicitly mention race as a factor in this obsession with Jamaican and other Caribbean migrants falling astray of immigration law. But it is difficult to see these trends as anything other than examples of the unofficial continuation of racism within Canadian immigration policy.[27] Also clear are the echoes of the historical practices of slaveowners and their governments in the administration of the SAWP, including the preoccupation with "running off" and the selection of workers based on notions of compliance.[28]

Caribbean Resistance

There can be no doubt that foreign workers – particularly those from the Caribbean – faced serious structural obstacles that almost certainly made them less likely to protest poor working or living conditions. But this didn't preclude them entirely from doing so. In contrast to the portrayals that cast them as meek and obedient (or the related narratives of total victimization), Caribbean workers did in fact push back against employers on numerous occasions, consequences be damned.

Like the European immigrants who had preceded them in the tobacco belt, Caribbean workers carried with them to Canada not only their persons and physical belongings, but also particular ideas and practices about work and politics, including traditions of workplace resistance. These went back as far as the period of slavery, when uprisings of enslaved people on plantations were a frequent occurrence in the West Indies and played an important role in the eventual abolition of slavery in the British Empire via the 1833 Slavery Abolition Act. By the mid-twentieth century, the major Caribbean sending countries in the SAWP – Jamaica, Barbados, and Trinidad and Tobago – all boasted robust traditions of trade unionism that dated back at least to the pan-Caribbean labour uprisings of the 1930s. Unlike in most of North America, union membership and organizing in the West Indies has historically extended to agricultural workers. Beyond official unionism, farm workers in each country – and in other sending countries in the SAWP – engaged in dramatic wildcat strikes during the twentieth century, including in the post–World War II period. A particularly noteworthy example – and one that occurred not long before the start of the SAWP – was the 1958 wildcat strike staged by sugar cane workers in Barbados, in which some 19,000 cane workers on 260 estates set down their tools, effectively closing down Barbados's sugar industry – which at that time accounted for 45 per cent of the island's gross domestic product and 95 per cent of its exports – for a full five weeks, before ending in a significant pay raise and other concessions for workers. Barbadian cane workers went on strike again in 1963–64 and 1968, while Trinidadian workers engaged in widespread protests on sugar estates in 1964–65.[29] While it is not possible to say whether West Indian SAWP workers consciously drew on these legacies of resistance when pushing back against substandard working conditions, given the experiences of many SAWP workers and their forebearers in sugar cane (Winston Bovell's parents, for example, worked in cane), this would certainly not be surprising.

Regardless, Caribbean workers' tactics of on-farm resistance differed little from those of their Canadian counterparts. Just like Canadians, West Indian guest workers frequently engaged in struggles for control over production, and as was the case with their colleagues, the most frequent site of disagreement was the kiln, specifically when growers attempted to fill the kiln with greater-than-customary amounts of tobacco without raising workers' piece rate. In an oral history interview, one Barbadian guest worker recalled engaging in an argument with his employer about the issue over the course of many days, reasoning that the practice was not only unfair to workers but also damaged the crop, causing the tobacco stems to swell. Eventually, he was able to convince the grower of this latter point, and the farmer conceded.[30] Occasionally, struggles at the kiln resulted in sabotage. Another Barbadian worker told an interviewee in 1975 that one way to retaliate against a bad employer was to break sticks of tobacco in the kiln, thereby slowing down the entire operation.[31] This act of sabotage does not appear to have been widely practised, however, which is unsurprising given its side effect of lengthening the workday.

Conflict also developed around the pace of work. The apparently slower pace of Caribbean workers was a frequent cause of complaint for growers, particularly in the early years of the program. Barbadian worker Leroy Rollins complained to researcher George Kinsman Lewis in the early 1970s that in Canada, someone was "driving you all time," and other workers in the same study voiced similar complaints.[32] But workers did push back against employers' need for speed. An excerpt from Lewis's study describes some of the give-and-take, as related by Leroy's brother, Talbot "Sherriff" Rollins: "Sherriff feels that work in Canada is more difficult than in Barbados as there are always Canadian farm owners or foremen bullying the migrant or exhorting them on with phrases such as 'come on, keep going.' When someone tells him to 'come on, let's go,' his rejoinder is to tell the exhorter 'Oh, slow down, Bill.' He added that if he were treated that way in Barbados he would leave the job."[33] It wasn't only employers and supervisors pushing the pace; West Indians' calmer work style could also cause tensions with Canadian co-workers, who were accustomed to working as quickly as possible in order to finish the work-day sooner. Notwithstanding pushback like Sherriff's, it appears that the more common outcome of this conflict was for West Indian workers to convert to the faster pace, whether as a result of employer discipline, pressure from co-workers, or the realization that filling the kiln more quickly meant a sooner end to the workday and greater opportunities for additional cash-paying jobs.[34]

A more overt and collective form of workplace resistance among Caribbean workers came in the form of wildcat strikes. The earliest known wildcats in the SAWP in fact occurred in 1967, the very first year that participants laboured in tobacco.[35] The trouble began a couple weeks into the harvest, when Trini-dadians on two tobacco farms discovered they were being paid less than their Canadian co-workers for the same work. Conditions were also found lacking, with poor quality food and accommodations and insufficient provision of work clothing – a crucial requirement for workers navigating dew-soaked to-bacco rows in the early morning cold. When the workers approached their bosses to demand improvements in pay and conditions, their "representations … were not well received," according to a Canadian official, and "the workers went back to the fields and caused unrest amongst their fellow-workers."[36]

Officials in both Canada and Trinidad and Tobago, promptly apprised of the situation, reacted with anxious concern. Not only was it Trinidad's first year in the program, but out of the 83 Trinidadians placed in Canada at that point, fully 20 were involved in the protests. Trinidad's top civil servant in the Ministry of Labour, J. Adams, quickly made plans to travel to Canada to meet with the workers, assess the situation, and make decisions about repatriating participants. Canadian officials, particularly in the Department of External Affairs, were extremely anxious about the potential for negative press around the story and wanted to ensure that if any workers were repatriated, it was done by Adams's orders rather than those of the Canadians. As a Canadian di-plomatic staffer in Trinidad explained in a telegram, "It is highly important that any decisions regarding possible repatriation be held if possible until Adams can be associated with them; that number of forced repatriations be kept as low as possible; and that we be informed immediately if any publicity appears in Canada. I am sure [it is] unnecessary [to] remind you that [the] movement of persons is [a] most delicate area of general Canadian-Trinidadian relations and that much damage could be done if [the] question is not – repeat – not handled in that light." Making matters even touchier was the fact that Trinidad and Tobago's prime minister, Eric Williams, was scheduled to visit Canada in a week's time.[37]

Both External Affairs and Manpower and Immigration agreed that the best course of action would be to repatriate a small number of workers. "Only those who have been formenting [*sic*] dissatisfaction" should be sent home, wrote a Manpower staffer. "This hopefully will serve as an example to the remainder."[38] External Affairs concurred that returning a few workers home "might have [a] sufficiently salutary effect" on the rest.[39] After his deliberations in Canada, Adams decided to repatriate seven workers, though in a debriefing meeting with Canadian officials, he irritated at least one External Affairs representative by appearing to sympathize somewhat with his countrymen's predicament. "He played down the seriousness of the problem," the official griped. Adams summarized the reasons for the workers' protest and commented that the conditions they were accustomed to in the Caribbean were typically better than what they had encountered in Ontario. "The foregoing was in the form of an apology or explanation for the behaviour of the seven workers," blustered the Canadian diplomat.[40]

Notwithstanding his capacity to understand some of the workers' complaints, Adams still authorized the repatriation of the seven men, A. Horsford, N. Rampersad, W. MacDonald, C. Hackshaw, Romona Ali, M. Lawrence, and James Nelson, who were flown back to Trinidad on 29 August.[41] Bureaucrats were largely successful in their goal of keeping the story out of the press, aside from one article in the *Trinidad Guardian* on one of the returned workers, James Nelson of Tobago, but Canadian officials were relieved to report that it was "not overly sensational," and that Trinidadian officials "believe they have been successful in keeping any other adverse reports out of newspapers here."[42]

The wildcat strikes of 1967 appear to have soured at least some tobacco growers to Caribbean workers, especially those from Trinidad and Tobago – likely a final reason for the slow incorporation of the SAWP in tobacco. Trinidadian workers were thought to be more demanding and less hard-working than those from other countries, a remarkable example of how rapidly racial and national stereotypes could be extrapolated from the (completely justifiable) actions of a few members of a group. Reporting on his experience with

Trinidadian workers in 1967, one grower complained that "they had two speeds, slow and reverse," and said that he didn't even use them for priming tobacco.[43] A 1970 Manpower report on the Caribbean program disclosed that "employers have shown an increasing reluctance to accept workers from Trinidad ... The workers from this island have a tendency to voice their grievances and requests for improvements in working and living conditions more frequently perhaps than Jamaicans, which is another reason why the latter are preferred over the other two nationalities." The association between Trinidadians and protest was likely encouraged in part by the conflicts in tobacco in 1967, but awareness of the country's growing militant Black Power movement also fuelled suspicions. As the Manpower document explained, "Newspaper reports on the recent unrest in that country may have contributed to [employers'] attitude."[44] Additionally, reminiscent of the concerns about mixing white workers from the American South and Black West Indians, it was widely accepted that Trinidadians of African and Indian heritage could not be housed together due to ethnic tensions, causing headaches for growers.[45] This again represented a very quick formulation of racial knowledge on the part of employers and Canadian authorities, with questionable supporting evidence. All of this amounted to negative impressions of Caribbean workers, for at least some employers. "Among tobacco growers, there was a fairly definite preference for Canadian workers," noted a review of the 1967 program, which then offered the qualification that "some operators, however, said they had no complaints against Caribbean workers." Negative impressions along similar lines seemed to linger for at least a few years; a 1973 report, for example, shared commentary by one disappointed grower who complained that West Indians were unwilling to perform tasks outside of those listed on their contracts.[46]

Resistance and Racism

As mostly Black men (with a smaller number of Indo-Trinidadians) in lily-white rural Ontario, Caribbean guest workers were often in the position of being conspicuous outsiders; as such, they were frequently on the receiving end of racist abuse, both at work and in host communities. In both scenarios, they worked out various strategies for dealing with such discrimination. Bigotry at work did not always come at the hands of employers; sometimes it was instigated by Canadian co-workers. Jamaican Headley Hutchinson, who worked in Canada in the 1970s and '80s, recalled being targeted by his employer's son and several of his friends who also worked on the farm, who wanted to make more money and blamed the Jamaican workers for their inadequate paycheques. "They want better money," he explained, "and they start curse we. They come fi fight we." But Hutchinson and his co-workers were not prepared to back down, boss's son or not. As he explained, they felt they had no choice but to fight back: "We have fi get serious and lick them. Yeah, we have fi lick them." The defeated Canadian boys went to tell the boss what had happened, and the farmer approached the Jamaican men to get their side of the story. Surprisingly, the boss took the Jamaicans' side, declaring the behaviour of his son and his friends to have been "out of order." The young aggressors "begged pardon," and according to Hutchinson the Jamaican crew got on fine with them from then on.[47]

West Indian migrants also encountered racism in the towns and villages they visited for grocery shopping and other outings. In shops, cashiers would sometimes refuse to take money directly from the hands of workers, instead directing them to place the money on the counter. Multiple workers reported being called the n-word in the towns and villages of rural Ontario. Winston Bovell was once walking down the street with his white Canadian girlfriend when a group of white men called her a "n——r lover." When Bovell confronted them, they backed down.[48] As that incident suggests, racism against Caribbean workers was often bound up with panic about Black sexuality. Canadian worker Michelle Vermeeren recalled that "there was such an … unwelcome-ness [toward Caribbean workers in Tillsonburg] … with all these white people looking at them, like, 'Don't touch my daughter.'"[49]

Others employed more internalized strategies for dealing with racial slurs. When David Moore of Barbados was called the n-word on the street, he chose to ignore the hateful insult, remembering his grandmother's words of wisdom: "Words can't hurt you, only sticks and stones."[50] These struggles over racism and the means by which they were settled also clearly intersected with ideas about masculinity and respectability – on the part of guest workers, local residents, and employers alike.

In addition to facing explicit racism, workers engaged in a more subtle battle with employers, locals, and Canadian officials in defining their identities as Black West Indian guest workers – a battle that was often intertwined with workplace struggles. In particular, workers repeatedly found themselves confronting the idea that they were naturally subservient – on account of their "race," nationality, or their poverty in their home country. A tobacco farmer (who didn't himself hire Caribbean workers) gave a fairly representative view in a 1985 oral history interview in which he explained the attractiveness of West Indian labour:

> Well, with the West Indians, they're a subservient type of people you see. They've always been hard up, and if they ever got fired off a job up here for any reason at all, their government would never let them come back up here. So they had a disadvantage right off the bat in working conditions. They would [do just] about anything you ask, and no questions. Whereas, somebody else if you told them … 'there's too many leaves laying around, you're tramping them.' They'd just keep right on tramping them. Not with Black people [*laughs*]. You just tell 'em once.[51]

Caribbean-employing tobacco farmers also referenced workers' poverty in accounting for their quality. One such tobacco farmer, Paul Donohue, explained in an oral history interview that "the offshore [workers], they were on the contract, and they needed the money. They were desperate."[52] Fellow farmer Walter Demeulenaere had similar reasoning: "If you make a dollar an hour [at home] … and they fly you to another country and you make triple the money, you gonna behave, right? Don't you think so? You're going to be on your best [behaviour]."[53] Employers' comments about the poverty of sending countries align neatly with one of the key justifications for the program, voiced by employers and government agents alike – namely, that it is a form of foreign aid from Canada to the Caribbean and Mexico.[54] This is itself a racialized trope, of course, one with a long historical lineage, that suggests that workers in the program should be grateful for their employment.[55]

Caribbean workers' narratives tell very different stories than the ones presented by farmers. For one thing, in a variety of ways, they push back against the conception that Caribbean workers come from "poor" countries or that they are "desperate." Sometimes this is done subtly. Jamaican worker Gladston Williams, for example, in explaining why he decided to work in Canada, was careful to say that the prime economic advantage wasn't so much that the wages were better, but rather that the work was steadier.[56] For other workers, the point was made more explicitly. As Tobagonian Hassel Kennedy explained,

The only thing we don't have, what Canada have here, is the cold weather. But we have everything [else] ... I come in the program to elevate myself, move on, learn something new. Because at the end of the day, you have to move on, you have to get experience ... *People say we're poor. We is not poor there* ... People come on these things [guest-worker programs] to just move on, just, you know, have some experience. Some people come for fun. Some people come for holidays.[57]

Kennedy's comment that some guest workers come for "holidays" or to "have some experience" was echoed by other interviewees who talked about being motivated to see more of the world, and of the enjoyment of learning about a new place and new culture and meeting different people.[58] Indeed, these were aspects of harvest work that appealed to workers across the labour force's diverse groups and eras, as we have seen elsewhere.

For some workers, rejecting racialized notions of poverty and desperation in their home countries went hand in hand with workplace resistance. We don't know if this was the case for the Trinidadian and Tobagonian wildcat strikers, not having the benefit of hearing their own thoughts on the matter, but it is not difficult to imagine that it was. It *was* clearly the case for Winston Bovell, who, in his second year in the program, again found himself participating in a wildcat strike on a tobacco farm. While priming tobacco on a ride-on priming aid, the Barbadian crew encountered a number of problems with the machine, which kept getting stuck in the mud. Since workers were paid at a piece rate, the problems with the machine meant that their day was being significantly extended with no additional compensation. Under these conditions, Bovell recalled, the men decided to stop working:

So when we get in the row, we stop pick tobacco. He [the farmer] come over, wants to know "what the fuck is going on here?" So we tell him, like, "We ain't picking more tobacco, because the ground is wet and the machine is sticking." We start arguing, and then his wife came out. Me, 'cause I was the guy who was leading, she look at me and tell me, "Get back on that fucking machine, you son of a bitch."

I was like [*long pause*] ... "If you are stupid? She really cursing me fi true? Me a free man. I tell you these words, listen to me, listen to me very carefully. I'm from Barbados. My passport come from Barbados, I'm not

Canadian. And I could go back to Barbados any time I want. Because I'm not going to go home and sleep on the streets. I have a house like you, I have the same flushing toilet, I have the same bath ... I have the same stove, fridge, everything like you. I don't live in a mud hut. I live in a proper home. So don't come and tell me ... I just come to Canada to get the experience for this. So you don't come and tell me that I'm this. So if I'm a son of a bitch, that mean you're the daughter of a [*pause*] ... Right?" So it escalate from there. They wanted me out of the farm. Because I was too strict for them.[59]

Bovell's narrative reveals not only a rejection of the alleged subservience of workers in the SAWP but also a complete reversal of the idea that Caribbean workers' poverty in their home countries makes them pliable while in Canada. He also clearly refuses racial ascriptions, declaring instead his individual and national identities. With his comment "I'm from Barbados," Bovell clearly states that his home country is not in fact poor and that he is under no compulsion to put up with workplace abuse. He does not reject entirely the idea that being from Barbados gives him a distinct identity, but he employs this concept to very different ends. Furthermore, his declaration "Me a free man" situates him within the long history of slavery and other forms of unfree agricultural labour while also distinguishing him from this history and the associated stereotypes about Black West Indians. Bovell rejects the racist ascription of subservience by asserting his freedom, humanity, and individuality.

In making connections between identity and resistance, workers did not simply lay claim to dignified identities for themselves. They also sometimes contributed to the essentialization of other groups of workers. In a group interview with Bovell and two other Barbadian workers, the men offered an explanation for why Barbados's representation in the SAWP had decreased while Mexico's and Jamaica's had not. The workers reasoned that Mexicans and Jamaicans do as they are told, while Bajans do not. When Barbadians' rights are violated in Canada, they go on strike.[60] The reverse of such intergroup essentialization also takes place. Sociologist Jenna Hennebry, for example, describes examples of Mexican workers comparing themselves favourably to Jamaicans, saying that Mexicans were able to overtake Jamaicans in the program because the latter complained too much.[61]

6.2 Vincenzo Pietropaolo (photographer), Caesar Uries, Errol Cain, and George Barber of Saint Vincent and the Grenadines in their bedroom, La Salette, Ontario, 1984.

Employers and bureaucrats also made distinctions between different groups of SAWP participants and their perceived levels of obedience or rebelliousness. This is most obvious in comparisons between Mexican and Caribbean SAWP workers,[62] but as seen in the earlier example of the striking Trinidadian workers, comparisons were also made between different West Indian nationalities. While Trinidadians were marked as particularly rebellious after their early experiences in the SAWP, others singled out Barbadians as the likeliest to protest their conditions. Gary Cooper, the former president of the grower agency that took over administration of the SAWP in 1987, made connections between the education and socio-economic levels of Barbadians and their propensity for dissent, in some ways echoing the comments made by Barbadian workers. In explaining why he and other farmers preferred Jamaican over Barbadian workers, Cooper said that

Barbadian workers were a little more educated and a little more demanding. Barbados as a country was a little better off financially than some of the other countries. So the workers had been exposed to more of ... you

know, the financial side of things. And I think in Barbados – I was always
told, I've never read the figures, but I was always told that ... there was
more unionized workers in Barbados, so they were more aware of what
they felt their rights were. So, they wanted to pick and choose their jobs
... Barbadians were a little bit more demanding.[63]

Cooper's comments, in addition to evoking slaveholders' comparisons of
the supposedly inherent characteristics of different groups of enslaved Africans
(including their proclivity for resistance),[64] demonstrate the heterogeneity of
employers' essentialization of workers in the sAWP. While the dominant logic
appears to have suggested that all sAWP workers were subservient, or that Mexicans were more pliable than West Indians, other essentialized theories also
circulated. Though the attribution of specific qualities like "reliability" or "rebelliousness" to certain groups differed between commenters, the connection
between workers' alleged degree of poverty and their subservience remained
a common theme. Just as other employers explicitly linked Jamaicans' poverty
with their subservience, so, too, did Cooper connect Barbadians' economic
stability with their supposed penchant for protest. For both employers and
workers, resistance was a key terrain on which battles over identity were fought.

Transnational Resistance: Caribbean Workers

Tobacco guest workers' resistance was not limited to the workplace, nor did it
take place only while workers were on contract in Canada. Rather, just as the
programs in which they laboured were transnational, so, too, was their resistance. For Caribbean workers, who found themselves working within a scheme
administered in part by their home governments, advocating for a better deal
within the program necessitated confrontation with those aspects of the arrangement that were organized by the sending countries. While under contract
in Canada, this included frequent negotiations with liaison officers. As Winston
Bovell's recollections at the start of this chapter indicate, workers often viewed
liaison officers with suspicion. When I asked another interviewee if he had a
favourable impression of the liaison officer, he simply laughed and chose to
pass on the question. Many workers clearly perceived liaison officers not as
advocates, but as yet another manifestation of power within the program –
someone to be wary of, another factor to negotiate.[65]

The end of the season in Canada did not bring an end to workers' dealings with the apparatuses of the SAWP. Caribbean workers' return home was often accompanied by conflict. A common spark was the compulsory savings scheme, under which a significant proportion of Canada-bound workers' wages (20 per cent initially, and 25 per cent in later years) were deducted and remitted directly to the home country's Ministry of Labour. Some of these funds covered program costs, but the vast majority constituted forced savings, transferred to a bank and only accessible to workers upon their return home.[66] While there have been mixed reviews from workers over the years about the practice – with some appreciating the lump sum received at the end of their contract and others disliking the scheme's paternalist aspects – participants representing both points of view could easily agree on the importance of being able to access their withheld wages immediately upon returning home.[67] In practice, particularly in Jamaica, this often did not occur – a fact at the root of many confrontations between returned workers, the Ministry of Labour, and the banks holding the funds. Headley Hutchinson, a Jamaican worker active in the program in the 1970s and '80s, recalled one year when the bank was slow to release workers' savings. To inquire about his money at the bank, Hutchinson had to travel from his home in Christiana to the city of Mandeville, more than an hour's trip by bus. After multiple visits and disruptions to their day-to-day lives, he and his fellow program participants were still unable to access their funds. As Hutchinson recalled, "Sometime when we come to the bank, they say the money no come from Canada yet. And we start quarrel and say, 'How the money no come?'" Hutchinson and his colleagues called the liaison officer and their employer in Canada, with the latter assuring them that the money had already been transferred to the bank. With this knowledge in hand, Hutchinson explained, "we go back to the bank and start quarrel and they give we the money."[68] Fellow Jamaican worker Gladston Williams remembered that banks sometimes shortchanged workers on their compulsory savings, and that most workers would carefully guard their pay slips to ensure they could prove what was owed them.[69]

Conflict over the release of compulsory savings also took place in the Caribbean-US farm-worker scheme. In 1961–62, a sharp increase in the number of Jamaican farm workers in that program created a bureaucratic backlog for the Agricultural Workers' Centre, the government agency that at that time was in charge of receiving and distributing workers' compulsory savings.

While the agency attempted to head off any problems by promising to mail cheques to workers, as opposed to having them travel to the office in person, these efforts came too late, and angry, shortchanged workers arrived en masse to demand their withheld pay. As Jamaican minister of finance D.B. Sangster reported, "Before any appreciable progress could be made in overtaking the arrears of work, the workers attended the Centre in large numbers, some 600 to 700 daily on pay days, demanding their savings ... On the 15th [of] August the workers invaded the offices of the Centre, tampering with the records so that work had to be suspended for more than five hours until the police were able to restore order." Unfortunately for the workers, civil servants estimated that they would have to wait until 29 September to receive their savings, more than three months after they had returned from the United States.[70]

European Student Resistance

There is no direct evidence of European students participating in wildcat strikes or other forms of on-farm resistance, though this does not, of course, mean that this didn't happen. But there is ample evidence of European student workers protesting their conditions of employment after the fact, through letters sent to departments of their home governments, Canadian consular offices, and to the organizers of the various schemes. In this sense, European students' resistance was also transnational in character. It is perhaps unsurprising that, among guest workers, epistolary protest was almost entirely the preserve of the European students, who possessed far greater levels of formal education than their rural proletarian counterparts from the Caribbean and southern United States.[71]

One such letter was sent in 1972 by British student Stephen Collett to Manpower and Immigration. Collett decried the lack of contracts governing the terms of employment and explained that participants, working in a foreign country with a fixed return date, found it nearly impossible to simply quit a bad job. "Moreover," he wrote, "striking is impracticable because of the threat of dismissal. In these circumstances, the farmer is free to exploit the imported labour." Like Canadian and Caribbean workers, he also reported the "overstuffing" of kilns, writing that the farmer "took advantage of our position" by using the end-of-harvest bonus to compel workers to start "over-filling the kilns by putting more leaves on the sticks and more sticks in the kilns," resulting in three extra hours of work per day.[72] German worker Egmonth Bilzhause and two companions made similar complaints about kiln-stuffing and the lack of a contract in a 1973 letter to Robert Andras.[73] In one instance, the parents of a student worker from France wrote to the Canadian ambassador in Paris to blast the conditions experienced by their son. An experience that was supposed to be "enrichissante" (enriching) had turned quickly into a "cauchemar," or nightmare, as their son was overworked and underpaid. The whole ordeal had soured their opinions of Canada. "Jusqu'ici, le Canada avait pour moi l'image d'un pays généereux où les étrangers étaient accueillis volontiers. Nous somme amenés à changer radicalement notre perception à la suite de l'expérience désastreuse que vient de vivre notre fils au cours de cet été." (Up to now, Canada had for me the image of a generous country, where foreigners were readily welcomed. After the disastrous experience that our son just went through over the course of this summer, we are prepared to radically change our point of view.)[74]

The most striking example of epistolary protest came in 1972, when dozens of German student tobacco workers sent letters to the German Central Labour Office complaining both about German organizers' management of the program, and about their own poor experiences in Canada. The Labour Office forwarded the letters to the Canadian Embassy in Berlin, which in turn translated them and passed them on to Manpower. The correspondence included two group letters, with nineteen and thirty-four signatories, respectively, along with multiple letters from individual workers detailing their particular grievances. The students had many complaints. From the letter signed by the thirty-four: "In most cases the students found themselves completely at the mercy of the farmers ... Our ignorance of the work process was taken advantage of by having us do, apart from the tobacco work, additional gratuitous jobs like potato harvest, lawn-mowing, car-washing etc. A person refusing to do these additional jobs was fired on the spot, thus, in the absence of any assistance on the part of ... [the German program organizers], getting in big trouble." The letter also complained about tobacco poisoning, workplace injuries, and poor accommodations. But "the determining factor of our indignation," the students continued, "is not only the hard work, but rather the bad pay and the treatment which amounted to a master-servant-relation." Individual letters made similar complaints. Peter Klein revealed that students were subject to "constant threatening to order them off the farm." Dirk W. Pohlmeyer claimed that "my ignorance about the work policy of the host country and my financial distress was taken advantage of in such a mean way that I was used as a strike-breaker and thus being brutally exploited as a cheap work slave."[75]

It is not clear what Pohlmeyer's strike-breaker comment referred to, but the level of dissatisfaction among the students is obvious. For all their determined anger and sense of injustice, the German students' letters demonstrate the limitations of this form of protest. The reaction of Manpower officials amounted to little more than a shrug. They chalked up the students' protest to the fact that the 1971 cohort had been a bit wealthier than previous groups and were more interested in sightseeing than engaging in hard work. As for the previously cited letters of complaint from British, German, and French students that landed on the desks of Manpower officials, there is no record at all of them receiving any consideration, let alone replies.[76]

◆◆◆

Guest workers frequently did not live up to the ideal of a pliable, orderly, legal labour force. They broke contracts, evaded immigration authorities, went on strike, wrote angry letters, and confronted representatives of their home governments. And while they still, despite these deviations from the ideal, offered employers an enhanced degree of labour control, the creation of new guest-worker schemes featuring workers from the Caribbean and Europe did not precipitate a rapid or radical reconfiguration of the agricultural workforce, in tobacco or elsewhere – in part because of workers' falling short of the ideal, but also for many other reasons, as we saw in the previous chapter. In tobacco, employers continued to employ temporary foreign workers to the same degree as they had for many years prior, and the newcomers to the workforce were simply slotted in as replacements for workers from the rapidly declining US movement. Eventually, of course, guest workers from the Global South did come to represent a much greater share of the agricultural workforce in labour-intensive crops such as fruits, vegetables, and tobacco. This shift would be justified in part by those extolling the virtues of guest workers while disparaging the depravity of Canadian labourers. But the true reasons for the shift had less to do with employer preference than popular narratives have led us to believe.

7

TOBACCO TRANSFORMED

It was August of 1985, and the streets of Delhi were eerily quiet. Gone were the crowds of job seekers packing the sidewalks, sleeping in parks, inconveniencing locals, and rankling authorities. At Delhi's CFLP office, only about two hundred and fifty transients had shown up looking for work that year, a fraction of the four to five thousand habitually received just a few years prior. The stark change in the harvest scene was the talk of the town. "There is absolutely no comparison (between now and 15 years ago)," remarked Dorothy Lindsay, a resident of Delhi for seventy-five years, to reporter Mark Hankinson of the *Delhi News-Record*. "We always dreaded civic holiday weekends because they just packed the streets. It used to be pretty grim. Now, the town is pretty quiet." Not everyone was thrilled about the change of pace; this was especially true of the local merchants who had benefitted from the rush of business each summer. As the owner of a men's clothing store explained, "Harvest is not what it used to be. At one time, harvest was our Christmas. Now, it's okay, but it's not like Christmas." The few remaining transients were themselves no less baffled. Fresh off a fourteen-hour hitchhiking odyssey to Delhi and installed at the traditional transient stomping grounds of Memorial Park, twenty-seven-year-old Paul Laflamme of Lévis, Quebec, told Hankinson that "the very first time I came here [in 1977], there would be 250 people in the same park." Continued Hankinson: "Now, when he looks across Memorial Park, he shakes his head in disbelief as he sees only 10 or 15 people." No matter who you talked to, everyone seemed to agree that transients' days were numbered. The *News-Record*'s headline aptly summed it up: "Transient Workers – Last of a Dying Breed."[1]

The *News-Record* had it right: within a few short years, the mass arrival of unattached migrant job seekers at harvest time became little more than a distant memory.[2] What had caused this monumental shift? Were government labour mobility schemes at last successful? Had growers, fed up with unreliable Canadian migrants, finally switched to Caribbean and Mexican guest workers? In fact, neither theory holds much explanatory water.

Instead, the root of the changes in tobacco labour lay not in government action or employer choice, but in the radical economic restructuring of the sector, a process that had begun in the 1960s but that accelerated dramatically in the 1980s. This restructuring left tobacco profoundly transformed, with the sector increasingly dominated by a smaller number of heavily capitalized operations as small growers were pushed out of business. It was only once this new economic order had taken hold that tobacco farms began employing Caribbean and Mexican guest workers in greater numbers. As early as the 1970s, however, tobacco growers – notably those who hired guest workers – were laying the groundwork for a very different interpretation of events. Disparaging the quality of Canadian workers while praising guest workers as their idealized opposite, the minority of growers who employed guest workers began ever more loudly making the case that they were experiencing a shortage of adequate labour and that temporary foreign workers represented the only solution.

Economic Challenges

Cracks began to appear in tobacco's previously golden edifice in the 1960s, as we saw in chapter 4. Rising costs, declining tobacco prices, and reduced production quotas pushed many smallholders to sell their farms in 1965 in what amounted to the first big instance of consolidation in the sector.[3] Small farmers got something of a break over the next few years, as production quotas returned to higher levels from 1966 to the end of the decade, in part due to the efforts of the Marketing Board to secure expanded export markets.[4] By the 1970s, however, challenges were again mounting for tobacco growers. An acreage cut in 1970 sparked more sell-offs. Another blow came when the United Kingdom entered into the European Common Market in 1973, and consequently began to phase out its preferential tariff on Canadian tobacco, an important factor in the tobacco belt's early success.[5]

As difficulties such as these pushed growers, and especially small growers, out of business, changes in Marketing Board policy made it more likely for their exit to result in the consolidation of production. Notably, in 1974, the

Marketing Board allowed tobacco production quotas to be detached from specific land and sold between growers. Under the previous rules, a tobacco quota was fixed to its assigned farm, and could only be sold along with the farm itself. Under the new rules, a tobacco grower getting out of the business could sell their quota while still keeping their farm. Conversely, larger operations could add production capacity to their existing land holdings, instead of having to manage multiple farms, some potentially at a distance from one another. The trend of consolidation was unmistakable. Between 1965 and 1975, the number of tobacco farm owners in Ontario decreased by more than 65 per cent, while acreage remained about the same. An especially big drop occurred from 1974 to 1975 after the introduction of the new rules on quota sales, when the number of tobacco farm owners plummeted by 12 per cent from one year to the next.[6]

These challenges soon turned to out-and-out catastrophe for tobacco growers, as demand for cigarettes plummeted. The causes were the growing awareness of the links between smoking and lung cancer, and the taxes on tobacco products that formed a key part of the policy response to the emerging public health crisis. But while the bottoming out of demand was perhaps the most ominous threat to tobacco farmers, it was not as if their other problems had simply gone away. Operating costs continued to rise, soaring by 100 per cent between 1974 and 1981, while gross revenue increased just 68 per cent. Next, farmers were hit by devastating natural disasters in 1979 and 1982 in the form of blue mould and a late-August frost. Finally, in the 1980s, in what must have seemed to weary tobacco growers the tenth plague of their proverbial Egypt, interest rates soared to between 17 and 22 per cent, meaning that the near-universal model of financing each season's crop by bank credit became untenable for all but the largest, most efficient farmers.[7]

By the early 1980s, the tobacco sector was in full-blown crisis. Domestic cigarette sales dropped by 17 per cent between 1981 and 1986, but tobacco production took an even greater hit, falling by 30 per cent over the same period. The differential drops in production and consumption are explained by two additional thorns in growers' sides: increased imports of leaf (from Brazil and Zimbabwe in particular), and changes in cigarette manufacturing that resulted in a 10 per cent drop in the amount of tobacco used in each cigarette. Under the weight of these cascading disasters, many tobacco growers found themselves in dire financial straights. In 1986, for example, tobacco farmers represented 4 per cent of Ontario's farm population but accounted for a whopping

25 per cent of applicants to the provincial Farm Debt Review Board. Unsurprisingly, this unrelenting economic drubbing had calamitous personal effects on farmers. Many farmers died by suicide in these years. One can surmise that countless more suffered from anxiety, depression, and strains on their personal relationships.[8]

Faced with such a dire situation in one of the country's most important crops, the provincial (and later the federal) government launched a series of initiatives to help tobacco farmers transition out of the business. The first, the Tobacco Transition Reduction Initiative, or "REDUX," purchased quota rights from growers in order to retire it permanently – in other words, to reduce tobacco production to better match demand while also compensating participating farmers. Running from 1983 to 1987, it succeeded in retiring approximately half of the province's total tobacco quota. Future programs in the 1980s and '90s were aimed at helping tobacco growers transition into other crops or businesses. A final quota-buyout scheme was announced in 2008 by the federal government, in which $300 million – part of a $1 billion fine paid by two tobacco multinationals as a penalty for cross-border tobacco smuggling – was paid out to about a thousand remaining quota holders.[9]

Due to these factors, the consolidation of tobacco production only accelerated in the 1980s, with the result that more and more small farmers were pushed out of business. In 1970, almost 4,600 tobacco farms dotted the province. By 1981, that number had been slashed by nearly half, to 2,650. In ten more years, it was again almost halved, to 1,418 tobacco farms in 1991. Overall tobacco production declined too, but not nearly at the same rate: a drop of 23 per cent between 1970 and 1991. With ever-thinning profit margins, only the biggest, most efficient farms could survive, a fact reflected in the changing levels of production per farm. In 1970, the average tobacco farm produced about 43,000 pounds of leaf. In 1991, the average farm's production more than doubled to 109,000 pounds. As figure 7.1 demonstrates, these trends would only accelerate in the decades to come.

A key factor enabling more heavily capitalized operations to stay in business was the adoption of a new wave of machinery. Tobacco's latest technological revolution began in the 1960s, and its crown jewel was the automatic harvester. It took just one or two operators to drive an automatic harvester through the tobacco rows, pick off individual leaves, and send them into a bin – thereby performing a job that previously required five or six workers. The other major

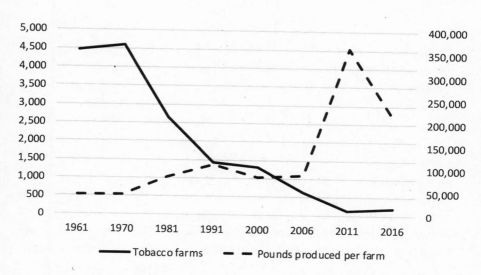

7.1 Number of tobacco farms and pounds produced per farm, Ontario, select years, 1961–2016. Sources: "Secretary's Report to the Fourth Annual Meeting," 13 July 1961, RG 27, vol. 667, file 6-5-26-1, part 3, LAC; OFCTGMB Annual Reports, 1970, 1975, 1976, 1982, 1986, 2001, Elgin County Archives; Census of Agriculture, 1981, 1991; Stewart, "Agricultural Restructuring in Ontario Tobacco Production," 163; *Recent Trends in Tobacco Agriculture in Canada* (Ottawa: Physicians for a Smoke-Free Canada, 2008); "Selected Crops, Historical Data," Statistics Canada; "Field Crops," Ontario Ministry of Agriculture.

innovation in this period were bulk kilns, which delivered the final blow to the traditional jobs at the tying table and kiln. Under this new productive order, bins or racks containing thousands of loose leaves of tobacco could be directly transferred from harvesting machine to kiln, eliminating entirely the previous job of tying tobacco to sticks or hanging those sticks in kilns. These changes revolutionized tobacco's production process. Four workers could now perform the labour of fourteen. The primers, tiers, handers, and curers who had dominated harvest workforces were replaced by two workers operating the harvesting machine, one driver transporting leaf and bins back and forth from the field, and one person loading and unloading the kilns.[10]

The early prototypes of automated harvesters and bulk kilns were first developed and adopted by a small number of growers in the 1960s and '70s, but their use did not become widespread until the 1980s and '90s, in part because of the enormous outlay of capital required and doubts about the reliability of the machines – and of automatic harvesters in particular.[11] Technological developments were encouraged by the federal government's experimental farm in Delhi and by the Marketing Board, via both educational programs and incentivization.[12] Tobacco-buying companies, Imperial chief among them, were also keen on mechanization. While stressing the advantages to farmers of having more modern, efficient production, the benefits to companies were of course clear: cheaper production would enable lower tobacco prices, and any risk of investing significant capital into costly (and often unproven) new machinery would fall on farmers.[13] Mechanization was also good business for manufacturers and sellers of agricultural equipment, who tirelessly promoted the latest and greatest in labour-saving technologies.[14] Intentional or not, encouraging mechanization had the effect of encouraging the further consolidation of tobacco production. This was particularly true of Marketing Board schemes. In 1970, for example, the Marketing Board announced that three farms trying out automatic harvesters – priced at $11,000 each – would be permitted a 5 per cent increase on their allotted acreage, a decision that provoked controversy among at least some farmers.[15]

Just as tobacco farming's worsening economic outlook increasingly pushed small farmers and sharegrowers out of business, so, too, did it curtail opportunities for social mobility on the part of wage labourers. With the soaring costs of farming – and all the other swirling crises – the social mobility that had been so common in the sector's early decades became increasingly difficult to attain; ultimately, it was effectively impossible. Into the 1960s, European immigrants in the tobacco belt still managed to climb from wage labourer to farm owner. Like their predecessors, these later arrivals – with Dutch, Polish, and Portuguese immigrants prominent among them – often combined wage labour in tobacco with work in other crops, as well as in manufacturing, construction, and/or resource extraction, in order to save capital to purchase a farm. But those who arrived earliest in Canada appear to have had the best chance of progressing to farm ownership. Out of dozens of consulted questionnaires conducted in 1977, the latest arriving immigrant to have purchased a tobacco farm arrived in the country in 1962, though many arriving after this date became sharegrowers.[16] Former tobacco grower John Ackner also recognized this trend, especially after the 1960s. Upward social mobility, he recalled, became more difficult to do when the price of land and quota [increased] … You could buy a 100-acre farm that had 40 acres of growing rights to it – you could buy that in the late sixties for like $100,000. Well, once you got into the mid-eighties it was like $600,000. I realize there was inflation there, but it wasn't that high. So, as a result, as the price of those farms went up and the quota and the equipment and all that, it just became a situation where you couldn't work yourself into it … From a labourer to a grower – it just was way too high.[17]

The Vanishing Transient

It was in this context of economic disaster that Canadian migrant workers began to disappear from the tobacco labour scene, after decades of being at centre stage. A gradual decline in the numbers of transients arriving each harvest had been observed as far back as the mid-1960s. By the mid-1980s, with an eerie quiet falling over Delhi's summertime streets, there could be no doubt that a decisive shift had occurred. Exact statistical indicators are difficult to muster, but the following figures are telling: whereas in 1969, 25 per cent of the workforce were Canadians from outside of Ontario, by 1980 that proportion had dropped to 17 per cent, a number that by all indications continued to plummet in the coming years.[18]

What caused the sudden disappearance of the transient, so long a feature of the tobacco belt at harvest time? Government officials were quick to credit themselves with the development, claiming victory for the labour mobility schemes whose efficacy they had preached for decades. This was true not only in the 1980s, but also in earlier periods when the numbers of transients appeared to be down. In the early 1970s, for example, a wave of radio spots broadcast throughout Quebec and Atlantic Canada were thought to have played a key role in convincing potential job seekers to avoid coming to the tobacco belt without pre-arranged work. "Following the harvest in 1970 we received congratulations from the industry because there had been a reduction in the number of transient workers. We were asked to continue the program again this year," wrote the assistant deputy minister of manpower. In 1971, it was again considered a success: "In view of the large numbers of unemployed workers and students it was surprising that the transient flow was reduced in

1971."[19] CFLP staffers again took credit for the final, permanent decline in transient arrivals in the early 1980s.[20]

In spite of official boosterism, there is limited evidence to suggest that the decline of transients was in fact a result of the efforts of the CFLP. For one, bureaucrats' purported victories over uncontrolled labour migration always seemed to be frustratingly short-lived, with increases in the usage of government mobility programs unfailingly giving way to declines in subsequent years. After three promising seasons between 1971 and 1973, for example, officials reported renewed challenges in 1974, with the creation of the CFLP. "Many if not all of the transients I have spoken to not just in the tobacco fields but as well as fruit and vegetable industry, have not heard of the Canada Farm Labour Pool programme nor the Student Mobility Programme," wrote Elizabeth Shea, the regional coordinator of Manpower's hostel program.[21] Dampening bureaucrats' declarations of victory even further was the fact that many CFLP placements did not involve workers who would otherwise have been unattached transients. Many of those Canadian migrants who came to the tobacco belt via the CFLP did so through the so-called Named Worker Program, meaning that they were returning to an employer who had employed them previously.[22] In such cases, the CFLP did not replace the movement of unattached transients into the region; instead, it simply injected a state travel subsidy into the recruitment of return workers, a practice that had been common throughout the sector's history, usually without any state involvement. Before the CFLP, growers would often contact workers individually to arrange payment of their transportation costs.[23] In such cases, it is not surprising that they would take advantage of a government program promising to deliver the same workers while footing the bill. Even with "named workers" inflating the statistics somewhat, estimates of CFLP usage remained modest. In 1977, for example, a Marketing Board survey found that only 21 per cent of growers had hired workers through Manpower programs, while the *Globe* reported that fewer than 10 per cent of tobacco workers were hired through the CFLP.[24]

Nor were unattached transients replaced by guest workers, as might be assumed from the vantage point of today. The number of Caribbean and Mexican workers in tobacco jumped to 1,691 in 1981, at that point an all-time high, but still a small percentage of the 30,000-strong workforce. In the next few years, however, those numbers shrank again, to about 1,000 per year in 1984 and 1985, as the federal government ordered reductions in the program's size.[25]

It wasn't until later in the decade, a full twenty years after the introduction of the SAWP, that its participants would begin to account for more than 10 per cent of the overall workforce, as we will see later in this chapter.

In fact, grower preferences appear to have played at most a marginal role in the transient's disappearance from the tobacco belt. Instead, over time Canadian migrant workers simply stopped coming. The reasons were not complicated: wages and conditions declined, making the sector a decidedly less attractive place to work compared to other opportunities. In 1965, the median wage paid to tobacco workers, eighteen dollars a day, was 2.25 times higher than what they would have made working an eight-hour day at the province's newly introduced minimum wage of a dollar per hour. By 1969, however, tobacco workers were earning only 1.73 times the daily pay of someone working for the minimum wage. That figure essentially plateaued through to the early 1980s, dropping slightly to 1.57 in 1984. The late 1970s and early 1980s also saw tobacco wages drop in relation to the Consumer Price Index (CPI), a tool measuring the cost of a fixed basket of consumer goods that Statistics Canada uses to track changes in purchasing power over time. Between 1978 and 1984, the median tobacco harvest wage in relation to the index declined by 27 per cent (see figure 7.2). Reductions in the real wages of tobacco workers were likely a combined result of the tightened cost-price squeeze facing tobacco growers, as well as the opportunities that mechanization afforded them to hire younger and less-skilled local workers. For more self-aware farmers, however, it was no mystery why finding quality labour was a growing problem. As a farmer having trouble locating workers for the 1973 planting season commented, "We wouldn't have labor problems if we could afford to pay what we should be paying. There are enough people to do the work if the price is right. If the farmer was paid more for his product everyone would benefit because the farmer turns his money back into the country."[26]

Desperate to cut costs in any way, some farmers adopted a more nefarious method of suppressing wages – namely, by firing workers just before the end of the harvest in order to avoid paying bonuses, as we saw in chapter 4.[27] The economic climate made the workplace unpleasant in other ways too. Workers bunking on farms in this era often described their living conditions as extremely poor. Among tobacco workers, sharegrowers developed a reputation for providing the worst accommodations and meals, unsurprising given their status as the most economically challenged employers. Sharegrowers' farm

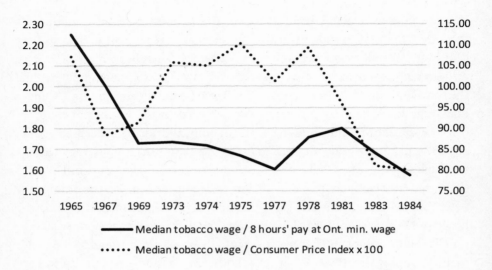

7.2 Tobacco wages in relation to Ontario minimum wage and Consumer Price Index,
select years, 1965–84. Sources: Immigration Branch (RG 76, vol. 1112), Department
of Manpower and Immigration (RG 118, vol. 246, 273 acc. 1985–86/071, vols 74–5), LAC;
Simcoe Reformer, 8 August 1975; *Toronto Star*, 23 September 1977; Barker and Kennedy,
The Tobacco Leaf Yesterday and Today; Canadian Farmworkers Union Collection, Simon
Fraser University Digitized Collections; Whyte, *The Experience of New Immigrants
and Seasonal Farmworkers*, 4.17; Employment and Social Development Canada;
Statistics Canada.

equipment was also thought to be in shoddy condition, likely to break down
and therefore lengthen the workday (with no increase in pay, given the piece-
rate system).[28]

Québécoise migrant worker Patricia, whom we met in chapter 4, recalled
extremely tense experiences working on tobacco farms. Both years that Patricia
worked in tobacco, she and her co-workers were victims of the bonus-payment
bait and switch – fired right before the end of the harvest with the most absurd
justifications. The second time this happened, the ostensible reason was that
the workers had taken an onion from the farm family's garden. "That's where
I decided that was it for tobacco," Patricia explained. She continued to work
seasonal farm jobs in southwestern Ontario – that autumn and also in future
years – but never again in tobacco. "We opted for tomatoes and apples because

... [you earned] roughly what you got with [tobacco] ... You could work more on your own – you didn't have to keep up to a machine with other guys. And ... honestly, it was the tension. I just hated it. I thought they were all crazy at the time .... [I]t just hit me as a crazy place to be."[29]

While farmers disparaged transients as unreliable quitters, as we'll see later in this chapter, things looked remarkably different from workers' perspectives. As wages, living, and working conditions worsened, and tobacco farms became ever-less pleasant places to work, Canadian migrants stopped coming in such large numbers to seek work in the harvest. Who could blame them? Whereas in previous decades, tobacco work had offered attractive opportunities for short-term wage earning, and even social mobility, by the 1980s this was no longer the case. Young job seekers moved on, even reversing the long-standing trend of tobacco poaching workers from other crops, as Patricia and other workers switched to different crops. Tobacco lost its status as the top destination for itinerant Canadian farm workers, a mantle that would soon be taken up by British Columbia's Okanagan Valley, where large numbers of Québécois (in particular) would begin travelling for seasonal farm jobs, starting in precisely this era.[30]

The void left by transients was principally filled not by workers in the CFLP or by foreign guest workers, but by local workers, especially young ones. With few other employment opportunities – and often not requiring room and board – they could frequently be hired for lower wages. Technological advances – particularly the ride-on priming machines and tying machines that predominated before the ascendance of the more automated production process adopted in the 1980s and '90s – also made tobacco work less strenuous and skilled, further enabling the hiring of younger workers. For at least one farmer, hiring a young crew provided a pathway to avoiding an immense expenditure on an automated harvester. George DeBock told the *Delhi News-Record* in 1974 that his priming crew now consisted entirely of boys aged thirteen to fifteen, whom he could hire for lower wages than those that older workers would expect. "If I can get by this way I have no intention of purchasing an automatic harvester. There must be hundreds of kids this age in nearby towns who are just walking around when they could each be earning in excess of $1,000 from the harvest," DeBock exclaimed.[31] In 1977, another farmer reported hiring an all-local crew of young people – in this case, all girls. The grower explained that he had employed Caribbean workers in the mid-1960s, but that the cost had been too high. "I have been using young women in field crews for several years now and they are the best workers I have ever had. I will hire a female over a male as a primer any day."[32]

Another attraction of local teenagers was that community ties and social norms lessened the likelihood of workplace conflict, early quitting, or absenteeism. A teenager working for the neighbour down the road, who was perhaps a family friend or who might have attended the same church, was unlikely to protest poor conditions. Of course, the inverse was likely also true – a grower in such a situation was probably much less likely to trick a local worker out of a bonus payment by firing them early.[33] Michelle Vermeeren of Tillsonburg, who in the 1980s worked many tobacco harvests in her youth alongside her siblings, explained in an interview how community ties and obligations helped ensure a reliable teenaged workforce: "I think [the farmers we worked for] were grateful to have a guaranteed workforce. You know, our parents would kill us [if we messed up the job]. Nobody called in sick ... there's no sickness, right? [Laughs.] I remember my brother hurt his hand at home, doing something stupid, [like] making his own firecrackers. And he ripped his hand open. And he had to prime. And my parents are like, 'Okay, we'll clean it up and do whatever and then wrap it up, and you're working tomorrow."[34]

Belated Turn to the SAWP

It was only in the transformed tobacco sector of the late 1980s and beyond that tobacco growers finally began employing guest workers from the Caribbean and Mexico in greater numbers, a full two decades after first gaining access to them. The belated turn to SAWP workers was part and parcel of the broader transformation taking place in the tobacco sector in this period. Just as it was the larger, more heavily capitalized growers who were able to purchase automatic harvesters and other machinery, enabling them to operate more efficiently and at greater scale, so, too, was this same group of growers the ones who could afford to hire workers through the SAWP. It is a broad misconception that SAWP workers are attractive because they are "cheap labour." SAWP workers have never been cheap. The standards of accommodation required by the program meant that most employers had to build entirely new bunkhouses in order to participate. Coupled with advancing funds for workers' flights, this meant that hiring guest workers required considerable advance expenditure.

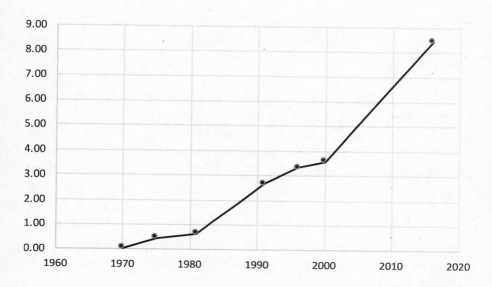

7.3 SAWP workers per farm, Ontario tobacco, select years, 1970–2016. Sources: Whyte, *The Experience of New Immigrants and Seasonal Farmworkers*, 4.5; Satzewich, *Racism and the Incorporation of Foreign Labour*, 112; Weston and Scarpa de Masellis, *Hemispheric Integration and Trade Relations*, 31; Basok, *Tortillas and Tomatoes*, 34; and sources for figure 7.1.

It was not wishful thinking when Manpower officials referred to the SAWP as a "premium" program, repeatedly resisting growers' calls to reduce their costs in accessing the scheme.[35]

It was the biggest growers who could afford to bring in workers via the SAWP, so it stands to reason that the growth of the SAWP within tobacco coincided very closely with the sector's consolidation. In 1981, Ontario's 2,650 tobacco farmers hired 1,691 workers through the SAWP, a rate of 0.65 SAWP workers per farm. Fifteen years later, in 1996–97, the number of farms had dwindled to 1,317, while the number of SAWP workers had surged to 4,382, representing 3.33 SAWP workers per farm, a fivefold increase from 1981. The ratio has continued its meteoric rise in the years since, with tobacco growers employing 8.45 SAWP workers per farm in 2016–18 (see figure 7.3). The operations with the capital and efficiency to survive into the 1990s and beyond were clearly pleased with their now SAWP-dominated workforce. In a survey of sixty-three

current and former tobacco farmers conducted in 1996–97 in which participants were asked to identify positive and negative "forces of change" in the
sector, "labour issues" was rated as the top positive trend, as growers specifically
pointed to "the ability to obtain offshore labour from Mexico and Jamaica."[36]

While the swirling crises and traumatic sell-offs of tobacco farms represent
a particularly dramatic example, the same general trend – the expansion of
temporary foreign worker programs correlated with agricultural consolidation
– can be observed in Canadian agriculture writ large (see figure 7.4). As public
policy researcher Robert Falconer explains in a recent report, "In the postwar
period, Canadian farms underwent a dramatic consolidation, creating significantly fewer farms of substantially larger size."[37] From a high of approximately
730,000 Canadian farms in 1941, this fell to 430,000 by 1966 and to 280,000 by
1991 – a decline of 60 per cent over fifty years. Over this same period, the total
acreage of crops remained fairly steady, meaning that the remaining farms
were ever larger in size. Whereas in 1941, the average agricultural operation
farmed 77 acres of cropland, by 1991 the figure had nearly quadrupled to 296
acres of cropland per farm. The trends have only accelerated in the years since,
with the average farm boasting 483 acres of cropland in 2016.

Other indicators tell the same story. For example, the percentage of farms
with revenue greater than $250,000 rose from 3 to 14 per cent of all operations
between 1981 and 2001 (in 2000 dollars). Between 1981 and 2016, the share of
farms with receipts over $500,000 (in 2010 dollars) has soared from 1 to 16 per
cent.[38] In 1981, 57 per cent of farms held capital valued at $500,000 or higher
(in 2016 dollars). In 2016, that designation was true of 78 per cent of farms.
Similarly, the average capital held per farm increased nearly fourfold between
1976 and 2016 (in 2016 dollars); by the latter date, the average Canadian farm's
capital was valued at $2.6 million.[39] Over these same years, the number of SAWP
workers – and later temporary foreign workers in other agricultural streams
– entering Canada also skyrocketed, with especially steep climbs coming in
the late 1980s, the late 1990s and 2000s, and the 2010s. As I do here in the case
of tobacco, Falconer argues that these two trends were not mere coincidence.
"The participation of foreign workers in Canadian food production may have
little to do with the *displacement of domestic workers* in comparison to the *consolidation of agriculture*," he writes, focusing especially on the impossibility of
family labour keeping up with labour requirements on ever-larger operations.[40]
Indeed, by 2018, 68.4 per cent of temporary foreign workers in agriculture were

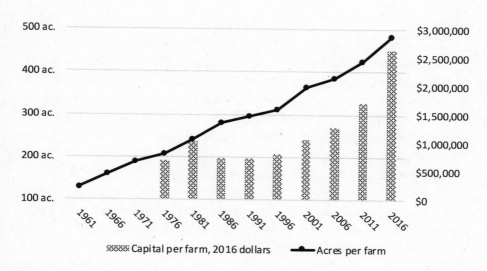

7.4 Acres and capital per tobacco farm, Ontario, select years, 1961–2016. "Total Area of Farms and Use of Farm Land, Historical Data," "Farm Capital, Selected Expenditures and Forest Product Sales, Historical Data," Statistics Canada; Census of Agriculture, 2016; "Inflation Calculator," Bank of Canada.

employed by farms with gross receipts of over $2 million, revenue that would place them in approximately the top 3 per cent of all Canadian farmers. In other words, by and large, it is the very largest of farming operations that hire temporary foreign workers.[41]

Of course, consolidation was not the sole cause of the SAWP's exponential growth from the 1980s to the 2010s, though, along with Falconer, I submit that it was the most important. Changes in Canadian federal policy helped open the door for growers to enjoy easier access to the program. Specifically, in 1987 administrative duties for the program were passed from the federal Department of Employment and Immigration to a private, farmer-run not-for-profit agency, the Foreign Agricultural Resource Management Services, or FARMS.[42] This change was the result of the cost-cutting efforts of the so-called Nielson Task Force under Brian Mulroney's Progressive Conservative government. As part of this arrangement, restrictions on the number of workers employers could request were lifted.[43] The immediate impacts of this change can be seen by a spike in program usage between 1985 and 1989. In 1985, 5,005 workers travelled to Canada under the SAWP. In 1988, after the changes had taken hold, 8,047 workers participated, and their numbers jumped to 11,302 in 1989 – a 126 per cent increase over 1985. But the program would plateau in size after that, and only began to creep up in size again in the early 2000s. Expansion reached its greatest heights in the 2010s, when the annual number of SAWP workers surged to over 40,000, about four times the 1989 levels. Again, this increase co-incided with a parallel surge in farm consolidation, as can be seen in figures 7.4 and 7.5.

The creation of FARMS helped growers in other ways too, notably by allow-ing them to significantly reduce their costs for using the program, thus eroding the "premium" aspect that had long characterized it. Airfare costs were a par-ticular target. Previously, all SAWP travel had been routed through a single Chatham travel agency, which, according to past FARMS president Gary Cooper, was making a fabulous profit both by marking up airfare and by charg-ing a $50 administration fee for each worker's flight. In Cooper's calculations, "5,000 workers at $50 [equals] $250,000. Pretty nice deal." FARMS first lobbied the government to allow growers to choose from multiple travel agencies, but after a few years they were still dissatisfied with the markup on flights. (Cooper suggested that this was a result of collusion between the firms.) Around the mid-1990s, FARMS went back to the government again, this time requesting permission to set up its own travel agency and cut out the profit-skimming middlemen. Permission was granted, and FARMS created a non-profit travel agency, CanAg Travel, that arranged air travel at cost to employers, drastically reducing prices.

FARMS was also very successful in gradually shifting the share of airfare onto workers' shoulders. For the first six years of the SAWP, employers covered the full cost of workers' airfare. That changed in 1972, when employers gained the right to deduct up to $60 from workers' paycheques to cover part of their travel costs – $374 in 2019 dollars (the dollar measurement used for the remainder of this paragraph to account for inflation). Between 1972 and 1983 (before FARMS), the amount that growers could deduct actually *decreased* to a maxi-mum of $164 in 1983. But the founding of FARMS reversed that trend; by 1996, growers could recover $489. That figure has stayed fairly steady, with the de-duction set at $456 in 2019.[44]

The increase and then plateau in workers' share of airfare has coincided with a dramatic reduction in the market costs of flights, especially in recent

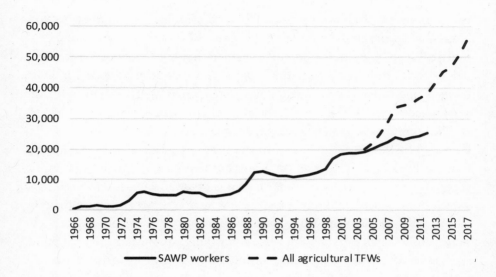

7.5 SAWP workers, 1966–2012, and all agricultural temporary foreign workers, 2004–17, Canada. Sources: Satzewich, *Racism and the Incorporation of Foreign Labour*, 111; Secretariat of the Commission for Labor Cooperation, *Protection of Migrant Agricultural Workers in Canada, Mexico and the United States*, 8; Citizenship and Immigration Canada, *Facts and Figures: Immigration Overview – Temporary Residents, 2009–16*.

years. In 1973, round-trip airfare between Kingston and Toronto cost $180, or $1,060 in 2019 dollars – though in 2019, flights could often be found for half that amount. With workers' costs remaining steady, those savings have gone entirely to employers. Since the creation of FARMS, growers have also gained the right to deduct costs for utilities from workers, something they could not do in the program's early decades.[45]

The Labour Shortage Narrative

In spite of the many sound material reasons for Canadian migrants to stop coming to the tobacco belt, and the strong correlation between consolidation and SAWP employment, popular memory has painted an altogether different picture of the changes in the tobacco workforce over the latter decades of the twentieth century. A typical example comes from an exhibit on tobacco farming on the website of the Elgin County Archives, text from which also appears in a permanent exhibit at the Delhi Tobacco Museum and Heritage Centre. "In the later part of the 20th century," it reads, "it became more difficult to find dedicated transient workers to bring in the harvest. Offshore workers were perceived as steady and dependable. Migrant workers from Jamaica, Barbados, Mexico, and other southern countries were increasingly brought in for the season and returned home when the harvest was done."[46]

The museum's version of events is entirely unremarkable. Indeed, the "labour shortage narrative," as I call it, has become so ingrained in understandings of the origins of guest-worker programs as to become an article of common sense. And yet, as we've seen so far in this chapter, the actual reasons for the switch from Canadian to foreign workers were much more complex than the labour shortage narrative would lead us to believe. It thus confuses and obscures more than it explains. But while confusion helps the narrative to persist, its origins do not lie in a simple misunderstanding of historical sequence. Instead, the labour shortage narrative owes its existence – and much of its persistence – to concerted efforts by growers to defend and expand their access to temporary foreign workers, a story we can observe very clearly in the case of tobacco.

In the same period that tobacco farmers' profit margins were thinning and the sector was becoming a decidedly less attractive place to work, a small but vocal group of tobacco growers began making ever more insistent claims about the depravity of Canadian migrant workers and the superiority of guest workers. Their attitudes cohered into a fairly consistent set of self-evident truths. Canadian migrants were drunks, drug addicts, and criminally inclined. They were unreliable – likely to quit without notice before the end of harvest. They had poor attitudes and were difficult to work with. And perhaps most importantly, they were not truly interested in farm jobs. "I had two boys here from New Brunswick this fall who got drunk and refused to work the next day," a tobacco farmer told the *Toronto Star* in 1971, in one typical example. "I had to fire them. In the harvest season people just can't stop and start like that."[47] Foreign guest workers, on the other hand, came to represent precisely the opposite qualities: they were reliable, morally upstanding, eager, compliant, and genuinely interested in performing agricultural labour. The contrast was summed up neatly in a letter written by a tobacco-farming couple to their member of Parliament in 1976: "Off-shore [Caribbean] workers are quiet people that spend their evenings cooking, washing and cleaning while transients are often drunkards, abusive and even violent with no respect for our property."[48]

These claims mirrored very closely ones that had been made by Ontario fruit and vegetable growers since the 1950s and '60s, especially in the context of lobbying for a West Indian guest-worker scheme. Typical examples can be found in reports by two different fruit and vegetable farmers' associations, in 1958 and 1965, which described Canadian migrant farm workers as a "poor calibre of men" besot with criminal records (per the 1958 report), and "drunks, half drunks, and winos who only work enough to get the price of a couple bottles of wine" (per the other). Special disdain was reserved for First Nations workers and the urban unemployed.[49] For tobacco growers, however, this sort of "character assassination," as Vic Satzewich aptly labels it, represented something of a discursive departure. While local residents and political figures in the Norfolk region had long grumbled about transient workers, growers had generally remained mum on the topic, content with the yearly rush of job seekers to their doorsteps.

These truisms fit comfortably within the broader "common sense" (to borrow Antonio Gramsci's term) of neoliberalism that was taking hold in much of the world in this era.[50] While on the policy side, neoliberalism featured an assault on Keynesianism and government-funded social programs, it also contained a powerful cultural element that featured, among other things, a moral rebuke of the subscribers to such programs. In keeping with these trends, tobacco growers' comparisons of Canadian and foreign workers often worked simultaneously as a critique of the welfare state.

A letter from tobacco farmer Elizabeth Pearce to Minister of Agriculture Eugene Whelan, sent in 1975 to protest proposed restrictions on the Caribbean scheme, offers a particularly striking example. The typical Canadian worker sent to the tobacco district by Manpower, Pearce explained, is "undoubtedly already on Unemployment Benefits … and at the end of the day he will collect his cheque for a day's work and will not return the following day." He is, Pearce continued, "unambitious, lazy and very often content with the way his life is." With "the benefits of Welfare and Unemployment to fall back on," he has no incentive to "work in the heat, the rain or cold." In sum, "The Unemployed Canadian is a pretty soft individual and has never been taught how to work."

Workers from the Caribbean were completely different, according to Pearce. "In the seven years that we have been fortunate enough to have Barbados Labour," she wrote, "we have never had to lay-off because of an absent, drunk or drugged employee. These men have come to Canada to work and this is the main reason for their coming." Just as social assistance programs were partly to blame for the shortcomings of Canadian workers, it was their assumed *absence* in Barbados that explained the superiority of those workers. "These labourers have no Old Age Pension Fund, no Unemployment Insurance or Welfare Benefits to fall back on if they don't work. They must work while they are able to provide for their families and for their old age."[51] (It should be noted that, contrary to Pearce's assumptions, Barbados did indeed have a national pension program at this time, the National Insurance Scheme, founded in 1967, six months after the island nation's independence.[52])

As if often the case with elements of "common sense," these truisms about Canadian and foreign workers were not pure fancy. There can be no doubt, for example, that guest workers were indeed more "reliable" than their Canadian counterparts. Of course, there were logical reasons for this that had little to do with these workers' good manners or superior morals. Guest workers, with no rights to labour mobility and obliged to return home at season's end, were far less likely to blow off work or quit before the end of harvest. And, despite the many examples of protest we've seen, they were still probably less likely to openly protest than their Canadian counterparts. The structural pressures ensuring "good behaviour" were especially true for migrant workers from the Caribbean, many of whose livelihoods became dependent on their earnings in Canada.

In moments of candour, growers and civil servants readily recognized the material bases for the "reliability" gap between Canadian migrants and guest workers – whether they came from the Caribbean or Europe. European students were "good workers, stable and dependable – mainly as they had no place else to go and are not allowed to change jobs without authority," tobacco growers reported to Manpower and Immigration in 1973.[53] "The West Indian workers are excellent," said one farmer in 1971. "You know that once you hire them they will stay."[54] Added another in 1977: "I like the Caribbean labour because I hold something over him. If he chatters too much or stays out too late at night, I can send him home, and that means something to him."[55] Indeed, government officials labelled both European and Caribbean workers as "captive labour" at various points.[56] The true attraction of guest workers, then, had little to do with labour shortages. Instead, as many other authors have pointed out, it was guest workers' *unfreedom* that fundamentally made them appealing to employers.[57] Grower narratives about Canadian migrants also undoubtedly contained some kernels of truth. Free to move and work where they liked with no prospect of deportation, there surely were Canadian tobacco workers who overindulged in drugs and alcohol, quit early, and generally comported themselves in ways unlikely to earn them "employee of the month" badges.

Neither were tobacco growers' labour problems mere fiction. While labour shortages were not a real concern in the 1960s and '70s, as thousands of job seekers continued to jam the district each summer, farmers did find it ever more difficult to retain workers until the end of harvest – especially as the workforce got younger. The high school and university students who increasingly populated the tobacco workforce had the annoying habit of wanting to return to school in early September, before the completion of the harvest. Growers met this challenge with a variety of tactics, instituting bonus systems that offered payouts to workers who stayed until the end of harvest, and – through the Marketing Board – lobbying the Ministry of Education and local high schools to delay the start of the school year until after the harvest (or at least permit enrolled tobacco workers to rejoin their classmates late).[58] Temporary foreign workers, contractually bound to farmers until the end of harvest, provided employers with an even more effective solution.[59] (Growers' headaches around absconding students presented a lucrative opportunity to those workers who did not have to – or wish to – return to school in September. Marc Chaussé of Rouyn-Noranda, Quebec, who worked in tobacco as a teenager in the 1970s, put it like this: "Me, I was not in a hurry to go back to school. So I stayed after [completing my original contract]. And then I was choosing my job ... I was taking the best job on the farm – what they were calling the boat driver, the guy that drives the tractor. So when I was walking on the street, and the farmers stopped and asked if I was available, I [would] say, 'Yes, but the only thing I do is boat driver.'" Chaussé recalled with a chuckle how he would be able to secure fifteen or even twenty days of extra work by this method. "For me, it was like overtime."[60])

Real though farmers' issues were – as were the material advantages offered by guest workers – they did not produce a significant change in how tobacco growers used guest-worker programs after the introduction of the European and Caribbean schemes, as we have already seen. And yet, the disparagement of Canadians and the pedestalling of guest workers became an increasingly common refrain among tobacco farmers, as it had been for some years with other growers. The similarities between tobacco and other farmers' rhetoric extended even further when, in the 1970s, tobacco farmers began also to complain of labour shortages, despite there being little evidence of real shortages occurring. Indeed, in many years – down to the early 1980s even – the tobacco belt continued to experience labour *surpluses* at harvest time, with repeats of the familiar scenes of the 1930s as hundreds of job seekers were turned away without having secured work.[61]

To begin to understand the seeming contradictions of growers' claims about labour shortages at a time when there were no labour shortages, and about the unemployability of Canadian migrants at a time when they remained a significant element of the workforce, we need to note two further characteristics of farmers' rhetoric. First, such claims came not from all tobacco farmers, or even a majority of them, but instead from a tiny minority – those who hired guest workers. Second, these comparisons tended to be voiced – and voiced most emphatically – at very specific moments: namely, at times when growers' access to foreign workers was threatened, a relatively common occurrence during these years. Growers' rhetoric, then, is best understood as part of a larger *narrative* – one that was articulated by a small minority of growers and deployed at strategic moments. In constructing this narrative, growers took what they claimed were the self-evident truths of Canadian migrant inferiority (aided and abetted by the welfare state) and guest-worker superiority and forged them into a logical sequence just like the one used by their counterparts in other crop sectors: Canadian migrants' disinterest in and profound unsuitability for farm work were to blame for farm labour shortages, and guest workers represented the solution. This was the tobacco sector's version of the labour shortage narrative, which over time transitioned from strategic message to hegemonic understanding of the origins of guest-worker schemes.[62]

One moment when the labour shortage narrative was strategically deployed in Ontario's tobacco belt took place in 1975, when Manpower implemented changes to the SAWP requiring the preferential hiring of Canadians before guest workers could be secured, and delaying the hiring of West Indians until 15 August, a date that fell two weeks into the tobacco harvest and was also disruptive to other farmers' plans. The changes enraged farmers – in tobacco and other crops. In March of that year, six hundred growers – representing the fruit and vegetable as well as tobacco sectors – packed into Delhi's German Hall for an emergency meeting called by the Norfolk Federation of Agriculture. Speaking to an audience of their peers, along with sympathetic Norfolk-Haldimand MP William Knowles and the manager of Simcoe's Manpower office, growers railed against the changes, spurred on by "applause, shouts of 'right on' and a few other choice expressions," as the *Delhi News-Record* reported. In making their case, growers did not limit themselves to arguments about the questionable logic of delaying the arrival of workers until after the start of harvest. Instead, to get their points across, they deployed the now familiar common sense about the hopeless inadequacy of Canadian workers. "Several in the audience complained [that] many of the people brought in from other parts of the country by Manpower could not do the jobs, or would not work," the *News-Record* recounted. "One lady said she was tired of dealing with alcoholics, drug addicts and Saturday night brawls. Off-shore labour seemed to be the solution and now you are taking them away from us, she declared."[63] Similar points were raised in Elizabeth Pearce's letter to Eugene Whelan, quoted earlier in this chapter, which was sent in protest against the same measures. Opponents of the change also raised the spectre of labour shortages. Recalling the tried-and-true farmers' plea about crops rotting in the fields for want of labour,[64] tobacco grower K.C. Emerson reasoned, "Tobacco is a very perishable crop, as well as being expensive to grow, and it is important to the economy of the area. The association feels very strongly that no effort should be spared in securing the best, most dependable worker for the planting and harvesting of the tobacco crop."[65] Despite Emerson's concern, 1975 was yet another year in which a surplus of job seekers entered the tobacco belt, forcing many to leave the region without having secured work.[66]

In each of the next two years, 1976 and 1977, growers in the program were again on the defensive, first when employers in the Tillsonburg area were limited to two Caribbean workers per farm, and next when tobacco growers were barred from hiring West Indians for springtime planting. Growers launched a spirited letter-writing campaign to protest the 1976 limits, flooding their MPs' offices with letters of protest, matters that were duly taken up with Minister of Manpower and Immigration Robert Andras by MPs for Oxford and Norfolk-Haldimand. The letter writers also sought to revive long-standing anxieties about race mixing on tobacco farms, in living quarters in particular.

"There is *no* way we can house 2 races of people together in harmony due to differences in food and living conditions," wrote one tobacco farming couple, voicing a sentiment echoed by many other correspondents.

Incredibly, this particular argument had been encouraged by Jamaican liaison officer Noel Heron in correspondence with farmers about how to protest the new regulations. Heron had advised farmers that Jamaica would refuse to send workers to farms with accommodations shared between Jamaicans and other nationalities. To their credit, Manpower officials – perhaps having learned from the debacle of the integration of the US-Ontario program ten years earlier – swiftly rebuked this line of argumentation.[67] Up in arms again in 1977, growers' comments at a meeting with Manpower representatives revealed what was really problematic about Canadian migrant workers. "The most prominent concern among farmers as indicated Thursday seemed to be the transience of Canadian labour," summarized the *Delhi News-Record*. One grower present at the meeting bluntly asked, "Isn't there some way we can force seasonal labour to stay put?"[68] Comparisons between guest workers and Canadian migrant workers were also marshalled to make arguments for maintaining or expanding the European student scheme, such as in 1977 when the Marketing Board requested a doubling of that program's quota. "Many producers who have turned to the off-shore workers have had a bad experience with the Canadian workers," reported the *Reformer*.[69]

Civil servants readily recognized growers' strategic use of the labour shortage narrative. "It is apparent that some of the growers are launching a publicity campaign in the Simcoe and Tillsonburg area to have all their requests for Caribbean workers approved," explained a Manpower memorandum in 1976. "Canadian labour was strongly criticized while the Caribbean workers were praised."[70] They also saw through to the true advantage offered by guest workers. "The quality of the Canadian workers selected and recruited are invariably measured against the Caribbean workers. Since the Caribbeans are recruited under specific contract terms and conditions, they are essentially a captive labour force," wrote one official.[71] Similarly, the European program was described by a 1984 Manpower report as a "source of captive labour."[72]

With farmers of other crops, too, officials frequently questioned their claims of labour shortages and the inadequacy of Canadian workers. In Manpower and Immigration's major 1973 report on seasonal farm labour in southwestern Ontario, bureaucrats reported meeting with a cucumber and tomato grower

on his farm near Chatham. Officials noted the irony when, "after an angry ti-
rade about Canadians not wanting to work, and other familiar themes," the
grower proceeded to explain his farm's extremely parsimonious pay structure,
according to which almost two-thirds of employees' wages were withheld until
the end of the season. "It is not hard to understand why, under these circumstances, there is a high turnover," the report observed. The report went on to
describe a visit to a very different farm, whose owner paid higher wages, offered
better conditions, and experienced few labour troubles.[73]

Tobacco growers were very successful in enlisting the assistance of elected
representatives in their campaigns for sustained or increased access to guest-
worker programs. Particularly loyal to farmers in this regard were two regional
Progressive Conservative MPs, William Knowles of Norfolk-Haldimand and
Bruce Halliday of Oxford, as well as Liberal MP for Essex-Windsor and two-
time minister of agriculture (1972–79 and 1980–84) Eugene Whelan.[74] For Whelan, who had played an important role in lobbying for the SAWP from 1964 to
1966,[75] going to bat for farmers often meant butting heads with fellow Liberals,
a task from which he did not shy away. In one sizzling exchange, we can see
not only Whelan's tenacious advocacy, but also his adoption of some of the
growers' tenets of common sense about Canadian workers. Writing to Minister
of Manpower and Immigration Robert Andras about the 1975 limitations on
the hiring of West Indians, Whelan did not mince words: "As Minister responsible for food production in Canada, I am appalled, dismayed and disillusioned
by the lack of consultation you have had with me concerning the problems I
am confronted with to ensure that we have proper food production in Canada.
You cannot do that, Bob, with sending as many as thirty inexperienced persons
per week to farms – people who would probably rather receive welfare or unemployment insurance than do farm work."[76]

Though growers deployed the labour shortage narrative strategically, this
does not mean that they did not sincerely believe it. As Ian McKay reminds us,
the creation of "common sense" is seldom an "outright invention or hoax."[77]
Regardless of the exact balance of strategy versus sincerity, over the subsequent
decades, the tactical nature of its use and the numerous holes in its logic were
forgotten, and the narrative did indeed become an article of common sense,
not only among growers and sympathetic politicians, but in broader popular
understandings of farm labour and the reasons for the existence of temporary
foreign worker programs – even among former farm workers. Evident enough

in textual sources, the dominance of the labour shortage narrative becomes unmistakable when oral history interviews are considered, recalling Luisa Passerini's arguments about the peculiar value of oral history as a source. "Oral history," Passerini writes, "consists not just [of] factual statements, but is pre-eminently an expression and representation of culture."[78] The cultural hegemony of the labour shortage narrative – and in particular the idea that Canadians are simply uninterested in farm work – is on display whether talking to growers (Linda Scott: "Canadian people as a whole … don't want to work seven days a week, 12 hours a day … It could be cold, it could be raining, you know, and for the most part, Canadian people just don't want to do that anymore."); local workers (Oneida tobacco worker Mercy Doxtator in 1998: "I guess you can't find anyone to work in tobacco anymore … a lot has changed. The young people won't agree to work [in tobacco], it's too dirty."); or even Caribbean guest workers (Anthony Lowe of Barbados: "The Canadians don't want to work … That's why you see them get people [from] the Caribbean, Mexico.").[79]

The labour shortage narrative also, in short order, began to shape people's historical understanding of the creation of guest-worker schemes, fulfilling Antonio Gramsci's observation that "common sense creates the folklore of the future."[80] This was evident as early as 1982, for example, when the manager of Tillsonburg's Canada Employment Centre, Tony Murphy, recalled that the origins of West Indians' involvement in the tobacco harvest stemmed from labour shortages in the mid-1960s.[81] (Of course, no such shortages occurred, and tobacco's West Indian workers numbered less than two hundred for each year in the 1960s that they participated.) And the labour shortage narrative is on prominent display today in seemingly every accounting for the existence of agricultural guest-worker programs that has any historical perspective at all. A 2017 article in the *Toronto Star* provides a typical example, with the author recounting that the SAWP "was launched in 1966 as a stopgap initiative to fill labour shortages."[82] Appearing a third of the way into the article, in the middle of a sentence that itself sits in the middle of a paragraph, the explanation is located in exactly the sort of place you would expect to find a tenet of common sense, something so obvious that it hardly requires mentioning – and if it does, it is only for the seriously uninitiated. It is not the *Star* journalist's fault of course; scholars haven't given him much of an alternative to work with. One of two major books on the history of the SAWP, for example, Tanya Basok's *Tortillas and Tomatoes: Transmigrant Mexican Harvesters in Canada*, advances a nearly identical version of events: "The [SAWP] was put in place in 1966 to alleviate labour shortages experienced by Canadian fruit and vegetable farmers."[83]

Of course, Basok's statement is not about tobacco farmers, and it does seem apparent that fruit and vegetable farmers did have somewhat more legitimate claims to labour struggles. In any event, it is beyond the scope of this book to provide an in-depth assessment of these other crop sectors. But the insights opened up here, from the case study of tobacco, do beg some questions about the application of the labour shortage narrative in other crop sectors. If labour shortages were so acute in fruit and vegetable sectors, if crops were rotting in the fields and guest workers represented the only solution, then how was it that a tiny guest-worker program, which never accounted for more than 10 per cent of Ontario's waged farm workforce during its first twenty years, was able to adequately solve this crisis? Why, moreover, did only a small percentage of farmers make use of it? In 1981, for example, out of 34,023 farmers in Ontario who reported hiring paid labour, only 1,050 utilized the SAWP, a total of 3 per cent. Zooming into some specific crop sectors: out of 6,202 farms reporting vegetables, 293 hired SAWP workers (5 per cent). Out of 3,125 apple orchards, 126 hired SAWP workers (4 per cent). The sector with the most farmers hiring SAWP workers that year was, in fact, tobacco, where 355 out of the sector's 2,650 farms hired Caribbean and Mexican migrants, making it also the crop with the greatest percentage of growers utilizing the SAWP – 13 per cent.[84] Considering the more detailed portrait of tobacco's labour force, and the role of guest workers within it, that we've been able to paint in this chapter and throughout the book – in other words, a picture of what a sector in which 13 per cent of employers hired SAWP workers actually looked like up close – we might well begin to view the labour shortage narrative in all agricultural sectors with a (re)invigorated scepticism.

✦✦✦

The eventual shift to guest workers from the Global South in tobacco does not fit most preconceptions of how this story unfolded. Labour-short farmers did not turn to West Indians and Mexicans in desperation. They did not tally up a comparison between their various labour options and choose SAWP workers. They did not hire guest workers because they represented cheap labour. And the turn to guest workers was not the inevitable result of government-created labour programs and campaigns to control the flows of transient labour. Instead, the key to understanding why growers in tobacco (and other crops) turned – belatedly – to temporary foreign workers lies in the changing economics of agriculture. It was only after a series of crises ravaged the tobacco belt, pushing out thousands of farmers and leaving a radically transformed, heavily consolidated sector in their wake, that greater numbers of sawp workers began labouring in Ontario tobacco. Only large operations – the same ones that could afford expensive machinery and produce at a large enough scale to remain profitable – could afford to construct new bunkhouses and advance cash for plane tickets to bring in workers from Mexico and the Caribbean. While the restructuring of tobacco was particularly dramatic, the story of consolidation has been essentially the same across all Canadian agriculture – and, for that matter, across most of the capitalist world – over the last few decades. Examining in detail how consolidation and the transformations in the labour force played out in one sector allows us to gain new insights into the intimate links between these two processes, and prompts us to cast a critical gaze on the labour shortage narrative writ large.

CONCLUSION: COVID, CLIMATE, AND THE FUTURE OF AGRI-FOOD PRODUCTION

On 16 March 2020, as the SARS-COV-2 virus, better known as Covid-19, took hold in earnest in North America, the Canadian federal government announced a slate of emergency immigration measures aimed at preventing the further entry of the virus into Canada. With the exception of US citizens and workers in limited occupational categories, all foreign nationals were barred from entering the country – including migrant farm workers. The Canadian farm lobby responded quickly and forcefully. Growers' groups from across the country warned of labour shortages and threats to Canada's food security should foreign workers be kept out. Worker advocacy groups also lambasted the government's decision, citing the economic havoc it would wreak on the lives of the men and women who grow Canada's food. "There is no public health reason to shut out non-permanent residents, while allowing American and Canadian citizens and permanent residents in" read a statement by the Migrant Rights Network released the same day as the government's announcement. "This is simply racism. The economic impact of this decision will gravely hurt racialized, low-waged, migrants around the world." Despite their very different reasons for opposing the decision, both groups – farmers and advocates – could agree on one thing: Canadian food production, and especially fruit and vegetable farming, was utterly dependant on migrant workers from the Global South.[1]

The government was rapidly swayed, and within four days it had reversed course: migrant farm workers would now be permitted to enter Canada, with the stipulation that they enter into a fourteen-day quarantine before commencing work. The next month, federal authorities announced $50 million of funding to assist farmers with the costs of providing appropriate quarantine accommodations and paying workers during their limbo. Growers breathed a sigh of relief. Advocates were less satisfied and almost immediately pivoted to sounding the alarm about what additional measures would be needed to keep farm workers safe. Advocates pointed out that, while the measures would protect Canadians from contracting Covid from migrant workers, they gave little thought to the protection of those workers once they had completed their two-week quarantine. As countless journalistic exposés, documentary films, reports, and first-hand accounts have shown over the years, migrant farm workers often live in cramped (not to mention abject) quarters, with bedrooms often shared between four, six, or even more workers sleeping in bunk beds. Many migrant bunkhouses don't have bedrooms at all, but rather are converted warehouses or barns in which dozens of workers sleep in one large room. And while much farm work takes place outdoors, this is not always the case – and notably so in greenhouse agriculture, the sector that employs the largest number of migrant farm workers.[2] As critics pointed out, such conditions are incredibly conducive to the spread of an infectious disease such as Covid-19.[3]

And spread it did. By the end of 2020, approximately 2,000 migrant farm workers had contracted the virus, mostly in Ontario, where they were *ten times* more likely than the general population to be infected during the first year of the pandemic.[4] At one particularly hard-hit farm – Scotlynn Group, a vegetable farm located in Norfolk County, the heart of the historic tobacco belt – a staggering 199 out of 216 workers contracted the virus. One of the Scotlynn Group workers died: fifty-five-year-old father of four Juan López Chaparro. Two more migrant farm workers, also from Mexico, died from Covid in 2020: thirty-one-year-old Bonifacio Eugenio Romero and twenty-four-year-old Rogelio Muñoz Santos.[5] In 2021, migrant deaths surged even further. As of July 2021, at least 9 more SAWP workers – from Jamaica, Trinidad and Tobago, Saint Vincent, and Mexico – had perished, a minimum of 6 of them during their two-week quarantines after arriving in Canada. One of those deaths, that of Mexican Fausto Ramirez Plazas, was declared due to Covid, while the causes of the other workers' deaths were not released. Regardless of the precise causes, the rate of death was staggering. Between 1994 and 2011, 39 SAWP workers died while in Canada, just over two deaths per year, making 2021 more than four times as deadly as an average year.[6]

For many Canadians, the Covid crisis on the country's farms was the first time they became aware of the plight of Canada's migrant workers. Investigative reporting by the *Globe and Mail* and *Toronto Star*, along with television documentaries on CTV and CBC, revealed the crowded conditions of bunk-houses, the pervasive fear of reprisal that discourages workers from speaking out, and the repeated mistakes – and ignoring of warnings – on the part of provincial and federal authorities responsible for ensuring the health and safety of migrant farm workers.[7] Political leaders were forced to account for the unfolding catastrophe. Long hidden away down obscure rural roads, migrant farm workers suddenly found themselves the subject of politicians' press conferences. "We know that there are many issues – from living conditions ... [to] labour standards – that require looking at," mused Prime Minister Justin Trudeau in June 2020. "We should always take advantage of moments of crisis to reflect: Can we change the system to do better?" Ontario premier Doug Ford, for his part, alternated between falsely accusing migrant workers of hiding symptoms and urging employers to co-operate with widespread testing efforts.[8]

Of course, Covid alone did not create the disasters that unfolded on Canadian farms. Instead, the pandemic merely lifted the veil on long-standing injustices, ones that critics had been calling attention to for years. It was not only the substandard living conditions that were all of a sudden on display; so, too, were the stark power imbalances and culture of fear that permeate the world of migrant farm labour. Canadian newspaper readers and television audiences learned that Gabriel Flores, co-worker and bunkmate of Juan López Chaparro, the Scotlynn employee who died from Covid-19, had been fired the day after his friend's death, after raising concerns about health and safety conditions on the farm in comments made to supervisors and to the media. Scheduled to be put on a plane and sent home to Mexico, Flores fled the farm and was taken in by advocates who put him up in a safe house, from which he continued to fight his case.[9] Flores was hardly the first worker to complain about conditions at Scotlynn. In fact, as Sara Mojtehedzadeh of the *Toronto Star* reported, between 2016 and 2018 the Mexican Ministry of Labour received thirty-three complaints from Mexican program participants about conditions on the farm, the most of any Canadian farm during those years.[10]

Flores's situation, ghastly though it was, was by no means unique or even unusual. As numerous reports have demonstrated, participants in the SAWP and other agricultural temporary foreign worker schemes are strongly discouraged from voicing complaints about living or working conditions. In order to continue uninterrupted participation in the SAWP year after year, workers must be requested by name by an employer, resulting in strong dis-incentives against not only complaining, but also against taking time off for illness or doctor's appointments, or reporting injuries. The many workers who avoid doing these things to the fullest possible extent are not overreacting, but instead are behaving in an entirely rational manner: the blacklisting of pro-testing workers within the program has been well-documented.[11] Workers in the SAWP are further marginalized by their inability, in Ontario, Quebec, and Alberta, to join or form labour unions recognized under provincial labour legislation. (Those provinces respectively have the first-, third-, and fifth-lar-gest contingents of SAWP workers, with about half of all SAWP participants working in Ontario.[12])

Canadian readers and viewers paying close attention might also have learned one final, critical fact about migrant farm workers: that they effectively have no access to permanent residency. Many workers labour in Canada for ten, twenty, even thirty growing seasons – which might be as long as eight months per year – but receive no credit for this experience that might facilitate their staying in Canada permanently. Typically hailing from poor rural backgrounds and with little formal schooling, very few migrant farm workers are able to qualify for entry to Canada via the Federal Skilled Worker Program (or "points system"). It is not surprising, then, that out of all temporary foreign workers, those in the SAWP have by far the lowest rate of transition into permanent resi-dency status. On average, only 2 per cent of SAWP workers secure permanent residency status by the time they've worked five years in the program; by the ten-year mark, it's just 3.4 per cent.[13]

Vulnerable, bullied, and, in the words of one scholar, "permanently tem-porary": this is the condition of migrant farm workers in Canada at the start of the 2020s.[14]

◆ ◆ ◆

This book has attempted, in part, to show that none of this was inevitable.

It was not inevitable that Canadian farmers should come to depend on tem-porary foreign workers from the Global South, or that these workers would be employed under such oppressive conditions, or that farm work would be so poorly paid and unappealing as to fail to attract Canadian workers. As this study of Ontario's flue-cured tobacco sector has shown, Canadian agriculture has not always and everywhere been a site of poverty and abuse for wage labourers. For decades, the tobacco sector was a very popular destination for temporary job seekers, attracting tens of thousands of workers each harvest, from local areas, elsewhere in Canada, and from beyond Canada's borders. The reason was not complicated: tobacco paid good wages, higher than most other crops, and even higher than certain industrial and urban jobs. Even more appealing for working people with aspirations of making a living on the land, for three or four decades after the sector's takeoff in the late 1920s, tobacco offered working families rare opportunities for social mobility by progressing from wage labour to sharegrowing to farm ownership.

The tobacco bonanza did not last forever, of course, and by the 1960s cracks were beginning to appear in its foundation. Rising costs and declining prices for tobacco made it harder and harder for small farmers to stay in business. By the 1980s, the trickle of change had become a tidal wave. With the links between smoking and lung cancer established beyond any shadow of a doubt, and governments taking action (through taxation and public education) to discourage smoking, demand for tobacco fell rapidly. These profound challenges to the tobacco farming sector spelled doom for thousands of farmers – but not for the sector as a whole. Indeed, the sector would survive – and still survives to this day – but in a radically transformed condition in which the thousands of tobacco farms that previously dotted the landscape of Norfolk, Oxford, Elgin, and neighbouring counties, have been replaced by fewer than two hundred.[15]

As small growers sought desperately to hang on within a sector in crisis, it became more and more difficult to pay good wages or offer attractive conditions. Canadian migrants took notice and fairly quickly stopped showing up on the streets of Delhi, Simcoe, and Tillsonburg each summer in search of work, shifting to other crop sectors in Ontario, or, in the case of young itinerant workers from Quebec, travelling much farther down the road to British Columbia's Okanagan Valley. Meanwhile, the large operations snatching up the farms and tobacco quota put up for sale by their out-of-luck neighbours saw no need to try to convince Canadian migrants to come back. Highly capitalized operations, they did not face the same barriers to employing foreign workers as small growers. The capital requirements for constructing appropriate bunkhouses and advancing airfare posed no real difficulty for these larger farms. And the workforce they could access by jumping over these barriers was one that, given the structural conditions of their employment, was far less likely to quit before the end of harvest, protest poor conditions, or request higher wages.[16] It was only at this moment, once the radical restructuring of the to-bacco sector had taken hold, in the late 1980s and beyond, that the remaining tobacco growers began to switch in significant measure to hiring guest workers from the Caribbean and Mexico. Though other crop sectors did not undergo the dramatic fall from grace experienced by tobacco, the story across Canadian agriculture has been more or less the same: consolidation preceded the turn to temporary foreign workers.[17]

This sequence of events is very different from the dominant narrative about farm labour and the employment of guest workers in Canadian agriculture. That narrative, especially as advanced by the agri-food industry, maintains that Canadian workers are simply not interested in performing farm work, and that employers – often represented as struggling family farmers – have had no choice but to turn to temporary foreign workers. The supposed refusal of Canadians to accept farm jobs is – with varying degrees of subtlety – chalked up to their softness or lack of work ethic, both of which are often pinned on the overgenerosity of welfare programs or the too-high minimum wage.[18] Few commentators call these assumptions into question. Such commentary fails to ask why on earth people would travel to hard-to-reach rural regions to take up dangerous, temporary jobs that pay minimum wage. It doesn't take a labour economist (or labour historian) to point out that this is not the way to attract workers. Of course, the stories told by growers and their allies are not intended to accurately represent reality. Rather, they are advanced in order to defend employers' access to temporary foreign workers, and to preserve a status quo that, under the weight of negative attention – never more so than during the Covid-19 crisis – is appearing to employers to be increasingly under siege.

This book has sought to call these easy narratives about farm labour into question, through a case study of one particularly important crop sector. But Ontario tobacco is hardly the only example we could use to debunk popular claims about the reasons for Canadian farmers' dependence on temporary for-eign workers. Evidence to the same effect was on prominent display during the first year of the coronavirus pandemic. The response of at least one em-ployer to the pandemic, for example, puts under the light of scrutiny the idea that agricultural employers have no other viable choice than to hire temporary foreign workers. After Scotlynn Group's entire 216-person Mexican workforce was placed into quarantine, the company began offering twenty-five dollars an hour to locals to harvest the asparagus crop – a full eleven dollars above the minimum wage that migrant workers are almost always paid. "People responded in droves," reported the *Hamilton Spectator*. Said Scotlynn CEO Scott Biddle: "It was unbelievable, the amount of people who came out to show support and gave us a hand."[19] Biddle's enthusiasm notwithstanding, perhaps it was not so unbelievable that the offer of a competitive wage appeared to trump any inherent Canadian aversion to farm labour.

Furthermore, the precise locations of farm outbreaks provided a window into the types of operations that hire temporary foreign workers: mostly large, heavily capitalized ones. Scotlynn Group, for example, is a multinational trucking and agricultural company with farms in Ontario, Florida, and Georgia. Its Norfolk County farms produce a number of crops, including approximately 18 per cent of the total asparagus crop in Ontario. As its website attests, it is "one of Ontario's largest farming operations."[20] Another major outbreak of at least 180 cases occurred at Nature Fresh Farms, a Leamington-based greenhouse grower that, like Scotlynn, also boasts operations in the United States. With greenhouses spanning over two hundred acres, Nature Fresh, according to its website, is "one of the largest independent greenhouse produce growers in Canada, as well as one of the largest greenhouse Bell Pepper growers in North America."[21]

This is not merely an impression gleaned from the Covid crisis. A survey conducted in 2017 by the Canadian Agricultural Human Resource Council, in which approximately 40 per cent of SAWP employers in Ontario and Atlantic Canada participated, found that the average SAWP employer had gross receipts of $1.78 million, a figure that would put an operation in the top 3 or 4 per cent of Canadian farms.[22] And it is not a question of a few of the very largest operations skewing the average stats. Fifty per cent of SAWP employers in the survey grossed over $1 million, placing them in the top 4.8 per cent of Canadian farmers; 71 per cent of SAWP employers grossed over $500,000, putting them in the top 11 per cent overall; and 88 per cent of SAWP employers grossed over $250,000, placing them in the top 22 per cent.[23] There is no mistaking the trend: SAWP workers are overwhelmingly employed by large agribusiness operations, not struggling family farmers.

✦✦✦

Just as Canadian growers' dependence on foreign migrants and the conditions under which they labour was not inevitable, neither has it ever been guaranteed that farm workers would simply accept their lot. This of course has been another major plank of growers' narratives about domestic and foreign farm workers: that temporary foreign workers are more obedient and less likely to complain than their Canadian counterparts. Of course, there is undoubtedly some truth to this, but it has little to do with the inherent characteristics of either group and everything to do with the vastly inferior conditions of migrant workers' terms of employment. In fact, narratives describing the apparent docility of farm workers stretch back to long before the days of state-managed guest-worker schemes; like the more recent stories, those older ones tended to confuse the results of material conditions (geographically dispersed workers in short-term jobs with high rates of yearly turnover) for innate traits of the workforce.[24] But as the case of Ontario's tobacco sector shows, even in spite of the structural barriers stacked against them, farm workers have never stuck to the script of obedience, either within or outside of state-managed guest-worker schemes. Throughout the twentieth century, diverse forms of worker protest proliferated among the tobacco workers of Ontario, facilitated in part by the sector's geographic concentration and mass gatherings of harvest job seekers each summer in the tobacco belt's main towns and villages.

In the 1930s and '40s, these favourable conditions were seized upon by local radicals – Hungarian and other immigrant Communists most conspicuous among their ranks – who waged multiple struggles to improve the lives and working conditions of wage labourers, sharegrowers, and small farm owners alike. This local infrastructure of dissent was bolstered during harvest times by the masses of unemployed job seekers who descended on the region each year in search of work – a combination that was never more potent than in 1939, when migrant workers and local activists joined together to form a union, and pickets and wildcat strikes spread throughout the tobacco zone.

As immigrant communities and their politics evolved, radical organizations became a rarer sight in the Norfolk area. But this by no means spelled an end to worker protest. While local oppositional politics within the sector became solely concerned with the interests of small farmers, migrant workers and job seekers continued to organize for better conditions. Before harvest started, they protested the poor treatment of job seekers in the tobacco belt. Once employed on harvest crews, they negotiated for higher pay, went on strike, and engaged in countless other acts of resistance. This legacy did not disappear with the addition of migrant workers from the Caribbean and Mexico to the tobacco workforce. Instead, like the Hungarians, Belgians, and Québécois before them, these workers brought their own traditions of working-class politics and organization to the tobacco belt. And though their disincentive to protest was many times stronger than that of Canadian or permanent resident workers – for whom losing a job did not mean being deported – they still engaged in the same sorts of workplace resistance.

Migrant worker resistance was not unique to tobacco, and it has not abated in recent decades. Despite it all, migrant workers have continued to engage in all manner of protest – from individual acts to work stoppages to multi-city caravans to testifying before parliamentary committees – in pursuit of more humane and just conditions.[25] This fact, too, was evident during the first year of the Covid-19 pandemic. Returning to Scotlynn Group and the case of Mexican employee Gabriel Flores, who was fired for making health-related complaints one day after his bunkmate died from Covid-19, we find a story of continued resistance even in the face of truly appalling employer behaviour. Having just fled from the farm in order to avoid being unceremoniously returned to Mexico, Flores did not lay low. Instead, he doubled down on his efforts to agitate for better conditions, not just at Scotlynn, but for all migrant workers. On 30 July 2020, he wrote an open letter to Minister of Immigration Marco E.L. Mendicino that was remarkable for its courage and directness – all the more so considering that Flores was at the time without legal immigration status. "I am sending this letter to you and hope you respond not just to me, but to all migrant and undocumented people in the country. My story is the story of many others," began the letter. "I have come here with a message for your government: We will not be silenced by bad employers or bad laws," wrote Flores. "And I have a message for all my fellow migrant farmworkers and all migrants in Canada: I am not afraid. It is our responsibility to speak up, for ourselves and for everyone. We are not alone." Flores ended his letter with a very clear appeal: "We demand full immigration status for all. Minister Mendocino, do the right thing."[26]

Flores didn't stop there but went on to file a complaint of unfair dismissal to the Ontario Labour Relations Board. The board ultimately ruled in his favour, ordering Scotlynn to pay him $20,000 in lost wages and $5,000 in damages. In victory, Flores again directed attention toward the broader situation faced by migrant workers. "We have won this battle but we have to keep fighting for equal rights for migrants in this country," Flores said at a press conference, through a translator. "We need a change in the system now. For now I am happy, but much remains to be done. My coworkers don't have the same opportunities as me. The government needs to do more, by guaranteeing permanent residency." Speaking to his fellow migrant workers, Flores implored them, "Do not be afraid. Dare to raise your voice. Dare to use this valuable weapon. It is important that we do not remain silent. United we are stronger."[27] Flores was hardly the only worker who took action during the pandemic to demand better conditions. In November 2020, for example, Jamaican and Trinidadian workers on Martin's Family Fruit Farm in Elgin County engaged in a wildcat strike after a Covid-19 outbreak, refusing to work until they had received negative test results.[28]

✦✦✦

The experience of the Covid-19 pandemic on farms also demonstrated the critical role of international factors in shaping Canadian agriculture and its labour force, another important theme of this book. Even after the Canadian government relaxed its travel restrictions for migrant farm workers, the actual transport of workers to and from Canada required close co-operation with authorities in sending countries. Such negotiations frayed diplomatic relations on at least two occasions.[29]

The rollercoaster ride of migrant worker travel regulations during the first year of the pandemic, shaped by diplomatic, epidemiological, and economic considerations, revealed the profound vulnerability of Canada's food production system. Seemingly overnight, the availability of the workforce on which critical agricultural sectors such as fruit and vegetable farming and canning depend was in jeopardy. While in the end, tens of thousands of migrant farm workers were able to travel to Canada in 2020, farms across the country were deprived of significant numbers of their usual foreign employees due to the multi-layered chaos of the pandemic and the government response. Disruptions to labour markets have been cited by the authors of *Canada's Food Price Report* as a key factor in the rapid increase in food prices (which rose by about 4 per cent over 2021 and are predicted to increase another 5 to 7 per cent in 2022).[30]

As the effects of climate change take ever greater hold, these sorts of disruptions to the food production system – in Canada and globally – will only become more commonplace. Given the well-documented role of climate change in producing conditions amenable to the emergence of zoonotic diseases, it is entirely plausible that pandemics will become a much more frequent fixture of twenty-first-century life.[31] So, too, will extreme weather events, whose increased incidence as a result of global warming is by now well-known. Instead of being positioned to confront these crises and the extreme stresses they place on the food system with a secure, well-paid labour force – one that enjoys the full rights of citizenship and shares in the benefits of the sector – Canada has an extremely vulnerable system with even more vulnerable workers.

This book has shown that it was not inevitable that such an agri-food system should have come to be. Nor is it inevitable that it should continue. For at least two decades, a vibrant constellation of farm workers, immigration activists, trade unionists, academics, and others have been calling attention to the plight of migrant farm workers in Canada and agitating for a fairer deal for the men and women who plant, tend, harvest, and process Canada's crops.[32] In recent years, these advocates have increasingly been linking the conditions and struggles of migrant workers with the worsening climate emergency. As Gabriel Allahdua, a former migrant farm worker from Saint Lucia who is now one of the strongest voices of the migrant justice movement, explains, climate change is a major factor in driving out-migration, something he experienced himself after 2010's Hurricane Tomas devasted his livelihood and compelled him to join the SAWP. As Allahdua saliently points out, there is a particularly bitter irony in the fact that, while Canada is a major contributor to climate change, it is countries such as Saint Lucia that suffer – and in the process are forced to send more migrants to places such as Canada. "Canadian extraction, climate change contributions, and neocolonial trade policies force people off the land and make local business completely unsustainable," Allahdua explained in one interview. And he put it even more pointedly in another: "Canada contributes so much to climate change, but we are the ones it affects."[33]

In confronting the already-here climate emergency, the world as we know it will be drastically remade. Exactly *how* it will be remade is still to be determined. Will weather take the reins, with states continuing their ambivalence toward large-scale, preventative action, choosing instead a "strategy" of ad hoc reaction to weather and related events? Or, more terrifyingly, will the global tide of right-wing politics continue its ascent, adapting its nationalism, xenophobia, and extreme individualism to the climate emergency and ever more stridently excluding migrants and other "outsiders" not only from cross-border movement, but also from relief from extreme weather events, access to social programs, and the body politic writ large (a tendency that has been labelled "eco-fascism")? Or will it be possible to secure a future that is not only sustainable but also just? Such is the emerging project of a burgeoning global climate justice movement that, like Allahdua, places front and centre of the climate conversation the deeply disproportionate effects of climate change on different regions of the world and on different groups within the contemporary world's many intertwined, historically constructed social hierarchies. This movement, in some places assembling under the banner of the "Green New Deal," argues for addressing the climate emergency and inequality in all its guises at the same time. To do this, they argue for a bold political project of massive public investment not only in the sorts of infrastructure projects needed to curb greenhouse gas emissions – renewable energy, low-emission transportation, housing retrofits, for example – but also in the caring sectors that are low-emission, essential in confronting the effects of the climate emergency, and whose workers deliver the sorts of services that, quite simply, make our societies more humane places to live – health care and education, in particular. Such a project would create hundreds of thousands of jobs (in Canada), and – in the fullest manifestation of the dreams of climate justice advocates – would entail a significant transfer of power and resources to poor communities, migrants, racialized and Indigenous peoples, and those from the Global South – all of whom, as Allahdua points out, have done the least to cause climate change but stand to suffer the most.[34]

As a major source of greenhouse gas emissions – particularly through synthetic fertilizers and livestock raising, but also though fossil fuel use and land management practices such as tilling – capitalist agriculture represents critical terrain for the transformation of our economies and societies that is necessary in order to build any sort of sustainable future.[35] Furthermore, increasingly common but unpredictable extreme weather events – just like pandemics – pose a significant risk to food security. In tackling both these projects – the creation of a more sustainable agriculture and the bolstering of food security – farm workers will play (and indeed, are already playing) a critical role.

Whether they will do so as exploited temporary foreign workers, excluded from the body politic, or as full members of society, well-compensated for their essential labour and with a rigorous set of rights and protections, is a question that is yet to be answered.

NOTES

Introduction

1 "Riot Act Read, Arrest 9," *Simcoe Reformer*, 4 August 1966; "The Cause: Cold, Hunger," *Simcoe Reformer*, 4 August 1966; "Workers March," *Globe and Mail*, 4 August 1966; "Tobacco Pickers Say Police Beat Them Up," *Toronto Star*, 12 August 1966; "Charge Unlawful Assembly," *Simcoe Reformer*, 4 August 1966.

2 "Charge Color Bar in Tobacco Fields," *London Free Press*, 16 August 1966; "Tobacco Farmers Refused to Hire Us, 24 Negroes Say," *Toronto Star*, 13 August 1966; "More Migrants Stranded in City as Jobs Fall Through," *Buffalo Evening News*, 15 August 1966; "21 Negroes Stranded after Being Refused Work on Canada Farms," *Poughkeepsie Journal*, 13 August 1966; "Negroes Claim They Refused Work in Canada," *Danville Register*, 14 August 1966; Dunsworth, "Race, Exclusion, and Archival Silences."

3 Proctor, "The History of the Discovery of the Cigarette–Lung Cancer Link"; Canadian Cancer Society, "Canada's War on Tobacco Turns 50," 17 June 2013, https://www.newswire.ca/news-releases/r-e-p-e-at——canadas-war-on-tobacco-turns-50-512598301.html.

4 "Says Work Available on Farms," *The Globe*, 9 August 1935; "Summary Record of Work Performed by Offices in Tobacco Area," 10 November 1944, RG27, vol. 667, file 6-5-26-1, part 2, Library and Archives Canada (hereafter LAC); "OFCTGMB Annual Report," 1970, Records of the Flue-Cured Tobacco Growers' Marketing Board, RG 16-250, box B388334, file "Tobacco Plan: Regulations & Annual Report, 1970," Archives of Ontario (hereafter AO); Duncan R. Campbell to J. Edwards, 20 February 1984, RG118, vol. 273, file 7905-14 (84), LAC.

5 Previously the designation had been held by the Prairies and the region's grain farms, but the massive annual "harvest excursions" were quickly curtailed in the late 1920s and early 1930s with the widespread adoption of combine harvesters. See Danysk, *Hired Hands*, chap. 8; Cherwinski, "A Miniature Coxey's Army," 163.

6 Ken Forth, "Clearing the Air over Seasonal Farm Workers," *Hamilton Spectator*, 29 January 2018, https://www.thespec.com/opinion-story/8098237-clearing-the-

air-over-seasonal-farm-workers/. Forth was responding to Janet McLaughlin and Donald MacLean Wells, "Immigrant Workers Suffer So We Can Have Cheaper Food," *Hamilton Spectator*, 20 January 2018, https://www.thespec.com/opinion-story/8082170-immigrant-workers-suffer-so-we-can-have-cheaper-food/. McLaughlin and Well's article echoed many of the core criticisms that have been lobbed at the SAWP for years, including poor working and living conditions, payment of employment insurance premiums without full access to benefits, and the toll of migrant labour on separated families.

7   The two prominent historical portrayals of the SAWP are Satzewich, *Racism and the Incorporation of Foreign Labour*, and Basok, *Tortillas and Tomatoes*.

8   In addition to the books by Satzewich and Basok, cited in the previous note, see, for example, Preibisch, "Pick-Your-Own Labor"; Reid-Musson, "Grown Close to Home"; Binford, "Assessing Temporary Foreign Worker Programs"; McLaughlin, "Trouble in Our Fields."

9   The scholarship on guest-worker programs represents a terrain of rigorous debate about the role of the state in labour markets. A more orthodox Marxist position of the state as "handmaiden" of capital is still present in the literature, and it received a regendered update in geographer Don Mitchell's important 2012 book on the Mexico-US Bracero program when Mitchell characterized the state as the "foreman" of agricultural employers. But that position has been under attack for over thirty years – for example, by Vic Satzewich in his 1991 book on farm labour migration to Canada, in which he demonstrated, quite convincingly, that – in the Canadian case at least – the state has by no means been beholden to the interests of agri-food capitalists. State officials are instead informed by myriad competing agendas, and in fact are often in disagreement and conflict with one another other – an altogether messier picture than the foreman-of-capital portrait suggested by Mitchell. Neither of these broad perspectives within the literature, however, have paid much (or any) attention to the *historical* aspect of state involvement in the farm labour market: namely, its change over time. Instead, they have presented the fundamental nature of the state-employer relationship as somewhat unchanging, even as the precise outcomes of that relationship change. Fortunately, some of the non-Canadian literature has provided more historicized accounts. Of particular value in this regard is the work of Cindy Hahamovitch, who, in her books on migrant farm workers in the eastern United States and on Jamaican guest workers, details the rise, evolution, and complexities of state involvement in those domains. Mitchell, *They Saved the Crops*; Satzewich, *Racism and the Incorporation of Foreign Labour*; Hahamovitch, *The Fruits of Their Labor*; Hahamovitch, *No Man's Land*.

10   See, for example, Chilton, "Managing Migrants"; Hoy, *A Line of Blood and Dirt*; Fahrmeir, Faron, and Weil, eds, *Migration Control in the North Atlantic World*.

11 I am particularly influenced here by the scholarship on state formation. See especially Greer and Radforth, eds, *Colonial Leviathan*. More recent efforts to this end are sometimes classified as the "new political history"; some notable texts, among many, are Loo, *Moved by the State*; Tillotson, *Give and Take*; Heaman, *Tax, Order, and Good Government*. For more, see Hayday, Kelm, and Loo, "From Politics to the Political: Historical Perspectives on the New Canadian Political History."

12 Marx, *The Eighteenth Brumaire of Louis Bonaparte*.

13 Out of a vast literature, see, for example, McKercher and Van Huizen, *Undiplomatic History*; Madokoro, McKenzie, and David Meren, *Dominion of Race*; Mills, *A Place in the Sun*; Dubinsky, Perry, and Yu, *Within and Without the Nation*; Chang, *Pacific Connections*; Meren, *With Friends like These*; Chilton, *Agents of Empire*.

14 Marx, *Capital*, vol. 1; Williams, *Capitalism and Slavery*; Wallerstein, *The Modern World-System I*; Beckert, *Empire of Cotton*. Other notable authors and titles, among many, include James, *The Black Jacobins*; Rodney, *How Europe Underdeveloped Africa*; Panitch and Gindin, *The Making of Global Capitalism*.

15 For example, Lipman, *Guantánamo*; Greene, *The Canal Builders*; Mapes, *Sweet Tyranny*; Putnam, *The Company They Kept*; Linebaugh and Rediker, *The Many-Headed Hydra*; van der Linden, *Transnational Labour History*; van der Linden, *Workers of the World*; Hoerder, van Nederveen Meerkerk, and Neunsinger, eds, *Towards a Global History of Domestic and Caregiving Workers*; Fink, ed., *Workers across the Americas*; Peck, *Reinventing Free Labor*.

16 Mathieu, *North of the Color Line*; Flynn, *Moving beyond Borders*.

17 Examples of comparative labour histories include Milloy, *Blood, Sweat, and Fear*; High, *Industrial Sunset*; Neumann, *Remaking the Rust Belt*; Parnaby, "Indigenous Labor in Mid-Nineteenth-Century British North America"; Finkel, "Workers' Social-Wage Struggles during the Great Depression and the Era of Neoliberalism."

18 Karen Flynn is again an exception here. Her chapter in *Within and Without the Nation* is one of the only (if not the only) contributions to the major collections on transnational history in Canada that features workers as the key subjects. Flynn, "She Cannot Be Confined to Her Own Region." Two more important exceptions are Chang, *Pacific Connections*, and Mills, *A Place in the Sun*, chap. 6.

19 Loza, *Defiant Braceros*; Johnson, "To Ensure That Only Suitable Persons Are Sent"; Snodgrass, "Patronage and Progress"; Miller, *Turkish Guest Workers in Germany*.

20 Hahamovitch makes similar findings about the comportment of liaison officers in the US–West Indian program, but there are some subtle differences between our portrayals. Hahamovitch's analysis tends to privilege the power of American growers in compelling sending-country governments to compete in a "race to the

bottom" to provide the most reliable, problem-free workers, a portrayal that maintains the primacy of North-South power relations within the scheme. My findings suggest a greater deal of agency for sending-country representatives, who did not appear to need much (or any) coercion to adopt stances that prioritized jobs over the protection of workers. Hahamovitch, *No Man's Land*, chap. 5. See also Hahamovitch, "Risk the Truck."

21   See, for example, Encalada Grez, "Mexican Migrant Farmworker Women Organizing Love and Work," chap. 4; Paz Ramirez, "Embodying and Resisting Labour Apartheid," 64–81; Loza, *Defiant Braceros*; Miller, *Turkish Guest Workers in Germany*; Cohen and Hjalmarson, "Quiet Struggles"; Binford, "From Fields of Power to Fields of Sweat."

22   Some examples of books already discussed or cited in this introduction include Mitchell, *They Saved the Crops*; Mapes, *Sweet Tyranny*; Satzewich, *Racism and the Incorporation of Foreign Labour*.

23   In her award-winning book *No Man's Land*, Cindy Hahamovitch makes use of Jamaican government documents obtained by American attorneys during the discovery process of a number of lawsuits, but too readily dismisses the holdings of Jamaica's national archives, the Jamaica Archives and Records Department (JARD), writing that the Jamaican Ministry of Labour's records "were neither at the National Archives nor at the Ministry itself." While undoubtedly an honest mistake by a first-rate scholar, this is simply untrue. To be sure, the Ministry of Labour's records at JARD are sparse – and the reasons for this may well be, as Hahamovitch suggests, nefarious – but they are not entirely missing, much less devoid of interpretive value. In particular, JARD holds at least a dozen submissions to cabinet made by the minister of labour (or a surrogate) concerning the farm-worker arrangements with Canada and the United States, dating from the 1950s to the 1980s. Many of these reports are quite rich in detail and are therefore quoted and cited throughout this book. This methodological distinction of course informs the subtle differences between Hahamovitch and me on the question of transnational power in guest-worker schemes, as addressed in an earlier note. Hahamovitch, *No Man's Land*, 9–10.

24   Works of Canadian migration history that employ transnational research methodologies include Ramirez, *On the Move*; Chilton, *Agents of Empire*; Takai, *Gendered Passages*; Fernandes, "Moving the 'Less Desirable'"; Mills, *A Place in the Sun*. Examples of guest-worker literature doing the same, in addition to Hahamovitch, include Johnson, "To Ensure That Only Suitable Persons Are Sent"; Loza, *Defiant Braceros*; Miller, *Turkish Guest Workers in Germany*; Snodgrass, "Patronage and Progress."

25   Urquhart and Buckley, eds, *Historical Statistics of Canada*, 355; "Labour Force at Census Dates," Series D1-123, Table D1-7, Statistics Canada, accessed 19 February

2022, https://www150.statcan.gc.ca/n1/pub/11-516-x/sectiond/D1_7-eng.csv; "Civilian Employment in Agriculture and Non-Agricultural Industries, by Class of Worker and Sex, Annual Averages, 1946 to 1975," Series D236-259, Table D236-259, Statistics Canada, accessed 19 January 2022, https://www150.statcan.gc.ca/n1/pub/11-516-x/sectiond/4057750-eng.htm; "Work Force, by Industrial Category and Sex, Census Years, 1911 to 1971," Series D1-123, Table D8-85, Statistics Canada, accessed 19 January 2022, https://www150.statcan.gc.ca/n1/pub/11-516-x/sectiond/4057750-eng.htm.

26 For a superb account of this intellectual movement, particularly in the Canadian context, see Heron, *Working Lives*, vii–xx.

27 The exception was Danysk, *Hired Hands*. The articles and chapters include Thompson and Seager, "Workers, Growers and Monopolists"; Seager, "Captain Swing in Ontario?"; Cherwinski, "The Incredible Harvest Excursion of 1908"; Cherwinski, "A Miniature Coxey's Army"; Parr, "Hired Men"; Crowley, "Rural Labour."

28 See, for example, Paige Raibmon's chapter on Indigenous hop pickers in *Authentic Indians*, chap. 4; Patrias, "More Menial than Housemaids?"; Dunsworth, "Race, Exclusion, and Archival Silences."

29 There are of course exceptions to the focus on state policy – for example, Wong, "Migrant Seasonal Agricultural Labour," a PhD dissertation in sociology about racial and ethnic relations within the Okanagan agricultural sector that considers Chinese, Doukhobor, Japanese, Indigenous, and French-Canadian workers. Another exception is Reid-Musson, "Historicizing Precarity," about transient tobacco workers in the 1960s and '70s that is concerned not only with state labour mobilization policy, but also with worker agency and experience. Two further examples of non-guest-worker-focused studies – both about Indigenous workers – serve as examples of the predominance of state policy as line of enquiry: Laliberte and Satzewich, "Native Migrant Labour in the Southern Alberta Sugar-Beet Industry," and Laliberte, "The 'Grab-a-Hoe' Indians."

30 See, for example: Basok, *Tortillas and Tomatoes*, and McLaughlin, "Trouble in Our Fields." Other examples of the burgeoning scholarship on migrant farm workers – and the SAWP in particular – include the works of Kerry Preibisch, Leigh Binford, Gerardo Otero, Jenna Hennebry, Anelyse Weiler, Evelyn Encalada Grez, and Emily Reid-Musson, many of whose texts are cited throughout this book and listed in the bibliography.

31 James, *A Brief History of Seven Killings*, 671.

32 High, "Foreward," xv–xx; Freund, *Oral History and Ethnic History*; Epp and Iacovetta, eds, *Sisters or Strangers?*, 3–18.

33 Portelli, "The Peculiarities of Oral History"; Portelli, *The Death of Luigi Trastulli*; High, *Oral History at the Crossroads*.

34 Passerini, "Work Ideology and Consensus under Italian Fascism"; Gabaccia and Iacovetta, eds, *Borders, Conflict Zones, and Memory*.

35 Sangster, "Politics and Praxis in Canadian Working-Class Oral History."

36 Vosko, "Blacklisting as a Modality of Deportability."

37 Goodman, *Tobacco in History*, 3–4; Winter, "Native Americans"; Nee, "Origin and Diffusion."

38 In addition to Goodman, *Tobacco in History*, see the following entries in *Tobacco in History and Culture*: Baud, "Brazil"; Menard, "British Empire"; Náter, "Caribbean"; Kellman, "French Empire" (all in volume 1); Winter, "Native Americans"; Nee, "Origin and Diffusion"; Kerr-Ritchie, "Slavery and Slave Trade"; Rodríguez Gordillo, "Spanish Empire" (all in volume 2).

39 McQuarrie, "From Farm to Firm," 11, 105–6; Winter, "Native Americans."

40 Labelle, *Dispersed but Not Destroyed*; Trigger, "The French Presence in Huronia"; Miller, *Compact, Contract, Covenant*, chaps 3–4.

41 Wood, *Making Ontario*.

42 There is some debate about this. See McQuarrie, "From Farm to Firm," 111; Clarke, *The Ordinary People of Essex*, 189, 560n184.

43 Clarke, *The Ordinary People of Essex*, 262.

44 McQuarrie, "From Farm to Firm."

45 Enstad, *Cigarettes, Inc.*, 10.

46 McQuarrie, "From Farm to Firm"; Tait, *Tobacco in Canada*.

47 Flue-cured tobacco refers not to a specific variety of *tabacum*, but more accurately to the set of processes used to produce tobacco for manufacture into cigarettes. A number of varieties of *tabacum* are grown as flue-cured tobacco. McQuarrie, "From Farm to Firm," 3; Hahn, *Making Tobacco Bright*.

48 I am indebted to Naomi Klein's framing of these questions in *On Fire* and elsewhere.

Chapter One

1 Mr and Mrs Yates Eaker, interview by Anne Schooley, 14 June 1985, Oral History Interviews, Delhi Tobacco Collection, ref. AME-14131-EAK, Multicultural Historical Society of Ontario (hereafter MHSO); "Report of Admissions and Rejections at the Port of Niagara Falls, Ont.," 18 August 1929, Border Crossings: From US to Canada, 1908–1935, Ontario, Manifests, Ancestry.ca; Marriage Affadavit, Joseph Yates Eaker and Nina Jeanne Harper, 19 August 1930, Ontario, Canada, Marriages, 1826–1937, Ancestry.ca.

2 As noted in the introduction, "flue-cured" refers more accurately to a process of production involving a select number of varieties of tobacco, rather than to a specific variety. McQuarrie, "From Farm to Firm"; McQuarrie, "Tobacco Has

Blossomed like the Rose in the Desert," 33–62; Tait, *Tobacco in Canada*; Niewójt, "From Waste Land to Canada's Tobacco Production Heartland," 355–77.

3   On "crop booms," and for a comparative case in Southeast Asia, see Hall, "Where the Streets Are Paved with Prawns," 507–30.

4   "Norfolk Tobacco Growers Will Reap Two-Million Dollar Crop," *Simcoe Reformer*, 23 August 1928.

5   Agricultural Representatives' Field Reports, Norfolk, 1927–28, RG 16-66, microfilm MS 597, Reel 40, AO; "Flue Tobacco Being Grown on 10,000 Acres in Norfolk," *Simcoe Reformer*, 8 August 1929; "Record of Flue Industry in Ontario over 60 Years," *Simcoe Reformer*, 25 February 1988.

6   *Toronto Star*, 29 July 1939; "Delhi Makes Astonishing Progress," *Delhi Reporter*, 18 December 1930; "Norfolk – the New Virginia," *Simcoe Reformer*, 8 October 1931; Table 34, Agriculture, Census of Canada, 1941, 920.

7   Rudy, *The Freedom to Smoke*; Robinson, "Cigarette Marketing and Smoking Culture in 1930s Canada," 63–105; Cox, *The Global Cigarette*; Rudy, "Cigarettes," 144–9.

8   In 1930, 54 per cent of the tobacco used by Canadian manufacturers was grown in Canada. By 1939, the figure had risen to 90.4 per cent. McQuarrie, "From Farm to Firm," 32, 203; "New Riches for Canada from Tobacco Growing," *Simcoe Reformer*, 19 May 1927.

9   For examples of large estates in twentieth-century Cuba, California, and Florida, see, for example, McGillivray, *Blazing Cane*; Barajas, *Curious Unions*; Bardacke, *Trampling out the Vintage*; Hahamovitch, *No Man's Land*.

10 Haviland, "Ontario Tobacco Farm Organization," 127.

11 "Ontario Tobacco Plantations Ltd Advertisement," *Toronto Star*, 6 December 1927.

12 "Norfolk Tobacco Growers," *Simcoe Reformer*, 23 August 1928; "Norfolk – the New Virginia," *Simcoe Reformer*, 8 October 1931; "Company Will Own 90 Tobacco Farms Following Merger," *Simcoe Reformer*, 20 April 1939.

13 "Norfolk Agricultural Representative's Field Report," 1928–29, Agricultural Representatives' Field Reports, RG 16-66, microfilm MS 597, Reel 40, AO; "Imperial President Tells Simcoe Audience Canadian Tobacco's Future Bright," *Simcoe Reformer*, 20 January 1938; Imperial Leaf Tobacco Company of Canada Limited to Producer Members of the Flue-Cured Tobacco Marketing Association of Ontario, 25 April 1939, Premier Mitchell Hepburn Private Correspondence, box 296, file "Agriculture Department General Correspondence," AO.

14 "Flue Tobacco Being Grown on 10,000 Acres in Norfolk," *Simcoe Reformer*, 8 August 1929; "Norfolk – The New Virginia," *Simcoe Reformer*, 8 October 1931; Vance, "The Tobacco Economy," 39.

15 Wilson, *Tenants in Time*.

16   On sharecropping in American tobacco, see Petty, *Standing Their Ground*, and
     Daniel, *Breaking the Land*.

17   "New Issue: $500,000, Ontario Tobacco Plantations Limited," *Simcoe Reformer*,
     24 November 1927; "News of Delhi," *Delhi Reporter*, 2 October 1930.

18   It still, however, split its holdings into individual farms. "Norfolk Tobacco
     Growers Will Reap Two-Million Dollar Crop," *Simcoe Reformer*, 23 August 1928;
     Barker and Kennedy, *The Tobacco Leaf Yesterday and Today*, 6.

19   Haviland, "Ontario Tobacco Farm Organization," 128; T.B. Pickersgill to A. Mac-
     Namara, 30 June 1943, RG 27, vol. 667, file 6-5-26-1, part 1, LAC; Barker and Ken-
     nedy, *The Tobacco Leaf Yesterday and Today*, 37–9; "OFCTGMB Annual Report,"
     1970, Records of the Flue-Cured Tobacco Growers' Marketing Board, RG 16-250,
     box B388334, file "Tobacco Plan: Regulations & Annual Report, 1970," AO; Walter
     Wallis, "Farm Diary," 1928–53, Howard Bilger-Walter Wallis textual records,
     F 1405-60-35, microfilm reel MFN 202, AO.

20   One farm's balance sheet from 1950 recorded spending $8,450 on labour and
     board, out of total expenditures of $13,850 (61 per cent). In 1949, another farm
     spent $6,154 out of $10,179 in expenses (60 per cent) on wages alone (board not
     calculated). Plantations spent less on wages – typically 20–30 per cent of their
     expenditures – but this is because sharegrowers would have been paying all
     on-farm wages except for, in many cases, half the cost of the curer. Hall, "The
     Introduction of Flue-Cured Tobacco," 329; Haviland, "Ontario Tobacco Farm
     Organization," 128; plantation balance sheets in Corporations Branch sous-fonds,
     RG 95-1, vols 2048, 1881, 941, files "Windham Plantations, Limited," "St Williams
     Plantations, Limited," "Southern Canada Tobacco Plantations, Limited," LAC.

21   "20,000 Acres of Tobacco Predicted for Norfolk County," *Simcoe Reformer*, 29
     January 1931; "Hands Imported," *The Globe*, 13 August 1931; "Says Work Available
     on Farms," *The Globe*, 9 August 1935; "Summary Record of Work Performed by
     Offices in Tobacco Area," 10 November 1944, RG 27, vol. 667, file 6-5-26-1, part 2,
     LAC.

22   "Norfolk Agricultural Representative's Field Report," 1935–36, Agricultural Repre-
     sentatives' Field Reports, RG 16-66, microfilm MS 597, Reel 40, AO. See chapter 4
     for examples of tobacco paying higher than industrial jobs.

23   Haythorne and Marsh, *Land and Labour*, 355; "Norfolk Agricultural Represen-
     tative's Field Report," 1928–29, Agricultural Representatives' Field Reports, RG 16-
     66, microfilm MS 597, Reel 40, AO.

24   Tait, *Tobacco in Canada*, 96–8; McQuarrie, "From Farm to Firm," 7; John Kenneth
     Galbraith, *Does It Pay?*, 456; "Norfolk – the New Virginia," *Simcoe Reformer*, 8 Oc-
     tober 1931; Smit, Johnston, and Morse, "Labour Turnover on Flue-Cured Tobacco
     Farms in Southern Ontario," 153–68; Tait, *Tobacco in Canada*, 98–120; Wallis,
     "Farm Diary," AO.

25 Daniel, *Breaking the Land*, 24–5; "Starlings Real Problem for Cherry Growers," *Simcoe Reformer*, 21 July 1932; "Norfolk Agricultural Representative's Field Report," 1932–33, Agricultural Representatives' Field Reports, RG 16-66, microfilm MS 597, Reel 40, AO; "Norfolk Agricultural Representative's Field Report," 1933–34, Agricultural Representatives' Field Reports, RG 16-66, microfilm MS 597, Reel 40, AO; "Imperial President Tells Simcoe Audience Canadian Tobacco's Future Bright," *Simcoe Reformer*, 20 January 1938; Barker and Kennedy, *The Tobacco Leaf Yesterday and Today*, 27.

26 Garner, *A Hugh Garner Omnibus*, 673. On the story being inspired by Garner's experiences working as a primer in 1939, see Garner, *One Damn Thing after Another*, 35–6.

27 Stompin' Tom Connors, "Tillsonburg," *My Stompin' Grounds*, Boot Records, 1971.

28 The disease's other side effects included "vomiting, dizziness, abdominal cramps, breathing difficulty, abnormal temperature, pallor, diarrhoea, chills, fluctuations in blood pressure or heart rate, and increased perspiration and salivation." McBride et al., "Green Tobacco Sickness," 294.

29 "Two Tobacco Workers Die in Heat Wave," *Simcoe Reformer*, 11 August 1949; "'I'll Quit' – But Men like Him Don't," *Toronto Telegram*, 7 September 1961. Interviewee James Bryon Long reported vomiting a few times while priming – perhaps due to the heat, perhaps in reaction to pesticide or herbicide spray. Long, interview.

30 See chapter 4.

31 "Norfolk – the New Virginia," *Simcoe Reformer*, 8 October 1931. For video of tying tobacco, see "Hand Tying Tobacco," YouTube video, 0:51, posted by Ron Warris, 21 April 2012, https://www.youtube.com/watch?v=hunbnvmCeTM.

32 Chaussé, interview; Hall, "The Introduction of Flue-Cured Tobacco," 100; Haviland, "Ontario Tobacco Farm Organization," 127.

33 In researching this book, I only encountered two explicit references to sexual violence against tobacco workers, both involving the assault of female workers by their employers. The incidence of such events, however, was undoubtedly much more widespread, given the deep silences around sexual assault and the findings of researchers from other agricultural contexts. Scott, *A Communist Life*, 53; *To Pick Is Not to Choose*, directed by John Greyson (Toronto: Tolpuddle Farm Labour Information Centre, 1985), DVD. On sexual violence against women in agriculture, see Galarneau, "Farm Labor, Reproductive Justice"; Castañeda and Zavella, "Changing Constructions of Sexuality and Risk," 249–68.

34 Elm, "Learning to Work in Tobacco." On tension between primers and tiers: Donohue, interview.

35 Passmore, interview.

36 Interview with George Fulop, 26 July 1977, 1956 Hungarian Memorial Oral History Project, Simon Fraser Digital Collections, accessed 28 August 2021,

https://digital.lib.sfu.ca/hungarian-65/hungarian-interview-george-fulop; Scott, *A Communist Life*, 52–4; "Voice of the People," *Toronto Star*, 5 August 1937; McQuarrie, "Farm to Firm," 47–8. Food has been an important component of labour recruitment and retention in other seasonal industries as well. See, for example, Radforth, *Bushworkers and Bosses*, 96–102.

37 See, for example, "Wedding Soloist Prefers 'Plain' Cooking," *Canadian Tobacco Grower*, April 1969, 62–3; "12 Desserts from One Basic Mix," *Canadian Tobacco Grower*, June 1969, 45; "Her Table's Always Full," *Canadian Tobacco Grower*, May 1973, 26–7.

38 DeDecker, interview; Donohue, interview; Knowles, interview.

39 Doxtator, "All About Tobacco."

40 For a critical analysis of the discursive construction of "expertise" in Ontario tobacco, see McQuarrie, "From Farm to Firm," 85–93.

41 "Norfolk – the New Virginia," *Simcoe Reformer*, 8 October 1931.

42 McQuarrie, "From Farm to Firm," 8; Tait, *Tobacco in Canada*, 113–20.

43 McQuarrie, "From Farm to Firm," chaps 1 and 6; Cox, *The Global Cigarette*, 116–17; Tait, *Tobacco in Canada*, 516–29; "Half-Million Dollar Tobacco Plant Being Built at Delhi," *Simcoe Reformer*, 3 April 1930; "Imperial Tobacco Company Plant a Boost for Delhi," *Delhi Reporter*, 18 December 1930; "Delhi Makes Astonishing Progress," *Delhi Reporter*, 18 December 1930. Imperial's share of tobacco purchases derived from Canada, *Investigation into an Alleged Combine*, 30; "Record of Flue Industry in Ontario over 60 Years," *Simcoe Reformer*, 25 February 1988.

44 Cox, "British American Tobacco"; Cox, *The Global Cigarette*; Parham, *Tobacco in the Blood*.

45 McQuarrie, "From Farm to Firm," 79–80; Canada, *Statistical Handbook of Canadian Tobacco*, 3–15.

46 "Norfolk – the New Virginia," *Simcoe Reformer*, 8 October 1931.

47 Takai, "Bridging the Pacific."

48 Magee, *The Belgians in Ontario*, 92–3. On Belgian and American migration from Essex-Kent, see also "Tobacco Growing in Norfolk," *Simcoe Reformer*, 26 May 1927; "Delhi Makes Astonishing Progress," *Delhi Reporter*, 18 December 1930; Stanley Gehring, interview by Anne Schooley, 10 July 1985, Oral History Interviews, Delhi Tobacco Colleciton, ref. MUL-14131-GER, MHSO; "John DePauw," "Omer Sanders," and "Mr and Mrs Fred Ellington," all 1977, Delhi Tobacco Belt Project Papers (hereafter DTBPP), F 1405-61, B440612, files 9959.2 and 9959.1, AO. Other ethnic groups also transmigrated from Essex-Kent. See Gellner and Smerek, *The Czechs and Slovaks in Canada*; "Tobacco Growing Epidemic in Norfolk County," *Simcoe Reformer*, 8 September 1927; "Carl Szues," 1977, DTBPP, F 1405-61, B440614, file 9961.1, AO.

49 Avery, *Reluctant Host*, 82–113.

50 "Mrs K. Simutis," 1977, DTBPP, F 1405-61, B440613, file 9960.4, AO.

51 "John Mayer," 1977, DTBPP, F 1405-61, B440612, file 9959.4, AO.

52 Wallis, "Farm Diary," AO.

53 "Many Seeking Work at Imperial Tobacco Plant," *Simcoe Reformer*, 20 October 1938; "Imperial Factory at Delhi Is Model Industrial Plant," *Simcoe Reformer*, 13 January 1938; "Imperial Tobacco Company Plant a Boost for Delhi."

54 On Six Nations workers in the tobacco labour force as late as the 1980s, see Berggold, interview.

55 A couple civil servant estimates from the 1940s and '50s placed the number of seasonal farm workers (in both tobacco and fruits) from Six Nations at 1,000 – with no indication of how many of those worked specifically in tobacco. The one available tobacco-specific statistic is from a 1944 report of the wartime National Selective Service (NSS) that enumerated the "office of origin" of adult male workers registered to work in tobacco – a requirement for such workers in 1944 and 1945. This report counted 49 adult male workers whose home offices were labelled "Reserves (Indian)." This is obviously a large undercount, considering the failure to include both women and young workers, as well as the reported reluctance of some Indigenous peoples to register with the NSS, as discussed in chapter 3. But it seems unlikely that the number of First Nations workers surpassed about 1,000 in most years, in light of the above estimates and statistic, the scant mentions of Indigenous workers in other sources, and the total populations of the major source reserves – approximately 4,500 in Six Nations; 1,500 in the reserves outside of London, and 600 in Saugeen. T.W. Wells to G.W. Ritchie, 29 July 1944, RG 27, vol. 668, file 6-5-26-4, LAC; R.J. Stallwood to J.E. Morris, 25 January 1956, RG 10, vol. 8429, file 401/21-5, part 1, LAC; "Summary Record of Work Performed by Offices in Tobacco Area," 10 November 1944, RG 27, vol. 667, file 6-5-26-1, part 2, LAC; Hill, *The Clay We Are Made Of*, 246; "Census Profile for Canada, Provinces and Territories, Census Divisions and Census Subdivisions, 1981 Census – Part A," entries Caradoc 42, R; Oneida 41, R; Saugeen 29, R; Six Nations (Part) 40, R (two entries), Census of Canada, 1981, accessed 14 August 2021, https://www12.statcan.gc.ca/datasets/Index-eng.cfm?Temporal=1981&Theme=1&VNAMEE=&GA=3&S=0.

56 Elm, "Learning to Work in Tobacco"; Doxtator, "All About Tobacco"; Kennedy, "My First Job in Tobacco"; "Teeterville," *Simcoe Reformer*, 10 August 1936.

57 Many decades since the sale of the family farm, Byer is still friends with some of the people from Six Nations whom he worked alongside as a young man. Byer and Byer, interview.

58 Byer and Byer, interview; Ackner (pseudonym), interview. Similar bigotry in other crop sectors' hiring patterns is mentioned in Satzewich, *Racism and the Incorporation of Foreign Labour*, 151–2, and Basok, *Tortillas and Tomatoes*, 31–2.

59   Cornelius, "A Lifetime Working," 227–33.

60   "Virginia Comes to Norfolk County," *Simcoe Reformer*, 30 August 1937.

61   On southerners in Ontario tobacco, see Dunsworth, "Race, Exclusion, and Archival Silences," 563–93; Sheldon, "Ontario's Flue-Cured Tobacco Industry," 195–212; Daniel, *Breaking the Land*, 212–14.

62   Badger, *Prosperity Road*; Petty, *Standing Their Ground*.

63   Agricultural Representatives' Field Reports, Norfolk, 1931–37, RG 16-66, microfilm MS 597, Reel 40, AO; Satzewich, *Racism and the Incorporation of Foreign Labour*, 108.

64   Cox, "British American Tobacco"; Enstad, *Cigarettes, Inc.*

65   Daniel, *Breaking the Land*, 202.

66   Enstad, *Cigarettes, Inc.*, 2, 12. See also Enstad, "To Know Tobacco," 6–23.

67   For a detailed examination of the exclusion of Black workers from the US-Ontario movement, see Dunsworth, "Race, Exclusion, and Archival Silences." On Canada's unofficial colour bar, see Winks, *The Blacks in Canada*, 307–13; Hastings, "The Limits of 'Brotherly Love,'" 38–53; "Immigration Act, 1910," Canadian Museum of Immigration at Pier 21, accessed 20 September 2017, https://www.pier 21.ca/research/immigration-history/immigration-act-1910.

68   Travelling with four white companions, the Black border-crosser, Fred Moore, was permitted entry, an example of the occasional exceptions made to Canada's colour bar. "Report of Admissions and Rejections at the Port of Bridgeburg, Ont.," 1928–35, Border Crossings: From US to Canada, 1908–1935, Ontario, Manifests, Ancestry.ca. For Fred Moore's crossing, see report from 21 August 1928.

69   The importance of elite brokers in organizing the migration process and serving as interlocutors between immigrant and host communities has been an important topic of consideration among migration historians, particularly, it seems, among scholars of Chinese migration to North America. For three of the most important texts, see Mar, *Brokering Belonging*; Chang, *Pacific Connections*; McKeown, *Melancholy Order*.

70   "Lynedoch Leads in New Industry," *Simcoe Reformer*, 6 January 1927; "Half-Million Dollar Tobacco Plant Being Built at Delhi," *Simcoe Reformer*, 3 April 1930; Magee, *The Belgians in Ontario*, 87–8; Barker and Kennedy, *The Tobacco Leaf Yesterday and Today*, 7; "Local Happenings," *Simcoe Reformer*, 24 February 1927; "Hollanders Arrive," *Simcoe Reformer*, 28 April 1927; Hall, "The Introduction of Flue-Cured Tobacco," 46.

71   Tait, *Tobacco in Canada*, 64–6; Sheldon, "Ontario's Flue-Cured Tobacco Industry," 196–7; McQuarrie, "From Farm to Firm," 79–85; Lyal Tait, interview by Michael Lipowski and Stacia Johnson, 11 April 1985, Oral History Interviews, Delhi Tobacco Collection, ref. MUL-14131-TAI, MHSO; Bowling, *Granville County Revisited*, 104; "Thursday, October 16," *Daveblackonline* (blog), October 2008 Blog Archives,

16 October 2008, http://www.daveblackonline.com/october_2008_blog_archives.htm; F.R. Gregory to A. MacNamara, 6 September 1945, RG 27, vol. 667, file 6-5-26-2, LAC.

72 "Oral History Sources' Collection: The Delhi & Tobacco District Hungarian House," *Polyphony* 2, nos 2–3 (1979–80): 81–8, Hungarian Canadian photographs, F 1405-19-42, B115689, AO.

73 For examples of informal networks in action, see Elizabeth Johnson, interview by Stacia Johnson, 10 April 1985, Oral History Interviews, Delhi Tobacco Collection, ref. AME-14131-JOH, Multicultural History Society of Ontario; "May Settle in Norfolk," *Simcoe Reformer*, 3 September 1931; "Hollanders Arrive," *Simcoe Reformer*, 28 April 1927; Magee, *The Belgians in Ontario*, 96; Byer and Byer, interview.

74 "Order-in-Council PC 1931-695, 1931," Canadian Museum of Immigration at Pier 21, accessed 21 September 2017, http://www.pier21.ca/research/immigration-history/order-in-council-pc-1931-695-1931.

75 Delhi Women's Institute, *History of Delhi, 1812–1970*; Patrias, *Patriots and Proletarians*, 157–65; "Associations Will Hold Meetings to Discuss Acreage," *Simcoe Reformer*, 20 February 1939; "Delhi Makes Astonishing Progress," *Delhi Reporter*, 18 December 1930; Eaker and Eaker, interview.

76 "Lynedoch," *Simcoe Reformer*, 12 January 1928; "South Middleton," *Simcoe Reformer*, 7 March 1929; "Atherton West," *Simcoe Reformer*, 16 August 1928; "Granville Man Died Monday in Canada," *Oxford Public Ledger*, 2 August 1927; "Granville Man Poisoned in Canada," *Oxford Public Ledger*, 23 September 1927.

77 "The Delhi Reporter," *Simcoe Reformer*, 20 December 1934; "Belgians Take Autos Back to Impress Home Folk," *Simcoe Reformer*, 14 January 1937; McQuarrie, "From Farm to Firm," 41–2; "Conditions in Troubled Europe Vividly Related by Former Staff Writer," *Simcoe Reformer*, 27 August 1936; "Carilloneur Gives Fine Program Here," *Simcoe Reformer*, 10 September 1936.

78 Bardacke, *Trampling Out the Vintage*, 1.

79 "Crossing Crash Kills Five," *Simcoe Reformer*, 23 March 1936.

80 "Condition Is Still Critical," *Simcoe Reformer*, 10 September 1942. For another example of a car accident involving tobacco workers, see "News of Delhi," *Delhi Reporter*, 2 October 1930. For a more extensive consideration of farm workers and automobile accidents, see Edward Dunsworth, "Not so Accidental: Farmworkers, Car Crashes, and Capitalist Agriculture," ActiveHistory.ca, 13 September 2018, https://activehistory.ca/2018/09/not-so-accidental-farmworkers-car-crashes-and-capitalist-agriculture/.

81 "20,000 Acres of Tobacco Predicted for Norfolk County," *Simcoe Reformer*, 29 January 1931; "Delhi Expects to Get Tobacco Grading Station," *Simcoe Reformer*, 20 June 1929; "Tobacco Growing Epidemic in Norfolk County," *Simcoe Reformer*,

8 September 1927; "Workers Besiege New Tobacco Plant," *Simcoe Reformer*, 29 September 1932.

82　"Population by Census Subdivisions, 1871–1941," Census of Canada, 1941.

83　"Norfolk Agricultural Representative's Field Report," 1927–28, Agricultural Representatives' Field Reports, RG 16-66, microfilm MS 597, Reel 40, AO.

84　"Lynedoch Leads in New Industry," *Simcoe Reformer*, 6 January 1927.

85　Sheldon, "Ontario's Flue-Cured Tobacco Industry," 201; Vance, "The Tobacco Economy," 46; Barker and Kennedy, *The Tobacco Leaf Yesterday and Today*, 5.

86　Hall, "The Introduction of Flue-Cured Tobacco," 63.

87　Vance, "The Tobacco Economy," 46, 94, 98; Hall, "The Introduction of Flue-Cured Tobacco," 4, 65; "Judge Says Foreigners Too Prone to Lawsuits," *Globe and Mail*, 3 December 1943; "Here and There," *Simcoe Reformer*, 13 December 1928; Dunsworth, "Green Gold, Red Threats," 105–42.

88　Vance, "The Tobacco Economy," 101.

89　"Simcoe Rotary Club Has Fine Record of Service to District," *Simcoe Reformer*, 2 May 1935; "Simcoe Tries the Better Way," *Simcoe Reformer*, 31 December 1931.

90　"Here and There," *Simcoe Reformer*, 31 May 1928. These types of sentiments were of course consistent with broader patterns of discrimination against southern and eastern Europeans in this period. See Avery, *Reluctant Host*.

91　"Half-Million Dollar Tobacco Plant Being Built at Delhi," *Simcoe Reformer*, 3 April 1930; "Delhi Makes Astonishing Progress," *Delhi Reporter*, 18 December 1930; "Reeve-Elect of Delhi Has Fine Record," *Simcoe Reformer*, 6 January 1938; "Norfolk's County Council for 1944," *Simcoe Reformer*, 24 January 1944.

92　The tobacco belt's European diasporic communities played an important role in the 1956–57 campaign for a new growers' organization, and subsequent chairmen of the new Marketing Board hailed from these communities – for example, George Demeyere (of Belgian descent) and Ted Raytrowsky (of German and Belgian descent). Both men were prominently involved in a number of other local organizations. "George Arthur Demeyere: Obituary," Maurice J. Verhoeve Funeral Homes, accessed 20 January 2022, https://www.verhoevefuneralhomes.com/memorials/george-demeyere/3716936/service-details.php; "Theodore Raytrowsky," Remembering.ca, 30 July 2015, https://www.remembering.ca/obituary/theodore-raytrowsky-1073361148; Tait, *Tobacco in Canada*; Dunsworth, "Green Gold, Red Threats."

Chapter Two

1　"Daily Data Report for August 1939, Brantford, Ontario," Historical Climate Data, Government of Canada, accessed 3 August 2020, https://climate.weather.gc.ca/climate_data/daily_data_e.html?timeframe=2&Year=1939&Month=8&Day=

19&hlyRange=%7C&dlyRange=1876-01-01%7C1963-06-30&mlyRange=1876-01-01%7C1963-12-01&StationID=4734&Prov=ON&urlExtension=_e.html&search Type=stnName&optLimit=yearRange&StartYear=1939&EndYear=1939&selRow PerPage=25&Line=0&searchMethod=contains&txtStationName=Brantford.

2   "Sikeres piknik volt Delhiban!," *Kanadai Magyar Munkás* (hereafter *Munkás*), 8 August 1939. *Munkás* articles were translated from Hungarian into English by Krisztina Helga Fally, Attila Kis, and Károly Gabor Mathe. For more on Hungarian Communists in southwestern Ontario, see Patrias, *Patriots and Proletarians*.

3   The details in this passage are drawn from the extensive coverage that the crisis received. See "Delhi Village Swamped With 10,000 Jobless," *London Free Press*, 1 August 1939; "Posters Blamed for Jobless Flood," *London Free Press*, 2 August 1939; "Warned From Tobacco Area," *London Free Press*, 2 August 1939, evening ed.; "Delhi Not Forcing Jobless to Move," *London Free Press*, 3 August 1939; "The Delhi Crisis," *London Free Press*, 3 August 1939; "Delhi Job Rush is Credit to Men," *London Free Press*, 3 August 1939; "12,000 Unemployed Invade Norfolk," *Simcoe Reformer*, 3 August 1939; "Here and There," *Simcoe Reformer*, 3 August 1939; "Tobacco Organization," *Simcoe Reformer*, 3 August 1939; "Attempt Organization of Transient Unemployed," *Simcoe Reformer*, 3 August 1939; "Jobless Army Goes Broke As Norfolk County Folk Resent Transient Influx," *Toronto Telegram*, 5 August 1939; "They DO Want Work!," *Clarion*, 12 August 1939, magazine section; "Pet Bunny, Corn, and Spuds Go; Probably Stew," *London Free Press*, 8 August 1939, evening ed.; "Nation-Wide Ads Lured Boys to Tobacco Fields," *Clarion*, 19 August 1939 (reprinted from the *Dunnville Gazette*); "Chief Issues Warning," *Simcoe Reformer*, 25 April 1938; "Delhi Council Planning to Have Jobless Moved from Village in Week," *London Free Press*, 9 August 1939, evening ed. See also, Dunsworth, "Green Gold, Red Threats."

4   "Sikeres piknik volt Delhiban!," *Munkás*, 8 August 1939.

5   Danysk, *Hired Hands*, 52–6; Parr, "Hired Men," 100–1.

6   Tait, *Tobacco in Canada*, 69–70; McQuarrie, "From Farm to Firm," 43–5; "Delhi Tobacco Belt Project Papers," 1977, F 1405-61, B440614, file 9961.1, AO.

7   Corporations Branch sous-fonds, RG 95-1, vol. 1881, file "St Williams Plantations, Limited"; vol. 2048, file "Windham Plantations, Limited"; vol. 435, file "Simcoe Tobacco Plantations Limited, The," LAC; Stewart, "Agricultural Restructuring in Ontario Tobacco Production," 36; Hall, "The Introduction of Flue-Cured Tobacco," 45–6.

8   Stewart, "Agricultural Restructuring in Ontario Tobacco Production," 33–4.

9   Sheldon, "Ontario's Flue-Cured Tobacco Industry," 206; Hall, "The Introduction of Flue-Cured Tobacco," 46; Stewart, "Agricultural Restructuring in Ontario Tobacco Production"; "Teeterville," *Simcoe Reformer*, 1 November 1945; Donohue,

interview; "Buying Land for Tobacco," *Simcoe Reformer*, 27 November 1939; "Stephanie de Leemans," 1977, Delhi Tobacco Belt Project Papers, F 1405-61, B440612, file 9959.2, AO.

10   The metaphor of the agricultural ladder was first developed in 1916 by American economists Henry C. Taylor and Richard T. Ely. My arguments join those of a long list of scholars who have criticized the metaphor for ignoring contexts of downward social mobility (or stasis) and for homogenizing the economic goals and life trajectories of all agriculturalists. Historian Joshua M. Nygren argues that the metaphor "recast the prototypical farmer as well capitalized, highly efficient, and white," and "naturalized the agricultural capitalism and racialized tenancy that prevented poorer farmers from owning their own farms," in the process bolstering its creators conservative, capitalist, and social Darwinist politics. Nygren, "In Pursuit of Conservative Reform"; Dorman, *Revolt of the Provinces*, 188–9; Alston and Kauffman, "Up, Down, and Off the Agricultural Ladder"; Wilson, "Tenancy as a Family Strategy in Mid-Nineteenth Century Ontario"; Wilson, *Tenants in Time*, 190.

11   DTBPP, F 1405-61, AO.

12   "Theodore Brinker," 1977, DTBPP, F 1405-61, B440612, file 9959.1, AO; "Peter and Helen Sterczer," 1977, DTBPP, F 1405-61, B440612, file 9959.5, AO; "Mr and Mrs Medard Van De Walle," 1977, DTBPP, F 1405-61, B440612, file 9959.1, AO. See also "Marcel Opdecam," 1977, DTBPP, F 1405-61, B440612, file 9959.1, AO.

13   Kosa, *Land of Choice*, 27.

14   Danys, *DP, Lithuanian Immigration to Canada*, 177–8.

15   Mrs K. Simutis, DTBPP, AO.

16   Peter and Helen Sterczer, DTBPP, AO.

17   "Farming? Yes, It's Woman's Work," *Toronto Star*, 14 July 1977; Scott and Van Londersele, interview.

18   "A Very Good Year," *Vittoria Booster*, Summer 2012.

19   Jaenen, *The Belgians in Canada*, 15. For similar interpretations, see Hall, "The Introduction of Flue-Cured Tobacco," 62–3; Vance, "The Tobacco Economy," 47.

20   "Wyecombe," *Simcoe Reformer*, 31 March 1927; "Houghton," *Simcoe Reformer*, 2 April 1931; "May Settle in Norfolk," *Simcoe Reformer*, 3 September 1931; "Virginia Comes to Norfolk County," *Simcoe Reformer*, 30 August 1937.

21   "P. Vindasius," 1977, DTBPP, F 1405-61, B440613, file 9960.4, AO.

22   Danys, *DP, Lithuanian Immigration to Canada*, 176–80.

23   "John Ligetti," 1977, DTBPP, F 1405-61, B440612, file 9959.5, AO; Danys, *DP, Lithuanian Immigration to Canada*, 177.

24   McQuarrie, "From Farm to Firm," 38–45; "Virginia Comes to Norfolk County," *Simcoe Reformer*, 30 August 1937.

25   "Police Called to Hungarian's Farm," *Simcoe Reformer*, 3 September 1936.

26 See, for example, "Windham Woman Charged in Court with Assault," *Simcoe Reformer*, 12 June 1934; "Dispute Ends in Court," *Simcoe Reformer*, 1 November 1934; "Charge Worker as Employer Injured," *Simcoe Reformer*, 2 July 1936.

27 "Cyriel Rabaey," 1977, DTBPP, F 1405-61, B440612, file 9959.2, AO.

28 "Stanley Tokarz," 1977, DTBPP, F 1405-61, B440612, file 9959.6, AO.

29 McQuarrie, "From Farm to Firm," 43; Kosa, *Land of Choice*, 27–8.

30 "Joseph Toth," 1977, DTBPP, F 1405-61, B440614, file 9961.1, AO; "Albert Mikulskis," 1977, DTBPP, F 1405-61, B440613, file 9960.4, AO; "S. Styra," 1977, DTBPP, F 1405-61, B440613, file 9960.4, AO.

31 "Report of the Indian Affairs Branch for the Fiscal Year Ended March 31, 1946," reprinted from Canada, *Annual Report of the Department of Mines and Resources*.

32 See, for example, Wallis, "Farm Diary," AO; Walter Wallis, interview by David Judd, 26 July 1977, Oral History Interviews, Delhi Tobacco Collection, ref. BRI-1162-WAL, Multicultural History Society of Ontario.

33 Sears, *The Next New Left*, 1–23.

34 The next most common sectors for strikes were sugar beets (three reported strikes), and greenhouses (three reported strikes). Finding aid, Strike and Lockout Files, AO.

35 The field of labour geography posits that we can understand the geography of capitalism as a contested site, where both capitalists and workers strive to arrange landscapes to suit their interests. Furthermore, as Andrew Herod argues, "Geography plays a role in structuring workers' lives, and … workers and their organizations may play important roles in shaping landscapes as part of their social self-reproduction." Herod, *Labor Geographies*, 5. For a fine labour geography study on struggles over "transient" camps in Ontario tobacco during the 1960s and '70s, see Musson, "Historicizing Precarity."

36 On barriers to farm labour organizing, see, for example, Mooney and Majka, *Farmers' and Farm Workers' Movements*, xxii–xxiv; Danysk, *Hired Hands*, 120–31. The other two strike-prone agricultural sectors – sugar beets and greenhouses – shared some important similarities with tobacco. Sugar beets featured a similar concentration of farms within restricted geographic areas and large annual influxes of harvest workers. Greenhouses, on the other hand, bear more of a resemblance to factories than farms in many ways, most notably for the present argument, by bringing workers together into one place. See Thompson and Seager, "Workers, Growers and Monopolists"; Seager, "Captain Swing in Ontario?"

37 Kealey, *Enlisting Women for the Cause*, 14.

38 Patrias, *Patriots and Proletarians*, 157–9, 165; Kealey and Whitaker, eds, *R.C.M.P. Security Bulletins*, 1 November 1938, bulletin no. 904, pp. 325–7.

39 Kealey and Whitaker, eds, R.C.M.P. *Security Bulletins*, 25 September 1935, bulletin no. 774, pp. 499–500.

40 "Vörös zászlós avatás a delhi-i kempen," *Munkás*, 24 August 1934. Article discovered via Patrias, *Patriots and Proletarians*, 223.

41 "Growers Group Agrees to Hold Crops for 34 ½ Cent Figure," *Simcoe Reformer*, 4 November 1937.

42 "Foreign-Born Growers Voice Dissatisfaction," *Simcoe Reformer*, 3 November 1938.

43 Magee, *The Belgians in Ontario*, 93; Strikwerda, *A House Divided*, 298.

44 "Buck Asserts Naziism Must be Squashed," *Simcoe Reformer*, 5 September 1939.

45 McKay, *Rebels, Reds, Radicals*, 155–69; Palmer, *Working-Class Experience*, 226–9; MacPherson and Magwood, "New Political Directions," plate 46; Priestland, *The Red Flag*, chap. 5; Avakumovic, *The Communist Party in Canada*.

46 Thompson and Seager, "Workers, Growers and Monopolists"; Seager, "Captain Swing in Ontario?"

47 These findings are consistent with other studies that have found that Communist activists, while striving to conform with party objectives, still very much directed their organizational work toward local concerns. See, for example, Kelley, *Hammer and Hoe*, xiii–xiv, 175; Culligan, "The Practical Turn," 3; Storch, *Red Chicago*, 1–8.

48 On beet workers, see Thompson and Seager, "Workers, Growers and Monopolists." For *Munkás* coverage, see for example, the issues from 30 May 1936 and 15 October 1936.

49 Kealey and Whitaker, eds, R.C.M.P. *Security Bulletins*, 24 June 1936, bulletin no. 812, p. 260; "Delhi Tobacco Belt Project Papers," 1977, F 1405-61, B440614, file 9961.1, AO; Patrias, *Patriots and Proletarians*.

50 Sears, *The Next New Left*, 1–2.

51 "Nyomorban szenvedők tanyája," *Munkás*, 5 January 1933. Article discovered via Patrias, *Patriots and Proletarians*, 223, 284n57.

52 Strike 254 (1937), D 21, Strike and Lockout Files, Microfilm Collection, AO. For other examples, see Strike 134 (1935) and Strike 129 (1938), in the same collection.

53 Readers may wonder whether there was a big shift in Communist organizing in tobacco between the Third Period and Popular Front, but it is difficult to provide a satisfactory answer. For one thing, the sources on Communist organizing up to 1935 are sparse, and the organizing that took place in that era, as the discussed examples suggest, was rather fleeting. The much higher-profile moments of Communist activism in the tobacco belt occurred in 1937 and 1939, well into the Popular Front era, and these are naturally also the campaigns with the richest source base. The later maturation of the tobacco belt's infrastructure of dissent is hardly surprising when one remembers that the sector was in its early stages of

development in the later 1920s and early 1930s, and that Hungarians only began moving into the district in significant numbers after 1933. Second, as mentioned, CPC leadership does not appear to have had much – or any – interest in the tobacco sector, at least until it exploded in labour revolt in 1939. So organizational efforts in the sector don't appear to have been closely linked with party directives. In short, the tobacco belt is not a particularly useful case study for examining the transition from the Third Period to the Popular Front.

54 Thompson and Seager, "Workers, Growers and Monopolists." The CPC's position was part of a larger debate that can be called the "class question," which sought, in essence, to understand who exactly constituted the agricultural proletariat that must be organized against capital. For more, see Dunsworth, "Green Gold, Red Threats," 123–5; McKay, *Reasoning Otherwise*, 198–208; Danysk, *Hired Hands*, 9–23; Avakumovic, *The Communist Party in Canada*, 84; Monod, "Agrarian Struggle."

55 Thompson and Seagear, "Workers, Growers and Monopolists"; Seager, "Captain Swing in Ontario?"

56 "Tobacco Harvest Men Said Ready in West," *Globe and Mail*, 26 July 1937; "Tobacco Showdown Next Week," *Globe and Mail*, 29 July 1937; "Premier Told Agitators Busy in Tobacco Area," *Globe and Mail*, 24 July 1937; "Violence Flares as Tobacco Men Cry for Helpers," *Toronto Star*, 28 July 1937; "To Use Provincials if Disorder Occurs," *Toronto Star*, 30 July 1937; "Hepburn to Inquire Into Labor Situation," *Simcoe Reformer*, 26 July 1937.

57 "Thinks Canadians May Supplant Foreigners," *Simcoe Reformer*, 29 July 1937.

58 "Tobacco Harvest Men Said Ready in West," *Globe and Mail*, 26 July 1937; "Tobacco Showdown Next Week," *Globe and Mail*, 29 July 1937; "Premier Told Agitators Busy in Tobacco Area," *Globe and Mail*, 24 July 1937; "Violence Flares as Tobacco Men Cry for Helpers," *Toronto Star*, 28 July 1937; "To Use Provincials if Disorder Occurs," *Toronto Star*, 30 July 1937; "Notes and Comments," *Globe and Mail*, 12 August 1937.

59 In a study of farm worker strikes in 1930s California, historical geographer Don Mitchell argues convincingly that the labelling of union organizers as "outside agitators" serves both to delegitimize migrant workers based on their lack of local ties, and conversely to legitimize locally entrenched growers who lay sole claim to the rights of local belonging and respectability. See Mitchell, "The Scales of Justice," 160–2.

60 "Will It Be 'Eastward Ho'?" *Globe and Mail*, 29 July 1937.

61 "Tovább fujja a régi nótát a nagykompániák hü dudása," *Munkás*, 7 August 1937.

62 The original organization had a slightly different name, the Ontario Flue-Cured Tobacco Marketing Board. The organization was reorganized and renamed in 1936, but the two iterations are properly considered as a single entity.

63 McQuarrie, "From Farm to Firm," 242–55; Tait, *Tobacco in Canada*, 125–47.

64 See the following articles from *Munkás*: "Növekvö dohánytermö-vidék," 14 August 1937; "Egy rókának két börét," 19 August 1937; "Tovább fujja a régi nótát a nagykompániák hü dudása," 7 August 1937; "Ontarió dohánytermelöi magasabb dohányárakéert," 2 November 1937.

65 John H. Teall to Patrick M. Dewan, 16 January 1939; Jack Sawyer to Dewan, 16 February 1939; Dewan to John H. Teall, 21 January 1939; W.E. MacDonald to Dewan, 20 June 1939; Dewan to J.E. Carter, 18 September 1940 – all letters in Patrick Michael Dewan fonds, box 2, file "Tobacco #2," AO.

66 MacDonald to Dewan, 20 June 1939, Patrick Michael Dewan fonds, box 2, file "Tobacco #2," AO; See McQuarrie, "From Farm to Firm," 252–7, for more examples of opposition to the association.

67 Unfortunately, a thorough search for more information about who E. Holwell was and how he came to participate in the 1937 growers' movement proved fruitless. "Növekvö dohánytermö-vidék," *Munkás*, 14 August 1937.

68 It appears growers had expected higher prices due to the quality of their crop and the low stocks of manufacturers as a result of reduced production in 1936. Buyers on the other hand felt that they had paid too dearly for tobacco in 1936 and sought to restore a more favourable price. "Delhi dohánytermelöi az alacsony árak ellen," *Munkás*, 14 September 1937; "Growers Group Agrees to Hold Crops for 34 ½ Cent Figure," *Simcoe Reformer*, 4 November 1937.

69 "A Communist Writes," *Simcoe Reformer*, February 9, 1939; Carl Hichin, "Communism's False Front," *Maclean's*, 1 February 1939.

70 "Tobacco Growers' Meeting," *Simcoe Reformer*, 13 September 1937; "Price of Tobacco Crop Discussed at Delhi Meeting," *Simcoe Reformer*, 16 September 1937; "Discontented Growers to Meet Dewan Today," *Simcoe Reformer*, 8 November 1937.

71 "Ask Cross to Intercede Before Leaf Price Set," *Simcoe Reformer*, 18 October 1937; "Ontarió dohánytermelöi magasabb dohányárakéert," *Munkás*, 2 November 1937.

72 "Growers Group Agrees to Hold Crops for 34 ½ Cent Figure," *Simcoe Reformer*, 4 November 1937; "Nö is van a delhi-iak farmerdelegáció-jában," *Munkás*, 6 November 1937.

73 "Discontented Growers to Meet Dewan Today," *Simcoe Reformer*, 8 November 1937.

74 "Group of Growers Seek Intervention Federal Minister," *Simcoe Reformer*, 11 November 1937.

75 "Prof. Leitch Issues Statement on Tobacco," *Simcoe Reformer*, 8 November 1937.

76 "Strike is Threat to industry," *Simcoe Reformer*, 11 November 1937.

77 "A dohánytermelök figyelmébe," *Munkás*, 27 November 1937.

78 "Birálat," *Munkás*, 23 November 1937.

79   "Tobacco Market Ends as Essex Crop Sold," *Simcoe Reformer*, 18 November 1937; "Birálat," *Munkás*, 23 November 1937.

80   "Foreign-Born Growers Voice Dissatisfaction," *Simcoe Reformer*, 3 November 1938; "Five Hundred at Annual Meeting of Marketing Board," *Simcoe Reformer*, 27 July 1939.

81   Tait, *Tobacco in Canada*, 171–203.

82   The term "politics of indignation" is borrowed from historian David Thompson, who describes indignation as a crucial way in which the unemployed express their disgust for and rejection of the socio-economic order that produces their unemployment and poverty, and also as a key step along the way to developing ideas of alternative worlds. See Thompson, "Working-Class Anguish and Revolutionary Indignation."

83   This estimation is gleaned both from press reports on the union and from Jack Scott's memoir, in which he characterizes his time working in Ontario agriculture as a period in which he was *not* actively involved in Party work. Scott, *A Communist Life*, 52–3.

84   *London Free Press*, 1 August 1939; *Globe and Mail*, 1 August 1939; *London Free Press*, 3 August 1939; *Toronto Star*, 1 August 1939.

85   "Delhi Not Forcing Jobless to Move," *London Free Press*, 3 August 1939; "The Delhi Crisis," *London Free Press*, 3 August 1939; "Delhi Job Rush Is Credit to Men," *London Free Press*, 3 August 1939; "12,000 Unemployed Invade Norfolk," *Simcoe Reformer*, 3 August 1939; "Here and There," *Simcoe Reformer*, 3 August 1939; "Tobacco Organization," *Simcoe Reformer*, 3 August 1939; "Attempt Organization of Transient Unemployed," *Simcoe Reformer*, 3 August 1939; "Lendülettel indul a dohánymunkások zervezése," *Munkás*, 5 August 1939; "Sikeres piknik volt Delhiban!," *Munkás*, 8 August 1939; "Döntö napokat," *Munkás*, 8 August 1939; "A dohányvidék nagy prolémája 2. rész," *Munkás*, 8 August 1939.

86   "Transients Refuse to Quit Ontario Town," *Toronto Telegram*, 3 August 1939.

87   "Jobless Army at Delhi Is Dispersing," *London Free Press*, 4 August 1939.

88   "Delhi Not Forcing Jobless to Move," *London Free Press*, 3 August 1939.

89   "9,000 Transients Jam Tobacco Belt; Alarm Authorities," *Globe and Mail*, 1 August 1939.

90   Strike 83 (1939), D 21, Strike and Lockout Files, Microfilm Collection, AO; "Single Officer Quickly Halts Tobacco Strike," *Toronto Telegram*, 12 August 1939.

91   "Denies Job-Hunters to Be Shooed Away," *Toronto Star*, 3 August 1939; "Hold Out for Tobacco Pay, Circulars Urge Transients," *Toronto Star*, 1 August 1939; "Danger of Disorder in Delhi Diminishes," *Toronto Star*, 4 August 1939.

92   "Single Officer Quickly Halts Tobacco Strike," *Toronto Telegram*, 12 August 1939; "Delhi Reeve Insists Taxpayers Be Left Room to Get Around," *Globe and Mail*, 4 August 1939.

93   "Hold Out for Tobacco Pay, Circulars Urge Transients," *Toronto Star*, 1 August 1939; "Súlyos mérgezések Delhi körül!" *Munkás*, 26 August 1939.

94   For examples of police repression in Alberta, Alabama, and California, see, respectively, Thompson and Seager, "Workers, Growers and Monopolists," 169; Kelley, *Hammer and Hoe*, 40–1, 166; and Barajas, *Curious Unions*, 153–5, 173. Violence against organizers in Alabama, characterized by virulent racism, was particularly horrific, as activists were frequently beaten, kidnapped, and murdered.

95   Scott, *A Communist Life*, 53.

96   "Too Costly to Live in Delhi," *London Free Press*, 4 August 1939, evening ed.

97   "Súlyos mérgezések Delhi körül!" *Munkás*, 26 August 1939.

98   "Delhi Council Planning to Have Jobless Moved from Village in Week," *London Free Press*, 9 August 1939, evening ed.; "Jobless Army at Delhi Is Dispersing," *London Free Press*, 4 August 1939; "Transients Raid Town; Officer on Duty," *London Free Press*, 18 August 1939.

99   Strike 83 (1939), D 21, Strike and Lockout Files, Microfilm Collection, AO; "Single Cop Ends Strike Near Delhi," *Globe and Mail*, 12 August 1939.

100 "More Strike Threats Heard in Tobacco Area," *Globe and Mail*, 14 August 1939.

101 "Langton Now Storm Centre," *Brantford Expositor*, 14 August 1939.

102 "Súlyos mérgezések Delhi körül!," *Munkás*, 26 August 1939.

103 "Too Much 'Tim Buck,'" *Simcoe Reformer*, 7 September 1939.

104 "Buck Asserts Naziism Must Be Squashed," *Simcoe Reformer*, 5 September 1939.

105 For examples of continued instances of protest during the war, see "Start Movement to Probe Operation of Tobacco Association," *Simcoe Reformer*, 28 December 1939; "Mr. Carter's Mistakes," *Simcoe Reformer*, 4 January 1940; "Farm Labor Converges on Delhi after Election," *Simcoe Reformer*, 9 August 1943.

Chapter Three

1   Dunsworth, "Green Gold, Red Threats"; "Pet Bunny, Corn, and Spuds Go; Probably Stew," *London Free Press*, 8 August 1939; "Chief Issues Warning," *Simcoe Reformer*, 25 April 1938; "Delhi Council Planning to Have Jobless Moved from Village in Week," *London Free Press*, 9 August 1939, evening ed.; Strike 83 (1939), D 21, Strike and Lockout Files, Microfilm Collection, AO; "Says Work Available on Farms," *The Globe*, 9 August 1935; "'Little Budapest' Springs Up in Heart of 'New Virginia,'" *Simcoe Reformer*, 1 September 1932; "Many Foreigners Making Headquarters at Delhi," *Simcoe Reformer*, 10 August 1933; "County Authorities to Wage War on Transient Laborers," *Simcoe Reformer*, 3 June 1935.

2   This perspective is critically informed by historical scholarship on state formation. See especially Greer and Radforth, eds, *Colonial Leviathan*.

3   "Simcoe Worried by Unemployed," *The Globe*, 10 August 1932; "Simcoe Mistaken; Windsor Jobless not Dumped There," *The Globe*, 11 August 1932.

4   The *London Free Press* summarized the prime suspects, writing that the culprits were either "tobacco growers seeking cheap labor, municipalities in other parts of the country wanting to get rid of unemployed, or political extremists wishing to create a focus for agitation." "The Delhi Crisis," *London Free Press*, 3 August 1939; Dunsworth, "Green Gold, Red Threats."

5   "Tobacco Growers Besieged for Work," *The Globe*, 7 September 1935.

6   Dunsworth, "Green Gold, Red Threats," 126; Struthers, *The Limits of Affluence*.

7   Struthers, *No Fault of Their Own*, 9–11, 70, 110, 138; Struthers, *The Limits of Affluence*, chap. 3; Owram, *The Government Generation*, 220–38; "Simcoe Applies for Slice of Government Relief Funds," *Simcoe Reformer*, 30 October 1930; "Camp for Single Unemployed Men Secured for Norfolk," *Simcoe Reformer*, 23 November 1933; "Delhi Moves to Move Transients," *Simcoe Reformer*, 10 August 1939; "The Transient Problem," *Simcoe Reformer*, 10 August 1939. For another example of locals lobbying higher levels of government, see "Claim Relief Regulations Make Hardship," *Simcoe Reformer*, 11 March 1935.

8   Dunsworth, "Green Gold, Red Threats," 126, 137; "County Authorities to Wage War on Transient Laborers," *Simcoe Reformer*, 3 June 1935; "Workers Are Thronging In," *Simcoe Reformer*, 13 June 1935; "Registration System for Transients Is Discussed," *Simcoe Reformer*, 19 January 1939.

9   "Nation-Wide Ads Lured Boys to Tobacco Fields," *The Clarion*, 19 August 1939; "Delhi Reeve Insists Taxpayers Be Left Room to Get Around," *Globe and Mail*, 4 August 1939; Dunsworth, "Green Gold, Red Threats," 137–8; "Tobacco Pickers Say Police Beat Them Up," *Toronto Star*, 12 August 1966; "Delhi Village Swamped with 10,000 Jobless," *London Free Press*, 1 August 1939; "Pet Bunny, Corn, and Spuds Go; Probably Stew," *London Free Press*, 8 August 1939, evening ed.; "Money a Drawback Transient Learns," *Simcoe Reformer*, 17 August 1936.

10 "Transients Cleared Out of Village Each Night," *Simcoe Reformer*, 14 August 1939; "Transients Raid Town; Officer on Duty," *London Free Press*, 18 August 1939.

11 "Influx of Tobacco Curers Causes False Alarm," *Simcoe Reformer*, 21 August 1930.

12 Parham, *Tobacco in the Blood*, 25–6.

13 "Influx of Tobacco Curers Causes False Alarm," *Simcoe Reformer*, 21 August 1930; "Simcoe Applies for Slice of Government Relief Funds," *Simcoe Reformer*, 30 October 1930; "20,000 Acres of Tobacco Predicted for Norfolk County," *Simcoe Reformer*, 29 January 1931.

14 "Order-in-Council PC 1931-695, 1931," Canadian Museum of Immigration at Pier 21, accessed 21 September 2017, http://www.pier21.ca/research/immigration-history/order-in-council-pc-1931-695-1931.

15 Putnam, *Radical Moves*; FitzGerald and Cook-Martín, *Culling the Masses*.

16 Roberts, *Whence They Came*; Avery, *Reluctant Host*.

17 "Important Notice Sent to Tobacco Farm Owners," *Simcoe Reformer*, 25 June 1931;

"Influx of Tobacco Help to Be Greatly Curtailed," *Simcoe Reformer*, 19 February 1931.

18 Sid Williams, interview by Leonard Rapport, 1939, Leonard Rapport Works Progress Administration interviews, in author's possession.

19 F.S. Thomas to Mitchell Hepburn, 8 August 1935, Premier Mitchell F. Hepburn Private Correspondence, RG 3-10, B307922, file "Agriculture Dept, re: Tobacco Industry, 1935," AO; Mitchell Hepburn to Thomas Magladery, 7 August 1935, Premier Mitchell F. Hepburn Private Correspondence, RG 3-10, B307922, file "Agriculture Dept, re: Tobacco Industry, 1935," AO; Deputy Minister to David A. Croll, 7 August 1935, Premier Mitchell F. Hepburn Private Correspondence, RG 3-10, B307922, file "Agriculture Dept, re: Tobacco Industry, 1935," AO; W. Davison to G.V. Haythorne, 30 July 1944, RG 27, vol. 667, file 6-5-26-1, part 2, LAC; "Tobacco Curer Situation Is Clarified; 825 May Enter," *Simcoe Reformer*, 12 August 1935; "Expect 1,400 Curers to Help with Tobacco Crop," *Simcoe Reformer*, 30 June 1938.

20 F.S. Thomas to Mitchell Hepburn, 8 August 1935, Premier Mitchell F. Hepburn Private Correspondence, RG 3-10, B307922, file "Agriculture Dept, re: Tobacco Industry, 1935," AO; Mitchell Hepburn to Thomas Magladery, 7 August 1935, Premier Mitchell F. Hepburn Private Correspondence, RG 3-10, B307922, file "Agriculture Dept, re: Tobacco Industry, 1935," AO; Deputy Minister to David A. Croll, 7 August 1935, Premier Mitchell F. Hepburn Private Correspondence, RG 3-10, B307922, file "Agriculture Dept, re: Tobacco Industry, 1935," AO; W. Davison to G.V. Haythorne, 30 July 1944, RG 27, vol. 667, file 6-5-26-1, part 2, LAC; "Tobacco Curer Situation Is Clarified; 825 May Enter," *Simcoe Reformer*, 12 August 1935; "Expect 1,400 Curers to Help with Tobacco Crop," *Simcoe Reformer*, 30 June 1938; "Native Tobacco Workmen Protected by Government," *Simcoe Reformer*, 6 April 1933; "Norfolk Agricultural Representative's Field Reports," 1933–36, Agricultural Representatives' Field Reports, RG 16-66, microfilm MS 597, Reel 40, AO; "Southern Curers, Primers Available to Harvest Leaf," *Simcoe Reformer*, 14 August 1941; George V. Haythorne to Brigadier General Rose, 15 May 1944, RG 27, vol. 667, file 6-5-26-2, LAC.

21 F.S. Thomas to Mitchell Hepburn (B), 9 August 1935, Premier Mitchell F. Hepburn Private Correspondence, RG 3-10, B307922, file "Agriculture Dept, re: Tobacco Industry, 1935," AO; "Says Curers Cost Closer to $200,000," *Simcoe Reformer*, 7 April 1938; "Train Our Own Curers," *Simcoe Reformer*, 14 April 1938; "Pass Resolution to Give Training In Curing Tobacco," *Simcoe Reformer*, 12 May 1938; "Approve Scheme to Train Young Canadian Curers," *Simcoe Reformer*, 7 July 1938; "Will Train 50 to Cure Leaf," *Simcoe Reformer*, 8 June 1939.

22 "Guarding Tobacco Industry," *Simcoe Reformer*, 30 July 1931; W. Davison to Fred Sloan, 29 October 1947, Extension Service, RG 33, NC-117 Entry 3A, box 72, file "Farm Labor – Canada, 1947–1948," National Archives and Records Administra-

tion (hereafter NARA); "District Superintendent to Immigration Inspector-in-Charge, Fort Erie, ON," 9 August 1948, RG 76, vol. 853, file 553-164, LAC; W. Davison to B.G. Sullivan, 13 August 1954, RG 27, vol. 667, file 6-5-26-1, part 3, LAC; W.W. Dawson to A.H. Brown, 2 March 1956, RG 27, vol. 668, file 6-5-26-2, part 4, LAC.

23 For a brilliant discussion of immigration agents' use of discretion in their decision-making processes, see Satzewich, *Points of Entry*.

24 "Report of Admissions and Rejections at the Port of Bridgeburg, Ont.," 21 August 1928, Border Crossings: From US to Canada, 1908–1935, Ontario, Manifests, Ancestry.ca; "Order-in-Council PC 1931-695, 1931," Canadian Museum of Immigration at Pier 21, accessed 21 September 2017, http://www.pier21.ca/research/immigration-history/order-in-council-pc-1931-695-1931.

25 See, for example, Schrover and Moloney, eds, *Gender, Migration and Categorisation*, 8; Madokoro, *Elusive Refuge*, 6–7.

26 "Illiteracy Bars Tobacco Curers," *Simcoe Reformer*, 18 August 1932. Given the exclusion of African American tobacco workers, one question that comes to mind is whether these curers might have been Black. There is no evidence to suggest that they were, however. I could not locate the rejected workers' entries within the border crossing manifests, so no definitive information about this – or any other details of the workers' case – is available. "Report of Admissions and Rejections at the Port of Fort Erie, Ont.," 10–17 August 1928, Border Crossings: From US to Canada, 1908–1935, Ontario, Manifests, Ancestry.ca.

27 "Special Investigator Rounds Up Six for Illegal Entry," *Simcoe Reformer*, 22 August 1935; F.S. Thomas to Mitchell Hepburn, 8 August 1935, F.S. Thomas to Mitchell Hepburn, 9 August 1935, and Thomas Magladery to Mitchell Hepburn, 3 September 1935, all in Premier Mitchell F. Hepburn Private Correspondence, RG 3-10, B307922, file "Agriculture Dept, re: Tobacco Industry, 1935," AO; W. Davison to W.W. Dawson, 14 June 1948, RG 27, vol. 667, file 6-5-26-2, LAC; F.R. Gregory to Officer-in-Charge, Fort Erie, 5 August 1952, RG 27, vol. 668, file 6-5-26-2, part 3, LAC; L.G. Irving to Regional Director, Toronto, 14 August 1967, RG 76, vol. 1112, file 553-164, LAC.

28 Pierson, *"They're Still Women After All,"* 9–61; Keshen, *Saints, Sinners, and Soldiers*, 43, 55; Bjørge, "The Workers' War"; Mosby, *Food Will Win the War*.

29 Patrias, "More Menial than Housemaids?," 98–9; Keshen, *Saints, Sinners, and Soldiers*, 59, 68.

30 Stevenson, *Canada's Greatest Wartime Muddle*, 4–5.

31 "Report of a Special Committee of the Dominion-Provincial Agricultural Conference with Respect to Farm Manpower," n.d. (c. 1942), RG 27, vol. 2270, file "Agricultural Manpower Policy, 1942–1946," LAC; Humphrey Mitchell and Arthur MacNamara, "A Message to Men Who Work on Farms," 9 August 1943, RG 27,

vol. 134, file 601.3-9, part 1, microfilm reel T-10116, LAC; Humphrey Mitchell and Arthur MacNamara, "A Message to Canadian Farmers," 17 April 1944, RG 27, vol. 134, file 601.3-9, part 1, microfilm reel T-10116, LAC; "Army Personnel on Extended Leave from District Depots, 1945," 1945, RG 17, vol. 3129, file 66-5, part 5, LAC.

32   Satzewich, *Racism and the Incorporation of Foreign Labour*, 70.

33   Owram, *The Government Generation*, 288–91; Struthers, *No Fault of Their Own*, 138–207.

34   Haythorne and Marsh, *Land and Labour*. Haythorne later published his own book, *Labor in Canadian Agriculture*, in 1961, in which he continued to make the case for active state involvement in farm labour.

35   Perrett et al., "Memorandum Re Tobacco Industry," 6 October 1943, attached to A. MacNamara to G.W. Ritchie et al., 19 January 1944, RG 27, vol. 667, file 6-5-26-1, part 1, LAC; Wallis, "Farm Diary," AO; "Poor Outlook for Tobacco," *Simcoe Reformer*, 1 August 1940; "Labour Cost for Tobacco Crop Higher," *Simcoe Reformer*, 17 August 1942.

36   E. Poste to B.G. Sullivan, 7 June 1943, RG 27, vol. 667, file 6-5-26-1, part 1, LAC.

37   "Tobacco Growers Pay Fancy Wages This Year," *Globe and Mail*, 16 August 1943; Gordon Bell to H.R. Hare, 27 August 1943, RG 27, vol. 667, file 6-5-26-1, part 1, LAC; A.H. Brown to A. MacNamara, 2 July 1943, RG 17, vol. 3130, file 66-5-3, LAC.

38   T.H. Robinson to Sheldon Ross, 16 April 1943, RG 27, vol. 667, file 6-5-26-1, part 1, LAC.

39   A.H. Brown to A. MacNamara, 2 July 1943, RG 17, vol. 3130, file 66-5-3, LAC. See also the following letters, all located in Department of Labour, RG 27, vol. 667, file 6-5-26-1, part 1, LAC: C.F. Needham to A. MacNamara (A), 22 April 1943; Allan Mitchell to A. MacNamara, 10 July 1943; T.B. Pickersgill to C.F. Needham, 12 July 1943; N.A. MacRae to George V. Haythorne, 18 May 1943; W.R. Reek to T.B. Pickersgill, 15 June 1943.

40   "Order-in-Council," 6 August 1943, RG 27, vol. 668, file 6-5-26-4, LAC.

41   Stevenson, *Canada's Greatest Wartime Muddle*, 10–11.

42   A.H. Brown to A. MacNamara, 13 July 1943, RG 27, vol. 667, file 6-5-26-1, part 1, LAC; T.B. Pickersgill to C.F. Needham, 12 July 1943, RG 27, vol. 667, file 6-5-26-1, part 1, LAC; Allan Mitchell to C.F. Needham, 16 July 1943, RG 27, vol. 667, file 6-5-26-1, part 1, LAC.

43   T.B. Pickersgill to C.F. Needham, 12 July 1943, RG 27, vol. 667, file 6-5-26-1, part 1, LAC; W.R. Reek to T.B. Pickersgill, 15 June 1943, RG 27, vol. 667, file 6-5-26-1, part 1, LAC; "Tobacco Labour," *Simcoe Reformer*, 15 July 1943; Merrell, "Memo: Flue-Cured Tobacco Crop in Ontario," 16 August 1944, War Manpower Commission, RG 211, I6 Entry 113, box 3, file "Canada – Agriculture: Conditions in the Labor Market," NARA; W.H. Mills to A. MacNamara, 29 June 1944, RG 27, vol. 668, file 6-5-26-4, LAC; "Minutes of Tobacco Advisory Committee Meeting," 10 May 1945, RG

27, vol. 667, file 6-5-26-1, part 3, LAC; "5,000 Tobacco Permits Issued," *Simcoe Reformer*, 10 August 1944; "Tobacco Labor," *Simcoe Reformer*, 27 March 1944.

44 H.R. Hare to Allan Mitchell, 20 July 1943, RG 27, vol. 667, file 6-5-26-1, part 1, LAC; Allan Mitchell to A. MacNamara, 16 August 1943, RG 27, vol. 668, file 6-5-26-4, LAC.

45 "Tobacco Men Protest," *Simcoe Reformer*, 30 March 1944, RG 27, vol. 667, file 6-5-26-1, part 1., LAC; Perrett et al., "Memorandum Re Tobacco Industry"; G.V. Haythorne to A. MacNamara, 17 July 1944, RG 27, vol. 667, file 6-5-26-1, part 2, LAC; A. MacNamara to W.T. Henderson and J.G. Gillanders, 17 July 1944, RG 27, vol. 667, file 6-5-26-1, part 2, LAC; "T.W. Wells to G.W. Ritchie," 29 July 1944, RG 27, vol. 668, file 6-5-26-4, LAC.

46 F.R. Gregory to A. MacNamara, 29 July 1944, RG 27, vol. 668, file 6-5-26-4, LAC.

47 On First Nations' resistance to the NRMA, see Stevenson, *Canada's Greatest Wartime Muddle*, chap. 2. On life under the paternalistic, invasive Indian Act on Ontario reserves, see Brownlie, *A Fatherly Eye*.

48 Tillotson, *Give and Take*, 182.

49 Perrett et al., "Memorandum Re Tobacco Industry."

50 N.A. MacRae to George V. Haythorne, 18 May 1943, RG 27, vol. 667, file 6-5-26-1, part 1, LAC. See also David Sim to A. MacNamara, 10 April 1944, and David Sim to A. MacNamara, 10 April 1944, RG 27, vol. 668, file 6-5-26-4, LAC.

51 H.J. Collins, "The Tobacco Forum," *Delhi News-Record*, 23 March 1944, RG 27, vol. 667, file 6-5-26-1, part 1, LAC; H.J. Collins, "Selective Service and the Tobacco Industry," *Delhi News-Record*, May 1944, RG 27, vol. 667, file 6-5-26-1, part 1, LAC.

52 Perrett et al., "Memorandum Re Tobacco Industry"; G.V. Haythorne to A. MacNamara, 17 July 1944, and G.G. Bramhill to George V. Haythorne, 21 March 1944, RG 27, vol. 667, file 6-5-26-1, part 1, LAC; "Minutes of Meeting," 18 May 1944, RG 27, vol. 667, file 6-5-26-1, part 1, LAC.

53 G.G. Bramhill to George V. Haythorne; "Minutes of Meeting," 18 May 1944; "National Selective Service: Order," 6 June 1944, RG 27, vol. 667, file 6-5-26-1, part 2, LAC; "Minutes of Meeting Held in Simcoe on Tobacco Growers Situation," 17 April 1944, RG 27, vol. 667, file 6-5-26-1, part 1, LAC.

54 F.R. Gregory to A. MacNamara, 15 April 1944, and G.V. Haythorne to A. MacNamara, 20 July 1944, RG 27, vol. 667, file 6-5-26-1, part 2, LAC; A. MacNamara to W.H. Taylor, 18 April 1944, RG 27, vol. 667, file 6-5-26-1, part 1, LAC; David Sim to A. MacNamara, 11 August 1944, RG 27, vol. 668, file 6-5-26-4, LAC; C.A. Yeager to W. Davison, 28 July 1944, RG 27, vol. 667, file 6-5-26-1, part 2, LAC.

55 F.R. Gregory to A. MacNamara, 19 July 1944, RG 27, vol. 668, file 6-5-26-4, LAC; "F.R. Gregory Asks Tobacco Investigation," *Simcoe Reformer*, 24 July 1944.

56 Norfolk County Clerk to Humphrey Mitchell, 5 May 1944, RG 27, vol. 668, file 6-5-26-4, LAC; Arthur Phillips et al. to A. MacNamara, 25 July 1944, RG 27, vol. 668, file 6-5-26-4, LAC.

57   See for example, "Minutes of Meeting," 18 May 1944, and A. MacNamara to
     F.R. Gregory, July 17, 1944, RG 27, vol. 668, file 6-5-26-4, LAC.

58   A. MacNamara to J.K. Perrett, 14 April 1944, RG 27, vol. 667, file 6-5-26-1, part 1,
     LAC. See also G.G. Bramhill to George V. Haythorne, and A. MacNamara to
     W.L. Pelton, 19 April 1944, RG 27, vol. 667, file 6-5-26-1, part 1, LAC; "Appeals for
     Harvest Help," *Simcoe Reformer*, 10 August 1944.

59   A. MacNamara to George V. Haythorne, 10 May 1944, and A. MacNamara to
     G.V. Haythorne, 22 May 1944, RG 27, vol. 667, file 6-5-26-2, LAC.

60   F.R. Gregory to W.L. Mackenzie King, 10 August 1944, RG 27, vol. 667, file 6-5-26-
     1, part 2, LAC. See also telegrams to the ministers of finance and labour in the
     same file: H.J. Collins to James G. Gardiner, 10 August 1944, and David Sim to
     A. MacNamara, 11 August 1944, RG 27, vol. 668, file 6-5-26-4, LAC.

61   "Report: Tobacco Advisory Counsel," 10 August 1944, RG 27, vol. 667, file 6-5-26-1,
     part 2, LAC; G.W. Ritchie to A. MacNamara, 10 August 1944, RG 27, vol. 667, file
     6-5-26-1, part 2, LAC.

62   T.W. Wells to A. MacNamara, 18 August 1944, RG 27, vol. 668, file 6-5-26-4, LAC;
     "10-Hour Day in Field for NRMA's," *Globe and Mail*, 19 August 1944.

63   "Summary Record of Work Performed by Offices in Tobacco Area," 10 November
     1944, RG 27, vol. 667, file 6-5-26-1, part 2, LAC; W. Davison to G.V. Haythorne,
     25 January 1945, RG 27, vol. 667, file 6-5-26-1, part 2, LAC.

64   "Record of Flue Industry in Ontario over 60 Years," *Simcoe Reformer*, 25 February
     1988.

65   J.K. Perrett to A. MacNamara, 20 March 1945, RG 17, vol. 3129, file 66-5, part 5,
     LAC; "Minutes of Tobacco Advisory Committee Meeting," 1 November 1944, and
     David Sim to A. MacNamara, 30 August 1944, RG 27, vol. 667, file 6-5-26-1, part 2,
     LAC; F.R. Gregory to A. MacNamara, 6 April 1945, RG 27, vol. 667, file 6-5-26-1,
     part 3, LAC; A. MacNamara to F.R. Gregory, 23 November 1944, RG 27, vol. 667,
     file 6-5-26-1, part 2, LAC.

66   "Minutes of Tobacco Advisory Committee Meeting," 10 May 1945, RG 27, vol. 667,
     file 6-5-26-1, part 3, LAC; "Tobacco Growers Not Following Regulations," *Simcoe
     Reformer*, 27 August 1945; "Record of Flue Industry in Ontario over 60 Years,"
     Simcoe Reformer, 25 February 1988.

67   On labour shortages in the United States, see Hahamovitch, *The Fruits of Their
     Labor*, chap. 7.

68   Similar agreements were also struck with the colonial governments of the Baha-
     mas, Jamaica, and other West Indian islands. See Loza, *Defiant Braceros*; Haha-
     movitch, *No Man's Land*; Henderson, "Bracero Blacklists," 199–217; Hahamovitch,
     "Risk the Truck."

69   "Resolution (No. 9)," 27 February 1942, RG 76, vol. 842, file 553-66-637, part 2,
     LAC. The two countries struck a similar deal to enable the movement of Cana-

dian woods workers to the northeastern United States. "Memorandum for the Minister," 23 May 1958, RG 25, vol. 6374, file 3629-40, part 4.1, LAC; "Memorandum," 29 March 1943, RG 76, vol. 475, file 731622, microfilm reel C-10411, LAC; Robert C. Goodwin to Jerry R. Holleman, 15 March 1961, Bureau of Employment Security, RG 183, A1 Entry 1, box 31, file "403, 1957," NARA.

70 Jolliffe's position here was not out of character. The veteran civil servant had forged his career in Vancouver, where in 1922, as controller of Chinese immigration, he recommended new federal legislation to limit the entrance of Chinese immigrants, a suggestion that came to fruition the following year with the passage of the Chinese Immigration Act. Later, as deputy director (under F.C. Blair) and from 1943 director of the Immigration Branch, Jolliffe played a leading role in the exclusion of asylum-seeking Jews attempting to flee the unfolding horrors in pre-war and wartime Europe, despite by all appearances not harbouring the same personal antisemitism as his predecessor. McEvoy, "A Symbol of Racial Discrimination," 29–30; Ward, *White Canada Forever*, 132; Abella and Troper, *None Is Too Many*, 156.

71 A.L. Jolliffe, "Memorandum," 24 June 1942, RG 76, vol. 475, file 731622, microfilm reel C-10411, LAC; A.L. Jolliffe to N.A. Robertson, 29 June 1942, RG 76, vol. 475, file 731622, microfilm reel C-10411, LAC; Director to N.A. Robertson, 9 July 1942 (second letter), RG 76, vol. 475, file 731622, microfilm reel C-10411, LAC; A.L. Jolliffe, "Memorandum," 9 July 1942, RG 76, vol. 475, file 731622, microfilm reel C-10411, LAC. For a more detailed discussion, see Dunsworth, "Race, Exclusion, and Archival Silences."

72 Fred Sloan to C.W.E. Pittman, 28 August 1946, RG 33, NC-117 Entry 3A, box 36, file "Farm Labor – North Carolina, 1946–1947," NARA (emphasis added); D.A. Tucker, "Virginia Annual Report," 1947, RG 33, PI-83 Entry 48, box 50, file "Virginia – Farm Labor Supervisor's Annual Narrative Report, 1947," NARA; C.E.S. Smith to Deputy Minister, 18 October 1960, RG 26, vol. 124, file 3-33-6, part 2, LAC.

73 T.B. Pickersgill to A. MacNamara, 9 June 1944, RG 27, vol. 667, file 6-5-26-2, LAC; J.K. Perrett to Tobacco Growers, 14 June 1944, RG 27, vol. 667, file 6-5-26-2, LAC.

74 Both instances of illicit recruitment were reported to the NSS by North Carolina Extension Service officials. W. Davison to G.V. Haythorne, 30 July 1944, RG 27, vol. 667, file 6-5-26-1, part 2, LAC; A. MacNamara to F.R. Gregory, 30 August 1945; F.R. Gregory to A. MacNamara, 6 September 1945; J.F. Dwyer to G.V. Haythorne, 14 September 1945 – all in Department of Labour, RG 27, vol. 667, file 6-5-26-2, LAC.

75 J.W. Crawford to C.W.E. Pittman, 8 June 1946, Department of Labour, RG 27, vol. 667, file 6-5-26-2, LAC.

76 "Minutes: Meeting of United States and Canadian Farm Labour Officials Re International Farm Labour Movements," 29 May 1946, RG 17, vol. 3637, file N-3-9, LAC; "North Carolina Annual Report, 1946," 1946, Extension Service, RG 33, PI-83

Entry 48, box 37, file "North Carolina – Annual Report, 1946," NARA; J.W. Crawford to C.W.E. Pittman, 8 June 1946.

77 R.M. Macdonnell to G.V. Haythorne, 23 August 1946, RG 27, vol. 667, file 6-5-26-2, LAC. Punctuation and spelling are rendered as they appear in the original letter.

78 W. Davison to G.V. Haythorne, 29 August 1946, RG 27, vol. 667, file 6-5-26-2, LAC; "North Carolina Annual Report, 1947," 1947, Extension Service, RG 33, PI-83 Entry 48, box 47, file "North Carolina – Annual Report, 1947," NARA; W.K. Rutherford to G.V. Haythorne, 3 February 1947, RG 27, vol. 667, file 6-5-26-2, LAC.

79 W. Davison to G.V. Haythorne, 18 July 1947, RG 27, vol. 667, file 6-5-26-2, LAC; Barnard Joy to R.E. Smith, 22 July 1947, Extension Service, RG 33, NC-117 Entry 3A, box 72, file "Farm Labor – Canada, 1947–1948," NARA; "North Carolina Annual Report, 1947," 1947, Extension Service, RG 33, PI-83 Entry 48, box 47, file "North Carolina – Annual Report, 1947," NARA.

80 "North Carolina Annual Report, 1947," 1947, Extension Service, RG 33, PI-83 Entry 48, box 47, file "North Carolina – Annual Report, 1947," NARA; G.V. Haythorne to W.J. Bambrick, 3 September 1947, RG 27, vol. 667, file 6-5-26-2. LAC.

81 For examples of later procedural problems, see Immigration Inspector-in-Charge, Niagara Falls, ON, to Eastern District Superintendent, 10 August 1948, RG 76, vol. 853, file 553-164, LAC; Don Larin to W.W. Dawson, 28 August 1953, Bureau of Employment Security, RG 183, UD-WW Entry 14, box 22, file "Georgia – 200, 1952," NARA; Don Larin to W. Davison, 28 August 1957, Bureau of Employment Security, RG 183, A1 Entry 1, box 33, file "411, July 1957," NARA; F.M. Hereford to G.V. Haythorne, 30 August 1961, RG 27, vol. 668, file 6-5-26-2, part 5, LAC.

Chapter Four

1 Patricia, interview. Last name omitted at interviewee's request.

2 W. Davison to R.E.O., 30 September 1955, RG 27, vol. 668, file 6-5-26-2, part 4, LAC; "For 36 Years Straight He's Cured Flue in Area," *Simcoe Reformer*, 18 September 1966, Ontario Flue-Cured Tobacco Growers' Marketing Board Scrapbooks (hereafter OFCTGMB Scrapbooks), Delhi Tobacco Museum and Heritage Centre (hereafter DTMHC).

3 Barker and Kennedy, *The Tobacco Leaf Yesterday and Today*, 37; "Small Tobacco Men Feel Pinch," *Globe and Mail*, 27 July 1965, OFCTGMB Scrapbooks, DTMHC; "Norfolk Agricultural Representative's Field Report, 1965–66," 1966, Agricultural Representatives' Field Reports, RG 16-66, microfilm MS 597, Reel 41, AO.

4 Barker and Kennedy, *The Tobacco Leaf Yesterday and Today*, 37; Donohue, interview; Alleyne, interview.

5 A.R. McCourt to R.G. Bennett, 13 September 1961, Program files of the Marketing and Special Services Division of the Ministry of Agriculture and Food (hereafter

MSSDMAF), RG 16-102, box B354994, file "Agricultural Manpower Services," sub-file: "Temporary Tobacco Placement Office, Delhi, 1961," AO.

6   E. Allen, "Meeting of the Provincial Agricultural Manpower Committee – Onta-rio," 3 November 1967, RG 118, acc. 1985–86/071, vol. 84, file 3315-11-551, part 1, LAC.

7   "OFCTGMB Annual Report," 1970, Records of the Flue-Cured Tobacco Growers' Marketing Board, RG 16-250, box B388334, file "Tobacco Plan: Regulations & Annual Report, 1970," AO.

8   "Labor Lack Seen Boon In Future," *Simcoe Reformer*, 18 February 1966; "Dem-eyere: Use Tried, True Ways," *Simcoe Reformer*, 20 July 1967, OFCTGMB Scrap-books, DTMHC; "Flue Board Helps Harvester Users," *Aylmer Express*, 21 December 1970, OFCTGMB Scrapbooks, DTMHC; "Minutes of a Meeting of the OFCTGMB," 17 December 1970, Records of the Flue-Cured Tobacco Growers' Marketing Board, RG 16-250, box B388334, file "Tobacco Plan – Minutes," AO.

9   "The World Renowned Hawk Tobacco Tying Machine," *Simcoe Reformer*, 12 March 1964; "Introducing BALTHES for Simcoe and District," *Simcoe Reformer*, 25 April 1966. See also issues of the *Canadian Tobacco Grower* from 1969 to 1973.

10 "The Ontario Flue-Cured Tobacco Harvest – 1969," 28 October 1969, RG 118, acc. 1985–86/071, vol. 75, file 3300-13, part 1, LAC. See also Allen, "Meeting of the Prov-incial Agricultural Manpower Committee – Ontario"; "Tobacco Harvest Mech-anization Eases Delhi Transient Problems," *Globe and Mail*, 10 August 1967.

11 "Tobacco Harvest Mechanization Eases Delhi Transient Problems," *Globe and Mail*, 10 August 1967.

12 A.R. McCourt to R. Gauvreau and G.H. Kidd, 9 August 1967, MSSDMAF, RG 16-102, box B353591 (catalogue location: box B236051), file "Ontario Federal-Provincial Farm Labour Committee: Tobacco Labour, 1966–," AO.

13 Allen, "Meeting of the Provincial Agricultural Manpower Committee – Ontario."

14 In 1943, for example, tiers earned $6 per day while primers earned between $6 and $8. In 1956, tiers earned $14 per day; primers $12 to $14. Contrast this with 1978, when women on the table crew made $35 a day, compared with $40 for field workers, or 1981, when the median wage for tiers was $42.50, compared with $47.50 for primers. For wage data for primers and tiers from 1942, 1943, and 1956, see "Labour Cost for Tobacco Crop Higher," *Simcoe Reformer*, 17 August 1942; "Tobacco Growers Pay Fancy Wages This Year," *Globe and Mail*, 16 August 1943; F.R. Gregory to Milton F. Gregg, 31 December 1956, RG 27, vol. 667, file 6-5-26-1, part 3, LAC; F.K. Ashbaugh to M.F. Gregg, 9 October 1956, RG 27, vol. 668, file 6-5-26-2, part 4, LAC. For 1978 and 1981, see Barker and Kennedy, *The Tobacco Leaf Yesterday and Today*, 39; "Minutes," 22 August 1981, Canadian Farmworkers Union Collection, Simon Fraser University Digitized Collections, http://digital.lib.sfu.ca/cfu-5078/ontario-organizing-evaluation-summary-minutes.

15 See, for example, Cohen, *Women's Work, Markets, and Economic Development in Nineteenth-Century Ontario*, chap. 5.

16 "Labor Lack Seen Boon In Future," *Simcoe Reformer*, 18 February 1966; "Encourage Hiring Women for Flue Field Gangs," *Tillsonburg News*, 15 July 1970, OFCTGMB Scrapbooks, DTMHC.

17 "Five Ladies Prime Tobacco For 10 Bulk Curing Units," *Delhi News-Record*, 25 September 1968, OFCTGMB Scrapbooks, DTMHC; "Debbie Takes Tobacco Road to Beauty Field," *Toronto Star*, 23 September 1977; "Five Female Primers Have Just the Right Touch," *Simcoe Reformer*, 8 August 1975, OFCTGMB Scrapbooks, DTMHC.

18 "Debbie Takes Tobacco Road to Beauty Field," *Toronto Star*, 23 September 1977.

19 "OFCTGMB Annual Report," 1970.

20 "Debbie Takes Tobacco Road to Beauty Field," *Toronto Star*, 23 September 1977.

21 "OFCTGMB Annual Report," 1970.

22 Patricia, interview.

23 "Growers Agree Negotiator Might Aid Flue Price Talks," *Simcoe Reformer*, 6 March 1975.

24 Ted Raytrowsky to J.L. Manion, 24 December 1974, RG 118, acc. 1985–86/071, vol. 74, file 3300-6-12, LAC.

25 "Flue Board," *Simcoe Reformer*, 14 February 1975.

26 "Growers Agree Negotiator Might Aid Flue Price Talks," *Simcoe Reformer*, 6 March 1975.

27 Palmer, *Canada's 1960s*, 216.

28 Radforth, *Bushworkers and Bosses*, 160–1.

29 Ackner, interview.

30 Sangster, *Transforming Labour*, chap. 1, conclusion.

31 "Small Tobacco Men Feel Pinch," *Globe and Mail*, 27 July 1965, OFCTGMB Scrapbooks, DTMHC.

32 "Letters to the Editor," *Tillsonburg News*, 28 February 1964, OFCTGMB Scrapbooks, DTMHC.

33 Some statistics from the report: The percentage of families living on less than $3,000 per year in Norfolk was 10 per cent higher than the national average. Between 5 and 10 per cent of the fifteen-and-older population had four or fewer years of schooling. Two thousand of the county's roughly 50,000 people (about 4 per cent) depended on welfare or family allowance funds. And perhaps most shockingly, Norfolk County's infant mortality rate was between 26 and 35 per 1,000, almost three times the national average. "Norfolk Poor Object to Plea for Poor-Area Status," *The Globe*, 19 May 1965; "Norfolk's Tobacco Road: Wrecked Cars, Debris, and Children," *Globe and Mail*, 21 May 1965.

34 "Norfolk's Tobacco Road: Wrecked Cars, Debris, and Children," *Globe and Mail*,

21 May 1965; "Norfolk Poor Object to Plea for Poor-Area Status," *The Globe*, 19 May 1965.

35 Chaussé, interview. Other interviews of Canadian migrants discussing adventure include Participant 26 and Craig Berggold.

36 Ladell, interview.

37 Passmore, interview and email correspondence, 15 August 2017.

38 Chaussé, interview.

39 Interviews with Chaussé, Ladell, Passmore, and Vermeeren.

40 Kennedy, "My First Job in Tobacco." See also Doxtator, "All about Tobacco," and Elm, "Learning to Work in Tobacco." Consumer goods also mentioned in Long, interview.

41 "Thousands Flock to District to Await Work in Tobacco," *Simcoe Reformer*, 6 August 1954.

42 Chaussé, interview.

43 Interviews with Long, Patricia, and Vermeeren; "Debbie Takes Tobacco Road to Beauty Field," *Toronto Star*, 23 September 1977.

44 "Population by Origin and Sex, for Counties and Census Divisions," Census of Canada, 1941–61. In 1941, the title began "Population by Racial Origin and Sex." Table numbers for 1941, 1951, and 1961, respectively: 31, 34, 37; Danys, *DP, Lithuanian Immigration to Canada after the Second World War*, 177–80; Delhi Tobacco Belt Project Papers, F 1405-61, AO.

45 Dégh, *People in the Tobacco Belt*; "Mrs. K. Simutis," 1977, Delhi Tobacco Belt Project Papers, F 1405-61, B440613, file 9960.4, AO.

46 One interesting indication of this can be found in the coverage of an oft-criticized business scheme whereby drivers of taxis or trucks transported migrants to the tobacco belt with a false guarantee of work. In the 1930s, the "trucking racket" was noted in particular for its Hungarian victims, while postwar reports did not specify passengers' ethnicities or origins. "Outside Jobless Again Being Dumped in Delhi," *Simcoe Reformer*, 26 July 1934; "Trucker Dupes Workers, Guarantees $11 per Day," *Simcoe Reformer*, 14 August 1950; W. Davison to Buckley, 16 September 1958, RG 27, vol. 667, file 6-5-26-1, part 3, LAC.

47 "Delhi Police Constable Assaulted by Transients," *Simcoe Reformer*, 10 August 1944.

48 "Here and There," *Simcoe Reformer*, 17 August 1944.

49 "Summary Record of Work Performed by Offices in Tobacco Area," 10 November 1944, RG 27, vol. 667, file 6-5-26-1, part 2, LAC; "OFCTGMB Annual Report," 1969.

50 W. Davison to B.G. Sullivan, 13 August 1954, RG 27, vol. 667, file 6-5-26-1, part 3, LAC. See also "Tobacco Harvest Is General in District; Leaf of Good Quality," *Simcoe Reformer*, 13 August 1951; "Thousands Flock to District to Await Work in Tobacco," *Simcoe Reformer*, 6 August 1954.

51 G.V. Haythorne to Anthime Charbonneau, 23 July 1946, RG 27, vol. 667, file 6-5-26-2, LAC; W. Davison to Buckley, 12 November 1956, RG 27, vol. 667, file 6-5-26-1, part 3, LAC; "Stephanie de Leemans," 1977, Delhi Tobacco Belt Project Papers, F 1405-61, B440612, file 9959.2, AO.

52 "OFCTGMB Annual Report," 1970.

53 From 1960 to 1975, unemployment in Ontario averaged about 4 per cent annually, below the national average. Quebec's jobless rate stood at 7.3 per cent, while Atlantic Canada's was more than double Ontario's at 8.8 per cent. "Table D491-497: Unemployment Rates, by Region, Annual Averages, 1946 to 1975," Statistics Canada, accessed 9 November 2018, https://www150.statcan.gc.ca/n1/pub/11-516-x/sectiond/D491_497-eng.csv. For northern Ontario and regional inequalities, see Weller, "Hinterland Politics," 727–9.

54 Mazer, "Making the Welfare State Work for Extraction," 18–34; Mazer, "Mining Mobility"; Langford, "Helping People Help Themselves," chaps 5 and 6.

55 G.J. Primeau, "Quebec Region: Agricultural – Placements, January 1st 1966 to October 31st 1966," 1966, RG 118, acc. 1985–86/071, vol. 75, file 3300-13, part 1, LAC; Director, Canadian Service to Deputy Minister, 11 March 1966, RG 76, vol. 842, file 553-67, part 3, LAC; Manager, CMC, Tillsonburg to G.H. Kidd, 25 September 1968, RG 118, vol. 244, file 9-6-4, part 59, LAC.

56 There had been an earlier attempt at such labour mobilization in Ontario in the mid-1950s, when Indian Affairs officials tried to place First Nations workers from Ontario reserves on sugar beet farms in southwestern Ontario. Officials found it difficult to locate workers interested in beet labour, since many already worked each year on tobacco, fruit, and vegetable farms, work they preferred and which paid higher wages. No more than a couple hundred workers were placed and the initiative was abandoned by the late 1950s. Department of Indian Affairs, RG 10, vol. 8429, file 401/21-5, part 1, LAC.

57 "500 Indians from James Bay to Help Harvest Tobacco," *Brantford Expositor*, 8 July 1965, OFCTGMB Scrapbooks, DTMHC; Laliberte and Satzewich, "Native Migrant Labour in the Southern Alberta Sugar-Beet Industry"; Laliberte "The 'Grab-a-Hoe' Indians"; Regional Director, Toronto to Regional Settlement Supervisor, Toronto, 21 March 1966, RG 76, vol. 1112, file 553-164, LAC.

58 Correspondence between R. Biddle and J. LeBlanc, 10–21 November 1967, RG 118, acc. 1985–86/071, vol. 73, file 3300-1, "Farm Labour – General Series," part 1, LAC.

59 See, for example, "A Conference on the Problems Raised by Itinerant Tobacco Workers," 6 December 1949, United Church of Canada Haldimand-Norfolk Presbytery, fonds 1014, series 2, acc. 1984.028C, file 3-25, United Church of Canada Archives; "Students and Ex-Convicts Populate Tobacco Camps," *Globe and Mail*, 9 August 1965; "Claims Tobacco Towns Menaced at Night by 'Lazy Slob' Migrants," *Toronto Star*, 8 August 1966.

60   Palmer, *Canada's 1960s*; Henderson, *Making the Scene*; Milligan, *Rebel Youth*;
      Mills, *The Empire Within*.

61   "Workers March on Delhi; Riot Act Read," *Globe and Mail*, 4 August 1966; "Time
      to Re-establish Hostels," *Simcoe Reformer*, 15 August 1969.

62   Walter Demeulenaere, interview; Joe Demeulenaere, interview; anonymous em-
      ployer A, interview by Kimberly Knowles, c. 1996, in author's possession; "Many
      Summer Student Transients Used Drugs," *Simcoe Reformer*, 24 February 1971.

63   "Cartoon," *Delhi News-Record*, 7 August 1968, OFCTGMB Scrapbooks, DTMHC;
      on Yorkville, see Henderson, *Making the Scene*.

64   See, for example, Igartua, *The Other Quiet Revolution*, 215–23.

65   "'Separatist' Trouble-Makers Blamed for Delhi near-Riot," *London Free Press*, 5
      August 1966, OFCTGMB Scrapbooks, DTMHC; "Few Quit Transient Tent Camp,"
      Simcoe Reformer, 5 August 1966; "Police Stem First Trouble as Harvest Transients
      Arrive," *Simcoe Reformer*, 31 July 1969.

66   "Morose Tobacco Pickers Bemoan Lack of Work," *Toronto Star*, 15 August 1970;
      "Four Guilty of Beating Transient Workers," *Simcoe Reformer*, 5 November 1975;
      On the Tobacco Road, dir. Maurice Bulbulian (1977; Montreal: National Film
      Board of Canada, 2007), DVD.

67   Patricia, interview.

68   Gripped by Cold War paranoia, officials believed that Communist states were
      commissioning rogue agents to pose as refugees and infiltrate government
      agencies and immigrant communities in Canada, and they went to great effort
      to try to weed out Communists from the ranks of prospective immigrants.
      Iacovetta, *Gatekeepers*, 9, 43–5; Whitaker, *Double Standard*, 25–32, 74–6.

69   Priestland, *The Red Flag*, chap. 8. Such confrontations with the realities of Soviet
      rule also played themselves out within many ethnic communities, where new ar-
      rivals found themselves in regular contact and conflict with already-established
      immigrants who had come to Canada a generation earlier with much more posi-
      tive opinions of the workers' state. While political divisions endured within these
      communities, newcomers' stories did change the views of some old guard Com-
      munists. For some excellent examples of these dynamics at play, see Danys,
      DP, Lithuanian Immigration to Canada, 101–3, 122–3, 227–8.

70   Whitaker, *Double Standard*, 74; Iacovetta, *Gatekeepers*, 43.

71   Patrias, *The Hungarians in Canada*, 19–22.

72   "Less Tobacco Smoke and More Fire Around Simcoe," *Simcoe Reformer* (re-
      printed from the *Financial Post*), 17 July 1952.

73   Ramsey et al., "Agricultural Restructuring of Ontario Tobacco Production," 84.

74   "'I'll Quit' – But Men like Him Don't," *Toronto Telegram*, 7 September 1961. For
      earlier examples, see "Farm Labor Converges on Delhi After Election," *Simcoe
      Reformer*, 9 August 1943; "Town Writes Selective Service about Transients on
      Streets," *Tillsonburg News*, 2 August 1943, RG 27, vol. 667, file 6-5-26-1, part 1, LAC.

75   "Transient Problems Not Serious Say Police," *Simcoe Reformer*, 9 August 1974.

76   Reid-Musson, "Historicizing Precarity," 166.

77   "Women Share Men's Work on Ontario Tobacco Farms," *Toronto Star*, 1 October 1966.

78   "Workers March on Delhi; Riot Act Read," *The Globe*, 4 August 1966; "The Cause: Cold, Hunger," *Simcoe Reformer*, 4 August 1966.

79   "Belgian Students 6-Week Farmers," *Globe and Mail*, 2 August 1966.

80   The job seekers' turn to activism was possibly spurred in part by an organization attempt that had taken place two weeks earlier, when a group of about twenty Québécois migrants staged a sit-down protest in Simcoe's Lynnwood Park and formed the United Transient Labourers Association. However, no explicit links between the two events could be found in consulted sources. "Quebec Workers Focus Attention on Problem," *Delhi News-Record*, 20 July 1966.

81   "Riot Act Read, Arrest 9," *Simcoe Reformer*, 4 August 1966; "The Cause: Cold, Hunger," *Simcoe Reformer*, 4 August 1966; "Workers March," *The Globe*, 4 August 1966; "Police Reinforced" *Telegram*, 4 August 1966; "The Riot Act: Disperse and Depart or Jail for Life," *The Globe*, 30 May 1953; "What Is the Riot Act?" *Hamilton Spectator*, 24 November 2007; "Tobacco Pickers Say Police Beat Them Up," *Toronto Star*, 12 August 1966.

82   "Charge Unlawful Assembly," *Simcoe Reformer*, 4 August 1966.

83   Reid-Musson, "Historicizing Precarity," 166.

84   See, for example, "Transient Problems Not Serious Say Police," *Simcoe Reformer*, 9 August 1974; "Disturbance Charge against Quebec Youth Dismissed," *Simcoe Reformer*, 1 August 1969.

85   "Canadian Farmworkers Union Chronology 1978 to 1997," Simon Fraser University Library, accessed 28 September 2017, https://www.lib.sfu.ca/about/branches-depts/special-collections/canadian-farmworkers-union-chronology.

86   Canadian Farmworkers Union – National, "Proposal to the Ontario Federation of Labour Executive Council," 15 January 1981, Canadian Farmworkers Union Collection, Simon Fraser University Digitized Collections, http://digital.lib.sfu.ca/cfu-2833/ontario-canadian-farmworkers-union; "Minutes," 22 August 1981, Canadian Farmworkers Union Collection, Simon Fraser University Digitized Collections, http://digital.lib.sfu.ca/cfu-5078/ontario-organizing-evaluation-summary-minutes.

87   Berggold, interview; Berggold, "Organizing Tobacco Workers Notes," 23 August 1981, Canadian Farmworkers Union Collection, Simon Fraser University Digitized Collections, http://digital.lib.sfu.ca/cfu-5091/ontario-organizing-tobacco-workers-notes; "1983 CFU Report – Draft 2," 20 October 1983, Canadian Farmworkers Union Collection, Simon Fraser University Digitized Collections, http://digital.lib.sfu.ca/cfu-2028/epho108-117; "Minutes," 22 August 1981, Cana-

dian Farmworkers Union Collection, Simon Fraser University Digitized Collections, http://digital.lib.sfu.ca/cfu-5078/ontario-organizing-evaluation-summary-
minutes; Berggold, "How Contact Was Made," 10 August 1981, Canadian
Farmworkers Union Collection, Simon Fraser University Digitized Collections,
http://digital.lib.sfu.ca/cfu-5010/ontario-how-contact-was-made%E2%80%A6-
pesticide-poisoning-or-tobacco-poisoning.

88 "Minutes," 22 August 1981, Canadian Farmworkers Union Collection, Simon
    Fraser University Digitized Collections, http://digital.lib.sfu.ca/cfu-5078/ontario-
    organizing-evaluation-summary-minutes.

89 "1983 CFU Report – Draft 2."

90 National representative Judy Cavanaugh described the conditions prompting the
    CFU's decision to suspend activities in Ontario in a letter to an allied organiza-
    tion: "The gains farmworkers have made in BC are under attack; we lost the en-
    forcement of workers compensation regulations, one farm under contract was
    sold, our organizing drives have been at a standstill, the growers are banding to-
    gether and our resources are stretched to their limit. The reality of the erosion of
    our gains makes it crucial for us to pull together all our resources." Judy Cava-
    naugh to Jean Christie, 27 April 1983, Canadian Farmworkers Union Collection,
    Simon Fraser University Digitized Collections, http://digital.lib.sfu.ca/cfu-
    2256/eph0179-001.

91 Reid-Musson, "Historicizing Precarity," 161.

92 Berggold, "Organizing Tobacco Workers Notes"; "Charter Flight to Delhi and
    That's All Brother," Globe and Mail, 25 August 1966.

93 "Tobacco Report," 1973, RG 118, acc. 1985–86/071, vol. 75, file 3300-13-1 (73), LAC.

94 Berggold, "Organizing Tobacco Workers Notes."

95 Patricia, interview; Karl Beveridge and Carol Condé, "Canadian Farmworkers
    Union," Fuse 5, no. 10 (March 1982): 321.

96 Berggold, "Organizing Tobacco Workers Notes."

97 Bartsch, interview; Participant 7, interview; Stephen Collett to Department of
    Manpower and Immigration, 16 October 1972, RG 118, acc. 1985–86/071, vol. 84,
    file 3315-11-636, part 2, LAC.

98 Patricia, interview.

99 Donohue, interview.

100 "Farming? Yes, It's Woman's Work," Toronto Star, 14 July 1977.

101 Bulbulian, On the Tobacco Road; "Tobacco Pickers Say Police Beat Them Up,"
    Toronto Star, 12 August 1966.

102 "'Burg Police Burn Huts of Transients," Simcoe Reformer, 15 August 1960; "Till-
    sonburg Police Burn Tobacco Workers' 'Jungle,'" London Free Press, 15 August
    1960; "Burning Workers' Shacks an Act of Cruelty," London Free Press, 16 August
    1960; "Mayor Raps Critics of Police Action against Transients," London Free Press,
    18 August 1960.

103 - On the 1950s hostel, see "A Conference on the Problems Raised by Itinerant To-bacco Workers," 6 December 1949, United Church of Canada Haldimand-Norfolk Presbytery, fonds 1014, series 2, acc. 1984.028C, file 3-25, United Church of Canada Archives; "Correction of Bad Situation Needs Action," *Simcoe Reformer*, 5 September 1958. On camps, see "Tobacco Harvest Workers Co-Ordinating Committee: Meeting Minutes," 28 September 1962, RG 27, vol. 667, file 6-5-26-1, part 3, LAC; "No Shelters for Tobacco Jobless," *Toronto Star*, 27 July 1967, RG 76, vol. 1112, file 553-164, LAC. On the 1970s hostels, see "Flue Transients Will Not Get Hostel Program This Year," *Simcoe Reformer*, 4 June 1975.

104 "Labor Hostel Registrations Reach 1,400," *Simcoe Reformer*, 30 August 1951; G.H. Kidd to Mr. Cummings, 28 November 1962, MSSDMAF, RG 16-102, box B354994, file "Agricultural Manpower Services," AO.

105 "Answers Middleton Complaint," *Simcoe Reformer*, 5 July 1967; "Tobacco Transient Camp Site Killed," *London Free Press*, 5 July 1967, OFCTGMB Scrapbooks, DTMHC.

106 "Labor Hostel Committee Lacks Funds, Disbands," *Simcoe Reformer*, 24 March 1952; J.A. Carroll to Bernard B. Acton, 25 August 1954, MSSDMAF, RG 16-102, box B354994, file "Agricultural Manpower Services," AO; "Correction of Bad Situation Needs Action," *Simcoe Reformer*, 5 September 1958; "Describe Program of Flue Workers Harvest Committee," *Simcoe Reformer*, 24 September 1962, OFCTGMB Scrapbooks, DTMHC.

107 "Flue Board Grants $400 for Hostel," *Simcoe Reformer*, 11 July 1956; "Six Attempts Failed to Find Campsite," *Tillsonburg News*, 19 July 1962, OFCTGMB Scrapbooks, DTMHC; "Tobacco Workers' Hostel: Final Financial Report," 30 January 1974, Ontario Federation of Labour Research Department subject files, F 4180-24, box B394763, file "Farm Labour. Correspondence and Reports – 1973–1975," AO; "Flue Transients Will Not Get Hostel Program This Year," *Simcoe Reformer*, 4 June 1975.

108 "Flue Transients Will Not Get Hostel Program This Year."

109 W. Davison to W.W. Dawson, 24 March 1950, RG 27, vol. 668, file 6-5-26-2, part 3, LAC.

110 Loo, *Moved by the State*, 11.

111 Loo, 11; Scott, *Seeing like a State*.

112 Loo, *Moved by the State*, 8–11; Grundy, *Bureaucratic Manoeuvres*, chap. 3; Mazer, "Making the Welfare State Work for Extraction"; Mazer, "Mining Mobility," chaps 2 and 3; Director, Canadian Service to Deputy Minister, 11 March 1966, Department of Citizenship and Immigration, RG 26, vol. 145, file 3-41-15, part 4, LAC.

113 "Federal Provincial Farm Labour Agreements," 1944–57, MSSDMAF, RG 16-102, box B354994, AO.

114 G.V. Haythorne to G.S.H. Barton, 7 November 1946, RG17, vol. 3129, file 66-5, part 6, LAC; "Better Farm Living for Workers on the Land," 1948, RG17, vol. 3637, file

N-3-9, LAC; "Norfolk Agricultural Representative's Field Report, 1965-66"; "Week Before Transient Tobacco Labor Needed," *Simcoe Reformer*, 26 July 1948; "Want Workers to Stay Home Until Harvest," *Delhi News-Record*, 19 July 1967, OFCTGMB Scrapbooks, DTMHC; Raoul Grenier to S.W. Kaiser, 21 December 1971, RG 118, acc. 1985–86/071, vol. 73, file 3300-1, "Farm Labour – General Series," part 2, LAC.

115   "Workers Housing: Payments – 1 April 1967 to 29 February 1968," 4 March 1968, RG 16-102, MSSDMAF, box B355678, file "Housing for Seasonal Farm Workers Applications," AO; W. Davison to R. Gordon Bennett, 14 October 1970, RG 16-102, MSSDMAF, box B355678, file "Housing for Seasonal Farm Workers Applications," AO; DeDecker, interview.

116   Satzewich, *Racism and the Incorporation of Foreign Labour*, chap. 3; George V. Haythorne, "Speech for Edmonton Chamber of Commerce," 20 February 1952, RG 17, vol. 3130, file 66-5-3, LAC.

117   Another outcome was the addition of Mexico as a sending country in what would become known as the SAWP (done in order to provide a legal, regulated alternative to the unsanctioned, unregulated migration of Mexican Mennonites to Ontario's fields). Satzewich, "Business or Bureaucratic Dominance in Immigration Policymaking in Canada."

118   "Farm Labour Pools, Work Camps Planned," *Delhi News-Record*, 13 February 1974, OFCTGMB Scrapbooks, DTMHC; J.D. Boyd to B. Ducharme, 25 February 1974, RG 118, acc. 1985–86/071, vol. 82, file 3315-5-5, part 2, LAC. The CFLPS also maintained some concern with alleviating regional unemployment, though this wasn't a central goal. Gaétan Lussier to Lloyd Axworthy, 14 December 1982, RG 76, vol. 1691, file 8040-16, part 1, LAC.

119   That year, the manager of Simcoe's NES office had mailed letters to 1,583 tobacco growers, asking them to report their labour requirements for the harvest. He received just 45 replies, but once the harvest started and growers found themselves short of workers, the office was flooded with over 2,500 requests from employers. "Tobacco Harvest Help Committee Appointed," *London Free Press*, 20 October 1959, OFCTGMB Scrapbooks, DTMHC.

120   "Annual Report: Farm Labour Service, 1 April 1961–31 March 1962," 15 May 1962, MSSDMAF, RG 16-102, box B353591 (catalogue location: box B236051), file "Fed.-Prov. Agric. Manpower Serv. Annual Reports, 1953–1968," AO; A.L. Ouimet to E. Allen, 16 March 1967, RG 118, acc. 1985–86/071, vol. 73, file 3300-1, "Farm Labour – General Series," part 1, LAC; "General Report of Agricultural Placement Activities," 1973, RG 118, acc. 1985–86/071, vol. 75, file 3300-13-1 (73), LAC; G.A. Demeyere to J.L. Manion, 5 April 1973, RG 118, acc. 1985–86/071, vol. 83, file 3315-11-1, part 2, LAC; Elizabeth Shea to E.M. Hutchinson, 22 August 1974, RG 118, acc. 1985–86/071, vol. 73, file 3300-1, "Farm Labour – General Series," part 4, LAC.

Chapter Five

1   Williams, interview.

2   Hahamovith, *No Man's Land*, chap. 1.

3   In the 1950s, small numbers of women tiers travelled to Ontario from the United States to meet shortages in that occupation, but technological changes soon resulted in a cut to the number of such positions, while the European program was exclusively male until 1975, when it was opened up to a small number of female participants in honour of International Women's Year; both changes were discussed in the previous chapter. For its part, the Caribbean scheme was restricted to men until the mid-1980s, when a small number of women (first from Barbados) began participating. Women have never accounted for more than 4 per cent of total program rolls. "Annual Report of the Department of Labour," 1984, 1986, Srl 9, Barbados Department of Archives; Silverman and Hari, "Troubling the Fields," 91–104.

4   Troper, "Canada's Immigration Policy since 1945," 255–81; FitzGerald and Cook-Martín, *Culling the Masses*, chap. 4.

5   W. Davison, "Report on a Visit to Tobacco Growing States," 1966, MSSDMAF, RG 16-102, B353591, file "Federal-Provincial Farm Labour Conferences," sub-file "1966 Federal-Provincial Agricultural Manpower Conference," AO; James Leathong, "Report of Committee Making Labour Survey in the Southern States," 26 April 1966, RG 76, vol. 1112, file 553-164, LAC.

6   "Civil Rights Act of 1964," *National Archives Catalog*, accessed 18 October 2017, https://catalog.archives.gov/id/299891.

7   "General Administration Letter No. 1036," 20 October 1966, RG 183, UD Entry 116, box 3, file "Fiscal GAL – GAL 1036 & Ch. 1," NARA. Such directives go back to at least February 1966 and can be found in the same file.

8   Davison, "Report on a Visit to Tobacco Growing States"; W. Davison to R.G. Bennett, 13 January 1966, MSSDMAF, RG 16-102, B353591, file "Federal-Provincial Farm Labour Conferences," sub-file "1966 Federal-Provincial Agricultural Manpower Conference," AO.

9   Davison, "Report on a Visit to Tobacco Growing States"; Leathong, "Report of Committee."

10 Davison, "Report on a Visit to Tobacco Growing States."

11 For demographic information for the sending counties see, "Total Population: Black, 1970," *Social Explorer* (based on data from US Census Bureau), accessed 20 February 2022, https://www.socialexplorer.com/90f0f9d479/view. Designations of major sending counties were made using a complete list of workers and their places of origin from 1948 (the latest such list available) and the itinerary of the Canadian delegation on their 1966 tour. Immigration Inspector-in-Charge, Fort Erie, ON to Eastern District Superintendent, 22 March 1949, RG 76, vol. 853, file 553-164, LAC; Leathong, "Report of Committee."

12   James Leathong, "Notes Made of Points Discussed Which May Prove Helpful to Labour Committee of the Ontario Flue-Cured Tobacco Growers' Marketing Board," 26 April 1966, RG 76, vol. 1112, file 553-164, LAC.

13   For two American stories, see "21 Negroes Stranded after Being Refused Work on Canada Farms," *Poughkeepsie Journal*, 13 August 1966; "Negroes Claim They Refused Work in Canada," *Danville Register*, 14 August 1966.

14   "Tobacco Farmers Refused to Hire Us, 24 Negroes Say," *Toronto Star*, 13 August 1966.

15   "Charge Color Bar in Tobacco Fields," *London Free Press*, 16 August 1966.

16   "More Migrants Stranded in City as Jobs Fall Through," *Buffalo Evening News*, 15 August 1966.

17   "Untitled Note," 16 August 1966, RG 76, vol. 1112, file 553-164, LAC; "Deny Tobaccomen Rejected Negroes," *Simcoe Reformer*, 15 August 1966; "Charge Color Bar in Tobacco Fields," *London Free Press*, 16 August 1966; "Tobacco Board Denies Bias against Negroes," *Globe and Mail*, 16 August 1966. See Dunsworth, "Race, Exclusion, and Archival Silences" for more on this episode.

18   Given that signs of decline were evident from early in the decade and that, within a few years, a number of tobacco growers were hiring Black Caribbean workers, it is doubtful that employer racism played a significant role in the withering of the US movement, however tempting it might be to draw that connection. "Program Directive: Canada-U.S.A. Agricultural Manpower Program," November 1969, RG 118, acc. 1986–86/071, vol. 73, file 3300-1, "Farm Labour – General Series," part 1, LAC; Robert C. Goodwin to All State Employment Security Agencies, 6 March 1964, RG 183, UD-WW Entry 22, box 8, file "411, Jan 1964," NARA; Hahamovitch, *No Man's Land*, 150.

19   The contemporary program name was not used until the early 1980s, when the parallel arrangements with the West Indies and Mexico began being referred to as the Commonwealth Caribbean SAWP and the Mexican SAWP. For the sake of clarity and economy, I do make use of "SAWP" in the pre-1980s context. For the earliest known usage of that acronym, see External Ottawa to Kingston, Port of Spain, Bridgetown, 8 December 1982, RG 76, vol. 1691, file 8040-16, part 1, LAC.

20   R.A. Pelletier to A.L. Cobb, 10 August 1979, RG 118, vol. 273, file 7905-14 (79), LAC; Preibisch and Binford, "Interrogating Racialized Global Labour Supply."

21   Satzewich, *Racism and the Incorporation of Foreign Labour*; Basok, *Tortillas and Tomatoes*.

22   Bourbonnais, *Birth Control in the Decolonizing Caribbean*, 9–31, 52–9, 81–9; Ittmann, *A Problem of Great Importance*, 76–8, 92, 127–8.

23   Richardson, *Caribbean Migrants*, chap. 1.

24   At home, information services were established to facilitate the voyages of prospective migrants. Barbados went even further, sponsoring emigration schemes to Great Britain (initially for health-care workers) and establishing a separate

program whereby emigrants to any destination could receive government loans. Davison, *West Indian Migrants*, 27–30.

25 "Case for West Indian Migration Into Canada," *Daily Gleaner*, 13 July 1966; C.M. Isbister to R.B. Curry, 25 March 1964, RG 26, vol. 124, file 3-33-6, part 3, LAC; G.C. McInnes to the Under-Secretary of State for External Affairs, Ottawa, 19 June 1963, RG 26, vol. 124, file 3-33-6, part 3, LAC.

26 With a significant portion of the populace dependent on agriculture for their livelihoods – often through a combination of wage labour and independent crop production – the improvement of production and standards of living in the countryside became a matter of keen interest for governments and public policy experts, who launched numerous programs, hosted countless conferences, and penned untold reports on everything from co-operative organization, to mechanization, to water infrastructure, to the rationalization of agricultural practices. In Jamaica, an entire ministry was formed to handle this file, the Ministry of Rural Land Development. "1st Report: Ministry of Rural Land Development, January 1969–March 1970," 1970, 1B/65/1/908, Jamaica Archives and Records Department (hereafter JARD); Francis, "A Note on the Agricultural Marketing Protocol and Vegetable Production in Barbados since 1968"; "Analytical Study of the Agricultural Sector of Barbados," 1971, HD1854.75 15, Barbados Department of Archives; Ali, "Towards the Rationalization of Land Use in Trinidad and Tobago."

27 L.B. Pearson to H.C. Collier, 1 December 1941, 1B/5/77/190, file "Air Force and Army – Training of Jamaicans in Canada & U.S.A.," JARD; "Canada-West Indies Conference," 1966, RG 26, vol. 125, file 3-33-6, LAC.

28 Johnson, "To Ensure That Only Suitable Persons Are Sent"; Carty, "African Canadian Women and the State"; Silvera, *Silenced*; Henry, "The West Indian Domestic Scheme in Canada," 83–91.

29 "Executive Council Submission: Recruitment of Jamaicans for Agricultural and Domestic Work in Canada," 21 April 1954, 1B/31/342, JARD; Satzewich, *Racism and the Incorporation of Foreign Labour*, 146–78.

30 Walker, *The West Indians in Canada*; Troper, "Canada's Immigration Policy since 1945"; FitzGerald and Cook-Martín, *Culling the Masses*, chap. 4.

31 George F. Davidson to Charles E. Hendry, 30 July 1962, RG 26, vol. 124, file 3-33-6, part 3, LAC; For Under-Secretary of State for External Affairs to Acting Director of Immigration, 22 August 1963, RG 76, vol. 824, file 552-1-577, LAC; Satzewich, "Racism and Canadian Immigration Policy," 77–97; "Peter Abraham's Commentaries: End of Canadain Migration Colour Bar," 23 January 1962, 3/9/1/263, JARD.

32 Satzewich, *Racism and the Incorporation of Foreign Labour*, 146–78; A.E. Ritchie, "Memorandum to the Minister: Seasonal Farm Labour from the West Indies," 5 April 1966, RG 118, acc. 1985-86/071, vol. 81, file 3315-5-1, part 1, LAC.

33 Tom Kent to R.B. Curry, February 7, 1966, RG 26, vol. 145, file 3-41-15, part 4, LAC.

34   "Jamaica, Canada Discuss Farm Labour Terms," *Daily Gleaner*, 4 May 1966.

35   As late as 1988, employment contracts did not specify that workers were required to return to their country of origin upon termination of the contract. Nowadays, no such confusion is likely, with the 2022 contract requiring workers to agree "to return promptly to the place of recruitment upon completion of the authorized work period." "Agreement for the Employment in Canada of Commonwealth Caribbean Seasonal Agricultural Workers," 1988, RG 76, vol. 1692, file 8040-16, folio, LAC; "Contract for the Employment in Canada of Commonwealth Caribbean Seasonal Agricultural Workers," 2022, Employment and Social Development Canada, available via http://web.archive.org/web/20220220142022/https://www.canada.ca/en/employment-social-development/services/foreign-workers/agricultural/seasonal-agricultural/apply/caribbean.html.

36   Harold Warren Danforth and John Carr Munro, "Immigration – Temporary Harvest Workers Remaining in Canada," 20 October 1966, *Hansard Parliamentary Debates*, retrieved from LiPaD: The Linked Parliamentary Data Project, https://www.lipad.ca/full/1966/10/20/26/#2441074.

37   R.M. Mackie to Black, 20 January 1967, RG 118, acc. 1985–86/071, vol. 82, file 3315-5-3, part 1, LAC.

38   Robert C. Goodwin to Jerry R. Holleman, 15 March 1961, Bureau of Employment Security, RG 183, A1 Entry 1, box 31, file "403, 1957," NARA; Satzewich, *Racism and the Incorporation of Foreign Labour*, 108.

39   Born in Jamaica, Edwards was the first Black person to hold the title of chief liaison officer. He was adored by US employers, whose interests he consistently upheld. On the occasion of his retirement in 1984, an apple farmer even wrote a poem in his honour. Hahamovitch, *No Man's Land*, 107.

40   H.F. Edwards, "CLO 720: Canada," 25 March 1960, RG 26, vol. 124, file 3-33-6, part 2, LAC.

41   After this important encounter in 1960, Edwards would remain a key player in the gradual development of the SAWP, which finally came to fruition in 1966: he remained in periodic communication with Canadian bureaucrats and employer groups throughout the intervening years, participated in meetings to determine the structure of the Canadian program, and in its first year was on call to travel north from Washington, DC, should his expertise be required to manage any problems. H.F. Edwards, "Letter," 1 September 1960, RG 26, vol. 124, file 3-33-6, part 2, LAC; C.E.S. Smith to Deputy Minister, 10 March 1961, RG 26, vol. 124, file 3-33-6, part 2, LAC; J.M. Sandham to J. Brown, 5 March 1964, RG 26, vol. 124, file 3-33-6, part 3, LAC; "Minutes of the First Meeting Between Canada/Jamaica Regarding Seasonal Agricultural Workers to Canada," May 1966, RG 118, acc. 1985–86/071, vol. 82, file 3315-5-4, part 1, LAC; Kingston to External, 4 April 1966, RG 118, acc. 1985–86/071, vol. 81, file 3315-5-1, part 1, LAC.

42 J.M. Sandham to J. Brown; "Cabinet Submission: Canada/Caribbean Talks –
    Report on Meetings of Officials," 1966, 1B/31/121, JARD; Satzewich, *Racism and the
    Incorporation of Foreign Labour*, 155–6; "File on Seasonal Agricultural Workers,"
    n.d., RG 76, vol. 842, file 553-67, parts 1–3, LAC. See also lobbying letters from
    Barbados and Jamaica in Department of Immigration, RG 76, vol. 842, file 553-67,
    parts 1–3, LAC.

43 G.H. Kidd to Mr. Black, 26 April 1966, RG 118, acc. 1985–86/071, vol. 81, file 3315-
    5-1, part 1, LAC.

44 "Cabinet Submission: Employment of Jamaican Farm Workers in Canada,"
    9 May 1966, 1B/31/401, JARD.

45 "Minutes of the First Meeting Between Canada/Jamaica Regarding Seasonal Agri-
    cultural Workers to Canada"; "Cabinet Submission: Employment of Jamaican
    Farm Workers in Canada"; P.E. Quinn to Benoit Godbout, 10 May 1967, RG 118,
    acc. 1985–86/071, vol. 81, file 3315-5-1, part 2, LAC; *Migrant Workers in Canada:
    A Review of the Canadian Seasonal Agricultural Workers Program* (Ottawa: North-
    South Institute, 2006), 9, http://www.nsi-ins.ca/wp-content/uploads/2012/10/
    2006-Migrant-Workers-in-Canada-A-review-of-the-Canadian-Seasonal-
    Agricultural-Workers-Program.pdf; Hahamovitch, *No Man's Land*, 48; S.W.
    Gibbons to Albert Dingemans, January 1969, RG 118, vol. 245, file 9-12-13-4, LAC.

46 D.E. Brandy, "Memorandum for File: Jamaican Seasonal Worker Movement,"
    13 May 1966, RG 118, acc. 1985–86/071, vol. 81, file 3315-5-1, part 1, LAC.

47 Hahamovitch, *No Man's Land*, 105.

48 "Cabinet Submission: Regional Labour Board – Appointment of Jamaica's Third
    Member," 16 February 1970, 1B/31/129, JARD; Hahamovitch, *No Man's Land*, 105;
    External to Kingston and Port of Spain, 31 March 1966, RG 118, acc. 1985–86/071,
    vol. 81, file 3315-5-1, part 1, LAC; Kingston to External, 1 April 1966, RG 118, acc.
    1985–86/071, vol. 81, file 3315-5-1, part 1, LAC; "Minutes of the Second Meeting
    between Representatives of the Jamaican and Canadian Governments Regarding
    the Employment of Seasonal Farm and Factory Workers in Canada," 27 April
    1967, RG 118, acc. 1985–86/071, vol. 81, file 3315-5-1, part 2, LAC; P.E. Quinn to Be-
    noit Godbout, 10 May 1967, RG 118, acc. 1985–86/071, vol. 81, file 3315-5-1, part 2,
    LAC; Port of Spain to External, 17 April 1967, RG 118, acc. 1985–86/071, vol. 81,
    file 3315-5-1, part 2, LAC.

49 "Cabinet Submission: Canadian Farm Workers Programme – Emergency and
    Welfare Fund," 28 March 1968, 1B/31/228, JARD; "Minutes of the Second Meeting
    ... Seasonal Farm and Factory Workers in Canada."

50 "Cabinet Submission: Employment of Jamaican Farm Workers in Canada." It
    is unclear why single men were preferred, and no statistics are available on the
    marital status of SAWP participants. A hallmark of the Mexican-Canadian pro-
    gram is that, with few exceptions, male participants must be married, the ration-

ale being that these workers are more likely to return home upon completion of their contracts, and more likely to send home remittances. Basok, *Tortillas and Tomatoes*, 98–9. For further evidence of the SAWP's curious literacy requirement, which only appeared to persist in its early years, see McLaughlin, "Trouble in Our Fields," 136.

51 "Cabinet Submission: Recruitment of Agricultural Workers for Employment in the U.S.A.," 27 March 1963, 1B/31/288, JARD; Hahamovitch, *No Man's Land*, 79, 192.

52 "Cabinet Submission: Employment of Jamaican Farm Workers in Canada."

53 Officer-in-Charge, Kingston to Director General, Foreign Service, 9 September 1969, RG 118, acc. 1985–86/071, vol. 81, file 3315-5-1, part 3, LAC.

54 Canadian High Commission, Kingston, to Under-Secretary of State for External Affairs, Ottawa, 16 March 1985, RG 76, vol. 1692, file 8040-16, part 2, LAC.

55 Oral history interviewees from both places made no mention of patronage politics in recruitment, and there is no reference to it in Canadian or Barbadian archives, though the latter's records on the Canadian program are sparse. (Trinidadian archives were not consulted as archivists reported no holdings on the program.) Patronage in Jamaica was repeatedly mentioned in both Canadian and Jamaican archives, and by interviewees.

56 Officer-in-Charge, Port of Spain to Director, Foreign Branch, Ottawa, 1 December 1967, RG 118, acc. 1985–86/071, vol. 81, file 3315-5-1, part 3, LAC.

57 R.M. Mackie to Black, 20 January 1967, RG 118, acc. 1985–86/071, vol. 82, file 3315-5-3, part 1, LAC. This trend of elevated urban participation was also noted by a former Jamaican participant in the program, pseudonym Tony, interviewed by Janet McLaughlin. McLaughlin, "Trouble in Our Fields," 136.

58 Officer-in-Charge, Kingston to Director General, Foreign Service; G.S. Conger to J.D. Boyd, 1 December 1975, RG 118, acc. 1989–90/039, vol. 76, file 3315-5-1, part 10, LAC.

59 See, for example, Preibisch and Binford, "Interrogating Racialized Global Labour Supply," 5–36; Hennebry, "Falling through the Cracks?," 369–88.

60 See, for example, Mark Ricketts, "Overseas Farm Workers Lighten Shadows at Home," *The Gleaner*, 12 May 2020, http://jamaica-gleaner.com/article/commen tary/20200512/mark-ricketts-overseas-farm-workers-lighten-shadows-home; "First Batch of Farm Workers for 2020 Depart for Canada," *Jamaica Observer*, 6 January 2020, http://www.jamaicaobserver.com/news/first-batch-of-farm-workers-for-2020-depart-for-canada_183863?profile=0; "PHOTOS: 113 Farm Workers off to Canada," *LOOP News*, 21 May 2019, http://www.loopjamaica.com/content/photos-113-farm-workers-canada. The knowledge of guest-worker programs serving as campaign issues comes from a conversation with Dr Michele A. Johnson, York University.

61 The only caveat for Manpower officials was that if new countries were added to

the scheme, the practice might need to be reviewed in order to ensure enough spots for new participants. "Minutes of the Second Meeting ... Seasonal Farm and Factory Workers in Canada"; P.E. Quinn to Benoit Godbout; Officer-in-Charge, Kingston to Director General, Foreign Service; D. Barbour, "Report on the Operation of the Caribbean Seasonal Workers Programme," 19 November 1974, RG 118, acc. 1985–86/071, vol. 81, file 3315-5-1, part 8, LAC.

62 FitzGerald and Cook-Martín, *Culling the Masses*, 182.

63 "Cabinet Submission: Visit of Minister of Labour and Employment to Canada, July 1973 – Farm and Domestic Workers' Programmes," 1 August 1973, 1B/31/456, JARD.

64 Cooper, interview.

65 "Cabinet Submission: Visit of Minister of Labour and Employment to Canada, July 1973 – Farm and Domestic Workers' Programmes."

66 "Report on the Operation of the Caribbean Seasonal Workers Programme," 1973, RG 118, acc. 1985–86/071, vol. 75, file 3300-13-1 (73), LAC.

67 In 1981, Caribbean countries were deciding among themselves how to split up vacancies in the program, but by the time program administration transferred to an employer-controlled agency in 1987, growers were able to select workers by country of origin. J.D. Love to Lloyd Axworthy, 1 September 1981, RG 76, vol. 1691, file 8040-16, part 1, LAC; Cooper, interview.

68 J.D. Boyd to J.L. Manion, 20 December 1973, RG 118, acc. 1985–86/071, vol. 81, file 3315-5-1, part 7, LAC; "Cabinet Submission: Visit of Minister of Labour and Employment to Canada, July 1973 – Farm and Domestic Workers' Programmes."

69 Satzewich, "Business or Bureaucratic Dominance in Immigration Policymaking in Canada," 255–75; Preibisch and Binford, "Interrogating Racialized Global Labour Supply."

70 "300 Farm-Factory Workers for Canada Next Month," *Daily Gleaner*, 25 April 1967, RG 118, acc. 1985–86/071, vol. 81, file 3315-5-1, part 2, LAC.

71 "Cabinet Submission: Jamaican Farm and Factory Workers to Canada – Workers Away Without Official Leave."

72 Similar competition for spots occurred in the US-West Indian program too. "Immigration Port of Spain to Immigration Ottawa," 3 August 1968, RG 118, acc. 1985–86/071, vol. 81, file 3315-5-1, part 3, LAC; Hahamovitch, *No Man's Land*, 105.

73 R.F. Dunkley to W.E. Allen, 14 July 1967, RG 118, acc. 1985–86/071, vol. 81, file 3315-5-1, part 2, LAC.

74 "Report on the Operation of the Caribbean Seasonal Workers Program, 1970," 20 November 1970, RG 118, acc. 1985–86/071, vol. 81, file 3315-5-1, part 4, LAC.

75 Representatives from Jamaica, Barbados, and Trinidad and Tobago all sent very similarly worded letters to Manpower and Immigration officials in July 1974. See Wills O. Isaacs to D.W. Findlay, 25 July 1974, RG 118, acc. 1985–86/071, vol. 81, file 3315-5-1, part 8, LAC.

76 D.W. Findlay to W.K. Bell, September 17, 1974, RG 118, acc. 1985–86/071, vol. 81, file 3315-5-1, part 8, LAC, cited in Satzewich, "Business or Bureaucratic Dominance?," 272–3.

77 Ishemo, Semple, and Thomas-Hope, "Population Mobility and the Survival of Small Farming." For a study on Mexican SAWP workers with similar findings, see Carvajal, "Farm-Level Impacts in Mexico."

78 Binford, *Tomorrow We're All Going to the Harvest*, chap. 5; Griffith, "The Promise of a Country"; Griffith, "Social Organizational Obstacles to Capital Accumulation among Returning Migrants"; Weiler, McLaughlin, and Cole, "Food Security at Whose Expense?"

79 Whyte, *The Experience of New Immigrants and Seasonal Farmworkers from the Eastern Caribbean to Canada*, 4.26–4.27.

80 For example, interviews with Williams and Moore.

81 Bovell and Lowe, interviews. Another example is the interview with Williams.

82 The multiple European arrangements were typically referred to by government and grower representatives in the singular as a "movement" or "program"; for clarity's sake, I frequently do the same. The program was also called different names at different times. The Marketing Board often called it the European Student Movement. The name I use here, the European Student Tobacco Worker Program, is drawn from Department of Employment and Immigration files in the late 1970s and early 1980s. Labour Market Planning and Adjustment, "European Student Tobacco Worker Program," 26 January 1979, RG 118, vol. 273, file 7905-14 (79), LAC.

83 Hoffman, *All You Need Is Love*, especially chap. 3; Brouwer, *Canada's Global Villagers*; Langford, *The Global Politics of Poverty in Canada*, especially chaps 7 and 8.

84 Brown, Hesketh, and Williams, "Employability in a Knowledge-Driven Economy," 107–26; Heath, "Widening the Gap," 89–103.

85 Hoffman, *All You Need Is Love*.

86 Assistant Deputy Minister (Immigration) to Deputy Minister, 10 March 1966, RG 26, vol. 145, file 3-41-15, part 4, LAC.

87 Meren, *With Friends like These*, 226–8; Mesli, *La coopération franco-québécoise dans le domaine de l'éduation*, chap. 3.

88 The most remarkable example of this must certainly be Australia's horticulture sector, in which over 70 per cent of the seasonal workforce is composed of people on working holiday visas. Reilly et al., "Working Holiday Makers in Australian Horticulture," 99–130. In Canada, the trend is most apparent in Banff, where a significant portion of tourism workers are part of similar programs. Smith and Staveley, "Toward an Ethnography of Mobile Tourism Industry Workers in Banff National Park," 435–47.

89 Helleiner, "Recruiting the 'Culturally Compatible' Migrant," 301–3.

90   For an interesting comparison to the European program with similarities in
      terms of program justification and participation, but important differences in
      terms of race, media attention, and geopolitical connections, see Loza, "The
      Japanese Agricultural Workers' Program," 661–90.

91   Officer-in-Charge, Woodstock, Ontario to Director, Canadian Services, Ottawa,
      17 December 1965, RG 118, acc. 1985–86/071, vol. 84, file 3315-11-517, part 1, LAC;
      A.A. Ewen, "Memorandum," 22 December 1965, RG 118, acc. 1985–86/071, vol. 84,
      file 3315-11-517, part 1, LAC; "Belgian Students to Work on Farms," *Delhi News-
      Record*, 2 March 1966, OFCTGMB Scrapbooks, DTMHC; "Belgian Students 6-Week
      Farmers," *Globe and Mail*, 2 August 1966.

92   For files broken down by source country (excepting Ireland), see Department
      of Manpower and Immigration, RG 118, acc. 1985–86/071, vol. 84, files 3315-11/513,
      3315-11/517, 3315-11/550, 3315-11/551, 3315-11/598, 3315-11/636, LAC. For start of Irish
      participation, see Labour Market Planning and Adjustment, "European Student
      Tobacco Worker Program."

93   Director, Planning Branch to Assistant Deputy Minister (Immigration), 5 August
      1966, RG 118, acc. 1985–86/071, vol. 83, file 3315-11-1, part 1, LAC.

94   Officer-in-Charge, Woodstock, Ontario to Director, Canadian Services, Ottawa,
      Immigration Branch; Officer-in-Charge, Woodstock, Ontario to Director, Home
      Branch, Ottawa, 30 August 1966, RG 118, acc. 1985–86/071, vol. 84, file 3315-11-517,
      part 1, LAC; P.E. Quinn to A.A. Ewen, 6 October 1966, RG 118, acc. 1985–86/071,
      vol. 84, file 3315-11-517, part 1, LAC; Assistant Deputy Minister (Immigration) to
      Assistant Deputy Minister (Manpower), 22 March 1967, RG 118, acc. 1985–86/071,
      vol. 84, file 3315-11-517, part 1, LAC.

95   G.A. Demeyere to Raoul Grenier, 5 December 1969, Department of Employment
      and Immigration, RG 118, vol. 246, file 9-12-29, LAC.

96   For two such instances, from France and West Germany, respectively, see J.P.
      Francis to J.A. Leathong, 8 May 1969, RG 118, vol. 246, file 9-12-29, LAC, and
      Norbert Guthling to J.A. Leathong, 8 March 1969, Department of Employment
      and Immigration, RG 118, vol. 246, file 9-12-29, LAC.

97   A.F. Murphy to G.D.A. Reid, 7 January 1969, RG 118, vol. 246, file 9-12-29, LAC;
      G.A. Demeyere to J.L. Manion, 5 April 1973, RG 118, acc. 1985–86/071, vol. 83, file
      3315-11-1, part 2, LAC; J.L. Manion to G.A. Demeyere, 5 June 1973, RG 118, acc.
      1985–86/071, vol. 83, file 3315-11-1, part 2, LAC; Robert Andras to Ted Raytrowsky,
      2 May 1974, RG 118, acc. 1985–86/071, vol. 74, file 3300-6-12, LAC.

98   Department of Manpower and Immigration, RG 118, vol. 273, file 7905-14 (84);
      "Delhi Celebrates Cultural Exchange," *Simcoe Reformer*, 10 September 1991.

99   Executive Assistant to the Assistant Deputy Minister (Immigration) to Director,
      Home Branch, 2 September 1966, RG 118, acc. 1985–86/071, vol. 84, file 3315-11-517,
      part 1, LAC; For Attache, Visa Office, Vienna to IMOS, Ottawa, 11 May 1966, RG 118,

acc. 1985–86/071, vol. 84, file 3315-11-513, LAC; For Director, Overseas Service to Attache, Visa Office, Vienna, 25 May 1966, RG 118, acc. 1985–86/071, vol. 84, file 3315-11-513, LAC.

100 For Director, Canadian Service to Assistant Deputy Minister (Immigration), 22 June 1966, RG 118, acc. 1985–86/071, vol. 84, file 3315-11-513, LAC; For Director, Canadian Service to Officer-in-Charge, London, Ontario, 24 June 1966, RG 118, acc. 1985–86/071, vol. 84, file 3315-11-513, LAC; Attache, Visa Office, Vienna to Director, Overseas Service, 7 June 1966, RG 118, acc. 1985–86/071, vol. 84, file 3315-11-513, LAC.

101 Director, Canadian Service, Immigration Branch to J.A. Leathong, 12 July 1966, RG 118, acc. 1985–86/071, vol. 84, file 3315-11-513, LAC.

102 Assistant Deputy Minister (Immigration) to Deputy Minister, 10 March 1966, RG 26, vol. 145, file 3-41-15, part 4, LAC. Similar reasoning had been provided the year before to two southwestern Ontario Liberal MPs (Herb Gray and Eugene Whalen) and the Essex County Associated Growers, who had pointed out the same incongruities while advocating for West Indian guest workers. Satzewich, *Racism and the Incorporation of Foreign Labour*, 166.

103 It is unclear if the scheme continued after 1967; I came across no mention of it beyond that year in my research. MSSDMAF, RG 16-102, box B355678, file "Farm Labour Recruitment in the United Kingdom: 1965 & 1966: A.G. Skinner," AO; "School Opening Upsets Part-Time Work on Farms," *Toronto Star*, 5 September 1967.

104 "Scots Farmworkers Seek Work in Canada," *Scottish Farmer*, 5 March 1966, in MSSDMAF, RG 16-102, box B355678, file "Farm Labour Recruitment in the United Kingdom: 1965 & 1966: A.G. Skinner," AO.

105 Parr, "Hired Men," 92; Satzewich, *Racism and the Incorporation of Foreign Labour*, 111; Glassco, "Harvesting Power and Subjugation," 126–7; Secretariat of the Commission for Labor Cooperation, *Protection of Migrant Agricultural Workers in Canada, Mexico and the United States*.

106 Whyte, *The Experience of New Immigrants and Seasonal Farmworkers from the Eastern Caribbean to Canada*, 4.5. Figures of tobacco SAWP workers are available up to 1985, when 1,089 West Indians and Mexicans worked in tobacco, and then not again until 1993, when they numbered 3,803. It is likely that SAWP workers in tobacco passed their previous high of 1,691 (in 1981) sometime between 1987 and 1989, over which time the SAWP surged to three times its 1985 size. Satzewich, *Racism and the Incorporation of Foreign Labour*, 112; Basok, *Tortillas and Tomatoes*, 34; Weston and de Masellis, *Hemispheric Integration and Trade Relations*, 31.

107 G.A. Demeyere to J.L. Manion, 5 April 1973, RG 118, acc. 1985–86/071, vol. 83, file 3315-11-1, part 2, LAC.

108 Robert Andras to Ted Raytrowsky, May 2, 1974, RG 118, acc. 1985–86/071, vol. 74, file 3300-6-12, LAC; J.L. Manion to D.W. Findlay, 22 January 1975, RG 118, acc. 1985–86/071, vol. 83, file 3315-11-1, part 2, LAC.

109 The most dramatic instance of this occurred in 1939, but the trend continued in the postwar period. Dunsworth, "Green Gold, Red Threats"; R.M. Macdonnell to G.V. Haythorne, 23 August 1946, RG 27, vol. 667, file 6-5-26-2, LAC; "Tillsonburg Police Burn Tobacco Workers' 'Jungle,'" *London Free Press*, 15 August 1960; "Luckless Job-Seekers Moving Out of Town," *Tillsonburg News*, 6 August 1975, OFCTGMB Scrapbooks; "Transients Frustrated in Flue Job Hunt," *Tillsonburg News*, 4 August 1982, OFCTGMB Scrapbooks, DTMHC.

110 E.P. Bensley to J.M. Sandham, 28 February 1964, RG 26, vol. 124, file 3-33-6, part 3, LAC.

111 J.K. Abbott to W. Thomson, 4 February 1966, Department of Manpower and Immigration, RG 118, acc. 1985–86/071, vol. 84, file 3315-11-637, LAC; J.L. Manion, "Meeting with Ontario Officials," 21 March 1966, RG 118, acc. 1985–86/071, vol. 84, file 3315-11-637, LAC; Regional Director, Toronto to Director, Canadian Services, Ottawa, 6 January 1966, RG 76, vol. 1112, file 553-164, LAC.

112 H.H. Sampson to D. Dunn, 14 June 1976, RG 118, acc. 1989–90/039, vol. 76, file 3315-5-3, part 3, LAC; J.L. Manion to D.W. Findlay, 22 January 1975, RG 118, acc. 1985–86/071, vol. 83, file 3315-11-1, part 2, LAC.

113 Benjamin Wilk to Allan J. MacEachen, 8 April 1970, RG 118, acc. 1985–86/071, vol. 81, file 3315-5-1, part 4, LAC; G.A. Demeyere to J.L. Manion, 5 April 1973, RG 118, acc. 1985–86/071, vol. 83, file 3315-11-1, part 2, LAC; C. Smith and C. Grigg to Jack Cardwell, 15 September 1973, RG 76, vol. 1057, file 5170-12-1, part 2, LAC.

114 J.M. DesRoches to Robert Andras, 1 March 1973, RG 118, acc. 1985–86/071, vol. 73, file 3300-1, "Farm Labour – General Series," part 3, LAC.

115 "Memorandum of Understanding … Mexican Seasonal Agricultural Workers Program," 3 February 1988, RG 76, vol. 1692, file 8040-16, folio, LAC; Bud Cullen to Eugene Whelan, 30 May 1978, Eugene Whelan Fonds, R12298, vol. 206, file 8, LAC.

116 Manion, "Meeting with Ontario Officials."

117 J.L. Manion, "Interview with Jamaican High Commissioner," 14 April 1966, RG 118, acc. 1985–86/071, vol. 81, file 3315-5-1, part 1, LAC.

118 Joe Demeulenaere, interview.

119 J.K. Abbott to W. Thomson; "Seasonal Workers from the Caribbean – Report of Departmental Committee," 2 March 1967, RG 118, acc. 1985–86/071, vol. 81, file 3315-5-1, part 2, LAC; "Memorandum to the Minister," 7 April 1970, RG 118, acc. 1985–86/071, vol. 81, file 3315-5-1, part 3, LAC; J.L. Manion, "Memorandum to the Minister," 28 June 1976, RG 118, acc. 1989–90/039, vol. 76, file 3315-5-1, part 10, LAC; Gaétan Lussier to Lloyd Axworthy, 14 December 1982, RG 76, vol. 1691, file 8040-16, part 1, LAC.

120 "Get the Jump on Harvest," Irene S. Anderson scrapbook, George Demeyere Library, Delhi Tobacco Museum and Heritage Centre. Advertisement discovered via Reid-Musson, "Historicizing Precarity," 165–6. Cartoon published in *Canadian Tobacco Grower*, June 1973, 4.

121 A superb resource on such tropes is the Jim Crow Museum of Racist Memorabilia, Ferris State University, accessed 9 October 2020, https://www.ferris.edu/HTMLS/News/jimcrow.

Chapter Six

1 Bovell, interview.
2 "Belgian Students," *Globe and Mail*, 2 August 1966.
3 While some of the US and global guest-worker literature has studied these topics historically, the Canadian scholarship has remained largely concerned with contemporary aspects of migrant worker resistance. See Loza, *Defiant Braceros*; Miller, *Turkish Guest Workers in Germany*. For contemporary-focused Canadian studies, see Encalada Grez, "Mexican Migrant Farmworker Women Organizing Love and Work Across Rural Canada and Mexico," chap. 4; Ramirez, "Embodying and Resisting Labour Apartheid," 64–81; Cohen and Hjalmarson, "Quiet Struggles"; Binford, "From Fields of Power to Fields of Sweat," 503–17.
4 Satzewich, "Business or Bureaucratic Dominance in Immigration Policymaking in Canada," 255–75.
5 International guest-worker scholars have also found the ideal of "managed migration" to be much messier on the ground. Griffith, ed., *(Mis)Managing Migration*; Loza, *Defiant Braceros*; Miller, *Turkish Guest Workers in Germany*.
6 Officer-in-Charge, Woodstock to Regional Director of Immigration, Toronto, 28 June 1967; G.H. Kidd to George Dennis, 29 June 1967; Ben Baldwin to George Dennis, 17 July 1967; L.G. Irving to Regional Director, Toronto, 14 August 1967 – all in Immigration Branch, RG 76, vol. 1112, file 553-164, LAC.
7 "Immigration Task Force – Elgin County, St Thomas," 5 September 1973, RG 76, vol. 1057, file 5170-12-1, part 2, LAC; Satzewich, "Business or Bureaucratic Dominance in Immigration Policymaking in Canada," 270–1.
8 J.P. Francis to J.A. Leathong, 8 May 1969, RG 118, vol. 246, file 9-12-29, LAC; A.L. May to Officers-in-Charge et al., 25 July 1969, RG 118, vol. 246, file 9-12-29, LAC; A. Dingemans to R. Gauvreau, 29 October 1969, RG 118, vol. 246, file 9-12-29, LAC; Arthur Hencher to Department of Manpower and Immigration, 7 May 1970, RG 118, acc. 1985–86/071, vol. 73, file 3300-1, "Farm Labour – General Series," part 1, LAC; Immigration Admissions Adviser to I.R. Stirling, 19 August 1969, RG 118, vol. 246, file 9-12-29, LAC; Officer-in-Charge, Woodstock, Ontario to Director, Canadian Services, Ottawa, 7 March 1966, RG 118, acc. 1985–86/071, vol. 84, file 3315-11-517, part 1, LAC.
9 Regional Admissions Supervisor to Deputy Regional Director, Toronto, 1 March 1967, RG 76, vol. 1112, file 553-164, LAC; Regional Director, Toronto to Regional Settlement Supervisor, Toronto, 10 April 1967, RG 76, vol. 1112, file 553-164, LAC.
10 W. Davison to W.W. Dawson, 18 October 1951, RG 27, vol. 668, file 6-5-26-2, part 3,

LAC; W. Davison to Buckley, 12 November 1956, RG 27, vol. 667, file 6-5-26-1, part 3, LAC.

11   C. Smith and C. Grigg to Jack Cardwell, 15 September 1973, RG 76, vol. 1057, file 5170-12-1, part 2, LAC; Knowles, interview.

12   Williams, interview; Walter Demeulenaere, interview.

13   "Caribbean Seasonal Farm Workers Program," October 1973, RG 118, acc. 1985–86/071, vol. 82, file 3315-5-8, part 1, LAC.

14   J.L. Manion to J.D. Boyd, 14 December 1973, RG 118, acc. 1985–86/071, vol. 81, file 3315-5-1, part 7, LAC.

15   "Caribbean Seasonal Farm Workers Program," October 1973, RG 118, acc. 1985–86/071, vol. 82, file 3315-5-8, part 1, LAC.

16   "J.A.G. Smith Guilty," *Daily Gleaner*, 20 July 1990; "Ex-Labor Minister Faces Trial Former Jamaican Official Mired in Farm-Worker Scandal," *Sun-Sentinel*, 1 April 1990, https://www.sun-sentinel.com/news/fl-xpm-1990-04-01-9002010438-story.html.

17   J.D. Boyd to Terry Wright, 4 January 1974, RG 118, acc. 1985–86/071, vol. 81, file 3315-5-1, part 7, LAC; Cooper, interview; Williams, interview.

18   See for example, RG 76, vol. 1057, file 5170-12-2, parts 1–2, LAC; Department of Manpower and Immigration, RG 118, acc. 1985–86/071, vol. 82, file 3315-5-9, LAC.

19   "Officers to Continue Checking for Illegal Tobacco Workers," *London Free Press*, 29 August 1975, OFCTGMB Scrapbooks, DTMHC; "Special Investigator Rounds Up Six for Illegal Entry," *Simcoe Reformer*, 22 August 1935.

20   Director, Home Branch to Director, Planning Branch, 27 February 1968, RG 118, acc. 1985–86/071, vol. 81, file 3315-5-1, part 3, LAC.

21   R.B. Curry to J.P. Francis, 5 April 1968, RG 118, acc. 1985–86/071, vol. 82, file 3315-5-9, LAC.

22   J.P. Francis to R.B. Curry, 18 April 1968, RG 118, acc. 1985–86/071, vol. 82, file 3315-5-9, LAC.

23   "Caribbean Seasonal Workers Program," 10 December 1969, RG 118, acc. 1985–86/071, vol. 75, file 3300-13, part 1, LAC; "Report on the Operation of the Caribbean Seasonal Workers Program," 11 December 1972, RG 118, acc. 1985–86/071, vol. 75, file 3300-13-1 (72), LAC.

24   P.E. Quinn to Benoit Godbout, 10 May 1967, RG 118, acc. 1985–86/071, vol. 81, file 3315-5-1, part 2, LAC.

25   "60 French Students Arrive for Harvest without Permits," *Simcoe Reformer*, 5 August 1970, OFCTGMB Scrapbooks, DTMHC; "May Deport Farm Worker," *Brantford Expositor*, 26 June 1974, OFCTGMB Scrapbooks, DTMHC; "Immigration Officials Order Cathcart Farm Worker Deported," *Brantford Expositor*, 27 June 1974, OFCTGMB Scrapbooks, DTMHC.

26   J.L. Manion, "Memorandum to the Minister," 10 November 1977, RG 118, acc. 1989–90/039, vol. 76, file 3315-5-4, part 3, LAC.

27 Numerous scholars have argued that the prevalence of racialized people among deportees is an important example of the ways in which racism continued to shape the Canadian immigration regime in the years following its liberalization in the 1960s. See, for example, Barnes, "Dangerous Duality," 191–202; Wright, "The Museum of Illegal Immigration," 31–54; Abu-Laban and Nath, "From Deportation to Apology," 71–98.

28 See, for example, Gomez, *Exchanging Our Country Marks*.

29 Alexander and Parker, *Organized Labor in the English-Speaking West Indies*, chaps 1, 12, 13; Bolland, *The Politics of Labour in the British Caribbean*; Sutton, "Continuing the Fight for Economic Justice."

30 Participant 7, interview.

31 Lewis, "The Acculturation of Barbadian Agriculture Workers in Canada," 82.

32 Lewis, 60, 71, 82, 141.

33 Lewis, 82.

34 Donohue, interview.

35 Like resistance in general, wildcat strikes among SAWP workers have not been as unusual as one might assume. In addition to the ones discussed in this chapter, on wildcat strikes among Mexican SAWP workers in the 2000s, see Becerril, "Transnational Work and the Gendered Politics of Labour," and Basok, *Tortillas and Tomatoes*, 111.

36 Officer-in-Charge, Port of Spain to Chief, Operational Services, Foreign Branch, 12 September 1967, Department of Manpower and Immigration, RG 118, acc. 1985–86/071, vol. 81, file 3315-5-1, part 3, LAC; McKinney (Port of Spain) to External, 22 August 1967, Department of Manpower and Immigration, RG 118, acc. 1985–86/071, vol. 81, file 3315-5-1, part 3, LAC.

37 McKinney (Port of Spain) to External. Shortened words in the telegram were replaced with unabbreviated versions for clarity's sake.

38 G.G. Duclos, "Memorandum to Under-Secretary of State for External Affairs," 28 August 1967, Department of Manpower and Immigration, RG 118, acc. 1985–86/071, vol. 81, file 3315-5-1, part 3, LAC.

39 External to Port of Spain, 23 August 1967, Department of Manpower and Immigration, RG 118, acc. 1985–86/071, vol. 81, file 3315-5-1, part 3, LAC.

40 Officer-in-Charge, Port of Spain to Chief, Operational Services, Foreign Branch.

41 E. Allen, "Caribbean Seasonal Workers – Trinidad & Tobago," 5 September 1967, Department of Manpower and Immigration, RG 118, acc. 1985–86/071, vol. 81, file 3315-5-1, part 3, LAC.

42 Port of Spain to External, 5 September 1967, Department of Manpower and Immigration, RG 118, acc. 1985–86/071, vol. 81, file 3315-5-1, part 3, LAC.

43 E. Allen, "Memorandum," 3 November 1967, RG 118, acc. 1985–86/071, vol. 82, file 3315-5-4, part 1, LAC.

44   "Report on the Operation of the Caribbean Seasonal Workers Program, 1970,"
     20 November 1970, RG 118, acc. 1985–86/071, vol. 81, file 3315-5-1, part 4, LAC.

45   "Report on the Operation of the Caribbean Seasonal Workers Program, 1970."

46   Buchanan, *Evaluation of the 1967 Caribbean Farm Labour Program*, 45; E. Allen,
     "Memorandum," 3 November 1967, RG 118, acc. 1985–86/071, vol. 82, file 3315-5-4,
     part 1, LAC; C. Smith and C. Grigg to Jack Cardwell, 15 September 1973, RG 76,
     vol. 1057, file 5170-12-1, part 2, LAC.

47   Hutchinson, interview.

48   Bovell, interview.

49   Vermeeren, interview.

50   Moore, interview.

51   Lyal Tait, interview by Michael Lipowski and Stacia Johnson, 11 April 1985, Oral
     History Interviews, Delhi Tobacco Collection, ref. MUL-14131-TAI, MHSO.

52   Donohue, interview.

53   Walter Demeulenaere, interview. Similar narratives have been articulated about
     Mexican workers, who are often portrayed as more quiescent than West Indians.
     Basok, *Tortillas and Tomatoes*, 110; Preibisch and Binford, "Interrogating Racial-
     ized Global Labour Supply," 5–36.

54   Bauder, "Foreign Farm Workers in Ontario (Canada)," 100–18.

55   On the historical lineage, see, for example, Boulukos, *The Grateful Slave*.

56   Williams, interview.

57   Kennedy, interview (emphasis added).

58   For example, Bovell, interview; Bovell and Lowe, interview.

59   Bovell, interview.

60   Alleyne, Bovell, and Participant 7, group interview.

61   Hennebry, "Globalization and the Mexican-Canadian Seasonal Agricultural
     Worker Program," 179–80.

62   Employers also developed essentialized and racialized ideas about which groups
     of workers were better suited to certain crops: West Indians for tobacco and
     apples; Mexicans for "stoop crops" such as tomatoes, for example. Preibisch
     and Binford, "Interrogating Racialized Global Labour Supply."

63   Cooper, interview.

64   See, for example, Gomez, *Exchanging Our Country Marks*.

65   Bovell, interview. This common perception of liaison officers is also confirmed
     by numerous informal conversations with migrant worker friends from Mexico,
     as well as activist (and former migrant worker) Gabriel Allahdua.

66   P.E. Quinn to Benoit Godbout, 10 May 1967, Department of Manpower and Im-
     migration, RG 118, acc. 1985–86/071, vol. 81, file 3315-5-1, part 2, LAC; "Cabinet Sub-
     mission: Canadian Farm Workers Programme – Emergency and Welfare Fund,"
     28 March 1968, 1B/31/228, JARD; "Annual Report of the Department of Labour,"
     1983, Srl 9, Barbados Department of Archives.

67 Whyte, *The Experience of New Immigrants and Seasonal Farmworkers from the Eastern Caribbean to Canada*, 4.28; "Jamaican Workers Take Control of Wages," *Vittoria Booster* (reprinted from *Simcoe Reformer*), Winter 2015.

68 Hutchinson, interview.

69 Williams, interview.

70 "Cabinet Submission: Agricultural Workers' Centre – Payment of Farm Workers' Savings," 5 September 1962, 1B/31/241, JARD.

71 The only known example of a letter of protest penned by US workers was discussed in chapter 3. R.M. Macdonnell to G.V. Haythorne, 23 August 1946, RG 27, vol. 667, file 6-5-26-2, LAC. The only letters from Caribbean or Mexican workers that I have located in the archives are enquiries about joining the program.

72 Stephen Collett to Department of Manpower and Immigration, 16 October 1972, RG 118, acc. 1985–86/071, vol. 84, file 3315-11-636, part 2, LAC.

73 Egmonth Bilzhause et al. to Robert Andras, 15 August 1973, RG 118, acc. 1985–86/071, vol. 75, file 3300-8-6, LAC.

74 Jacqueline and Francis Guinot to Son Excellence l'Ambassadeur, Ambassade du Canada, Paris, 5 November 1987, RG 76, vol. 1692, file 8040-16, part 2, LAC.

75 Assistant Attache, Canadian Embassy, Visa Section, Cologne to Director General, Foreign Service, 2 March 1972, RG 118, acc. 1985–86/071, vol. 84, file 3315-11-551, part 1, LAC.

76 Stephen Collett to Department of Manpower and Immigration; Egmonth Bilzhause et al. to Robert Andras; Jacqueline and Francis Guinot to Son Excellence l'Ambassadeur, Ambassade du Canada, Paris.

Chapter Seven

1 "Transient Workers – Last of a Dying Breed," *Delhi News-Record*, 7 August 1985, OFCTGMB Scrapbooks, DTMHC. For other references to the declining transient workforce in this period, see "Labor Shortage Misses Tobacco," *Simcoe Reformer*, 20 August 1984, OFCTGMB Scrapbooks, DTMHC; "Transient Workers Shut Out of Tobacco Harvest," *London Free Press*, 15 August 1984, OFCTGMB Scrapbooks, DTMHC; "Big Reduction in Farm Labour Demand," *Delhi News-Record*, 28 July 1982, OFCTGMB Scrapbooks, DTMHC.

2 Byer and Byer, interview; "Tobacco in Elgin – The Workers," Elgin County Archives, accessed 26 January 2021, https://www.elgincounty.ca/ElginCounty/CulturalServices/Archives/tobacco/workers.html.

3 "Small Tobacco Men Feel Pinch," *Globe and Mail*, 27 July 1965, OFCTGMB Scrapbooks, DTMHC.

4 Stewart, "Agricultural Restructuring in Ontario Tobacco Production," 53–5.

5 The Ontario Flue-Cured Tobacco Growers' Marketing Board, "Canadian Flue-Cured Tobacco Exports Generate Employment," 1976, Eugene Whelan Fonds,

R12298, vol. 425, file 10, LAC; "Flue Buyers Get 5 Cent Export Incentive," *Simcoe Reformer*, 26 December 1975.

6   "440 Fewer Growers of Flue," *Delhi News-Record*, July 16, 1975, OFCTGMB Scrapbooks, DTMHC; "The Ontario Flue-Cured Tobacco Growers' 1976 Marketing Board Report," 1976, box 182, file 8, Elgin County Archives; Stewart, "Agricultural Restructuring in Ontario Tobacco Production," 51.

7   Stewart, "Agricultural Restructuring in Ontario Tobacco Production," 48; Ramsey and Smit, "Impacts of Changes in the Flue-Cured Tobacco Sector on Farmers in Ontario, Canada"; Ramsey et al., "Agricultural Restructuring of Ontario Tobacco Production."

8   Stewart, "Agricultural Restructuring in Ontario Tobacco Production," 66; Ramsey and Smit, "Impacts of Changes in the Flue-Cured Tobacco Sector on Farmers in Ontario, Canada"; Ramsey et al., "Agricultural Restructuring of Ontario Tobacco Production."

9   Ramsey and Smit, "Impacts of Changes"; Ramsey et al., "Agricultural Restructuring of Ontario Tobacco Production"; Ramsey and Smit, "Rural Community Well-Being"; Susan Mann, "Audit Takes Aim at Tobacco Buyout," *Better Farming*, 24 November 2011, https://www.betterfarming.com/online-news/audit-takes-aim-tobacco-buyout-4672.

10 DeDecker, interview.

11 "Bulk Curing Methods Seen as Big Boon to Tobacco Growers," *St Thomas Times-Journal*, 15 April 1967, OFCTGMB Scrapbooks, DTMHC; "Tobacco Farmers Concerned about Labor for Fall Crop," *Brantford Expositor*, 10 May 1974, OFCTGMB Scrapbooks, DTMHC; Barker and Kennedy, *The Tobacco Leaf Yesterday and Today*, 39; DeDecker, interview.

12 "Labor Lack Seen Boon in Future," *Simcoe Reformer*, 18 February 1966; "Demeyere: Use Tried, True Ways," *Simcoe Reformer*, 20 July 1967, OFCTGMB Scrapbooks, DTMHC; "Flue Board Helps Harvester Users," *Aylmer Express*, 21 December 1970, OFCTGMB Scrapbooks, DTMHC; "Minutes of a Meeting of the OFCTGMB," 17 December 1970, Records of the Flue-Cured Tobacco Growers' Marketing Board, RG 16-250, box B388334, file "Tobacco Plan – Minutes," AO.

13 D.B. Wales, "We Must Mechanize," *Aylmer Express*, 3 April 1974, OFCTGMB Scrapbooks, DTMHC.

14 "The World Renowned Hawk Tobacco Tying Machine," *Simcoe Reformer*, 12 March 1964; "Introducing BALTHES for Simcoe and District," *Simcoe Reformer*, 25 April 1966. See also issues of the *Canadian Tobacco Grower* from 1969 to 1973.

15 "Flue Board Helps Harvester Users," *Aylmer Express*, 21 December 1970, OFCTGMB Scrapbooks, DTMHC.

16 "Artur Figueiredo," 1977, Delhi Tobacco Belt Project Papers, F 1405-61, B440613, file 9960.2, AO. In the same fonds, see other questionnaires in B440613, files 9960.2 and 9960.3; B440612, files 9959.3, 9959.6, and 9969.7.

17   Ackner (pseudonym), interview.

18   Smit, Johnston, and Morse, "Labour Turnover on Flue-Cured Tobacco Farms in Southern Ontario," 153–68; "OFCTGMB Annual Report," 1969.

19   Raoul Grenier to S.W. Kaiser, 21 December 1971, RG 118, acc. 1985–86/071, vol. 73, file 3300-1, "Farm Labour – General Series," part 2, LAC. For an earlier example, see "Tobacco Workers Arrive at Camp, Harvest in Week," *Brantford Expositor*, 4 August 1965, OFCTGMB Scrapbooks, DTMHC.

20   "Farm Pool 'Getting Better,'" *Simcoe Reformer*, 10 February 1982, OFCTGMB Scrapbooks, DTMHC; "Transient Workers – Last of a Dying Breed," *Delhi News-Record*, 7 August 1985, OFCTGMB Scrapbooks, DTMHC.

21   "Elizabeth Shea to E.M. Hutchinson," 22 August 1974, Department of Manpower and Immigration, RG 118, acc. 1985–86/071, vol. 73, file 3300-1, "Farm Labour – General Series," part 4, LAC. For examples of downturns in mobility program usage following closely behind increases in the 1960s, see "Annual Report: Farm Labour Service, 1 April 1961–31 March 1962," 15 May 1962, Program files of the Marketing and Special Services Division of the Ministry of Agriculture and Food, RG 16-102, box B353591 (catalogue location: box B236051), file "Fed.-Prov. Agric. Manpower Serv. Annual Reports, 1953–1968," AO; "A.L. Ouimet to E. Allen," 16 March 1967, Department of Manpower and Immigration, RG 118, acc. 1985–86/071, vol. 73, file 3300-1, "Farm Labour – General Series," part 1, LAC.

22   "Finding Workers That Tobacco Farmers Don't Need," *Globe and Mail*, 9 August 1977; "Big Reduction in Farm Labour Demand," *Delhi News-Record*, 28 July 1982, OFCTGMB Scrapbooks, DTMHC.

23   "Tobacco Growers Travel Greyhound," *Simcoe Reformer*, 20 July 1939; Participant 26, interview.

24   "Labor Brief Submitted by Flue Board," *Tillsonburg News*, 19 December 1977, OFCTGMB Scrapbooks, DTMHC; "Finding Workers that Tobacco Farmers Don't Need," *Globe and Mail*, 9 August 1977.

25   Whyte, *The Experience of New Immigrants and Seasonal Farmworkers from the Eastern Caribbean to Canada*, 4.5; Satzewich, *Racism and the Incorporation of Foreign Labour*, 112; "Agreement Reached on Offshore Labor," *Tillsonburg News*, 27 April 1983, OFCTGMB Scrapbooks, DTMHC; "Annual Review Meeting of the Commonwealth Caribbean Seasonal Agricultural Workers Program: Minutes," 13 December 1983, RG 76, vol. 1691, file 8040-16, part 1, LAC.

26   "Tobacco Exports," *Simcoe Reformer*, 11 June 1973.

27   Patricia, interview; Beveridge and Condé, "Canadian Farmworkers Union," *Fuse* 5 no. 10 (March 1982): 321.

28   Joan Duerden to John Eleen, 24 October 1974, Ontario Federation of Labour Research Department subject files, F 4180-24, box B394763, file "Farm Labour. Correspondence – 1971–1974," AO; Berggold, interview.

29   Patricia, interview.

30   Wong, "Migrant Seasonal Agricultural Labour"; *Okanagan Dreams*, dir. Annie
      O'Donoghue (Montreal: National Film Board of Canada, 2001), available at
      https://www.nfb.ca/film/okanagan_dreams/; Couture, "Les jeunes migrants qué-
      bécois dans les vallés fruitières de la Colombie-Britannique." Linguist Patricia
      Lamarre is also conducting some research on this topic. See "Publications et
      activités," *Un Canadien Errant*, accessed 30 January 2021, https://uncanadien
      errant.ca/publications-et-activites/.
31   "Tobacco Gang 15 and Under on George DeBock Farm," *Delhi News-Record*,
      4 September 1974, OFCTGMB Scrapbooks, DTMHC.
32   "Debbie Takes Tobacco Road to Beauty Field," *Toronto Star*, 23 September 1977;
      "Transient Workers Shut Out of Tobacco Harvest," *London Free Press*, 15 August
      1984, OFCTGMB Scrapbooks, DTMHC; "Labor Shortage Misses Tobacco," *Simcoe
      Reformer*, 20 August 1984, OFCTGMB Scrapbooks, DTMHC.
33   A number of local workers interviewed for this project talked about working for
      neighbours or family friends. For examples, see interviews with Bartsch, Byer and
      Byer, Knowles, Passmore, and Long. On paternalism in agricultural labour rela-
      tions in another context, see Danysk, *Hired Hands*.
34   Vermeeren, interview.
35   J.L. Manion to Robert Andras, 24 May 1973, RG 118, acc. 1985–86/071, vol. 73,
      file 3300-1, "Farm Labour – General Series," part 3, LAC; R.A. Girard to K.C.
      Emerson, 19 April 1974, RG 118, acc. 1985–86/071, vol. 74, file 3300-6-12, LAC; M.A.
      Schellenberger to E. Allen, 26 November 1975, RG 118, acc. 1989–90/039, vol. 76,
      file 3315-5-1, part 10, LAC.
36   Ramsey and Smit, "Impacts of Changes in the Flue-Cured Tobacco Sector," 353–4;
      "Memorandum of Understanding ... Mexican Seasonal Agricultural Workers
      Program," 3 February 1988, RG 76, vol. 1692, file 8040-16, folio, LAC.
37   Falconer, "Family Farmers to Foreign Fieldhands," 1.
38   Sparling, Quadri, and van Duren, "Consolidation in the Canadian Agri-Food
      Sector and the Impact on Farm Incomes," 32; "Total Area of Farms and Use of
      Farm Land, Historical Data," Table 32-10-0153-01, Statistics Canada, accessed
      26 January 2022, https://www150.statcan.gc.ca/t1/tbl1/en/tv.action?pid=3210015
      301&pickMembers%5B0%5D=1.1&pickMembers%5B1%5D=3.1&cubeTime
      Frame.startYear=1941&cubeTimeFrame.endYear=2016&referencePeriods=1941
      0101%2C20160101; "Land Use, Census of Agriculture, 2011 and 2016," Table 32-10-
      0406-01, Statistics Canada, accessed 26 January 2022, https://www150.statcan.
      gc.ca/t1/tbl1/en/tv.action?pid=3210040601; "Farms Classified by Total Gross Farm
      Receipts, Census of Agriculture, 2011 and 2016," Table 32-10-0436-01, Statistics
      Canada, accessed 26 January 2022, https://www150.statcan.gc.ca/t1/tbl1/en/tv.
      action?pid=3210043601; Chen et al., "A Historical Review of Changes in Farm
      Size in Canada."

39   "Farm Capital, Selected Expenditures and Forest Product Sales, Historical Data,"
     Table 32-10-0164-01, Statistics Canada, accessed 26 January 2022, https://open.
     canada.ca/data/en/dataset/37cea0fa-4ee0-4dfb-b865-4d6cb43bc051.
41   Falconer, "Family Farmers to Foreign Fieldhands," 3 (emphasis added).
41   "COVID-19 Disruptions and Agriculture: Temporary Foreign Workers," Statistics
     Canada, 17 April 2020, https://www150.statcan.gc.ca/n1/pub/45-28-0001/2020001/
     article/00002-eng.htm; "Farms Classified by Total Gross Farm Receipts, Census
     of Agriculture, 2011 and 2016," Table 32-10-0436-01, Statistics Canada, accessed 26
     January 2022, https://www150.statcan.gc.ca/t1/tbl1/en/tv.action?pid=3210043601.
42   Such a public-to-private transfer of administrative powers is common in the
     history of guest-worker programs. Griffith, *(Mis)managing Migration*, xiv.
43   Gaétan Lussier to John P. van Der Zalm, 8 April 1987, Employment and Social
     Development Canada (Access to Information Request); Cooper, interview; Pre-
     ibisch, "Local Produce, Foreign Labor," 423; Muller-Clemm and Barnes, "A His-
     torical Perspective on Federal Program Evaluation in Canada," 47–70; Larkin,
     "Workin' on the Contract," 120; Miller, "Testing the Boundaries of Employer-
     Driven Agricultural Migration"; Andre, "The Genesis and Persistence of the
     Commonwealth Caribbean Seasonal Agricultural Workers Program in Canada,"
     243–302.
44   Raoul Grenier to O.H. Jackman, 26 April 1972, RG 118, acc. 1985–86/071, vol. 81,
     file 3315-5-1, part 5, LAC; Whyte, *The Experience of New Immigrants and Seasonal
     Farmworkers from the Eastern Caribbean to Canada*, 4.64; "Inflation Calculator,"
     Bank of Canada, accessed 26 August 2021, https://www.bankofcanada.ca/rates/
     related/inflation-calculator/.
45   J.L. Manion to A.E. Gotlieb, 4 September 1973, RG 118, acc. 1985–86/071, vol. 81, file
     3315-5-1, part 6, LAC; "Program Related Costs," FARMS, accessed 26 January 2022,
     https://farmsontario.ca/things-to-know/program-related-costs/.
46   "Tobacco in Elgin – The Workers," Elgin County Archives, accessed 26 January
     2021, https://www.elgincounty.ca/ElginCounty/CulturalServices/Archives/
     tobacco/workers.html.
47   "Farm Labor: The Dirty Work that Canadians Won't Do," *Toronto Star*, 18 Sep-
     tember 1971.
48   Walter and Stella Kozuck to Bruce Halliday, May 5, 1976, RG 118, acc. 1989–90/039,
     vol. 76, file 3315-5-1, part 10, LAC.
49   Basok, *Tortillas and Tomatoes*, 31–2; Satzewich, *Racism and the Incorporation of
     Foreign Labour*, 151–2.
50   On common sense, see Gramsci, *Selections from the Prison Notebooks*; Crehan,
     Gramsci's Common Sense. On neoliberalism and its cultural aspects, see, for
     example, Cooper, *Family Values*.
51   Elizabeth Pearce to Eugene Whelan, April 8, 1975, Eugene Whelan Fonds, R12298,

vol. 206, file 4, LAC; "50% of Transients Are Bums," *Delhi News-Record*, 24 September 1969, OFCTGMB Scrapbooks, DTMHC; "Farm Labor: The Dirty Work that Canadians Won't Do," *Toronto Star*, 18 September 1971; "Farm Laborer a Dying Occupation, Lethargy Is Blamed," *Globe and Mail*, 11 December 1972.

52   "National Insurance Scheme: Celebrating 50 Years," Nation Publishing, 17 June 2017, https://issuu.com/nationpublishing/docs/national_insurance_scheme_celebrati.

53   C. Smith and C. Grigg to Jack Cardwell, 15 September 1973, RG 76, vol. 1057, file 5170-12-1, part 2, LAC.

54   "Farm Labor: The Dirty Work that Canadians Won't Do," *Toronto Star*, 18 September 1971.

55   "Offshore Labour Program Debated at Federation Meeting," *Delhi News-Record*, 16 February 1977, OFCTGMB Scrapbooks, DTMHC.

56   A.E. Gotlieb, "Memorandum to the Minister," 18 June 1976, RG 118, acc. 1989–90/039, vol. 76, file 3315-5-1, part 10, LAC; "Duncan R. Campbell to J. Edwards," 20 February 1984, RG 118, vol. 273, file 7905-14 (84), LAC.

57   See, for example, Satzewich, *Racism and the Incorporation of Foreign Labour*; Preibisch, "Pick-Your-Own Labor"; Basok, *Tortillas and Tomatoes*.

58   "Tobacco Report," 1973, RG 118, acc. 1985–86/071, vol. 75, file 3300-13-1 (73), LAC; George A. Demeyere to William G. Davis, 28 April 1967, MSSDMAF, RG 16-102, box B353591 (catalogue location: box B236051), file "Ontario Federal-Provincial Farm Labour Committee: Tobacco Labour, 1966–", AO; G.A. Demeyere to J.R. McCarthy, 16 June 1967, MSSDMAF, RG 16-102, box B353591 (catalogue location: box B236051), file "Ontario Federal-Provincial Farm Labour Committee: Tobacco Labour, 1966–", AO; J.R. McCarthy to G.A. Demeyere, 30 August 1968, MSSDMAF, RG 16-102, box B353591 (catalogue location: box B236051), file "Ontario Federal-Provincial Farm Labour Committee: Tobacco Labour, 1966–", AO; J.L. Manion to Robert Andras, 24 May 1973, RG 118, acc. 1985–86/071, vol. 73, file 3300-1, "Farm Labour – General Series," part 3, LAC.

59   G.A. Demeyere to Raoul Grenier; "General Report of Agricultural Placement Activities," 1972, RG 118, acc. 1985–86/071, vol. 75, file 3300-13-1 (72), LAC.

60   Chaussé, interview.

61   "No Harvest Jobs Either," *Simcoe Reformer*, 9 July 1982, OFCTGMB Scrapbooks, DTMHC; "Transients Frustrated in Flue Job Hunt," *Tillsonburg News*, 4 August 1982, OFCTGMB Scrapbooks, DTMHC; "Transient Workers Shut Out of Tobacco Harvest," *London Free Press*, 15 August 1984, OFCTGMB Scrapbooks, DTMHC.

62   This interpretation is inspired by the brilliant work of historian Madhavi Kale, whose book *Fragments of Empire* demonstrates how, in the post-emancipation British West Indies, claims of "labour shortages," deployed by planters to lobby for indentured workers from India to replace allegedly unwilling-to-work

freedpeople, hardly reflected objective reality; they were, rather, an "idiom" by which planters sought strategically to advance their interests. Kale's argument serves simultaneously as a critique of the bulk of scholarship on this subject, which has uncritically reproduced planters' characterizations. In a passage that rings eerily true in the context of postwar Ontario, Kale identifies a "new orthodoxy about labor shortage," which "stated that, in the aftermath of abolition, sugar production in the British Caribbean ... was suffering due to acute shortages of labor, that former apprentices were responsible for the shortages," and that only the importation of indentured labourers "could avert the economic catastrophe and moral decline that threatened this part of the British empire" (38).

63 "Farmers Voice Concerns about Flue Workers," *Delhi News-Record*, 26 March 1975, OFCTGMB Scrapbooks, DTMHC; Eugene Whelan to Robert Andras, 8 April 1975, Eugene Whelan Fonds, R12298, vol. 33, file 10, LAC; "No Off-Shore Farm Workers If Canadians Are Available," *Aylmer Express*, 9 April 1975, OFCTGMB Scrapbooks, DTMHC; "Tobacco Grower Prefers Offshore Workers," *London Free Press*, 8 May 1975, OFCTGMB Scrapbooks, DTMHC.

64 Satzewich, *Racism and the Incorporation of Foreign Labour*, 157.

65 "No Off-Shore Farm Workers If Canadians Are Available."

66 "Luckless Job-Seekers Moving Out of Town," *Tillsonburg News*, 6 August 1975, OFCTGMB Scrapbooks, DTMHC.

67 Walter and Stella Kozuck to Bruce Halliday, 5 May 1976, RG 118, acc. 1989–90/039, vol. 76, file 3315-5-1, part 10, LAC (emphasis in the original); Bruce Halliday to Robert Andras, 14 June 1976, RG 118, acc. 1989–90/039, vol. 76, file 3315-5-1, part 10, LAC; William D. Knowles to Robert Andras, 27 May 1976, RG 118, acc. 1989–90/039, vol. 76, file 3315-5-1, part 10, LAC. For the official rebuke, see J.D. Boyd to G. Demeyere, June 15, 1976, RG 118, acc. 1989–90/039, vol. 76, file 3315-5-1, part 10, LAC, and other letters in the same file.

68 "Offshore Labour Program Debated at Federation Meeting," *Delhi News-Record*, 16 February 1977, OFCTGMB Scrapbooks, DTMHC; "Knowles Says Foreign Worker Curb Hits Tobacco Planting," *Tillsonburg News*, 2 May 1977, OFCTGMB Scrapbooks, DTMHC.

69 "Flue Board Seeks Overseas Student Workers This Year," *Simcoe Reformer*, 19 January 1977.

70 J.L. Manion, "Memorandum to the Minister," 28 June 1976, RG 118, acc. 1989–90/039, vol. 76, file 3315-5-1, part 10, LAC. See also A.E. Gotlieb, "Draft Memorandum to the Minister," 10 June 1976, RG 118, acc. 1989–90/039, vol. 76, file 3315-5-1, part 10, LAC.

71 A.E. Gotlieb, "Memorandum to the Minister," 18 June 1976, RG 118, acc. 1989–90/039, vol. 76, file 3315-5-1, part 10, LAC.

72 Duncan R. Campbell to J. Edwards, 20 February 1984, RG 118, vol. 273, file 7905-14 (84), LAC.

73 *The Seasonal Farm Labour Situation in Southwestern Ontario: A Report* (Ottawa: Department of Manpower and Immigration, 1973), cited in Basok, *Tortillas and Tomatoes*, 62–3. See also Satzewich, *Racism and the Incorporation of Foreign Labour*, 157–9.

74 For examples of Halliday's and Knowles's advocacy, see Bruce Halliday to Robert Andras, 14 June 1976, and Knowles to Andras, 27 May 1976, RG 118, acc. 1989–90/039, vol. 76, file 3315-5-1, part 10, LAC.

75 Satzewich, *Racism and the Incorporation of Foreign Labour*, 157.

76 Eugene Whelan to Robert Andras, 8 April 1975, Eugene Whelan Fonds, R12298, vol. 33, file 10, LAC.

77 McKay, *The Quest of the Folk*, 16.

78 Passerini, "Work Ideology and Consensus under Italian Fascism," 84.

79 Doxtator, "All about Tobacco," 264–6; Scott and Van Londersele, interview; Bovell and Lowe, interview. Other examples include interviews with Vermeeren and Cooper.

80 Gramsci, *Selections from the Prison Notebooks*, 326. For an excellent discussion, see Crehan, *Gramsci's Common Sense*, especially the preface and chap. 3.

81 "Harvest Draws Foreign Workers," *Tillsonburg News*, 30 July 1982, OFCTGMB Scrapbooks, DTMHC.

82 Nicholas Keung, "He's Worked Legally in Canada for 37 Years but the Government Considers Him 'Temporary,'" *Toronto Star*, 5 October 2017, https://www.thestar.com/news/canada/migrants/2017/10/05/hes-worked-legally-in-canada-for-37-years-but-the-government-considers-him-temporary.html. For other examples, see Kazi Stastna, "Canada's Migrant Farm Worker System – What Works and What's Lacking," *CBC News*, 8 February 2012, https://www.cbc.ca/news/canada/canada-s-migrant-farm-worker-system-what-works-and-what-s-lacking-1.11 42489; Mackenzie Britton, "'It's Been a Great Program': New Foreign Worker Requirements Help Okanagan Fruit Industry," *Kelowna Capital News*, 19 February 2020, https://www.kelownacapnews.com/news/its-been-a-great-program new-foreign-worker-requirements-help-okanagan-fruit-industry/; Bethany Hastie, "The Coronavirus Reveals the Necessity of Canada's Migrant Workers," *The Conversation*, 12 May 2020, https://theconversation.com/the-coronavirus-reveals-the-necessity-of-canadas-migrant-workers-136360; Chantal Braganza, "What You Need to Know to Understand Migrant Labour in Canada," TVO.org, 26 September 2016, https://www.tvo.org/article/what-you-need-to-know-to-understand-migrant-labour-in-canada.

83 Basok, *Tortillas and Tomatoes*, 25.

84 Labour Market Planning and Adjustment, "Caribbean and Mexican Seasonal Agricultural Workers Programs," October 1981, RG 76, vol. 1691, file 8040-16, part 1, LAC; "Tree Fruits and Nuts, Berries and Grapes, Vegetables, Nursery and Green-

house Products and Mushrooms," "Agricultural Paid Labour, Operating Expenses and Receipts" Census of Agriculture, 1981, available via https://web.archive.org/web/20190326062443/https://library.queensu.ca/madgic/free/agriculture/1981/CANADA818.xls.

Conclusion

1 "CFA Extremely Pleased with Government's Response to Looming Agri-Food Worker Shortage," Canadian Federation of Agriculture/Fédération Canadienne de L'Agriculture, 20 March 2020, https://www.cfa-fca.ca/2020/03/23/cfa-extremely-pleased-with-governments-response-to-looming-agri-food-worker-shortage/; "Farmers and Migrant Workers Need Immediate Support for 2020 Growing Season," National Farmers Union, 20 March 2020, https://www.nfu.ca/media-release-farmers-and-migrant-workers-need-immediate-support-for-2020-growing-season/; Shelby Thevenot, "Agriculture Labour Shortage Feared amid COVID-19 Travel Bans," *Canada Immigration News*, last modified 18 March 2020, https://www.cicnews.com/2020/03/agriculture-labour-shortage-feared-amid-Covid-19-travel-bans-0313913.html#gs.s5vxdp; Joanna Chiu and Rosa Saba, "Migrant Workers Help Grow Our Food. Coronavirus Is Leaving Them in Limbo," *Toronto Star*, last modified 2 November 2020, https://www.thestar.com/news/canada/2020/03/17/migrant-workers-help-grow-our-food-coronavirus-is-leaving-them-in-limbo.html; Grant LaFleche, "Travel Restrictions on Migrant Workers Threaten Canada's Food Supply, Says Growers Group," *St Catharines Standard*, last modified 17 March 2020, https://www.stcatharinesstandard.ca/news/niagara-region/2020/03/17/travel-restrictions-on-migrant-workers-threaten-canada-s-food-supply-says-growers-group.html; Anelyse Weiler et al., "Protecting the Health and Rights of Migrant Agricultural Workers during the COVID-19 Outbreak Should Be a Priority," *Policy Note*, 1 April 2020, https://www.policynote.ca/migrant-workers/; Brent Lale, "Balancing Workers' Safety and Crop Production amid COVID-19 Crisis," *CTV News*, 29 March 2020, https://london.ctvnews.ca/balancing-workers-safety-and-crop-production-amid-Covid-19-crisis-1.4873364; Shree Paradkar, "Migrant Worker Groups Slam New Canadian Border Restrictions," *Toronto Star*, 16 March 2020, https://www.thestar.com/opinion/2020/03/16/migrant-worker-groups-slam-new-canadian-border-restrictions.html; Migrant Rights Network (@MigrantRightsCA), "Updated Statement on Border Closures that Allow in Americans and Canadians – but Shut Out Everyone Else," Twitter, 16 March 2020, https://web.archive.org/web/20210127211059/https:/twitter.com/MigrantRightsCA/status/1239617785036185601.

2 "COVID-19 Disruptions and Agriculture: Temporary Foreign Workers," Statistics Canada, 17 April 2020, https://www150.statcan.gc.ca/n1/pub/45-28-0001/2020001/article/00002-eng.htm.

3   Immigration, Refugees and Citizenship Canada, "Canada Provides Update on
    Exemptions to Travel Restrictions to Protect Canadians and Support the Econ-
    omy," Government of Canada, last modified on 27 March 2020, https://www.
    canada.ca/en/immigration-refugees-citizenship/news/2020/03/canada-provides-
    update-on-exemptions-to-travel-restrictions-to-protect-canadians-and-support-
    the-economy.html; "Feds to Fund Quarantine of Seasonal Farm Workers in
    Canada amid COVID-19," *Global News*, 13 April 2020, https://globalnews.ca/news/
    6811071/coronavirus-measures-foreign-workers-seniors/; "CFA Extremely Pleased
    with Government's Response to Looming Agri-Food Worker Shortage"; Weiler et
    al., "Protecting the Health and Rights of Migrant Agricultural Workers during the
    COVID-19 Outbreak Should Be a Priority"; Tavia Grant, "Canada's Food Supply
    at Risk as Pandemic Tightens Borders to Farm Workers," *Globe and Mail*, 1 April
    2020, https://www.theglobeandmail.com/business/article-canadas-food-supply-
    at-risk-as-pandemic-tightens-borders-to-farm/; "Unheeded Warnings: COVID-19
    & Migrant Workers in Canada," 8 June 2020, Migrant Workers Alliance for
    Change, https://migrantworkersalliance.org/policy/unheededwarnings/.
4   Tahmina Aziz, "COVID-19 Test Requirement to Enter Canada a Burden for Mi-
    grant Workers, Advocacy Group Says," *CBC News*, last modified 14 January 2021,
    https://www.cbc.ca/news/canada/windsor/migrant-workers-Covid-19-testing-
    1.5872711; Mark Kelley et al., "Bitter Harvest" *CBC News*, 29 November 2020,
    https://newsinteractives.cbc.ca/longform/bitter-harvest-migrant-workers-
    pandemic.
5   Kate Dubinski, "Migrant Worker Who Died on Ontario Farm Identified as
    Mexican Father of Four," *CBC News*, last modified 22 June 2020, https://www.cbc.
    ca/news/canada/london/migrant-worker-mexico-juan-l%C3%B3pez-chaparro-
    1.5621866; Mary Caton, "Migrant Worker's Widow Awaits Return of Husband's
    Body," *Windsor Star*, 23 June 2020, https://windsorstar.com/news/local-news/
    migrant-workers-widow-awaits-return-of-husbands-body; Sara Mojtehedzadeh,
    "Migrant Worker Fired for Speaking Out about COVID-19 Wins a Rare Reprisal
    Case against an Ontario Farm," *Toronto Star*, 12 November 2020, https://www.
    thestar.com/news/gta/2020/11/12/migrant-worker-fired-for-speaking-out-about-
    Covid-19-wins-a-rare-reprisal-case-against-an-ontario-farm.html.
6   Edward Dunsworth, "Insecurity via Exclusion: Migrant Farm Workers in the Age
    of COVID-19," 30 June 2021, ActiveHistory.ca, http://activehistory.ca/2021/06/
    insecurity-via-exclusion-migrant-farm-workers-in-the-age-of-Covid-19/.
7   Kathryn Blaze Baum and Tavia Grant, "Essential but Expendable: How Canada
    Failed Migrant Farm Workers," *Globe and Mail*, 16 June 2020, https://www.the
    globeandmail.com/canada/article-essential-but-expendable-how-canada-failed-
    migrant-farm-workers/; Sara Mojtehedzadeh, "A Study Urged Better Standards
    for Migrant Workers' Housing. Nothing Was Done. Now COVID-19 Has Struck,"

Toronto Star, 11 May 2020, https://www.thestar.com/business/2020/05/11/a-study-urged-better-standards-for-migrant-workers-housing-nothing-was-done-now-Covid-19-has-struck.html.

8 Laura Stone and Tavia Grant, "Doug Ford Says He Was Wrong about Migrant Workers Hiding from COVID-19 Tests," *Globe and Mail*, 3 July 2020, https://www.theglobeandmail.com/canada/article-doug-ford-says-he-was-wrong-about-migrant-workers-hiding-from-Covid-1/; "Protect Migrant Workers or Face Consequences, Ford and Trudeau Warn Farmers," CTV *News*, last modified 22 June 2020, https://toronto.ctvnews.ca/protect-migrant-workers-or-face-consequences-ford-and-trudeau-warn-farmers-1.4995281.

9 Sara Mojtehedzadeh, "This Migrant Worker Spoke Out about a Massive COVID-19 Outbreak that Killed His Bunkmate. Then He Was Fired, a Legal Complaint Says," *Toronto Star*, 30 July 2020, https://www.thestar.com/business/2020/07/30/this-migrant-worker-spoke-out-about-a-massive-Covid-19-outbreak-that-killed-his-bunkmate-then-he-was-fired-a-legal-complaint-says.html.

10 Sara Mojtehedzadeh, "A Third Migrant Worker Is Dead and the Farm Where He Worked Had a Long History of Complaints – an Inside Look at Scotlynn Growers," *Toronto Star*, 23 June 2020, https://www.thestar.com/business/2020/06/24/a-third-migrant-worker-is-dead-and-the-farm-where-he-worked-had-a-long-history-of-complaints-an-inside-look-at-scotlynn-growers.html.

11 Vosko, "Blacklisting as a Modality of Deportability," 1371–87.

12 Tucker, "Farm Worker Exceptionalism," 30–56; UFCW Canada and the Agriculture Workers Alliance, *The Status of Migrant Workers in Canada, 2020 – Special Report: Marking Three Decades of Advocacy on Behalf of Canada's Most Exploited Workforce* (Toronto: UFCW Canada and the Agriculture Workers Alliance, n.d.), https://ml.globenewswire.com/Resource/Download/709696c3-7d67-4d2d-bf71-e600701a2c8c.

13 Elena Prokopenko and Feng Hou, "How Temporary Were Canada's Temporary Foreign Workers?," Statistics Canada, 29 January 2018, https://www150.statcan.gc.ca/n1/pub/11f0019m/11f0019m2018402-eng.htm.

14 Hennebry, "Permanently Temporary? Agricultural Migrant Workers and Their Integration in Canada."

15 There were 195 tobacco farms counted in Ontario in 2019, for example. "Farms Classified by Farm Type, Census of Agriculture, 2011 and 2016," Table 32-10-0403-01, Statistics Canada, 2016, https://www150.statcan.gc.ca/t1/tbl1/en/tv.action?pid=3210040301.

16 While all these "tendencies" of Canadian workers were used by growers to disparage them (and advocate for increased access to guest workers), they are of course utterly normal events in a free labour market, insofar as such a thing exists.

17 Falconer, "Family Farmers to Foreign Fieldhands."

18 See, for example, Forth, "Clearing the Air over Seasonal Farm Workers"; Basok, *Tortillas and Tomatoes*, chap. 3; Kelsey Johnson, "Help Wanted: The Job Crisis in Canadian Agriculture," *iPolitics*, 8 March 2015, https://webcache.googleuser content.com/search?q=cache:i8-uRVViccUJ:https://ipolitics.ca/2015/03/09/help-wanted-the-job-crisis-in-canadian-agriculture/+&cd=3&hl=en&ct=clnk&gl= ca&client=opera; Bethany Hastie, "Migrant Workers' Rights in Spotlight," *Winnipeg Free Press*, 22 May 2020, https://www.winnipegfreepress.com/opinion/anal ysis/migrant-workers-rights-in-spotlight-570685612.html; *The Grower*, "FARMS Whiteboard Video," YouTube video, 20 August 2017, https://www.youtube.com/ watch?v=bHDABct8zAo&feature=youtu.be.

19 J.P. Antonacci, "COVID-19 Outbreak Forces Norfolk Asparagus Farmer to Abandon 450 Acres," *Hamilton Spectator*, 3 June 2020, https://www.thespec.com/news/ hamilton-region/2020/06/03/Covid-19-outbreak-forces-norfolk-asparagus-farmer-to-abandon-450-acres.html.

20 "Produce," Scotlynn Group, accessed 27 January 2022, https://www.scotlynn.com/ produce/; Monte Sonnenberg, "Scotlynn Pulls Plug on Asparagus Harvest," *Simcoe Reformer*, 4 June 2020, https://www.simcoereformer.ca/news/local-news/ scotlynn-pulls-plug-on-asparagus-harvest.

21 "We. Are. Nature Fresh Farms," Nature Fresh Farms, accessed 30 January 2021, https://www.naturefresh.ca/about/; "Work Can Resume at Leamington Farm after COVID-19 Outbreak Shut Down the Facility," *CBC News*, last modified 6 July 2020, https://www.cbc.ca/news/canada/windsor/nature-fresh-Covid-19-testing-1.5639440.

22 In 2016, 4.8 per cent of farms grossed more than $1 million, while 2.8 per cent grossed more than $2 million. "Farms Classified by Total Gross Farm Receipts, Census of Agriculture, 2011 and 2016," Table 32-10-0436-01, Statistics Canada, accessed 26 January 2022, https://www150.statcan.gc.ca/t1/tbl1/en/tv.action? pid=3210043601.

23 Canadian Agricultural Human Resource Council, *A Review of Canada's Seasonal Agriculture Worker Program* (Ottawa: Canadian Agricultural Human Resource Council, 2017), https://cahrc-ccrha.ca/sites/default/files/Emerging-Issues-Research/A%20Review%20of%20Canada%27s%20SAWP-Final.pdf.

24 Dunsworth, "Green Gold, Red Threats," 105–6.

25 Encalada Grez, "Mexican Migrant Farmworker Women Organizing Love and Work Across Rural Canada and Mexico"; Cohen and Hjalmarson, "Quiet Struggles"; "Migrant Farmworkers Travel 1500km to Demand Permanent Residency in Canada on 50th Anniversary of Farmworker Program," Harvesting Freedom, 3 October 2016, https://harvestingfreedom.org/wp-content/uploads/ 2016/09/harvestingfreedomreachesottawa-mediaadvisoryfinal.pdf; "Committee

Report No. 4 – HUMA (42-1)," House of Commons of Canada, accessed 30 January 2021, https://www.ourcommons.ca/DocumentViewer/en/42-1/HUMA/report-4/page-126.

26 Luis Gabriel Flores Flores, "Letter from Luis Gabriel Flores Flores," Migrant Workers Alliance for Change, 30 July 2020, https://migrantworkersalliance.org/wp-content/uploads/2020/07/Letter-to-Immigration-Minister-English.pdf.

27 Kate Dubinski, "Ontario Migrant Worker Fired after Raising Concerns about Unsafe Conditions Awarded $25,000 by Labour Board," CBC News, last modified 12 November 2020, https://www.cbc.ca/news/canada/london/migrant-worker-wins-labour-board-ruling-1.5799587; Sara Mojtehedzadeh, "Migrant Worker Fired for Speaking out about COVID-19 Wins a Rare Reprisal Case against an Ontario Farm," Toronto Star, 12 November 2020, https://www.thestar.com/news/gta/2020/11/12/migrant-worker-fired-for-speaking-out-about-Covid-19-wins-a-rare-reprisal-case-against-an-ontario-farm.html.

28 Justicia for Migrant Workers, "Solidarity Actions with Migrant Farmworkers Demanding Justice at Martin's Family Fruit Farm," November 2020, https://docs.google.com/document/d/17uko8TUQ364Wlyedhi75gwHf-C8dYpiolecthDgTDZQ/mobilebasic.

29 Rachel Gilmore, "Mexico Won't Send Workers to Canadian Farms that Ignore COVID-19 Rules: Ambassador," CTV News, 22 June 2020, https://www.ctvnews.ca/health/coronavirus/mexico-won-t-send-workers-to-canadian-farms-that-ignore-Covid-19-rules-ambassador-1.4995354; Nicholas Keung, "Stuck in Canada, Hundreds of Migrant Farm Workers Get Help from Federal Government," Toronto Star, 16 December 2020, https://www.thestar.com/news/canada/2020/12/16/stuck-in-canada-hundreds-of-migrant-farm-workers-get-help-from-federal-government.html.

30 Dr Sylvain Charlebois et al., Canada's Food Price Report 2022, Dalhousie University, accessed 19 February 2022, https://cdn.dal.ca/content/dam/dalhousie/pdf/sites/agri-food/Food%20Price%20Report%20-%20EN%202022.pdf.

31 For example, "Climate and COVID-19: Converging Crises," The Lancet 397, no. 10269 (9 January 2021): 71, https://doi.org/10.1016/S0140-6736(20)32579-4.

32 Important organizations include Justicia for Migrant Workers, Migrant Workers Alliance for Change, the United Food and Commercial Workers and their Agricultural Workers Alliance centres, RAMA Okanogan (British Columbia), and the Immigrant Workers Centre (Quebec), among others.

33 Georgina Alonso, "Black Lives Matter in Rural Canada, Too," Briarpatch, 22 December 2020, https://briarpatchmagazine.com/articles/view/black-lives-matter-in-rural-canada-too; Melodie McCullough, "Migrant Workers' Rights: The Struggle Continues for Permanent Immigration Status," JOURNEY Magazine, 2 September 2016, https://journeymagazineptbo.com/2016/09/02/4121/.

34 For an excellent introduction to the struggle for a progressive Green New Deal,
     see Klein, *On Fire*. Other authors influencing my thinking here include DeGooyer
     et al., *The Right to Have Rights*, and the work of Ian McKay, including "A Half-
     Century of Possessive Individualism."
35 Stephen Russell, "Everything You Need to Know about Agricultural Emissions,"
     World Resources Institute, 29 May 2014, https://www.wri.org/blog/2014/05/every
     thing-you-need-know-about-agricultural-emissions; "Systemic Changes for
     1.5°C-Consistent Pathways," in *Global Warming of 1.5°C. An IPCC Special Report*,
     2018, https://www.ipcc.ch/sr15/chapter/chapter-4/4-3/.

BIBLIOGRAPHY

Archival and Manuscript Collections
Ancestry.ca (online)
  Border Crossings: From U.S. to Canada, 1908–1935, Ontario, Manifests
Archives of Ontario, Toronto, Ontario
  D 21, Strike and Lockout Files
  F 1405-19-42, Hungarian Canadian Photographs
  F 1405-60-35, Howard Bilger-Walter Wallis Textual Records
  F 4180-24, Ontario Federation of Labour Research Department Subject Files
  F 1405-61, Multicultural History Society of Ontario Fonds, Delhi Tobacco Belt Project
    Textual Records
  RG 16-102, Program Files of the Marketing and Special Services Division of the Minis-
    try of Agriculture and Food
  RG 16-250, Records of the Flue-Cured Tobacco Growers' Marketing Board
  RG 16-66, Agricultural Representatives' Field Reports
  RG 3-10, Premier Mitchell F. Hepburn Private Correspondence
Barbados Department of Archives, Bridgetown, Barbados
  General Collection
Delhi Tobacco Museum and Heritage Centre, Delhi, Ontario
  George Demeyere Library
  Ontario Flue-Cured Tobacco Growers' Marketing Board Scrapbooks
Elgin County Archives, St Thomas, Ontario
  General Collection
Jamaica Archives and Records Department, Spanish Town, Jamaica
  General Collection
Kimberly Knowles, interviews conducted for "The Seasonal Agricultural Workers Pro-
    gram in Ontario: From the Perspective of Jamaican Migrants" (MA thesis, University
    of Guelph, 1997) (in author's possession)
Leonard Rapport Works Progress Administration interviews (in author's possession)
Library and Archives Canada, Ottawa, Ontario

R12298, Eugene Whelan Fonds
RG 17, Department of Agriculture
RG 10, Department of Indian Affairs
RG 25, Department of External Affairs
RG 26, Department of Citizenship and Immigration
RG 27, Department of Labour
RG 76, Immigration Branch
RG 95-1, Corporations Branch sous-fonds
RG 118, Department of Manpower and Immigration
McGill Digital Archive (online)
Canadian Corporate Reports
Multicultural Historical Society of Ontario, Toronto, Ontario
Oral History Interviews, Delhi Tobacco Collection
National Archives and Records Administration, Washington, DC
RG 33, Extension Service
RG 183, Bureau of Employment Security
RG 211, War Manpower Commission
National Library of Jamaica, Kingston, Jamaica
General Collection
Serials Collection
Simon Fraser University Digitized Collections (online)
Canadian Farmworkers Union Collection
1956 Hungarian Memorial Oral History Project
United Church of Canada Archives, Toronto, Ontario
Fonds 1014, United Church of Canada Haldimand-Norfolk Presbytery
Western University Archives and Special Collections, London, Ontario
London Free Press Collection of Photographic Negatives

Newspapers, Magazines, Newsletters, and Journals

Aylmer Express
Brantford Expositor
Buffalo Evening News
Canadian Tobacco Grower (Delhi, ON)
Clarion (Toronto, ON)
Daily Gleaner (Kingston, JM)
Danville Register (Danville, VA)
Delhi News-Record
Delhi Reporter
Globe (Toronto, ON)
Globe and Mail (Toronto, ON)

Hamilton Spectator
Kanadai Magyar Munkás (Toronto, ON)
London Free Press
MacLean's
Oxford Public Ledger (Oxford, NC)
Poughkeepsie Journal
Simcoe Reformer
St Thomas Times-Journal
Tillsonburg News
Toronto Star
Toronto Telegram
Vittoria Booster

Oral History Interviews

Ackner, John (pseudonym). Interview by author, 24 July 2017, St Thomas, Ontario.
Alleyne, David. Interview by author, 6 May 2017, Chapman, Saint Thomas, Barbados.
Alleyne, David, Winston Bovell, and Participant 7 (group interview). Interview by author, 6 May 2017, Chapman, Saint Thomas, Barbados.
Bartsch, Peter. Interview by author, 8 August 2017, by telephone (interviewee was in Woodstock, Ontario).
Berggold, Craig. Interview by author, 1 July 2018, Kingston, Ontario.
Bovell, Victor, and Anthony Lowe. Interview by author, 5 May 2017, Saint Sylvan's, Saint Joseph, Barbados.
Bovell, Winston. Interview by author, 6 May 2017, Chapman, Saint Thomas, Barbados.
Byer, William, and Christie Byer. Interview by author, 2 August 2017, La Salette, Ontario.
Chaussé, Marc. Interview by author, 2 November 2017, Laval, Quebec.
Cooper, Gary. Interview by author, 28 March 2018, Simcoe, Ontario.
DeDecker, Edward. Interview by author, 17 August 2018, La Salette, Ontario.
Demeulenaere, Joe. Interview by author, 31 July 2017, Princeton, Ontario.
Demeulenaere, Walter. Interview by author, 2 August 2017, Vanessa, Ontario.
Donohue, Paul. Interview by author, 17 August 2017, Vanessa, Ontario.
Hutchinson, Headley. Interview by author, 24 April 2017, Christiana, Manchester, Jamaica.
Kennedy, Hassel. Interview by author, 18 October 2016, Simcoe, Ontario.
Knowles, William. Interview by author, 25 July 2017, Langton, Ontario.
Ladell, Kimberlie. Interview by author, 25 August 2017, London, Ontario.
Long, James Bryon. Interview by author, 27 August 2017, Toronto, Ontario.
Moore, David. Interview by author, 3 May 2017, King George V Memorial Park, Saint Philip, Barbados.

Participant 7. Interview by author, 6 May 2017, Chapman, Saint Thomas, Barbados.

Participant 26. Interview by author, 26 February 2018, by telephone (interviewee was in Marystown, Newfoundland).

Passmore, Joanne. Interview by author, 18 August 2017, Elmira, Ontario.

Patricia (last name omitted at interviewee's request). Interview by author, 28 March 2018, by telephone (interviewee was in Montreal, Quebec).

Scott, Linda, and Paul Van Londersele. Interview by author, 17 August 2017, Simcoe, Ontario.

Vermeeren, Michelle. Interview by author, 20 September 2017, by telephone (interviewee was in London, Ontario).

Williams, Gladston. Interview by author, 17 April 2017, New Bowens, Clarendon, Jamaica.

Published Sources, Reports, and Theses

Abella, Irving M., and Harold Martin Troper. *None Is Too Many: Canada and the Jews of Europe, 1933–1948*. Toronto: University of Toronto Press, 2012.

Abu-Laban, Yasmeen, and Nisha Nath. "From Deportation to Apology: The Case of Maher Arar and the Canadian State." *Canadian Ethnic Studies Journal* 39, no. 3 (2007): 71–98.

Alexander, Robert J., and Eldon M. Parker. *A History of Organized Labor in the English-Speaking West Indies*. Westport, CT: Praeger, 2004.

Ali, Ridwan. "Towards the Rationalization of Land Use in Trinidad and Tobago." In *Proceedings of the Eighth West Indian Agricultural Economics Conference*, edited by C.E. McIntosh, 44–53. St Augustine, TT: University of the West Indies, 1973. Accessed at the National Library of Jamaica.

Alston, Lee J., and Kyle D. Kauffman. "Up, Down, and Off the Agricultural Ladder: New Evidence and Implications of Agricultural Mobility for Blacks in the Postbellum South." *Agricultural History* 72, no. 2 (1998): 263–79.

Andre, Irving. "The Genesis and Persistence of the Commonwealth Caribbean Seasonal Agricultural Workers Program in Canada." *Osgoode Hall Law Journal* 28, no. 2 (1990): 243–302.

Avakumovic, Ivan. *The Communist Party in Canada: A History*. Toronto: McClelland and Stewart, 1975.

Avery, Donald. *Reluctant Host: Canada's Response to Immigrant Workers, 1896–1994*. Toronto: McClelland and Stewart, 1995.

Badger, Anthony J. *Prosperity Road: The New Deal, Tobacco, and North Carolina*. Chapel Hill: University of North Carolina Press, 1980.

Barajas, Frank P. *Curious Unions: Mexican American Workers and Resistance in Oxnard, California, 1898–1961*. Lincoln: University of Nebraska Press, 2012.

Bardacke, Frank. *Trampling Out the Vintage: Cesar Chavez and the Two Souls of the United Farm Workers*. New York: Verso, 2011.

Barker, Judy, and Donna Kennedy. *The Tobacco Leaf Yesterday and Today*. Delhi, ON: Township of Delhi Public Library, 1979.

Barnes, Annmarie. "Dangerous Duality: The 'Net Effect' of Immigration and Deportation on Jamaicans in Canada." In *Crimes of Colour: Racialization and the Criminal Justice System in Canada*, edited by Wendy Chan and Kiran Mirchandani, 191–202. Peterborough, ON: Broadview Press, 2002.

Basok, Tanya. *Tortillas and Tomatoes: Transmigrant Mexican Harvesters in Canada*. Montreal: McGill-Queen's University Press, 2002.

Baud, Michiel. "Brazil." In *Tobacco in History and Culture: An Encyclopedia*, vol. 1, edited by Jordan Goodman, 88–92. Detroit: Thomson Gale, 2005.

Bauder, Harald. "Foreign Farm Workers in Ontario (Canada): Exclusionary Discourse in the Newsprint Media." *Journal of Peasant Studies* 35, no. 1 (2008): 100–18.

Becerril, Ofelia. "Transnational Work and the Gendered Politics of Labour: A Study of Male and Female Mexican Migrant Farm Workers in Canada." In *Organizing the Transnational: Labour, Politics, and Social Change*, edited by Luin Goldring and Sailaja Krishnamurti, 157–72. Vancouver: UBC Press, 2007.

Beckert, Sven. *Empire of Cotton: A Global History*. New York: Alfred A. Knopf, 2014.

Beveridge, Karl, and Carol Condé. "Canadian Farmworkers Union." *Fuse* 5, no. 10 (March 1982): 321.

Binford, Arthur Leigh. "Assessing Temporary Foreign Worker Programs through the Prism of Canada's Seasonal Agricultural Worker Program: Can They Be Reformed or Should They Be Eliminated?" *Dialectical Anthropology* 43, no. 4 (2019): 347–66.

– "From Fields of Power to Fields of Sweat: The Dual Process of Constructing Temporary Migrant Labour in Mexico and Canada." *Third World Quarterly* 30, no. 3 (April 2009): 503–17.

– *Tomorrow We're All Going to the Harvest: Temporary Foreign Worker Programs and Neoliberal Political Economy*. Austin: University of Texas Press, 2013.

Bjørge, Mikhail. "The Workers' War: The Character of Class Struggle in World War II." PhD dissertation, Queen's University, 2017.

Bolland, O. Nigel. *The Politics of Labour in the British Caribbean: The Social Origins of Authoritarianism and Democracy in the Labour Movement*. Princeton, NJ: Markus Wiener, 2001.

Boulukos, George. *The Grateful Slave: The Emergence of Race in Eighteenth-Century British and American Culture*. Cambridge: Cambridge University Press, 2008.

Bourbonnais, Nicole C. *Birth Control in the Decolonizing Caribbean: Reproductive Politics and Practice on Four Islands, 1930–1970*. New York: Cambridge University Press, 2016.

Bowling, Lewis. *Granville County Revisited*. Charleston, SC: Arcadia Publishing, 2003.

Brouwer, Ruth Compton. *Canada's Global Villagers: CUSO in Development, 1961–86*. Vancouver: UBC Press, 2013.

Brown, Phillip, Anthony Hesketh, and Sara Williams. "Employability in a Knowledge-Driven Economy." *Journal of Education and Work* 16, no. 2 (2003): 107–26.

Brownlie, Jarvis. *A Fatherly Eye: Indian Agents, Government Power, and Aboriginal Resistance in Ontario, 1918–1939.* New York: Oxford University Press, 2003.

Buchanan, D.R. *Evaluation of the 1967 Caribbean Farm Labour Program.* Ottawa: Research Branch, Department of Manpower and Immigration, 1968.

Canada. *Investigation into an Alleged Combine of Tobacco Manufacturers and Other Buyers of Raw Leaf Tobacco in the Province of Ontario.* Ottawa: Department of Labour, 1933.

– "Report of the Indian Affairs Branch for the Fiscal Year Ended March 31, 1946," reprinted from the *Annual Report of the Department of Mines and Resources.* Ottawa: King's Printer, 1947.

– *Statistical Handbook of Canadian Tobacco.* Ottawa: Statistics Canada, 1941.

Carty, Linda. "African Canadian Women and the State: 'Labour Only, Please.'" In *"We're Rooted Here and They Can't Pull Us Up": Essays in African Canadian Women's History,* edited by Peggy Bristow, 193–229. Toronto: University of Toronto Press, 1994.

Carvajal, Lidia. "Farm-Level Impacts in Mexico of the Participation in Canada's Seasonal Agricultural Workers Program (CSAWP)." PhD dissertation, University of Guelph, 2009.

Castañeda, Xochitl, and Patricia Zavella. "Changing Constructions of Sexuality and Risk: Migrant Mexican Women Farmworkers in California." In *Women and Migration in the U.S.-Mexico Borderlands: A Reader,* edited by Denise A. Segura and Patricia Zavella, 249–68. Durham, NC: Duke University Press, 2007.

Chang, Kornel S. *Pacific Connections: The Making of the U.S.-Canadian Borderlands.* Berkeley: University of California Press, 2012.

Chen, Hongyu, Alfons Weersink, Martin Beaulieu, Yu Na Lee, and Katrin Nagelschmitz. "A Historical Review of Changes in Farm Size in Canada." Institute for the Advanced Study of Food and Agricultural Policy, Department of Food, Agriculture, and Resource Economics, University of Guelph. Working Paper Series – WP 19-03 (January 2019). http://forecastinstitute.com/documents/Farm-Size-Historical-Review-2019-03.pdf.

Cherwinski, W. J. C. "The Incredible Harvest Excursion of 1908." *Labour/Le Travail* 5 (1980): 57–79.

– "A Miniature Coxey's Army: The British Harvesters' Toronto-to-Ottawa Trek of 1924." *Labour/Le Travail* 32 (1993): 139–65.

Chilton, Lisa. *Agents of Empire: British Female Migration to Canada and Australia, 1860s–1930.* Toronto: University of Toronto Press, 2007.

Clarke, John. *The Ordinary People of Essex: Environment, Culture, and Economy on the Frontier of Upper Canada.* Montreal: McGill-Queen's University Press, 2010.

Cobbs Hoffman, Elizabeth. *All You Need Is Love: The Peace Corps and the Spirit of the 1960s*. Cambridge, M A: Harvard University Press, 1998.

Cohen, Amy, and Elise Hjalmarson. "Quiet Struggles: Migrant Farmworkers, Informal Labor, and Everyday Resistance in Canada." *International Journal of Comparative Sociology*, 5 December 2018. https://doi.org/10.1177%2F0020715218815543.

Cohen, Marjorie Griffin. *Women's Work, Markets, and Economic Development in Nineteenth-Century Ontario*. Toronto: University of Toronto Press, 1988.

Cooper, Melinda. *Family Values: Between Neoliberalism and the New Social Conservatism*. New York: Zone Books, 2017.

Cornelius, Clifford. "A Lifetime Working." Told to Mercy Doxtator, 1994. In *Glimpses of Oneida Life*, by Karin Michelson, Norma Kennedy, and Mercy Doxtator, 216–38. Toronto: University of Toronto Press, 2016.

Couture, Hugo. "Les jeunes migrants Québécois dans les vallés fruitières de la Colombie-Britannique: Ethnographie d'une forme de mobilité." M A thesis, Université Laval, 2009.

Cox, Howard. "British American Tobacco." In *Tobacco in History and Culture: An Encyclopedia*, edited by Jordan Goodman, 92–95. Detroit: Thomson Gale, 2005.

– *The Global Cigarette: Origins and Evolution of British American Tobacco, 1880–1945*. New York: Oxford University Press, 2000.

Crehan, Kate A.F. *Gramsci's Common Sense: Inequality and Its Narratives*. Durham, N C: Duke University Press, 2016.

Crowley, Terry. "Rural Labour." In *Labouring Lives: Work and Workers in Nineteenth-Century Ontario*, edited by Paul Craven, 13–103. Toronto: University of Toronto Press, 1995.

Culligan, Mark. "The Practical Turn of the Communist Party of Canada: How the Social Insurance Campaign Created 'a Party of the Unemployed,' 1931–1936." M A cognate essay, Queen's University, 2013.

Daniel, Pete. *Breaking the Land: The Transformation of Cotton, Tobacco, and Rice Cultures since 1880*. Urbana: University of Illinois Press, 1985.

– *Dispossession: Discrimination against African American Farmers in the Age of Civil Rights*. Chapel Hill: University of North Carolina Press, 2013.

Danys, Milda. *DP, Lithuanian Immigration to Canada after the Second World War*. Toronto: Multicultural History Society of Ontario, 1986.

Danysk, Cecilia. *Hired Hands: Labour and the Development of Prairie Agriculture, 1880–1930*. Toronto: McClelland and Stewart, 1995.

Davison, Robert Barry. *West Indian Migrants: Social and Economic Facts of Migration from the West Indies*. London: Oxford University Press, 1962.

Dégh, Linda. *People in the Tobacco Belt: Four Lives*. Ottawa: National Museums of Canada, 1975.

DeGooyer, Stephanie, Alastair Hunt, Lida Maxwell, Samuel Moyn, and Astra Taylor. *The Right to Have Rights*. New York: Verso, 2018.

Delhi Women's Institute. *History of Delhi, 1812–1970*. Simcoe, ON: Second Ave Printing, 1970.

Dorman, Robert L. *Revolt of the Provinces: The Regionalist Movement in America, 1920–1945*. Chapel Hill: University of North Carolina Press, 2003.

Doxtator, Mercy. "All about Tobacco." Told to Karin Michelson, 30 January 1998. In *Glimpses of Oneida Life*, by Karin Michelson, Norma Kennedy, and Mercy Doxtator, 246–66. Toronto: University of Toronto Press, 2016.

Dubinsky, Karen, Adele Perry, and Henry Yu, eds. *Within and Without the Nation: Canadian History as Transnational History*. Toronto: University of Toronto Press, 2015.

Dunsworth, Edward. "Green Gold, Red Threats: Organization and Resistance in Depression-Era Ontario Tobacco." *Labour/Le Travail* 79 (2017): 105–42.

– "Race, Exclusion, and Archival Silences in the Seasonal Migration of Tobacco Workers from the Southern United States to Ontario." *Canadian Historical Review* 99, no. 4 (2018): 563–93.

Elm, Olive. "Learning to Work in Tobacco." Told to Karin Michelson, 29 January 1998. In *Glimpses of Oneida Life*, by Karin Michelson, Norma Kennedy, and Mercy Doxtator, 238–46. Toronto: University of Toronto Press, 2016.

Encalada Grez, Evelyn. "Mexican Migrant Farmworker Women Organizing Love and Work Across Rural Canada and Mexico." PhD dissertation, University of Toronto, 2018.

Enstad, Nan. *Cigarettes, Inc.: An Intimate History of Corporate Imperialism*. Chicago: University of Chicago Press, 2018.

– "To Know Tobacco: Southern Identity in China in the Jim Crow Era." *Southern Cultures* 13, no. 4 (2007): 6–23.

Epp, Franca, and Franca Iacovetta. "Introduction." In *Sisters or Strangers? Immigrant, Ethnic, and Racialized Women in Canadian History*, 2nd ed., edited by Marlene Epp and Franca Iacovetta, 3–18. Toronto: University of Toronto Press, 2016.

Fahrmeir, Andreas, Olivier Faron, and Patrick Weil, eds. *Migration Control in the North Atlantic World: The Evolution of State Practices in Europe and the United States from the French Revolution to the Inter-war Period*. New York: Berghahn Books, 2005.

Falconer, Robert. "Family Farmers to Foreign Fieldhands: Consolidation of Canadian Agriculture and the Temporary Foreign Worker Program." *School of Public Policy Publications* 13 (2020). https://journalhosting.ucalgary.ca/index.php/sppp/article/view/70741.

Fernandes, Gilberto. "Moving the 'Less Desirable': Portuguese Mass Migration to Canada, 1953–74." *Canadian Historical Review* 96, no. 3 (2015): 339–74.

Fink, Leon, ed. *Workers across the Americas: The Transnational Turn in Labor History*. New York: Oxford University Press, 2011.

Finkel, Alvin. "Workers' Social-Wage Struggles during the Great Depression and the Era of Neoliberalism: International Comparisons." In *Workers in Hard Times: A Long View of Economic Crises*, edited by Leon Fink, Joseph Anthony McCartin, and Joan Sangster, 113–40. Urbana: University of Illinois Press, 2014.

FitzGerald, David, and David Cook-Martín. *Culling the Masses: The Democratic Origins of Racist Immigration Policy in the Americas*. Cambridge, MA: Harvard University Press, 2014.

Flynn, Karen. *Moving beyond Borders: A History of Black Canadian and Caribbean Women in the Diaspora*. Toronto: University of Toronto Press, 2011.

– "'She Cannot Be Confined to Her Own Region': Nursing and Nurses in the Caribbean, Canada, and the United Kingdom." In *Within and Without the Nation: Canadian History as Transnational History*, edited by Karen Dubinsky, Adele Perry, and Henry Yu, 228–49. Toronto: University of Toronto Press, 2015.

Francis, Gloria E. "A Note on the Agricultural Marketing Protocol and Vegetable Production in Barbados since 1968." In *Proceedings of the Eighth West Indian Agricultural Economics Conference*, edited by C.E. McIntosh, 84–94. St Augustine, TT: University of the West Indies, 1973. Accessed at the National Library of Jamaica.

Freund, Alexander. *Oral History and Ethnic History*. Immigration and Ethnicity in Canada Series, booklet no. 32. Ottawa: Canadian Historical Association, 2014.

Gabaccia, Donna R., and Franca Iacovetta, eds. *Borders, Conflict Zones, and Memory: Scholarly Engagements with Luisa Passerini*. New York: Routledge, 2017.

Galarneau, Charlene. "Farm Labor, Reproductive Justice: Migrant Women Farmworkers in the US." *Health and Human Rights* 15, no. 1 (2013): 144–60.

Galbraith, John Kenneth. *Does It Pay?* Dutton, ON: Village Crier, 2010.

Garner, Hugh. *A Hugh Garner Omnibus*. Toronto: McGraw-Hill Ryerson, 1978.

– *One Damn Thing after Another*. Toronto: McGraw-Hill Ryerson, 1973.

Gellner, John, and John Smerek. *The Czechs and Slovaks in Canada*. Toronto: University of Toronto Press, 1968.

Glassco, Clare. "Harvesting Power and Subjugation: Canada's Seasonal Agricultural Workers Program in Historical Context." MA thesis, Trent University, 2012.

Gomez, Michael Angelo. *Exchanging Our Country Marks: The Transformation of African Identities in the Colonial and Antebellum South*. Chapel Hill: University of North Carolina Press, 1998.

Goodman, Jordan. *Tobacco in History: The Cultures of Dependence*. New York: Routledge, 1993.

– ed. *Tobacco in History and Culture: An Encyclopedia*. 2 vols. Detroit: Thomson Gale, 2005.

Gramsci, Antonio. *Selections from the Prison Notebooks of Antonio Gramsci*. Translated and edited by Quintin Hoare and Geoffrey Nowell-Smith. New York: International Publishers, 1971.

Greene, Julie. *The Canal Builders: Making America's Empire at the Panama Canal.* New York: Penguin Press, 2009.

Greer, Allan, and Ian Radforth, eds. *Colonial Leviathan: State Formation in Mid-Nineteenth-Century Canada.* Toronto: University of Toronto Press, 1992.

Griffith, David, ed. *(Mis)Managing Migration: Guestworkers' Experiences with North American Labor Markets.* Santa Fe, NM: School for Advanced Research Press, 2014.

– "The Promise of a Country: The Impact of Seasonal U.S. Migration on the Jamaican Peasantry." PhD dissertation, University of Florida, 1983.

– "Social Organizational Obstacles to Capital Accumulation among Returning Migrants: The British West Indies Temporary Alien Labor Program." *Human Organization* 45, no. 1 (1986): 34–42.

Grundy, John. *Bureaucratic Manoeuvres: The Contested Administration of the Unemployed.* Toronto: University of Toronto Press, 2019.

Hahamovitch, Cindy. *The Fruits of Their Labor: Atlantic Coast Farmworkers and the Making of Migrant Poverty, 1870–1945.* Chapel Hill: University of North Carolina Press, 1997.

– *No Man's Land: Jamaican Guestworkers in America and the Global History of Deportable Labor.* Princeton, NJ: Princeton University Press, 2011.

– "'Risk the Truck': Guestworker-Sending States and the Myth of Managed Migration." In *(Mis)Managing Migration: Guestworkers' Experiences with North American Labor Markets*, edited by David Griffith, 3–31. Santa Fe, NM: School for Advanced Research Press, 2014.

Hahn, Barbara. *Making Tobacco Bright: Creating an American Commodity, 1617–1937.* Baltimore: Johns Hopkins University Press, 2011.

Hall, Derek. "Where the Streets Are Paved with Prawns: Crop Booms and Migration in Southeast Asia." *Critical Asian Studies* 43, no. 4 (2011): 507–30.

Hall, Robert Burnett. "The Introduction of Flue-Cured Tobacco as a Commercial Crop in Norfolk County, Ontario." PhD dissertation, University of Michigan, 1952.

Hastings, Paula. "The Limits of 'Brotherly Love': Rethinking Canada-Caribbean Relations in the Early Twentieth Century." In *Dominion of Race: Rethinking Canada's International History*, edited by Laura Madokoro, Francine McKenzie, and David Meren, 38–53. Vancouver: UBC Press, 2017.

Haviland, W.E. "Ontario Tobacco Farm Organization and Selected New Belt Production Problems." *Economic Annalist* 20, no. 6 (1950): 127–33.

Hayday, Matthew, Mary-Ellen Kelm, and Tina Loo. "From Politics to the Political: Historical Perspectives on the New Canadian Political History." *Canadian Historical Review* 100, no. 4 (2019): 564–71.

Haythorne, George V. *Labor in Canadian Agriculture.* Cambridge, MA: Harvard University Press, 1960.

Haythorne, George V., and Leonard C. Marsh. *Land and Labour: A Social Survey of Agriculture and the Farm Labour Market in Central Canada.* Toronto: Oxford University Press, 1941.

Heaman, Elsbeth. *Tax, Order, and Good Government: A New Political History of Canada, 1867–1917.* Montreal: McGill-Queen's University Press, 2017.

Heath, Sue. "Widening the Gap: Pre university Gap Years and the 'Economy of Experience.'" *British Journal of Sociology of Education* 28, no. 1 (2007): 89–103.

Helleiner, Jane. "Recruiting the 'Culturally Compatible' Migrant: Irish Working Holiday Migration and White Settler Canadianness." *Ethnicities* 17, no. 3 (2017): 299–319.

Henderson, Stuart. *Making the Scene: Yorkville and Hip Toronto in the 1960s.* Toronto: University of Toronto Press, 2011.

Henderson, Timothy J. "Bracero Blacklists: Mexican Migration and the Unraveling of the Good Neighbor Policy." *Latin Americanist* 55, no. 4 (2011): 199–217.

Hennebry, Jenna. "Falling through the Cracks? Migrant Workers and the Global Social Protection Floor." *Global Social Policy* 14, no. 3 (2014): 369–88.

– "Globalization and the Mexican-Canadian Seasonal Agricultural Worker Program: Power, Racialization and Transnationalism in Temporary Migration." PhD dissertation, University of Western Ontario, 2006.

– "Permanently Temporary? Agricultural Migrant Workers and Their Integration in Canada." Institute for Research on Public Policy, 28 February 2012. https://irpp.org/research-studies/permanently-temporary/.

Henry, Frances. "The West Indian Domestic Scheme in Canada." *Social and Economic Studies* 17, no. 1 (1968): 83–91.

Herod, Andrew. *Labor Geographies: Workers and Landscapes of Capitalism.* New York: Guilford Press, 2001.

Heron, Craig. *Working Lives: Essays in Canadian Working-Class History.* Toronto: University of Toronto Press, 2018.

High, Steven C. "Foreword." In *Oral History off the Record: Toward an Ethnography of Practice*, edited by Stacey Zembrzycki and Anna Sheftel, xv–xx. New York: Palgrave Macmillan, 2013.

– *Industrial Sunset: The Making of North America's Rust Belt, 1969–1984.* Toronto: University of Toronto Press, 2003.

– *Oral History at the Crossroads: Sharing Life Stories of Survival and Displacement.* Vancouver: UBC Press, 2014.

Hill, Susan M. *The Clay We Are Made Of: Haudenosaunee Land Tenure on the Grand River.* Winnipeg: University of Manitoba Press, 2017.

Hoerder, Dirk, Elise van Nederveen Meerkerk, and Silke Neunsinger, eds. *Towards a Global History of Domestic and Caregiving Workers.* Boston: Brill, 2015.

Hoy, Benjamin. *A Line of Blood and Dirt: Creating the Canada–United States Border across Indigenous Lands.* New York: Oxford University Press, 2021.

Iacovetta, Franca. *Gatekeepers: Reshaping Immigrant Lives in Cold War Canada.* Toronto: Between the Lines, 2006.

Igartua, José Eduardo. *The Other Quiet Revolution: National Identities in English Canada, 1945–71.* Vancouver: UBC Press, 2006.

Ishemo, Amani, Hugh Semple, and Elizabeth Thomas-Hope. "Population Mobility and the Survival of Small Farming in the Rio Grande Valley, Jamaica." *Geographical Journal* 172, no. 4 (2006): 318–30.

Ittmann, Karl. *A Problem of Great Importance: Population, Race, and Power in the British Empire, 1918–1973.* London: University of California Press, 2013.

Jaenen, Cornelius J. *The Belgians in Canada.* Ottawa: Canadian Historical Association with the support of the Multiculturalism Program, 1991.

James, C.L.R. *The Black Jacobins: Toussaint L'Ouverture and the San Domingo Revolution.* London: Penguin, 2001.

James, Marlon. *A Brief History of Seven Killings.* New York: Riverhead Books, 2014.

Johnson, Michele A. "'To Ensure That Only Suitable Persons Are Sent': Screening Jamaican Women for the West Indian Domestic Scheme." In *Jamaica in the Canadian Experience: A Multiculturalizing Presence,* edited by Carl James and Andrea Davis, 36–53. Halifax: Fernwood, 2012.

Kale, Madhavi. *Fragments of Empire: Capital, Slavery, and Indian Indentured Labor Migration in the British Caribbean.* Philadelphia: University of Pennsylvania Press, 1998.

Kealey, Gregory S., Reginald Whitaker, and Committee on Canadian Labour History, eds. *R.C.M.P. Security Bulletins: The Depression Years.* St John's, NL: Canadian Committee on Labour History, 1993.

Kealey, Linda. *Enlisting Women for the Cause: Women, Labour, and the Left in Canada, 1890–1920.* Toronto: University of Toronto Press, 1998.

Kelley, Robin D.G. *Hammer and Hoe: Alabama Communists during the Great Depression.* Chapel Hill: University of North Carolina Press, 1990.

Kellman, Jordan. "French Empire." In *Tobacco in History and Culture: An Encyclopedia,* vol. 1, edited by Jordan Goodman, 240–4. Detroit: Thomson Gale, 2005.

Kennedy, Norma. "My First Job in Tobacco." Told to Karin Michelson, 15 April 2012. In *Glimpses of Oneida Life,* by Karin Michelson, Norma Kennedy, and Mercy Doxtator, 266–74. Toronto: University of Toronto Press, 2016.

Kerr-Ritchie, Jeffrey R. "Slavery and Slave Trade." In *Tobacco in History and Culture: An Encyclopedia,* vol. 2, edited by Jordan Goodman, 525–33. Detroit: Thomson Gale, 2005.

Keshen, Jeff. *Saints, Sinners, and Soldiers: Canada's Second World War.* Vancouver: UBC Press, 2004.

Klein, Naomi. *On Fire: The (Burning) Case for a Green New Deal.* New York: Simon and Schuster, 2019.

Kosa, John. *Land of Choice: The Hungarians in Canada.* Toronto: University of Toronto Press, 1957.

Labelle, Kathryn Magee. *Dispersed but Not Destroyed: A History of the Seventeenth-Century Wendat People*. Vancouver: UBC Press, 2013.

Laliberte, Ron. "The 'Grab-a-Hoe' Indians: The Canadian State and the Procurement of Aboriginal Labour for the Southern Alberta Sugar Beet Industry." *Prairie Forum* 31, no. 2 (2006): 305–24.

Laliberte, Ron, and Vic Satzewich. "Native Migrant Labour in the Southern Alberta Sugar Beet Industry: Coercion and Paternalism in the Recruitment of Labour." *Canadian Review of Sociology/Revue canadienne de sociologie* 36, no. 1 (1999): 65–85.

Langford, William. "'Helping People Help Themselves': Democracy, Development, and the Global Politics of Poverty in Canada, 1964–1979." PhD dissertation, Queen's University, 2017.

Larkin, Sherrie Noreen. "Workin' on the Contract: St. Lucian Farmworkers in Ontario. A Study of International Labour Migration." PhD, McMaster University, 1998.

Lewis, George Kinsman. "The Acculturation of Barbadian Agriculture Workers in Canada." PhD dissertation, Ball State University, 1975.

Linden, Marcel van der. *Transnational Labour History: Explorations*. London: Taylor and Francis, 2017.

– *Workers of the World: Essays toward a Global Labor History*. Boston: Brill, 2008.

Linebaugh, Peter, and Marcus Rediker. *The Many-Headed Hydra: Sailors, Slaves, Commoners and the Hidden History of the Revolutionary Atlantic*. London: Verso, 2012.

Lipman, Jana K. *Guantánamo: A Working-Class History between Empire and Revolution*. Berkeley: University of California Press, 2009.

Loo, Tina. *Moved by the State: Forced Relocation and Making a Good Life in Postwar Canada*. Vancouver: UBC Press, 2019.

Loza, Mireya. *Defiant Braceros: How Migrant Workers Fought for Racial, Sexual, and Political Freedom*. Chapel Hill: University of North Carolina Press, 2016.

– "The Japanese Agricultural Workers' Program: Race, Labor, and Cold War Diplomacy in the Fields, 1956–1965." *Pacific Historical Review* 86, no. 4 (2017): 661–90.

MacPherson, Murdo, and Mary Magwood. "New Political Directions." In *Historical Atlas of Canada*, vol. 3, *Addressing the Twentieth Century*, edited by Deryck W. Holdsworth and Donald Kerr, 114–16. Toronto: University of Toronto Press, 2016.

Madokoro, Laura. *Elusive Refuge: Chinese Migrants in the Cold War*. Cambridge, MA: Harvard University Press, 2016.

Madokoro, Laura, Francine McKenzie, and David Meren, eds. *Dominion of Race: Rethinking Canada's International History*. Vancouver: UBC Press, 2017.

Magee, Joan. *The Belgians in Ontario: A History*. Toronto: Dundurn Press, 1987.

Mapes, Kathleen. *Sweet Tyranny: Migrant Labor, Industrial Agriculture, and Imperial Politics*. Urbana: University of Illinois Press, 2009.

Mar, Lisa Rose. *Brokering Belonging: Chinese in Canada's Exclusion Era, 1885–1945*. Toronto: University of Toronto Press, 2010.

Marx, Karl. *Capital: A Critique of Political Economy.* 3 vols. London: Penguin, 1990.

– *The Eighteenth Brumaire of Louis Bonaparte.* 1852. Marxists Internet Archive. https://www.marxists.org/archive/marx/works/1852/18th-brumaire/ch01.htm.

Mathieu, Sarah-Jane. *North of the Color Line: Migration and Black Resistance in Canada, 1870–1955.* Chapel Hill: University of North Carolina Press, 2010.

Mazer, Katie. "Making the Welfare State Work for Extraction: Poverty Policy as the Regulation of Labor and Land." *Annals of the American Association of Geographers* 109, no. 1 (2018): 18–34.

– "Mining Mobility: Uneven Development, Resource Labour, and the Canadian Staple State." PhD dissertation, University of Toronto, 2019.

McBride, Jeffrey S., David G. Altman, Melissa Klein, and Wain White. "Green Tobacco Sickness." *Tobacco Control* 7, no. 3 (1998): 294–8.

McEnvoy, F.J. "'A Symbol of Racial Discrimination': The Chinese Immigration Act and Canada's Relations with China, 1942–1947." *Canadian Ethnic Studies* 14, no. 3 (1982): 24–42.

McGillivray, Gillian. *Blazing Cane: Sugar Communities, Class, and State Formation in Cuba, 1868–1959.* Durham, NC: Duke University Press, 2009.

McKay, Ian. "A Half-Century of Possessive Individualism: C.B. Macpherson and the Twenty-First-Century Prospects of Liberalism." *Journal of the Canadian Historical Association* 25, no. 1 (2014): 307–40.

– *The Quest of the Folk: Antimodernism and Cultural Selection in Twentieth-Century Nova Scotia.* Montreal: McGill-Queen's University Press, 1994.

– *Reasoning Otherwise: Leftists and the People's Enlightenment in Canada, 1890–1920.* Toronto: Between the Lines, 2008.

– *Rebels, Reds, Radicals: Rethinking Canada's Left History.* Toronto: Between the Lines, 2005.

McKeown, Adam. *Melancholy Order: Asian Migration and the Globalization of Borders.* New York: Columbia University Press, 2008.

McKercher, Asa, and Philip Van Huizen, eds. *Undiplomatic History: The New Study of Canada and the World.* Montreal: McGill-Queen's University Press, 2019.

McLaughlin, Janet. "Trouble in Our Fields: Health and Human Rights among Mexican and Caribbean Migrant Farm Workers in Canada." PhD dissertation, University of Toronto, 2009.

McQuarrie, Jonathan. "From Farm to Firm: Canadian Tobacco c. 1860–1950." PhD dissertation, University of Toronto, 2016.

– "'Tobacco Has Blossomed like the Rose in the Desert': Technology, Trees, and Tobacco in the Norfolk Sand Plain, c. 1920–1940." *Journal of the Canadian Historical Association* 25, no. 1 (2014): 33–62.

Menard, Russell R. "British Empire." In *Tobacco in History and Culture: An Encyclopedia,* vol. 1, edited by Jordan Goodman, 96–101. Detroit: Thomson Gale, 2005.

Meren, David. *With Friends like These: Entangled Nationalisms and the Canada-Quebec-France Triangle, 1944–1970.* Vancouver: UBC Press, 2012.

Mesli, Samy. *La coopération franco-québécoise dans le domaine de l'éduation: De 1965 à nos jours.* Quebec: Septentrion, 2014.

Michelson, Karin, Norma Kennedy, and Mercy Doxtator. *Glimpses of Oneida Life.* Toronto: University of Toronto Press, 2016.

Miller, Christopher. "Testing the Boundaries of Employer-Driven Agricultural Migration: Privatization and the Temporary Foreign Worker Program, 2002–2011." PhD dissertation, Carleton University, 2018.

Miller, Jennifer A. *Turkish Guest Workers in Germany: Hidden Lives and Contested Borders, 1960s to 1980s.* Toronto: University of Toronto Press, 2018.

Miller, J.R. *Compact, Contract, Covenant: Aboriginal Treaty-Making in Canada.* Toronto: University of Toronto Press, 2009.

Milligan, Ian. *Rebel Youth: 1960s Labour Unrest, Young Workers, and New Leftists in English Canada.* Vancouver: UBC Press, 2014.

Milloy, Jeremy. *Blood, Sweat, and Fear: Violence at Work in the North American Auto Industry, 1960–80.* Vancouver: UBC Press, 2017.

Mills, Sean. *The Empire Within: Postcolonial Thought and Political Activism in Sixties Montreal.* Montreal: McGill-Queen's University Press, 2010.

– *A Place in the Sun: Haiti, Haitians, and the Remaking of Quebec.* Montreal: McGill-Queen's University Press, 2016.

Mitchell, Don. "Labor's Geography: Capital, Violence, Guest Workers and the Post-World War II Landscape." *Antipode* 43, no. 2 (2011): 563–95.

– *They Saved the Crops: Labor, Landscape, and the Struggle over Industrial Farming in Bracero-Era California.* Athens: University of Georgia Press, 2012.

Monod, David. "The Agrarian Struggle: Rural Communism in Alberta and Saskatchewan 1926–1935." *Histoire sociale/Social History* 18, no. 35 (1985): 99–118.

Mooney, Patrick H., and Theo J. Majka. *Farmers' and Farm Workers' Movements: Social Protest in American Agriculture.* New York: Twayne, 1995.

Mosby, Ian. *Food Will Win the War: The Politics, Culture, and Science of Food on Canada's Home Front.* Vancouver: UBC Press, 2014.

Muller-Clemm, Werner J., and Maria Paulette Barnes. "A Historical Perspective on Federal Program Evaluation in Canada." *Canadian Journal of Program Evaluation* 12, no. 1 (1997): 47–70.

Murji, Karim, and John Solomos, eds. *Racialization: Studies in Theory and Practice.* Oxford: Oxford University Press, 2005.

Náter, Laura. "Caribbean." In *Tobacco in History and Culture: An Encyclopedia,* vol. 1, edited by Jordan Goodman, 107–11. Detroit: Thomson Gale, 2005.

Nee, Michael. "Origin and Diffusion." In *Tobacco in History and Culture: An Encyclopedia,* vol. 2, edited by Jordan Goodman, 397–402. Detroit: Thomson Gale, 2005.

Neumann, Tracy. *Remaking the Rust Belt: The Postindustrial Transformation of North America*. Philadelphia: University of Pennsylvania Press, 2016.

Niewójt, Lawrence. "From Waste Land to Canada's Tobacco Production Heartland: Landscape Change in Norfolk County, Ontario." *Landscape Research* 32, no. 3 (2007): 355–77.

Nygren, Joshua M. "In Pursuit of Conservative Reform: Social Darwinism, the Agricultural Ladder, and the Lessons of European Tenancy." *Agricultural History* 89, no. 1 (2015): 75–101.

Owram, Doug. *The Government Generation: Canadian Intellectuals and the State, 1900–1945*. Toronto: University of Toronto Press, 1986.

Palmer, Bryan D. *Canada's 1960s: The Ironies of Identity in a Rebellious Era*. Toronto: University of Toronto Press, 2009.

– *Working Class Experience: Rethinking the History of Canadian Labour, 1800–1991*. 2nd ed. Toronto: McClelland and Stewart, 1992.

Panitch, Leo, and Sam Gindin. *The Making of Global Capitalism: The Political Economy of American Empire*. New York: Verso, 2004.

Parham, Robert A. *Tobacco in the Blood: An Autobiography*. London: World Tobacco, 1966.

Parnaby, Andrew. "Indigenous Labor in Mid-Nineteenth-Century British North America: The Mi'kmaq of Cape Breton and Squamish of British Columbia in Comparative Perspective." In *Workers across the Americas: The Transnational Turn in Labor History*, edited by Leon Fink, 109–35. New York: Oxford University Press, 2011.

Parr, Joy. "Hired Men: Ontario Agricultural Wage Labour in Historical Perspective." *Labour/Le Travail* 15 (1985): 91–103.

Passerini, Luisa. "Work Ideology and Consensus under Italian Fascism." *History Workshop Journal* 8, no. 1 (1979): 82–108.

Patrias, Carmela. *The Hungarians in Canada*. Canada's Ethnic Group Series, booklet no. 27. Ottawa: Canadian Historical Association, 1999.

– "More Menial than Housemaids? Racialized and Gendered Labour in the Fruit and Vegetable Industry of Canada's Niagara Region, 1880–1945." *Labour/Le Travail* 78 (2016): 69–104.

– *Patriots and Proletarians: Politicizing Hungarian Immigrants in Interwar Canada*. Montreal: McGill-Queen's University Press, 1994.

Paz Ramirez, Adriana. "Embodying and Resisting Labour Apartheid: Racism and Mexican Farm Workers in Canada's Seasonal Agricultural Workers Program." MA thesis, University of British Columbia, 2013.

Peck, Gunther. *Reinventing Free Labor: Padrones and Immigrant Workers in the North American West, 1880–1930*. New York: Cambridge University Press, 2000.

Petty, Adrienne Monteith. *Standing Their Ground: Small Farmers in North Carolina since the Civil War*. New York: Oxford University Press, 2013.

Physicians for a Smoke-Free Canada. *Recent Trends in Tobacco Agriculture in Canada*. Ottawa: Physicians for a Smoke-Free Canada, 2008. http://www.smoke-free.ca/pdf_1/MF%20and%20MP%20Fact%20sheet%20-long.pdf.

Pierson, Ruth Roach. *"They're Still Women After All": The Second World War and Canadian Womanhood*. Toronto: McClelland and Stewart, 1986.

Portelli, Alessandro. *The Death of Luigi Trastulli, and Other Stories: Form and Meaning in Oral History*. Albany: State University of New York Press, 1990.

– "The Peculiarities of Oral History." *History Workshop Journal* 12, no. 1 (1981): 96–107.

Preibisch, Kerry L. "Local Produce, Foreign Labor: Labor Mobility Programs and Global Trade Competitiveness in Canada." *Rural Sociology* 72, no. 3 (2007): 418–49.

– "Pick-Your-Own Labor: Migrant Workers and Flexibility in Canadian Agriculture." *International Migration Review* 44, no. 2 (2010): 404–41.

Preibisch, Kerry, and Leigh Binford. "Interrogating Racialized Global Labour Supply: An Exploration of the Racial/National Replacement of Foreign Agricultural Workers in Canada." *Canadian Review of Sociology/Revue Canadienne de Sociologie* 44, no. 1 (2007): 5–36.

Priestland, David. *The Red Flag: A History of Communism*. New York: Grove Press, 2009.

Proctor, Robert N. "The History of the Discovery of the Cigarette–Lung Cancer Link: Evidentiary Traditions, Corporate Denial, Global Toll." *Tobacco Control* 21, no. 2 (2012): 87–91.

Putnam, Lara. *The Company They Kept: Migrants and the Politics of Gender in Caribbean Costa Rica, 1870–1960*. Chapel Hill: University of North Carolina Press, 2002.

– *Radical Moves: Caribbean Migrants and the Politics of Race in the Jazz Age*. Chapel Hill: University of North Carolina Press, 2013.

Radforth, Ian. *Bushworkers and Bosses: Logging in Northern Ontario, 1900–1980*. Toronto: University of Toronto Press, 1987.

Raibmon, Paige. *Authentic Indians: Episodes of Encounter from the Late-Nineteenth-Century Northwest Coast*. Durham, NC: Duke University Press, 2005.

Ramirez, Bruno. *On the Move: French-Canadian and Italian Migrants in the North Atlantic Economy, 1860–1914*. Toronto: McClelland and Stewart, 1991.

Ramsey, Doug, and Barry Smit. "Impacts of Changes in the Flue-Cured Tobacco Sector on Farmers in Ontario, Canada." *Applied Geography* 21, no. 4 (2001): 347–68.

– "Rural Community Well-Being: Models and Application to Changes in the Tobacco-Belt in Ontario, Canada." *Geoforum* 33, no. 3 (2002): 367–84.

Ramsey, Doug, Carol Stewart, Michael Troughton, and Barry Smit. "Agricultural Restructuring of Ontario Tobacco Production." *Great Lakes Geographer* 9, no. 2 (2003): 71–93.

Reid-Musson, Emily. "Grown Close to Home™: Migrant Farmworker (Im)Mobilities and Unfreedom on Canadian Family Farms." *Annals of the American Association of Geographers* 107, no. 3 (May 4, 2017): 716–30.

– "Historicizing Precarity: A Labour Geography of 'Transient' Migrant Workers in Ontario Tobacco." *Geoforum* 56 (2014): 161–71.

Reilly, Alexander, Joanna Howe, Diane van den Broek, and Chris F. Wright. "Working Holiday Makers in Australian Horticulture: Labour Market Effect, Exploitation and Avenues for Reform." *Griffith Law Review* 27, no. 1 (2018): 99–130.

Richardson, Bonham C. *Caribbean Migrants: Environment and Human Survival on St Kitts and Nevis.* Knoxville: University of Tennessee Press, 1983.

Roberts, Barbara. *Whence They Came: Deportation from Canada, 1900–1935.* Ottawa: University of Ottawa Press, 1988.

Rodney, Walter. *How Europe Underdeveloped Africa.* New York: Verso, 2018.

Rodríguez Gordillo, Jose Manuel. "Spanish Empire." In *Tobacco in History and Culture: An Encyclopedia*, vol. 2, edited by Jordan Goodman, 585–93. Detroit: Thomson Gale, 2005.

Sangster, Joan. "Politics and Praxis in Canadian Working-Class Oral History." In *Oral History Off the Record: Toward an Ethnography of Practice*, edited by Stacey Zembrzycki and Anna Sheftel, 59–75. New York: Palgrave Macmillan, 2013.

– *Transforming Labour: Women and Work in Post-War Canada.* Toronto: University of Toronto Press, 2010.

Satzewich, Vic. "Business or Bureaucratic Dominance in Immigration Policymaking in Canada: Why Was Mexico Included in the Caribbean Seasonal Agricultural Workers Program in 1974?" *Journal of International Migration and Integration/Revue de l'integration et de La Migration Internationale* 8, no. 3 (2007): 255–75.

– *Points of Entry: How Canada's Immigration Officers Decide Who Gets In.* Vancouver: UBC Press, 2015.

– "Racism and Canadian Immigration Policy: The Government's View of Caribbean Migration, 1962–1966." *Canadian Ethnic Studies/Études Ethniques au Canada* 21, no. 1 (1989): 77–97.

– *Racism and the Incorporation of Foreign Labour: Farm Labour Migration to Canada since 1945.* New York: Routledge, 1991.

Schrover, Marlou, and Deirdre M. Moloney. "Introduction: Making a Difference." In *Gender, Migration and Categorisation: Making Distinctions between Migrants in Western Countries, 1945–2010*, edited by Marlou Schrover and Deirdre M. Moloney, 7–54. Amsterdam: Amsterdam University Press, 2013.

Scott, Jack. *A Communist Life: Jack Scott and the Canadian Workers Movement, 1927–1985.* Edited by Bryan Palmer. St John's, NL: Committee on Canadian Labour History, 1988.

Scott, James C. *Seeing Like a State: How Certain Schemes to Improve the Human Condition Have Failed.* New Haven, CT: Yale University Press, 1998.

Seager, Allen. "Captain Swing in Ontario?" *Bulletin of the Committee on Canadian Labour History/Bulletin du Comité sur l'Histoire Ouvrière Canadienne* 7 (1979): 3–5.

Sears, Alan. *The Next New Left: A History of the Future*. Halifax: Fernwood Publishing, 2014.

Secretariat of the Commission for Labor Cooperation. *Protection of Migrant Agricultural Workers in Canada, Mexico and the United States*. Washington, DC: Secretariat of the Commission for Labor Cooperation, 2002.

Sheldon, Sam. "Ontario's Flue-Cured Tobacco Industry: The Southern United States Legacy." *American Review of Canadian Studies* 18, no. 2 (1988): 195–212.

Silvera, Makeda. *Silenced: Talks with Working Class West Indian Women about Their Lives and Struggles as Domestic Workers in Canada*. Toronto: Sister Vision Press, 1989.

Smith, Angèle, and Jeremy Staveley. "Toward an Ethnography of Mobile Tourism Industry Workers in Banff National Park." *Anthropologica* 56, no. 2 (2014): 435–47.

Smit, Barry, Tom Johnston, and Robert Morse. "Labour Turnover on Flue-Cured Tobacco Farms in Southern Ontario." *Agricultural Administration* 20, no. 3 (1985): 153–68.

Snodgrass, Michael. "Patronage and Progress: The Bracero Program from the Perspective of Mexico." In *Workers across the Americas: The Transnational Turn in Labor History*, edited by Leon Fink, 245–66. New York: Oxford University Press, 2011.

Sparling, David, Terry Quadri, and Erna van Duren. *Consolidation in the Canadian Agri-Food Sector and the Impact on Farm Incomes*. Ottawa: Canadian Agri-Food Policy Institute, 2005. https://citeseerx.ist.psu.edu/viewdoc/download?doi=10.1.1.455.499&rep=rep1&type=pdf.

Stevenson, Michael D. *Canada's Greatest Wartime Muddle: National Selective Service and the Mobilization of Human Resources during World War II*. Montreal: McGill-Queen's University Press, 2001.

Stewart, Carol. "Agricultural Restructuring in Ontario Tobacco Production." MSc thesis, University of Western Ontario, 1996.

Storch, Randi. *Red Chicago: American Communism at Its Grassroots, 1928–35*. Urbana: University of Illinois Press, 2007.

Strikwerda, Carl. *A House Divided: Catholics, Socialists, and Flemish Nationalists in Nineteenth-Century Belgium*. Lanham, MD: Rowman and Littlefield, 1997.

Struthers, James. *The Limits of Affluence: Welfare in Ontario, 1920–1970*. Toronto: University of Toronto Press, 1994.

– *No Fault of Their Own: Unemployment and the Canadian Welfare State, 1914–1941*. Toronto: University of Toronto Press, 1983.

Sutton, Constance R. "Continuing the Fight for Economic Justice: The Barbados Sugar Workers' 1958 Wildcat Strike." In *Revisiting Caribbean Labour: Essays in Honour of O. Nigel Bolland*, edited by Constance R. Sutton, 41–64. Kingston, JM: Ian Randle Publishers, 2005.

Tait, Lyal. *Tobacco in Canada*. Toronto: T.H. Best, 1968.

Takai, Yukari. "Bridging the Pacific: Diplomacy and the Control of Japanese Transmigration via Hawai i, 1890–1910." In *Entangling Migration History: Borderlands and*

Transnationalism in the United States and Canada, edited by Alexander Freund and Benjamin Bryce, 141–61. Gainesville: University Press of Florida, 2015.

– *Gendered Passages: French-Canadian Migration to Lowell, Massachusetts, 1900–1920.* New York: Peter Lang, 2008.

Thompson, David. "Working-Class Anguish and Revolutionary Indignation: The Making of Radical and Socialist Unemployment Movements in Canada, 1875–1928." PhD dissertation, Queen's University, 2014.

Thompson, John Herd, and Allen Seager. "Workers, Growers and Monopolists: The ' Labour Problem' in the Alberta Beet Sugar Industry during the 1930s." *Labour/Le Travail* 3 (1978): 153–74.

Tillotson, Shirley. *Give and Take: The Citizen-Taxpayer and the Rise of Canadian Democracy.* Vancouver: UBC Press, 2017.

Trigger, Bruce G. "The French Presence in Huronia: The Structure of Franco-Huron Relations in the First Half of the Seventeenth Century." *Canadian Historical Review* 49, no. 2 (1968): 107–41.

Troper, Harold. "Canada's Immigration Policy since 1945." *International Journal* 48, no. 2 (1993): 255–81.

Tucker, Eric. "Farm Worker Exceptionalism: Past, Present, and the Post-Fraser Future." In *Constitutional Labour Rights in Canada: Farm Workers and the Fraser Case*, edited by Fay Faraday, Judy Fudge, and Eric Tucker, 30–56. Toronto: Irwin Law, 2012.

Urquhart, M.C., and K.A.H. Buckley, eds. *Historical Statistics of Canada.* Toronto: Macmillan, 1965.

Vance, R. Cameron. "The Tobacco Economy and Its Effect on the Lives of the People in Those Portions of the New Belt Lying in the Counties of Norfolk, Elgin, Oxford, Middlesex and Brant." MA thesis, University of Western Ontario, 1952.

Vosko, Leah F. "Blacklisting as a Modality of Deportability: Mexico's Response to Circular Migrant Agricultural Workers' Pursuit of Collective Bargaining Rights in British Columbia, Canada." *Journal of Ethnic and Migration Studies* 42, no. 8 (2016): 1371–87.

Wallerstein, Immanuel. *The Modern World-System I: Capitalist Agriculture and the Origins of the European World-Economy in the Sixteenth Century.* Berkeley: University of California Press, 2011.

Ward, Peter. *White Canada Forever: Popular Attitudes and Public Policy toward Orientals in British Columbia.* 3rd ed. Montreal: McGill-Queen's University Press, 2014.

Weiler, Anelyse M., Janet McLaughlin, and Donald C. Cole. "Food Security at Whose Expense? A Critique of the Canadian Temporary Farm Labour Migration Regime and Proposals for Change." *International Migration* 55, no. 4 (2017): 48–63.

Weller, G.R. "Hinterland Politics: The Case of Northwestern Ontario." *Canadian Journal of Political Science/Revue canadienne de science politique* 10, no. 4 (1977): 727–9.

Weston, Ann, and Luigi Scarpa de Masellis. *Hemispheric Integration and Trade Relations – Implications for Canada's Seasonal Agricultural Workers Program.* Ottawa: North-South Institute, 2004.

Whitaker, Reginald. *Double Standard: The Secret History of Canadian Immigration Policy*. Toronto: Lester and Orpen Dennys, 1987.

Whyte, Anne V. *The Experience of New Immigrants and Seasonal Farmworkers from the Eastern Caribbean to Canada: Final Report on Phase 1*. Toronto: Institute for Environmental Studies, University of Toronto, July 1984.

Williams, Eric. *Capitalism and Slavery*. Chapel Hill: University of North Carolina Press, 2021.

Wilson, Catharine Anne. "Tenancy as a Family Strategy in Mid-Nineteenth Century Ontario." *Journal of Social History* 31, no. 4 (1998): 875–96.

– *Tenants in Time: Family Strategies, Land, and Liberalism in Upper Canada, 1799–1871*. Montreal: McGill-Queen's University Press, 2009.

Winks, Robin W. *The Blacks in Canada: A History*. 2nd ed. Kingston: McGill-Queen's University Press, 2000.

Winter, Joseph. "Native Americans." In *Tobacco in History and Culture: An Encyclopedia*, vol. 2, edited by Jordan Goodman, 375–82. Detroit: Thomson Gale, 2005.

Wong, Lloyd. "Migrant Seasonal Agricultural Labour: Race and Ethnic Relations in the Okanagan Valley." PhD dissertation, York University, 1988.

Wood, J. David. *Making Ontario: Agricultural Colonization and Landscape Re-creation before the Railway*. Montreal: McGill-Queen's University Press, 2000.

Wright, Cynthia. "The Museum of Illegal Immigration: Historical Perspectives on the Production of Non-Citizens and Challenges to Immigration Controls." In *Producing and Negotiating Non-Citizenship: Precarious Legal Status in Canada*, edited by Luin Goldring and Patricia Landolt, 31–54. Toronto: University of Toronto Press, 2013.

INDEX

accommodations, workers': and female-male cohabitation, 116, 123; and inter-racial/inter-ethnic cohabitation, 185, 202, 235–6; during Covid-19 pandemic, 241–3; on-farm, 31, 115–16, 123, 184, 200–2, 211, 221, 236; pre-harvest, 3, 45–6, 137–8, 144–5; in SAWP, 184, 195, 200–2, 224, 236, 241–3, 255–6n6

activism. *See* protests; resistance; strikes

adolescents. *See* youth

adventure, 26, 115–16, 125–8, 205, 287n35

African Americans: and desegregation of US-Ontario scheme (1966), 3–4, 152–7; exclusion from US-Ontario migration, 7, 46–8, 109–10, 165, 185–6; and tobacco farming in nineteenth-century Ontario, 20

alcohol. *See* drug and alcohol use

Allahdua, Gabriel, 251–2, 308n65

American Tobacco Company (ATC), 20, 41, 46

Americans, 42, 46–50, 54, 63–4, 92–8, 107, 111, 113, 165, 185–9, 197

Andras, Robert, 147, 184, 235, 237

Atlantic Canada, 22, 130, 219

Australia, 18, 41, 301n88

Austrians, 177–80

Barbadians, 170, 190–1, 199–200, 205–8, 232

Barbados, 198, 230

Basok, Tanya, 238–9

Belgians, 6, 42, 49–51, 53–4, 65, 268n92; in European Student Tobacco Worker Program, 4, 176–8, 180, 191; political activity, 68–9, 75–6, 77–9; social mobility of, 60, 64. *See also* European Student Tobacco Worker Program

Belgium, 68–9, 176

Bennett, R.B., 93

Berggold, Craig, 126, 141–2

Bovell, Winston, 190–1, 199, 203, 205–6, 208

Bracero program, 108, 157, 256n9

Brazil, 18, 19, 215

British, 13, 19, 181, 210–11

British American Tobacco (BAT), 41

British West Indies: emigration from, 160; and guest-worker programs, 161–2, 165–7, 172; and rural development, 160, 296n26; socio-economic problems of, 159–60; traditions of workplace resistance, 198

Buck, Tim, 84

Buffalo, 3, 96, 156

Byer, Bill, 44, 265n57